Culture of Life – Culture of Death

Culture of Life – Culture of Death

Proceedings of the International Conference
on
'The Great Jubilee and the Culture of Life'

Edited by

Luke Gormally

London – The Linacre Centre

Published by The Linacre Centre for Healthcare Ethics
60 Grove End Road, London, NW8 9NH
www.linacre.org

Distributor in North America: St Augustine's Press,
Chicago Distribution Center, 11030 South Langley Avenue,
Chicago, IL 60628-3893, U.S.A.

Distributor in Australasia: Ignatius House Services,
P O Box 180, Sumner Park, Qld. 4074, Australia

British Library Cataloguing in Publication Data

A catalogue record for this book is available from
the British Library

ISBN 0 906561 24 8

Typeset by Academic and Technical, Bristol
Printed and bound by Bookcraft (CPI Group), Midsomer Norton

In memory of
Cardinal Thomas J Winning
and
Professor Elizabeth Anscombe
both valiant for Truth
and exemplary in the witness they gave.

Contents

CONTENTS

I

Introduction

LUKE GORMALLY

THIS VOLUME contains the majority of invited papers (1–16), and all the papers submitted on the initiative of their authors (17–22), which were delivered at an International Conference on 'The Great Jubilee and the Culture of Life'. The Conference was held in July 2000 at Queens' College, Cambridge. It was planned principally as an occasion for Catholics with an active interest in the ethics of healthcare to respond in a particular way to Pope John Paul II's invitation to celebrate the Great Jubilee of the Year 2000.

Ethical issues in the field of healthcare are apt to confront practitioners as discreet problems or difficulties. But it is clear enough in our society that orthodox Christian responses to those problems and difficulties confront characteristically secularist responses, and that secularism[1] has become a decisively shaping influence on clinical practice, biomedical research, and developments in the legal framework of those disciplines. However discreet the problems and difficulties may appear to be, then, responses to them tend to come from one or the other side of a 'clash of orthodoxies'[2]: the orthodoxy of contemporary liberal secularism or the orthodoxy of the Judaeo-Christian moral tradition. And these orthodoxies are the intellectual faces, so to speak, of profoundly opposed cultures, ways of living which embody deeply opposed understandings of human life. The opposition is indeed profound, characterised by Pope John Paul II as the conflict between the culture of life and the culture of death. Christians, and Catholics in particular, need to recognise this global reality if they are to take the true measure of the moral issues which confront them in clinical practice and biomedical research.

Since the ultimate source of the culture of life is the life, death and resurrection of Jesus, it seemed particularly appropriate that those of us confronting the ethical issues raised by contemporary healthcare practice should celebrate the second millennium of the birth of Jesus with a conference devoted to exploring salient features of both the culture of death and the culture of life. The overall framework for this exploration was set by themes suggested by a reading of Pope John Paul's great encyclical on 'The Gospel of Life', *Evangelium Vitae*, alongside his Apostolic Letter for the Jubilee, *Tertio Millennio Adveniente*. What those themes are, and how the contributions from invited speakers were intended to relate to them, are fully explained in the Opening Address given to the Conference by the late Cardinal

---

[1] For the meaning of the term see John Finnis's contribution to the present volume.
[2] See Robert P. George, *The Clash of Orthodoxies. Law, Religion and Morality in Crisis.* Wilmington, Delaware: ISI Books 2001.

Winning. Readers who require an overview of the main contents of this volume should begin by reading that Address, which follows this Introduction. It should be noted, however, that the ordering of the papers in this volume differs from the order of their presentation at the Conference.

Readers are entitled to some explanation in this Introduction for what has been included and what omitted from the original conference proceedings. Of the original twenty invited contributions sixteen are included – the first sixteen papers printed. Readers of Cardinal Winning's Address will notice his reference to six papers which appeared in the Conference Programme under the general heading of 'Medicine and the Culture of Life'. These were an important part of the programme and greatly appreciated by the audience of over 200 who took part in the Conference. Those familiar with conference presentations by doctors will realise, however, that they are often not based on a continuous text but frequently consist in a discourse commenting on a series of slides or overheads. At the end of the Conference I received two complete texts from our medical speakers, as it happened both from doctors discussing their experience of working in developing countries. Many months later my efforts to elicit other texts resulted in one preliminary draft from a medical contributor, who, like his remaining medical colleagues, had addressed issues which at present principally concern the practice of medicine in the developed world. I therefore decided to limit the published contributions on 'Medicine and the Culture of Life' to the two contributions by Professor Walley and Sr Miriam Duggan to be found in this volume under the general heading of 'Medicine, the Developing World and the Culture of Life'. These two contributions, which impressively reflect exemplary dedication to care, deeply informed by Christian vision and virtue, can be taken to also reflect the character of the other medical contributions to the Conference.

The final section of the volume contains what I have perhaps inelegantly called 'Supplementary Papers'. These are papers offered for presentation at the Conference by participants who wished to take advantage of a small number of parallel sessions in the Conference programme. Though they bear on the general themes of the Conference, it seemed sensible to keep them together as they were not part of the planned exposition of those themes.

It remains for me to thank a number of people on whom the success of the Conference depended. I am grateful to the Board of Governors of the Linacre Centre who warmly encouraged this undertaking as they had warmly encouraged our previous Cambridge conference in 1997.[3] Among Governors gratitude is particularly owing to the Chairman, Professor Michael Horan, to the Vice-Chairman, Dr John Keown, and to Professor John Finnis for their counsel and material assistance. The success of the July 2000 Conference was in very large measure owing to Mrs Clarissa Fleischer, Administrator of The Linacre Centre between May 1996 and April 2001. Her efficiency and her equanimity under pressure were decisive factors in making for a well-organised conference

---

[3] For the Proceedings of that Conference see L. Gormally (ed) *Issues for a Catholic Bioethic*. London: The Linacre Centre 1999.

characterised by a pleasantly relaxed atmosphere. My other colleagues at the Centre, Dr Helen Watt (now its Director) and Mr Don Smith (its Librarian) were unfailingly helpful whenever their assistance was sought. Don Smith has also been a great help in supplying me with details of bibliographical references during the preparation of this volume. At a crucial stage in preparing for the Conference I received invaluable research assistance from Mr Davide Lees, seminarian at the Redemptoris Mater House of Formation in Rome and student at the Gregorian University.

The Centre was greatly helped in bringing overseas speakers to the Conference by financial assistance from Ave Maria School of Law, Ann Arbor, Michigan, USA, and from the Culture of Life Foundation, Washington, DC. Gratitude is owing to Professor Bernard Dobranski, Dean of Ave Maria School of Law, and to Mr Robert Best, then President of the Culture of Life Foundation, for their personal support for the Conference. Attendance at the Conference was also generously supported by Archbishop George Pell (then of Melbourne, now of Sydney) and by Mr Joseph Santamaria QC.

Last but not least, I would like to thank all the contributors to this volume for their generous collaboration in its production.

The volume is dedicated to the memory of two outstanding witnesses to what a culture of life requires of us: love for those innocents whose right to life is systematically violated in our society and an unflinching witness to truth, and ultimately to the One who is the Truth.

Cardinal Winning is perhaps best remembered among the general public for his Pro-Life Initiative, run by the Sisters of the Gospel of Life, to support women tempted to have an abortion. He was also well-known for his trenchant interventions in public debate designed to challenge the anti-life and anti-family policies of Government. Less spectacularly, he played a crucial role, as Chairman of the Catholic Bishops' Joint Bioethics Committee, from its establishment in 1983 till his death last year, in guiding the preparation of measured responses by the Catholic Church in England and Wales, Scotland, and Ireland, to a range of ethical issues in the field of healthcare. It was in his capacity as Chairman of that committee of the three Conferences of Bishops that the Cardinal opened both of the Cambridge conferences organised by the Linacre Centre in 1997 and 2000. His support for, and appreciation of, the work of the Centre were important influences on the Centre's development.

Here is not the place to attempt to convey an impression of Elizabeth Anscombe's distinction as a philosopher. Let it suffice to quote Baroness Mary Warnock who, despite the fact that she is evidently no lover of many of the values which inspired Professor Anscombe, nevertheless referred to her as "the undoubted giant among women philosophers, a writer of immense breadth, authority and penetration".[4] Central to Elizabeth Anscombe's intellectual distinction was her capacity to call

---

[4] The context was an anthology of women philosophers from the seventeenth century to the present edited by Baroness Warnock. See Mary Warnock (ed) *Women Philosophers*. London: J. M. Dent; Vermont: Charles E. Tuttle 1996: 203.

into question prevailing intellectual fashions and all forms of what she used to call 'syndrome thinking'. This capacity well served the Church's witness to moral truth, as can be seen, for example, in her fundamental work on the concept of intention and in her writings on the conduct of warfare and in her vigorous defence of the Church's teaching on contraception. The Linacre Centre's own public witness owed a very important debt to her. The Centre's first substantial publication was a volume on *Euthanasia and Clinical Practice*,[5] which was the Report of a Working Party, convened by the Centre in late 1978, in which Elizabeth Anscombe played an active role. The core of the ethical argument of that influential Report, to be found in chapter 3 ('Murder and the morality of euthanasia: some philosophical considerations'), was her work. Though most photographs in the public domain of Elizabeth Anscombe show her in one or another armchair, she was no armchair philosopher. There is one published photograph of her – which the newspapers were careful not to identify as a photograph of *her* – in which she is shown being dragged semi-prone by two policemen from the front of an abortion 'clinic' where she had been peacefully protesting against the daily slaughter of the innocent which took place there. She was in her seventies at the time and already frail but nonetheless valiant in her witness in defence of innocent human life. The dedication of this volume to her memory and to the memory of Cardinal Winning is a very small token of gratitude for their witness to that living Truth who is the source of the culture of life.

Note on the Cover Picture

Gerrit van Honthorst's *Christ before the High Priest* can be seen as emblematic of the confrontation between the culture of life and the culture of death. According to the Gospels, the High Priest in the year in which Jesus was condemned to death was Caiaphas, and the Gospel of John records that it was Caiaphas who uttered the prototypical consequentialist judgment: "...it is better for one man to die for the people than for the whole nation to be destroyed" (*Jn* 11: 50). Willingness to sacrifice the innocent purportedly for 'the greater good' is central to the mind-set characteristic of the culture of death. As the evangelist notes, however, there is a prophetic truth to Caiaphas's words lying beyond their intended meaning: "Jesus was to die for the nation – and not for the nation only, but to gather together in unity the scattered children of God". Gerrit van Honthorst's Christ is the Suffering Servant whose sacrificial death redeems us from the sin which alienates us from the Father and from each other, and makes possible a culture of life. So the candlelight illuminates principally the figure of Christ (the true Light of the World) as he serenely confronts the testimony of the enemies of Truth – the false witnesses – who lurk in the shadows.

---

[5] First published in 1982. Subsequently reprinted as the first third of L. Gormally (ed) *Euthanasia, Clinical Practice and the Law*. London: The Linacre Centre 1994.

2

Opening address

CARDINAL THOMAS J. WINNING

MY DEAR FRIENDS,

It is almost three years since I had the pleasure of standing here and welcoming many of you to the Conference organised by The Linacre Centre on *Issues for a Catholic Bioethic*. That notably successful Conference was convened to celebrate the 20th anniversary of the Centre's foundation. This Conference, to which I warmly welcome all of you, has been convened to help us all understand more deeply some of the implications of the Great Jubilee which we are celebrating in this millennial year. The general theme of this Conference links the celebration of the Jubilee with the idea of the 'culture of life'. In this opening address I would like to offer some general observations on the significance of that link.

In my opening address to the 1997 Conference I spoke about the dual mission of The Linacre Centre, a mission both *within* the Church, to assist in expounding and developing a Catholic bioethic, and a mission to society at large to influence the thinking behind public policy so that it may genuinely promote the common good. In a parallel way, I now want to talk about dual and related dimensions of the celebration of the Jubilee, aspects of what it should mean within the life of the Church, and aspects of what it should mean for society at large. What I have to say will be inspired in large measure by Pope John Paul's Apostolic Letter for the Jubilee, *Tertio Millennio Adveniente*, and by his great Encyclical on 'The Gospel of Life', *Evangelium Vitae*. I have taken those as my texts of reference, because the conception of this Conference was itself inspired by them. So some introductory reflections inspired by those texts will also serve to show how the individual parts of this Conference are meant to serve the overall conception.

A year of Jubilee is a "year of the Lord's favour" – a year of special graces. In Ancient Israel it meant being freed from slavery, restored to the life of one's family and to the enjoyment of a reasonable portion of the resources of the world that God created for all. "The jubilee year was meant to restore equality among all the children of Israel,..."[1] who should not "remain for ever in a state of slavery, since God had 'redeemed' them for himself as his exclusive possession by freeing them from slavery in Egypt."[2] Early in his public ministry, in the synagogue of his home town, Jesus identified that ministry with the fulfilment of all that was symbolically promised in the institution of the Jubilee: "Taking the Book of the Prophet Isaiah, he read this passage: 'The Spirit of the Lord is upon me, because

---

[1] *Tertio Mellennio Adveniente* [henceforth *TM*] 13.
[2] *TM* 12.

the Lord has anointed me to bring good tidings to the afflicted; he has sent me to proclaim release to the captives and recovery of sight to the blind, to set at liberty those who are oppressed; to proclaim the year of the Lord's favour'. And he closed the Book and gave it back to the attendant, and sat down; and the eyes of all in the synagogue were fixed on him. And he began to say to them, 'Today this scripture has been fulfilled in your hearing'." [Lk 4:18–21][3] This year 2000 is a year of the Lord's favour for us just in so far as we are united with what Jesus accomplished in the fulness of time through his Incarnation, Death and Resurrection and the sending of the Holy Spirit.

But how should we understand the captivity from which the Lord releases us, the blindness he removes, the oppression from which he frees us? We are given a substantial part of the answer to these questions in understanding what the Holy Father refers to as 'the culture of death'.[4] He introduced the idea of 'the culture of death' to identify more concretely the face of evil in what he speaks of as "the enormous and dramatic clash between good and evil" which confronts us today. "We find ourselves not only 'faced with' but necessarily 'in the midst of' this conflict", he writes; "we are all involved and we all share in it, with the inescapable responsibility of choosing to be unconditionally pro-life."[5]

Pope John Paul in *Evangelium Vitae* presents the anatomy of the culture of death in terms of, first, its characteristic manifestations, secondly, its generic, pervasive features, and, thirdly, its root cause.

Among its characteristic manifestations are abortion, euthanasia, embryo experimentation, and the imperialism which imposes policies of contraception and abortion on countries with rapid population growth. This imperialism, which is a prominent manifestation of what the Pope calls a "conspiracy against life",[6] is pursued in ways that seem heedless of the grim fruits of the widespread practice of contraception and abortion in the 20th century. Contraception, in closing hearts to the gift of the child and disposing many to the murderous practice of abortion, has left most First World countries with below replacement fertility rates. Hence the prospect of aged populations disproportionately large in relation to the part of the population generating income, with the prospect that many of the aged may be regarded as insupportable. That is the scenario against which the legalisation of euthanasia – particularly non-voluntary euthanasia of the mentally impaired elderly – looks increasingly attractive to many movers and shakers in the political and administrative classes. And so the spiral of decline is set to become ever more intensely deadly.

What are the pervasive, generic features of this culture of death?

First, an ideology of autonomy unconstrained by any sense of the claims of objective moral truth, and limited only by the power of those it is prudent not to challenge or with whom it is self-interestedly prudent to cooperate. This kind

---

[3] See *TM* 11.
[4] See *Evangelium Vitae* [henceforth *EV*] *passim*.
[5] *EV* 28.
[6] *EV* 12, 17.

of autonomy, in the words of the Pope, "ends up becoming the freedom of 'the strong' against the weak who have no choice but to submit."[7]

Second, there is "a practical materialism, which breeds individualism, utilitarianism and hedonism . . . The only goal which counts is the pursuit of one's own material well-being."[8]

Third, in this cultural climate "broad sectors of public opinion justify certain crimes against life in the name of the rights of individual freedom."[9] In the case of abortion, the so-called 'right' to have it has been almost everywhere legally accommodated, and the growing drive is to secure similar legal accommodation for euthanasia. What is thereby established is what the Holy Father calls 'structures of sin', that is, institutional arrangements which consist not only of permissive legislation but the requirement, under administrative directives in the UK, that at least some doctors should carry out the moral crimes in question.[10]

The *root* of this culture of death, in the Pope's words, lies at the "heart of the tragedy being experienced by modern man: *the eclipse of the sense of God and of man*, typical of a social and cultural climate dominated by secularism, which, with its ubiquitous tentacles, succeeds at times in putting Christian communities themselves to the test."[11]

We shall hear shortly from Professor Finnis on the subject of secularism as the root of the culture of death. At the root of secularism itself is the primordial sin of acting as if it were down to us to determine what is good and what is evil. The fact that secularism is a manifestation of the endemic tendency to succumb to the great diabolical deception that we are the ultimate masters of our lives should preserve us from the illusion that as Christians we are immune to it. One of the special graces of this Jubilee year should be a heightening of our awareness of the extent to which we ourselves are under the influence of ideological currents characteristic of the culture of death. We can look forward to Professor Finnis's keynote paper this evening, and the papers from Dr Cuddeback, Fr Fenlon and Professor George tomorrow morning, to help us in that examination of conscience about our commitment to the culture of life which the Holy Father has urged upon us. "Too often it happens" [he says] "that believers, even those who take an active part in the life of the Church, end up by separating their Christian faith from its ethical requirements concerning life, and thus fall into moral subjectivism and certain objectionable ways of acting. With great openness and courage, we need to question how widespread is the culture of life today among individual Christians, families, groups and communities in our dioceses."[12]

This critical questioning is urgent if the community of the Church is to be the leaven of humanity, permeating all cultures and giving them life from within so

---

[7] *EV* 19.
[8] *EV* 23.
[9] *EV* 4.
[10] *EV* 11, 24.
[11] *EV* 21.
[12] *EV* 95.

that, in the words of John Paul, "they may express the full truth about the human person and about human life."[13] In face of the enormity of the manifestations of the culture of death there are grave temptations either to seek to close our eyes to them and so underestimate the reality of evil, or to succumb to defeatism and despair. These temptations are not to be overcome by denying the realities that motivate them. First, the reality of our own selfishness: we are too often inclined to be indifferent to the plight of others, to censor out of our perception of the world the brutal realities of abortion, of euthanasiast neglect of the elderly, of oppression of the poor. Second, if we do confront these realities, we seem to have to face the facts that there are well-entrenched structures of sin and that the numbers of those converted to the truth seem utterly remote from the sort of critical mass we think would be required to transform a culture.

In face of these temptations we need to remind ourselves about the *source* of our hope and the *object* of our hope.

The *source* of our hope is the One who is at the centre of our Jubilee celebrations, the Risen Lord: for it is his Incarnation, Death and Resurrection which have freed us from that slavery to sin which leads us to enslave and kill others. He has released us from the blindness which prevents us from seeing that the dominion of God is a loving dominion which sets us free. And it is this blindness which also prevents us from seeing the immense dignity of every human being who is called to friendship with God in the communion of the Trinity. No doubt Monsignor Melina, in his keynote paper this evening, will deepen our appreciation of these truths.

Let us not be daunted by our own weakness, by our temptations to indifference to the plight of the victims of the culture of death. If we want to be transformed, if we pray to be transformed, the Lord will open our hearts to the afflicted. This Jubilee year is a year of the Lord's favour, one during which we can become more clearly conformed to the Lord's own heart.

We need also, in face of the culture of death, to remind ourselves of the *object* of our hope: it is life with the Triune God and the saints in the heavenly Kingdom. We are offered no sure hope of the good society in our present terrestrial condition. So why work for a culture of life?

We need to see clearly why it is morally necessary to do so. If we recognise the fundamental dignity of every human being we will recognise the claim of each to flourish as a human being. The needs which have to be met – physical, moral and religious needs – if human beings are to flourish can only be met within various kinds of relationship of dependence – from dependence on the fundamental community of the family to dependence on institutions such as church and school and hospital, which in turn exist only in virtue of higher levels of social organisation. Each of us, because of our basic needs, has a vested interest in this complex network of collaborative institutions and the practices they sustain *being in good order*; practices such as worship, teaching and healthcare. And each of us has reason to recognise that every other human being has the same vested interest.

---

[13] *EV* 95.

The object of this interest is what is called the common good: that set of conditions which enables the members of a community to obtain for themselves reasonable objectives through which they come to flourish as human beings. Our common need for and consequent interest in these conditions is the basis of the obligation to work to foster the common good of the communities to which we belong.

Recognition of the right of every human being *not* to be unjustly killed, and the legal enforcement of that right, are obviously the most fundamental elements of the common good. Yet in the forms required by justice they are manifestly absent from our societies. A moral ecology which favours chastity is another basic element of the common good. For chastity is necessary to serious marital commitment, and serious marital commitment is necessary to the good of children, to "the receiving of them lovingly, the nourishing of them humanely, the educating of them religiously", as St Augustine puts it.[14] If there is a conspiracy against life in our society, as Pope John Paul claims, the subversion of the conditions for the cultivation of chastity is an important part of it. The subversion is at work in the papers, on television, on the billboards, in much of what passes for art in our era; it is rationalised by philosophers, and pointedly pursued in sex education programmes.

It is vain to look to democratic procedures *as such* to reverse our social and cultural plight. For in a society in which the minds of many are shaped by the culture of death, standard democratic procedures will not favour the common good but only serve to entrench that culture.

In face of the captive power of personal sin and sinful social structures we must look to the Church to be the leaven of society through the renewal of her members in the power of the Risen Lord. We ourselves need to be more profoundly evangelized and in turn we need to proclaim the Good News of our redemption from slavery to all those who labour under the insufferable burdens born of secularism. The fundamental task is evangelisation, for without evangelisation there cannot be those conversions of hearts from which a culture of life is built.

The Holy Father has called each of us to see clearly the role we have to play as members of the Church in working for a culture which favours the cherishing of every human being, however weak, however impaired.

In this Conference, Archbishop Pell will speak to us about the role of the Bishop, Fr Hogan about the role of the priest, and Professor Laura Garcia about the role of the family in promoting the culture of life. Fr Lorenzo Rossetti will discuss what is at stake in that necessary tension which should characterise every serious christian life: the tension between being *against* 'the world', against the present order, while simultaneously seeking a way of loving those who now belong within this present order.

No profession has been more deeply corrupted by the culture of death than the medical profession over the past century. And nothing has more deeply corrupted it than the practice of abortion and the attendant attitude that human life which is weak and vulnerable is disposable. So there is a very great need for a moral

[14] *De Genesi ad litt.* 9.7.

renewal of the medical profession. Perhaps the most effective way of disposing people to renewal *from within medicine itself* is to show them that it is possible to do medicine differently. Hence at this Conference we have six sessions on 'Medicine and the Culture of Life' in which six doctors discuss some of the challenges facing them in their areas of practice and what it is possible to do to meet those challenges in ways consistent with respect for human life and dignity.

Doctors have to work within a framework which is set by politicians through legislation and administrative directives. So on the final morning we will have a paper from Fr Anthony Fisher OP on questions of conscience which face politicians seeking to defend innocent human life through conventional political means. And because conventional political means have been so notably unsuccessful in recent decades in the defence of innocent human life, consideration needs to be given to what a private citizen may reasonably do in defence of innocent human life, a topic addressed by Professor Jorge Garcia.

Finally, Bishop Donal Murray will speak to us about the Church as a community of hope. We need the virtue of hope in face of the culture of death. We need the Church to sustain us in the true hope of the heavenly Kingdom if we are to be generous and courageous in working for a culture of life and are not to be crushed by disappointment.

Let me conclude by reminding you that the unconquerable heart of that culture is the Risen Lord. Each morning of this Conference begins with the celebration of the Eucharist in which we are united with Him in His victory over sin and death through His sacrificial Death and Resurrection. That must be the place in which our lives are continually renewed if we are properly to face the task of working for a society and a culture which cherishes the life of every human being. May the next few days help to renew our commitment to that task. May we all grow in knowledge and understanding, and in friendship and solidarity with each other in the service of the One who is the Way, the Truth and the Life. May God bless you all.

The Culture of Death

3

Secularism, the root of the culture of death

JOHN FINNIS

I

CULTURE IS WHAT we add, by our choices, to nature, i.e. to all that we find given in our minds, bodies, and environment, prior to human decisions to believe, plan, make, and do. So culture comprises ways of thinking, communicating, and behaving that have been shaped by decisions between alternative possibilities, and that last because they are carried on by more or less deliberate adoption.

When we hear of *a* culture, we need not think of some worldwide or nation-wide reality, as wide as 'civilisation'. The Queens' College Cambridge doubtless has a culture subtly different from University College Oxford's. There is a recognisably English culture of football hooliganism. Can it be said to be part of 'English culture'? In a sense. But most or perhaps all of us, even those of us who are immersed in English culture, can truthfully say that we are in no way involved in English football hooliganism. So it would be misleading to say that "English culture *is* a culture of football hooliganism", or that English culture as such is hooligan.

Similarly, the phrase adopted by the Church in recent years, "the culture of death", need not and, I think, should not be taken to say that modern culture as such, or Western culture as such, or the secular world as a whole, *is* a culture of death. Rather, it says that there is very powerfully present in our contemporary world a distinguishable set of interrelated practices, conventions, laws, institutions, ways of responding, thinking, and communicating, and learned and learnable patterns of ambition and desire, which as a set can well be called 'a culture of death'. As *Evangelium Vitae* puts it, "our societies and cultures, strongly marked though they are by the culture of death",[1] also contain within them forms of familial and other associative culture radically opposed to that culture-within-our-culture.

As an ongoing reality, any culture centres on *intentio* in both main senses of that Latin word: meanings and purposes. It centres on what people *mean*, in both main applications of that English word: what they mean by their words and other signs and communications, and what they mean to be doing, bringing about, achieving. It is meaning in this latter sense, essentially intention or intendings as purposes and choices, that is referred to by the word 'culture' in the phrase 'culture of death'. These kinds of intention and choice are the decisive moment

---

[1] Encyclical 25 March 1995 *Evangelium Vitae* (hereafter: *EV*) 26.1.

13

in a structure or pattern which extends from dispositions and willingness to act, through conditional choices, to unconditional choices to act here and now, carried out by actual conduct (acts and deliberate omissions or forbearances). The word 'culture' always picks out some more or less *lasting* reality, so 'culture of death' is a phrase picking out a more or less settled and shared *willingness* or disposition to make and carry out choices of a certain kind, a more or less stable and overt, publicly unashamed, pattern of *intention*.

"Of death". What is distinctive of this set of attitudes and practices is that those who share in them are willing to *intend* death. Properly speaking, one intends what, and only what one chooses to try to bring about either as an end wholly or partly for its own sake, or as a means to some such end. So a culture in which the death of human persons is *not* chosen, but also is not shuffled out of sight or veiled in euphemism or other tricks of evasion and denial, but is a subject of open discussion, artistic representation, contemplation, and personal preparation, is not what 'culture of death' refers to. No, the phrase refers to a more or less systematised willingness to intend death, as an end or as a means.

"Intending death": more precisely, choosing to bring about or hasten the death of a person. For when we speak of *life* in contexts such as 'the right to life', or 'the basic and inviolable good of life',[2] we properly mean the life of a person. And since the persons whose life we can preserve or terminate are human animals, we properly mean the life of a human being, a person from the time of his or her conception because from then until death a single organism at all times radically capable of participating, under the right conditions of health and maturity, in acts of meaning, choosing and carrying out choices. A human being's life, like the life of any organism, is a coordinated system of physico-chemical processes maintained in dynamic equilibrium by homeostatic controls, and one's death is correspondingly the collapse of that integrated organic functioning and its irreversible decomposition. So one's life, the life of any human being, is one's very reality as that being, that person, who came into being at conception, unless anomalously at the time of an event such as twinning by extrinsically initiated embryo-splitting. Death, and only bodily death, ends that personal reality (leaving a spiritual remnant of so reduced a kind that St Thomas could say, and repeat, *anima mea non est ego*: my soul is not me, and if only my soul is saved, I am not saved). The death we are considering, then, is the termination, the destruction of the very reality of a human person. There is a culture *of death* when and where there is a more or less systematised willingness to *choose to* hasten or otherwise bring about the death of human beings, that is, a readiness, however reluctantly, to act or forbear from acting with a purpose of killing someone.

Since one's reality as a person can be promoted, protected, respected, neglected, damaged, or destroyed by human choice, life, human life, figures most commonly in one's thinking as a *good*, a value, a *reason* for acting. But

---

[2] Note that the Latin title of *EV* is *De vitae humanae inviolabili bono* – 'On the inviolable good of human life'.

talk, accurate though it is, of the good or value of human *life* should not be allowed to obscure the fact that what we are talking of is in every case the very existence and reality of an individual *person*. A society in which people are treated as having the right to suppress life, whether of themselves or of others, is a society whose culture approves of acts *against the person* (EV 4.2), and thus is willing that some people (characteristically the strong) exercise a kind of power over others that is unbounded or absolute inasmuch as it is power over their very existence (cf. *EV* 12.1; 20.3; 23.4).

Experience shows that in our culture, neither of the facts to which I have been drawing attention is welcome to those whose attitudes and practices I am considering. There is much reluctance to admit that those whose lives they are willing to terminate are human persons. And there is much reluctance to admit that these deaths are *intended*, or that it matters that they are intended rather than simply accepted as a side-effect of something else. There is something healthy about this reluctance, though nothing healthy about what it generates by way of spurious argumentation or mere rhetoric and evasion. Conversely, there is something intellectually satisfactory but humanly deplorable about the clear-cut willingness of those who, like the American liberal philosopher Jeffrey Reiman, plainly articulate and defend the thesis that the constitutional and moral right to abortion is precisely the right to *kill* the unborn child, and to make sure that it dies, and that this great right would be unjustly denied if it were interpreted as merely the right to remove the foetus, or have it removed, from one's body[3] (the right famously defended in the early days of 'pro-choice' abortive feminism by Judith Jarvis Thomson). There is the same combination of the clear and the callousing in Reiman's associated thesis that – contrary to our law and tradition – even after birth one has no rights until one has a self-reflective consciousness, some years on in childhood. Positions like Reiman's remain uncomfortably advanced for the main body of those who treat abortion as a right and, in its way, a good – but 'advanced' is the right word: his position is at the point of their culture's, that is, their sub-culture's, trajectory or dynamic.

II

"In seeking the deepest roots of the struggle between the 'culture of life' and 'the culture of death' . . . we have to go to the heart of the tragedy being experienced by modern man: *the eclipse of the sense of God and of man*, typical of a social and cultural climate dominated by secularism . . ." (*EV* 21.1) ". . . the loss of contact with God's wise design is the deepest root of modern man's confusion . . . By living 'as if God did not exist', man loses sight not only of the mystery of God, but also of . . . the mystery of his own being." (*EV* 22.3–4) That is how the

---

[3] J. H. Reiman, *Critical moral liberalism: theory and practice.* Lanham: Rowman & Littlefield 1997: 190. See further my debate with him in R. P. George and C. Wolfe (eds.), *Natural Law and Public Reason.* Washington DC: Georgetown University Press 2000: 75–124.

encyclical of 25 March 1995 makes the causal link suggested in the title of my reflections. The encyclical's proposal of this causal link is a theological reflection rather than a teaching of faith; it has some grounding in theology's sources, as the encyclical itself reminds us by quoting *Romans* 1:28: "since they did not see fit to acknowledge God, God gave them up to a debased mind and to improper conduct." But that is only a phase in a more extended and complex causal analysis by St Paul, running from verses 21 to 32 of *Romans* 1, and this larger analysis the encyclical does not take up. All in all we have good reason to undertake our own reflections about secularism's bearing on the two issues I have pointed to: the worth and significance of human existence and personal reality, and the significance of intention and of misconceptions or misrepresentations of intention, in shaping a culture and shaping it as "a veritable *structure of sin*" (*EV* 12.1).

What is the secularism that the encyclical says is a fundamental root of a more or less systematised contemporary willingness to kill some sorts of weak and dependent people? It is not respect for the secular – that which is not divine, sacred, or ecclesiastical. After all, 'secular' is a word minted by Latin Christians. Jerome's Latin New Testament uses it for Greek words signifying the affairs of this world, sometimes neutrally the world of time rather than eternity,[4] and the daily life of any human society,[5] sometimes pejoratively as matters which distract us from realities and dispositions of lasting worth.[6] Aquinas uses it regularly, and often quite without negative connotations: he will say, for example, that in matters which concern the good of the political community {*bonum civile*}, Christians should generally obey the directives of the *secular* authorities rather than the ecclesiastical.[7] Nothing startling about that: the Lord's "Render to Caesar the things that are Caesar's, and to God the things that are God's" (*Mt* 22:21 & par.) points us away from theocracy or any other general supremacy of states over the Church or of the Church over states or their governments, laws, and citizens.

No doubt this Christian differentiating of the secular from the sacred is only one instance or aspect of wider processes called by social historians 'secularisation', processes which involve the extension of human understanding and control over fields of life formerly so little accessible to human science and technology that it seemed reasonable to attempt to manage them instead by prayer. Christianity encourages secularisation of this kind, by insisting on the transcendence of God and the intelligibility of creation, with its consequent accessibility to the *natural* sciences and, accordingly, to technological exploitation. Secularism is another matter.

Like all significant realities, this mind-set or family of mind-sets is not tied to any word such as 'secular', 'secularisation' or 'secularism'. What we call

[4] 2 *Tim* 1: 9; *Tit* 1: 2.
[5] 1 *Cor* 6: 3–4.
[6] See 2 *Tim* 2: 4; *Tit* 2: 12.
[7] II *Sent*. d. 44 exp. textus ad 4: ... magis obediendum potestati saeculari quam spirituali.

secularism, Elizabethan philosophers and academics called atheism. The philosophical works of John Case, Oxford's and England's leading academic philosopher of the last quarter of the 16th century,[8] are the first 3,000 pages of academic work published by the Oxford University Press, of which he was in many respects the real founder. In their introductions and dedicatory letters to the great politicians of the age, they express a strong sense that atheism has made vast inroads into English culture. To some extent what John Case was pointing to was literally the belief that there is no God; to a greater extent it was what Vatican II was to call forgetting God[9] and *Evangelium Vitae* was to call losing the sense of God and "living 'as if God did not exist'" (*EV* 22, 4). But here it will be useful to make some distinctions offered to us by Plato, who reflected deeply on secularism and atheism, without using those words.

In his great last work, *Laws*, Plato sketches a cluster of dispositions – if you like, cultures – which shape up around one or other of three propositions: there is no God; or, no God has any concern with human affairs; or, any such divine concern with the human is easily appeased by a superficial piety and requires no demanding reform of human vice.[10] The corresponding character types described by Plato are well recognisable in more recent times. And the three propositions – no God; God absent; God soft-spirited[11] – match closely modern secularism's characteristic forms: atheism; or a deistic assumption that human history knows no divine intervention, no revelation of God's intentions for us; or a "liberal" religiosity which presumes upon divine benevolence, and has no time for warnings of the alienation from God inherent in immorality and potentially final (as Plato too warns in his prophetic meditation on wrongdoing's retribution, the *Republic*'s myth of Er).[12]

Though Plato's strongest indignation is reserved for the position ascribing to God a soft-spirited fatuity contemptible in men and women, his most vigorous argumentation (foreshadowing Aristotle in *Metaphysics* book I.4) confronts the first and second positions, which deny mind's sway in the cosmos. Atheistic materialism's claim that all is ultimately sheer chance and brute inexplicable necessity truncates the investigative quest of science and philosophy for intelligibility and explanation wherever it can be found. And deistic denial of all-governing divine providence under-estimates the all-creative, all-sustaining and all-penetrating power of the maker's practical intellect.

But Plato judges that the practical significance of the three positions is in each case essentially the same: the withering away of reverence for God, of a steady,

---

[8] For an introduction to Case, see C. B. Schmitt, *John Case and Aristotelianism in Renaissance England*. Montreal: McGill-Queen's University Press 1983.

[9] Vatican II, pastoral Constitution on the Church in the Modern World, *Gaudium et Spes* (hereafter: *GS*) 36.

[10] See *Laws* X 885b, 888c, 901d, 902e–903a, 908b–d, 909a–b. Plato usually speaks of "gods" or "the gods", but when getting to the heart of the matter switches to talk of God or "the god" (see 902e, 903d, 910b).

[11] See *Laws* X 901e, 903a. Also *Republic* 365d–e.

[12] *Republic* X 614b–621d; see also *Laws* X 903d; *Gorgias* 523a–527e.

uncringing, inspiriting fear of the Lord.[13] We can readily see that secularism, in this practical inner manifestation or resultant, is part of the makeup even of a God-fearing believer, just insofar as one is sinning. In that sense, as Maritain could consider the Church a reality which occupies a part of the believer's spirit, so one can think of secularism as a kind of deficiency detectable to a greater or lesser degree in every human soul except the authentic saints. Many if not all of us, with our friends and colleagues, seem to live in some sense as secularists; we have motives of sympathy and affection, as well as reasons of principle, to turn sharply aside from Plato when he plans fierce penal repression of secularists by the Guardians of the Laws.[14] In reflecting on secularism, one is considering a public reality, the secularism which shapes public debate, deliberation, dispositions, and action, and is strong in our education and culture. One is considering the ideas, not the people as such. People are often less consistent, and better, than their theories and dispositions. There is little profit in trying to estimate whether and in what ways secularism's dominance now is greater than in Plato's Athens, or John Case's Oxford and London, or is lesser than in Andropov's Leningrad. Western secularism takes many different forms, often under the influence of the faith it supplants. What concerns us now is the inherent link between "the loss of contact with God's wise design" (*EV* 22.3) and the willingness to use the killing of human beings as a culturally approved, indeed publicly cultivated means, if not also to have it as an end (as it is in the nuclear final retaliation which remains a part of US and, in another way, UK public policy).

I think I see in one of Shakespeare's plays an extended and elaborate comic and bitter-sweet reminiscence of John Case, presented on stage for good reasons, a few months after his death. Be that as it may, one of the questions which the playwright, like Case, took up again and again, in work after work, is whether God intervenes in history by acts outside the order of nature. As the wise "old lord" Lafeu says in *All's Well that Ends Well* (2.3.1ff): "They say miracles are past; and we have our philosophical persons to make modern [usual] and familiar things supernatural and causeless." "Thing causeless" means perhaps something without natural, this-worldly causes, perhaps the uncaused cause itself, doubtless (in Shakespeare's way) both. Lafeu is commenting on the healing of the king by the heroine Helena, and in a moment will say that it was by "the very hand of heaven", showing "In a most weak and debile minister great power, great transcendence." In this he echoes what Helena had said when offering the king this healing:

> He that of greatest works is finisher
> Oft does them by the weakest minister:
> So holy writ in babes hath judgment shown,
> When judges have been babes; great floods have flown
> From simple sources; and great seas have dried,
> When miracles have by the greatest been denied.

---

[13] See *Laws* XII 967d: *bebaiôs theosebês*. Plato does not speak of the Lord; but the divine "mover of the pieces" (*petteutes*: 903d) has a similar dignity.

[14] See *Laws* X 907d–910d.

18

"I must not hear thee...", the King breaks in to say. Helena responds: "Inspired merit..." – resonant words indeed in late Elizabethan Protestant England –

> Inspirèd merit so by breath is barr'd:
> It is not so with Him that all things knows
> As 'tis with us that square our guess by shows;
> But most it is presumption in us when
> The help of heaven we count the act of men.

The proposition that "miracles are ceased" was a Protestant teaching – one favoured by the Bishop of London of the day – which Shakespeare, with knowing anachronism. had earlier put on the lips of the Archbishop of Canterbury at the outset of *Henry V* (1.1.68). In that earlier play, as in *All's Well*, the drama sets itself against the proposition, and suggests the opposite thought, which the king himself articulates after Agincourt:

> O God, thy arm was here,
> And not to us, but to thy arm alone
> Ascribe we all. When, without stratagem,
> But in plain shock and even play of battle,
> Was ever known so great and little loss
> On one part and on th'other? Take it God,
> For it is none but thine.
> *Exeter*   'Tis wonderful

And so on for several more exchanges, concluding with Henry's "Do we all holy rites: Let there be sung *Non nobis* and *Te Deum*..." – *Non nobis*: Not to us, O Lord, but to your name give glory... Our God is in the heavens; whatever pleases him he does.[15] As the editor of the play's current Oxford edition remarks, commenting on the night scene where Henry goes about his camp before the battle: "Out of that night's anguished recognition of his utter dependence on God comes the wonder of 'O God, thy arm *was* here' (4.8.104) – a line which demonstrates how easily in performance, 'The platitudes of piety can become ultimate statements of overwhelming power'."[16]

When Owen Chadwick here in Cambridge investigated what his book title calls *The Secularization of the European Mind in the Nineteenth Century* (1975) he concluded that "near the heart of that elusive shift in the European mind" is "the axiom, miracles do not happen". My point is not that we should locate the line between what is immediately from nature and what is immediately from beyond nature just where John Case or Shakespeare's heroes and heroines locate it, but that in 1600 thoughtful and penetrating minds like Case and his philosophical junior William S. could see a main hub of cultural change – or epicentre of cultural disintegration – just where the cultural historian of the period running up to 1900 can locate it. The 'axiom' that Protestants levelled

---

[15] *Ps* 115: 1, 3 (Vulgate 113*: 1).
[16] *Henry V*, ed. G. Taylor, *The Oxford Shakespeare* [1982] 1998: 48.

against transubstantiation and the interventions of the saints had, perhaps unrecognised by those who wielded it, hidden premises, and these would before long be turned against all sacred history and revelation itself – against the Resurrection of Jesus and the resurrection of anyone at the last day, against all sacraments and all petitionary prayer, and so, in the end, against the twin truths of Creation and Providence, in their clear Christian articulation (for what could be more miraculous than creation of the universe out of nothing?) and in their less clear but very firm prototypes in the philosophy, the searching judgments, of Plato and Aristotle.

It is a truth of the faith that the spiritual soul, "that by which [the human person] is most especially in God's image",[17] is in each and every case "created immediately by God".[18] "The human *body* shares in the dignity of 'the image of God': it is a human body precisely because it is animated by a spiritual soul . . . [and] the unity of soul and body is so profound that one has to consider the soul to be the 'form' of the body."[19] St Thomas puts this even more vigorously when he insists, again and again, that in animals (including us) soul is the body's very *act*, so that in human beings the immortal spiritual soul, whose most distinctive acts are of insight and free choice, is, in each of us, what makes one a *live* body and makes all one's bodily functions, even the least "mental", *human* bodily functions. God's creative causality *initiates* and is *in* one's life – one's very reality – in a way more direct and immediate than his causality of everything else in the order of nature, which is a causality that works not "immediately" but through the natural causes which with their effects are the subject-matter of the natural sciences.

So for each of us the gift of life, of our very self as given prior to our free choices, is more radically, because more directly, the *gift of the Creator* than is any other kind of reality in the universe known or knowable by the empirical natural sciences. This gift is in the first instance a set of radical capacities, capacities which are actual and present in one as a zygote even though as yet in their initial and least developed way of being. There is no evidence of any substantial change – from something else into me – after the time of conception, save perhaps in the case of monozygotic twinning. So: then and there, each of us was actually capable, albeit as yet only radically, of understanding, reflecting, judging, laughing, choosing, promising, and praying. So even then and there, as zygotes, each of us was by God's gift *superior* to the most sensitive, alertly conscious, responsive, and lovable mature dog or great ape, because even then we had capacities which included all the kinds of capacity that dogs or apes have *and some more*.

And the *some more* that we had and have, and that subrational animals cannot have, are those that are not only God-given but godlike, God-imaging, far more directly and essentially than any other kind of thing whose activities, capabilities, and nature we can study.

[17] *Catechism of the Catholic Church* (hereafter: CCC; 1992) London 1999: 363.
[18] CCC: 366; also *EV* 43 note 32.
[19] CCC: 365.

Our reason for judging that human capacities image God's actuality in a specifically close way is this. Our natural, that is common sense and philosophical knowledge that God created and sustains in act the universe – knowledge attainable independently of any divine acts of self-revealing communication – is reached by a process of inquiry, understanding, reflecting, and judging, a process in which one is conscious, to be sure, but with a consciousness not so much of undergoing experiences or having responses as of *acting* – in this case, of carrying forward the action of responsibly raising questions, pursuing reflections, wrestling with objections or counter-hypotheses, and following one's inner argument to its conclusion in the act of judgment. All this is an exercise of freedom, for the opportunity of turning aside from the process is always available, and can have many attractions. And all this is a paradigm, a salient instance, of that "interiority" {*interioritas*} in virtue of which, as Vatican II's *Gaudium et Spes* says, each of us oustrips/excels {*excedit*} the entire universe of things {*universitatem rerum*} (*GS* 14.2), an interiority described a little earlier as one's having been, or being, created "capable {*capax*} of knowing and loving one's Creator" (*GS* 12.3; *EV* 34.5). But this inquiring reflection is, moreover, an imaging of *God*. For, in freely and responsibly following these ways of seeking the ultimate explanation of each and every thing, the explanation of each and every system and process in this universe, what we conclude to is that there is a reality that needs no explanation, and needs no explanation because always and inherently and essentially *actual*, in need of nothing because never needing to be moved or changed from potentiality to act, never needing to be brought into existence or developed or sustained. And this reality (God) – unlike all other realities because its *what it is* includes *that it is* – has all that it takes to explain not only the reality of everything, of every system and process with which we are or can become acquainted, but equally the intelligibility, the orderliness which, though not unmixed with fortuity and disorderliness, is so characteristic of our world. The explanation of this orderliness is as, ultimately, a directedness: God has projected and is projecting the whole order of things and each of its sub-systems in something like the way one projects an intelligible proposal into reality by adopting it – choosing it – and putting it into effect – carrying out one's intention(s).[20]

The empirical scientific and philosophical understanding of the material world is a great work of spirit, that is, of human intelligence, purposeful mental effort, and intellectual and moral responsibility. The creation of the material world, even if it had not included intelligent bodily realities such as human beings, would have been an inconceivably greater work of spirit, of divine intelligence and freedom in envisaging the infinite range of possible universes, and choosing the one which would come into actuality by being intended and chosen for existence. Plato and Aristotle stand, as it were on Mount Nebo across the Jordan from Jericho, on the very edge of, and as if seeing by anticipation, the promised land, the philosophical understanding reached and articulated by

---

[20] See Finnis, *Aquinas: Moral, Political, and Legal Theory*. Oxford: Oxford University Press 1998: 298–312.

their Christian successors, that human willing includes free choices in which *nothing* either external or internal determines which of the options one will adopt, and that the universe is not only ordered by and to the supremely actual being but actually created *ex nihilo* by an utterly transcendent free choice, a choice among infinitely many incompatibly alternative and incommensurably very good universes, a choice determined by nothing save the act of choosing, the divine will(ing) itself. Contemplation of the truth of God's transcendent freedom and power, in creating and sustaining and ordering the entire universe of everything there will ever be beyond Himself, has vastly deepened philosophical and common-sense understanding and appreciation of human dignity, and of the significance of intention in human life and action. When the truth of creation and providential sustaining and ordering is misunderstood, rejected, or forgotten, there emerge as if inherently caused and reinforced by, and reinforcing, the misunderstanding, rejection, and forgetfulness of intention in human moral life, and the explicit or implicit denial of the equality of all human beings in personal dignity.

To speak of dignity is to speak both of superiority (e.g. in power, excellence, status) and of what has intrinsic worth for its own sake. Our capacity for acts of free choice is a capacity both bodily and intellectual, material and spiritual, for in human beings all that is material and bodily is informed and actualised by a soul that is not only living and animal but also intellectual-spiritual. So each of us has every level of being – the physical solidity and dynamisms of a star of a galaxy, the chemical and biological complexity and self-directedness of a zygote, a tree, or a lion, *and* then some more. The *more* we have is the capacity to understand all these other kinds of reality, to reason about them and about reasoning itself, to take steps towards replicating and transforming other beings on all those levels of reality, and with self-mastery's freedom to *choose* whether or not to do so and in these and other ways *how to live*. These spiritual capacities subsist even when our bodily makeup is too immature, injured, or decayed to allow them to be actualised fully, or perhaps perceptibly at all. It is possession of these capacities that makes us each human and the equal of each other in basic dignity, worth, value, and so in human rights.

Nietzsche denied the existence of God because (in the last analysis) he could not bear that there be any being so transcendently his superior.[21] So he surrendered the truth to his own feelings, to a kind of spiritual passion, to pride itself. With the truth about God there disappeared the truth about human equality, dignity, and worth as such, and there opened up the way to Nietzsche's expression of active contempt for the weak and impatience with anyone willing to prefer care for them in their weakness to terminating their impaired existence. It is not so easy, usually, to trace the motivations of standard contemporary academic materialism. John Searle testifies against some forms of that materialism, while also exemplifying another form of it himself, and his testimony is that there are

---

[21] This is demonstrated from Nietzsche's writings by Eric Voegelin in his *Science, Politics, and Gnosticism.* [1958] Chicago: Henry Regnery 1968: 53–73.

unstated assumptions behind the drive to adopt positions which are as absurd, but as commonplace among contemporary philosophers, as the denial of the existence of the mental – the denial even that anyone is conscious. And the most significant of these unstated assumptions, in his view, is what he calls a "terror" of what seem to be the alternatives, among which he gives prominence (right alongside "spiritualism") to "belief in the immortality of the soul".[22] One can only speculate whether some such terror lies behind Searle's own stated belief that one of "the obvious facts of physics" is "that the world consists entirely of physical particles in fields of force"[23] – as if physics were qualified to establish the non-existence of facts or realities of a kind other than those it studies, facts such as that I *mean* this, or that so-and-so was being economical with the truth when he said he was going to the Law Library to put "the finishing touches" to his conference paper. But in general it would be rash to assume that fear of one or another element in Christian moral teaching plays no great part in the genesis, defence, and successful diffusion of materialistic "scientific world views".

What the Holy See calls the culture of death is, as I said earlier, a culture or subculture constituted by two main dispositions: willingness publicly to regard and treat some human beings as not persons, inherently entitled to basic rights and justice; and publicly unashamed willingness to choose and intend to kill such human beings, and to carry out, promote, and legally protect such choices and intentions. The opposing "culture of life", then, is the culture or subculture – aspiring and entitled in reason to be a universal culture – which rejects those dispositions. Accordingly, the culture of life defends not only the reality of soul which is the root of human dignity, equality, and rights, but also the significance of *intention* in one's conscientious deliberations and accordingly also in moral teaching.

Thus the whole teaching of the *Catechism of the Catholic Church* about the kinds of act which are excluded by the fifth commandment, that is, the *Catechism*'s entire treatment of legitimate defence as distinct from the intrinsic homicidal wrongs of murder, abortion, euthanasia, and suicide, is all placed under the distinction between carrying out an intention to kill and doing what causes death only as a side-effect. Of course causing death as an unintended side-effect is often an injustice,[24] but that wrong is relative to the circumstances whereas the commandment protecting at least innocent human beings is not; in line with natural reason, it excludes all intentional killing, exceptionlessly, whatever the circumstances – as *Evangelium Vitae* 75.1 puts it, "always and everywhere, without exception". Intentional killing, sometimes called "direct" killing in one of the senses of that ambiguous word, is killing done in carrying out a choice to deprive someone of his life either as an end in itself or as a means to some other end, good or bad: see *EV* 57.5; 62.1; *CCC* 2271.

---

[22] J. Searle, *The Rediscovery of the Mind*. Cambridge, Mass. and London: MIT Press 1992, 1994: 13.
[23] *Ibid*. xii.
[24] *CCC*: 2290.

The teaching of the Church in defence of life, marking out the minimum elements and backbone of the culture of life, is thus a teaching founded precisely on intention understood in terms of what is chosen, willed, as an end or as a means, as distinct from what is *caused* perhaps with full *foresight* of lethal consequences but is for the chooser and causer neither an end nor a means (that is, is a side-effect, or, as is sometimes less clearly said, an indirect killing).

So one of the important results of secularism in our culture is loss of grip on the reality of intention, and its distinction from bringing about as a side-effect. One finds this result of secularism in many contexts besides the pronouncements and decisions of certain British ministers of Health and American courts. Germain Grisez, Joseph Boyle and I recently wrote a long article exploring the significance of intention in common-sense, Roman Law and common law, and in Catholic moral teaching, and developing a philosophical analysis of the concept, on the basis of which we both responded to criticisms which the Notre Dame theologian Jean Porter had levelled against our earlier discussions of it, and made our own criticisms of some of the discussion of intention in the works of some of our friends and collaborators such as William E. May and Fr Kevin Flannery SJ.[25] Since our work on intention had been the entire subject-matter of Jean Porter's article in *Theological Studies* in 1996, we submitted our article to the same journal, the leading Jesuit theological periodical at least in America. The editor, Fr Michael Fahey SJ, after six months' consultation, wrote praising the article for its quality, but rejecting it for its subject-matter. The distinction between intention and side-effect, or "direct" and "indirect", is, he said (summarising the advice of the moral theologians he had consulted), a distinction which:

> admittedly has relevance for some and indeed might have importance in inter-preting parts of the encyclical *Veritatis splendor*. But in the long run, it was seen, the logic is not judged as generally helpful for most moral theologians, let alone other theologians whose ministry lies elsewhere.[26]

I think this is probably all true. The distinction has indeed relevance for "some", such as John Paul II and other bishops responsible for the *Catechism*, and *Evangelium Vitae*, and for the entire tradition running from Aquinas to Pius XII and Paul VI, and behind Aquinas back to Augustine and implicitly the author of the Bible's book of Wisdom. But these "some" seem to count for little with "most moral theologians". Secularism has made an astonishingly rapid and far-reaching penetration among them. With striking completeness and casualness the leading theologians responsible for disseminating proportionalism began to make two particular errors. One error was and is about the tradition, the doctrine, that they were rejecting: it was their claim that the moral precepts they were rejecting, mostly in the field(s) of killing and sex, are precepts about what is "directly" or

[25] J. Finnis, G. Grisez, J. Boyle, ' "Direct" and "Indirect:" A Reply to Critics of Our Action Theory'. 65 (2001) *The Thomist*: 1–44.
[26] Letter of Michael A. Fahey SJ to John Finnis, 13 January 2000.

"indirectly" *caused*,[27] when in truth those precepts concerned kinds of intending, choosing, and carrying out one's intentions and choices. The other error was not historical but analytical or philosophical: it was and is their claim that what one causes as a side-effect is a *means* to the consequences one seeks to achieve by one's action. In the tradition, properly understood and clarified, and in a sound analysis, whatever is willed as a means is intended, and chosen, and is part of what *Veritatis Splendor* 78.1 calls the object of one's act. That object, as this encyclical makes clear, must be understood from "the perspective of the acting person", and is *not* "a process or an event of the merely physical order, to be assessed on the basis of its ability to bring about a given state of affairs in the outside world" but is rather "the proximate end of a deliberate decision which determines the act of willing on the part of the acting person". Understanding action from the perspective of the deliberating and acting person is the key to understanding the backbone of morality in the life and death issues that are our concern in this Conference. Adopting this perspective, I should add, makes demands on the thinking of those who uphold the "culture of life", and upon "traditional" theologians as well as on those who would sideline them as "some".

I have discussed elsewhere the collapsing of intention into foresight and causation in such witnesses of much contemporary culture as the judgments of the Federal Courts of Appeal in the assisting suicide cases *Compassion in Dying v. Washington* (9th circuit, 1996) and *Quill v. Vacco* (2nd circuit, 1997).[28] These misunderstandings of intention or purpose were prominent in official and semi-official reactions to recent attempts here in England to declare illegal the withholding of treatment, care, and sustenance "with a purpose of hastening or otherwise causing death". They reappear in many places, notably among those who write and speak explicitly or implicitly as "secular humanists".

I have already said today a good deal about why secularism can never be a genuine humanism. The loss of an understanding of intention and its significance among the many teachers of Catholic moral theology who are in revolt against Catholic faith and life should be of concern also to those theologians whose ministry, in Fr Fahey's engaging words, "lies elsewhere". For as James J. Walter remarked not so long ago, neither he himself "nor any other proportionalist can see here how God's moral will is only disposed indirectly or permissively vis-à-vis non-moral evil (natural defect)."[29] But the great tradition of theological reflection on the divine will and providence, expounded by St John Damascene, the last of the Fathers, and by Aquinas, insists that God indeed does not will even *natural* defects to *be*, but only wills to permit them, because for God to intend *anything* which intelligence would call an evil is inconsistent with his holiness.

---

[27] See the quotations from Peschke and Fuchs in my *Moral Absolutes*. Washington DC: CUA Press 1991: 77 n. 38.

[28] 79 F. 3d 790, reversed sub nom. *Washington v. Glucksberg*, 117 S. Ct. 2258 (1997); 80 F. 3d 716, reversed sub nom. *Vacco v. Quill*, 117 S. Ct. 2293 (1997).

[29] 'Response to John Finnis', in Thomas G. Fuechtmann (ed.), *Consistent Ethic of Life*. Kansas City: Sheed & Ward 1988: 182–195 at 186; see Finnis, *Moral Absolutes* 74–77.

God's holiness seems faint indeed in the works of proportionalist theologians – read them and see – and is denied, one way or another, in each of the forms of secularism differentiated and discussed by Plato. But we too can forget it, in one or other of the ways which the Lord speaks of in the parable of the Sower: lack of understanding of the Word (stony ground), lack of endurance in the face of trial (shallow roots), and lastly what Shakespeare's Bastard Falconbridge transposes to "los[ing] my way among the thorns and dangers of this world"[30]: "Other seeds fell among thorns, and the thorns grew up and choked them ... this is the one who hears the word, but the cares of the world and the lure of riches choke the word, and it yields nothing."[31] The cares of this world. *he merimna tou aiônos – sollicitudo* **saeculi** *istius* – our Lord's warning against a kind of secularism by default.

---

[30] *King John* 4.3, 140.
[31] *Mt* 13: 7, 22.

4

De-Christianising England: Newman, Mill and the Stationary State

DERMOT FENLON *Cong. Orat.*

Deism is not a new creation of the Enlightenment: it is merely the return of the *Deus otiosus* of the mythical religions.

Cardinal Ratzinger[1]

I ever tell friends that they must look among Catholics, not for natural excellence, but supernatural. *But many Catholics do not like to allow this.*

Newman to J. Spencer Northcote, June 18, 1862

IT IS WELL to remember that the mythical religions of antiquity subserved a purpose of social control. The same is true of the mythology of secularism in the contemporary world. The wars of the Reformation frightened men of property. In England, Deism after 1660 mounted, in the name of reason, science and history, an assault on the sacramental principle embedded in the Anglican liturgy.[2] A brand of Latitudinarian Christianity, minimising doctrine, established the preponderant tone of Anglican Christianity. The proposed emasculation of Christianity, the project of Hume and Gibbon was, however, postponed by the triumph of Wesley and the Evangelical Revival. The political requisite of a Christian Crusade against Napoleon ensured that it was only after 1815 that the attack on Christianity in the English speaking world was renewed and 'became routine'. The role of John Stuart Mill in that enterprise, the hidden, tactical character of his prose, and especially the importance of his private correspondence was first identified by Philip Hughes in 1950, and then by Maurice Cowling, in a work which became the prelude to a remarkably penetrating study of the assault on Christianity in England, *Religion and Public Doctrine in Modern England.*[3]

---

[1] J. Ratzinger, *The Feast of Faith*. San Francisco: Ignatius Press 1986: 22.

[2] J. A. I. Champion, *The Pillars of Priestcraft Shaken: The Church of England and its Enemies 1660–1730*. Cambridge 1992. Andrew Louth, *Discerning the Mystery: an essay on the nature of theology*. Oxford: Clarendon Press 1983: 128–129.

[3] Three volumes, Cambridge University Press: Volume 1 (1980), Volume 2 (1985) for the 'routine' character of the nineteenth century attack: 104–108. Volume 3 (2001). The author's earlier *Mill and Liberalism*. Cambridge University Press 1963 was republished in a second edition in 1990, with a political preface which may be thought unhelpful. See also my essay 'The "Aristocracy of Talent" and the "Mystery" of Newman': 15 (1990) *Louvain Studies*: 203–225. For the Enlightenment in England, J. G. A. Pocock, *Barbarism and Religion*. Cambridge University Press: 2 Volumes 1999. For Philip Hughes see the reference in footnote 23 below.

Cowling's achievement was to identify Mill as the father and teacher of a new clerical estate, 'the Clerisy' (Coleridge's description adopted by Mill). Newman, Pusey, Keble and Hurrell Froude called it the 'Aristocracy of Talent'. Each of the parties understood the process as a replacement for the clergy by a secular administration deferring to the supposedly empirical criteria deriving from the university intelligentsia. Within the clerisy, by the close of the nineteenth century, Mill came to exercise what John Morley, Secretary to the Liberal Party, described as 'pontifical authority'.[4] His function was to supply a doctrine – that of zero population growth – and a rhetorical strategy, applicable through Common Law institutions, to Africa, India and the Colonial World, based on a norm of 'scientific' conduct replacing the imperatives of traditional religion. After World War II that became the objective of American foreign policy, pursued through the United Nations and World Health Organisation. Reproductive medicine became the key to command of resources through control of population. The strategy was Anglo-American. Mill held an important place in the origination of that policy.

In this paper I wish to explore the role of Mill, especially as we see it reflected in his correspondence with Harriet Taylor. For it was through Harriet that Mill, the 'saint' of nineteenth century rationalism, became the 'pontifical authority' constantly invoked in legislation which throughout the twentieth century advanced the secularisation of the reproductive act. The emptying out of religious meaning from the encounter between man and woman entailed an increasing tendency to regard the human child as a threat, a burden, or a designer product, in which the designer was no longer God. The child became a utilitarian possession. It was through Mill and Harriet Taylor that the difference between the sexes increasingly came to be considered a matter of social construction, and therefore of potential reconstruction, rather than more fundamentally, and biologically, 'given.' The loss of that 'giveness' is at the root of the confusion of identity which is the hallmark of contemporary sexuality and human culture. It is the final *Entzauberung*, the loss of meaning, surrounding the reproductive act and invading the whole of human life. Already, Mill, who himself felt bitterly the taunt of being a 'manufactured man', a 'mere reasoning machine', sought to redress his dilemma by looking to Harriet Taylor for conversion to a credo of feelings, which in turn supplied the criterion of 'harm' proposed by Mill as the basis of

---

[4] Morley's description of Mill's 'pontifical authority' in his *Recollections*. New York: Macmillan 1917: 1:55, quoted in Janice Carlisle, *John Stuart Mill on the Writing of Character*. Athens and London: University of Georgia Press 1991: 324. The death of Gladstone in 1896 may be regarded as the moment of Mill's posthumous triumph and the final displacement of Christianity as the doctrine of the state.

moral legislation – 'harm', that is to say, which by the late twentieth century had come to mean, especially, to others' 'feelings'.[5]

It is no coincidence that Mill should have been invoked with canonical regularity in the legislation of the later twentieth century – in the discussion surrounding the Wolfenden Report on homosexuality in 1959; in the Abortion Law Reform Association's account of its victory in 1967; in Baroness Warnock's appeal to the *Uses of Philosophy*, where Mill is enlisted to sustain the recommended view of the Warnock Report on Human Fertilisation and Embryology, that "In real life morality … there is no single 'correct' view."[6] Finally, and most interestingly, in Conrad Lord Russell's recent guide to Liberalism, the views of Mill on liberty have become "for the first time", so we are told, "part of the essence of the Liberal [Party?] creed." That creed, he informs us, has gained its 'extra boost' from the contraceptive pill and the sexual revolution, which ensure that "there will never again be a single agreed standard of sexual morals." In such a world we must "whether we like it or not" adopt Mill's concept of Individuality.[7]

What Lord Russell understands by that is illustrated by his recollection of "an elderly Oxford Fellow" complaining in 1969 "that undergraduates were no longer content to be able to have their girlfriends in all night: they were demanding a *right* to do so." From that, Lord Russell concludes, the sexual revolution, as a matter of right, ensures that "the moral basis of authority has been changed." Given that change, he tells us, we are to call on Mill. What for? For the defence of liberty – the individual's 'right' to 'choose'.[8]

[5] Roger Scruton's *Sexual Desire*. London: Weidenfeld and Nicolson 1986, and his *An Intelligent Person's Guide to Modern Culture*. London: Duckworth 1998, identify the 'disenchantment of the sexual act' as constituting the essence of modern secularism. So, in a different way, does Alastair Macintyre's *After Virtue*, London: Duckworth 1981. The 'emptying out' of the sacramental presence of God finds its completion, therefore, in the destruction of matrimony. Scruton, though not Cowling, identifies the aesthetics of 'right feeling' as the only available substitute for faith – thereby adopting the aesthetic-moral criterion proposed in Mill's *Essay on Bentham and Coleridge* (1840) which, taken up by Matthew Arnold, and developed by F. R. Leavis, has remained the 'substitution for Christianity' proposed by English culture since the nineteenth century. I wish to acknowledge Professor Robert George's helpful identification of an 'ethos' of 'good feeling' as the proposed substitute for the Ten Commandments in contemporary Liberalism (viva voce contribution to the discussion following the first version of this paper at Cambridge in July 2000). For Mill's sensitivity to the taunt of being 'a manufactured man' see his *Autobiography*, ed. Jack Stillinger, Oxford: University Press 1969: 93. The standard edition of Mill's output is *Collected Works* published from Toronto (University of Toronto Press). I have used whatever editions have come to hand.

[6] Mary Warnock, *A Question of Life. The Warnock Report on Human Fertilisation and Embryology.* Oxford: Basil Blackwell 1985, Introduction, p. x. ["In real life morality is more complicated and more various than that. There is no single 'correct' view."] For Warnock's appeal to Mill as the authority for a utilitarian jurisprudence linked with an irreducible moral pluralism, see Mary Warnock, *The Uses of Philosophy*. Oxford: Blackwell 1992, Chapter 6: 'Towards a Moral Consensus': 84–101. See also Keith Hindell and Madeleine Simms, *Abortion Law Reformed: With a Foreword by David Steel, M.P.* London: Peter Owen 1971, with a preliminary citation of Mill's 'On Liberty'.

[7] *An Intelligent Person's Guide to Liberalism*. London: Duckworth 1999: 90.

[8] *Ibid.*

This is Mill's language alright. Is it also what he means? In what follows I wish to raise the question whether it is not merely an accurate, but a sufficient account of what Mill intended, and to examine Mill in the light of what his contemporary, John Henry Newman, thought about the issues he raised. For Mill and Newman stand to each other and to us as the very type of secularism and its opposite – Mill the rationalist, Newman, the shepherd of souls, uttering the response of the Church, in the mind of Christ, to the crisis of humanity at the end of a Millennium which has seen the progressive de-Christianisation of the industrial West.

To begin with Mill. Mill is modern. He was born and grew up without baptism "in London" he tells us, "on 20th May 1806 ... the eldest son of James Mill, the author of the History of British India." British India hung over Mill as a destiny from birth. His father worked for the East India Company. As a boy, the young Mill helped his father to correct the proofs of his *magnum opus*. As a man he rose to be "chief conductor of correspondence with the Native States of India." Father and son: Mill was a child of the eighteenth century; he became preceptor of the twentieth. His influence, more than that of Marx, was decisive for the contemporary world order.

Mill was educated to reform humanity. His father, the son of an Angus farmer, lost his Christian faith as a student for the Scottish Church. He embraced the faith of the Scots Enlightenment, and imported it to London. "My father" wrote Mill, "impressed upon me from the first ... that the question 'Who made me?' cannot be answered." At the same time "he taught me to take the strongest interest in the Reformation, as the great and decisive contest against priestly tyranny for liberty of thought."[9] What Mill understood by that was to become clear in his account, given in 1848, of the imminent replacement of Christianity by the 'principles' of 'political economy':

> The principles of the Reformation have reached as low down in society as reading and writing, and the poor will not much longer accept morals and religion of other people's prescribing.[10]

Instead, the poor were to accept the morals prescribed by Mill's 'principles' disseminated through the schools, the press, and the institutions of the state. Among these, the central principle was the education of the people in the prevention of birth. That was not an easy undertaking in the Christian climate of Victorian England. Indeed, it would only become, what Mill wanted it to become, a 'duty', in the following century. With the arrival of the concept of contraceptive 'duty', Christianity ceased to be the shaping influence in English life and culture.

Meanwhile, 'liberty of thought' meant for Mill's own early education at home, Greek at the age of three, the histories of Gibbon and Robertson between the ages

---

[9] *Autobiography*: 27.

[10] *Principles of Political Economy*. Seventh and final edition, republished 1994, ed. Jonathan Riley, Oxford and New York: Oxford University Press: 135.

of four and seven, Logic, leading on to Hobbes by the age of twelve, all preparing the young Mill to bring to completion the Scottish Enlightenment and to domesticate England in the principles of the French Revolution, not with the weaponry of steel but through a civil service grounded in the logic of Mill's *Principles of Political Economy*.

Mill's hero, he tells us, was Condorcet. In Bentham he found what he called his "unifying conception . . . a creed, a doctrine, a philosophy, in one among the best senses of the word, a religion." Through Auguste Comte he learned to call it the religion of humanity. It was to be propounded by the educational methods of von Humbolt with the consent and indeed co-operation of Christians. "From the winter of 1821, when I first read Bentham" – Mill was fifteen years old – "I had what might be called an object in life; to be a reformer of the world." Not just England, mind you, but the world; India, in the wake of the Napoleonic Wars, was secure, and India *meant* the world. It has become more so. Through its economy, and through its participation in British Common Law, India has become central to the mind of the twenty-first century.

In 1823 Mill followed his father into the East India Company. By the close of the decade he was proposing, through the pages of the *Westminster Review*, a change of public opinion on the fundamentals of moral conduct. Among Mill's youthful acquaintances "Malthus's population principle was a banner, and point of union." This 'great doctrine', he says, we took up 'in the contrary sense' to that intended by Malthus. To improve mankind the first step was to reduce it.

Malthus, a clergyman of the Church of England, had intended a warning against faith in the perfectibility of man through science and economics alone; in later life, he urged a limitation of population growth by self-restraint. The younger Mill and his associates now turned Malthus on his head. The indefinite improvement of humanity must be secured precisely by population restriction. Mill called it 'the sole means' of human improvement. The poor must be educated accordingly.[11]

Mill belonged to what may be called the 'Malthusian turning point'. The new Poor Law Act of 1834 made the children of the poor the target of the municipal ratepayer. The middle classes were resolved that the poor should no longer be what hitherto they had always been, their Christian responsibility. The Marriage Registry Act of 1835 and the Municipal Corporation Act of 1836 replaced the Christian idea of Charity with a purely secular regulation of human relations. When Darwin, on board the Beagle, in 1834, received a packet of booklets advocating sexual restraint as a way of escaping starvation, he distributed the booklets to the men on board. They were the 'politicol-economical tales' of delayed marriages and couples rescued from the poor house, written by the government sponsored novelist Harriet Martineau. In these booklets she described the poor as 'the gangrene of the State'. It was thus that Darwin in due course

---

[11] *Ibid*: 64. See Adrian Desmond and James Moore, *Darwin*. London: Penguin Books 1991: 153–154 for Harriet Martineau and the 'gangrene of the State'.

arrived at the metaphors of natural selection and the survival of the fittest. The doctrine of zero population growth as the basis of Sustainable Development, at once economic and biological, contraceptive and educational, the doctrine, in short, of the Reith Lectures and of the World Health Organisation as we know it today, was born of the Malthusian moment. Mill was among the earliest promoters of the creed. He was the philosopher who supplied the requisite mental equipment for the replacement of Christianity.

In the autumn of 1826, he experienced his first great crisis of faith:

> I was in a dull state of nerves, such as everyone is liable to; unsusceptible to enjoyment or pleasurable excitement; one of those moods when what is pleasure at other times becomes insipid or indifferent; the state, I should think, in which converts to Methodism usually are, when smitten by their first 'conviction of sin'. In this frame of mind it occurred to put the question direct to myself: 'suppose that all your objects in life were realised; that all the changes in institutions and opinions which you are looking forward to, could be completely effected at this very instant: would this be a great joy and happiness to you?' And an irrepressible self-consciousness distinctly answered No! At this my heart sank within me: the whole foundation on which my life was constructed fell down. All my happiness was to have been found in the continual pursuit of this end. The end had ceased to charm, and how could there ever again be any interest in the means? I seemed to have nothing left to live for.[12]

In this condition he read Wordsworth and discovered Coleridge. The Romantic revolt of the nineteenth century against the eighteenth – a world of inner feeling – seized him. In 1830, at the age of twenty-four, he met Harriet Taylor. She was twenty-three. She was married with young children. Mill's views on Women's Suffrage impressed her.

By the end of 1832 "she to whom my life is devoted" wrote Mill, had sought from him a memorandum, "a written exposition of my opinions" on divorce.[13] There was no liaison between them. Harriet insisted on Mill making this known when they eventually married in a registry office after her husband's death in 1851. But the twenty year friendship caused scandal, and accounts for much of Mill's alienation from and inner hatred of English society. That was the driving force behind his *Essay on Liberty*: his chosen target, Christian, and specifically English Protestant public opinion. Indeed if we would understand the motivations of Mill's published works, we must take full account of the inner life disclosed in the letters and papers of Mill and Harriet Taylor.

In his response to Harriet's appeal for a memorandum in 1832–1833, Mill considered that first choice in matrimony should "very generally [be] persevered

---

[12] *Autobiography*: 80–81.

[13] *Sexual Equality; Writings by John Stuart Mill, Harriet Taylor Mill, and Helen Taylor*. Ed. Ann P. Robson and John M. Robson, Toronto: University of Toronto Press 1994: 3.

in... repeated trials for happiness have the most mischievous effects on all minds"; children would be "better cared for if their parents remain together." The family remained, for Mill, the cradle of humanity.

Chastity before marriage was, however, an "arbitrary ceremonial". Affection was the sufficient criterion of conjugality.[14]

Harriet's memorandum of the same date strikes a different note. She is imbued with the vision of a brave new world:

> If I could be Providence to the world for a time, for the express purpose of raising the condition of women, I should come to you to know the *means* – the *purpose* would be to remove all interference with affection... I have no doubt that when the whole community is really educated, tho' the present laws of marriage were to continue they would be perfectly disregarded, because no one would marry...

And again:

> ... on this plan, it would be in the woman's *interest* not to have children...[15]

In such a world, libido 'educated' in 'affection' would be its own objective. The 'condition of women' would be 'raised' by the replacement of Christian maternity. The ideal of the Female Eunuch would substitute for Providence a New World Order. It would provide for a 'really' educated rearrangement of the world's population and resources. It would be left to Mill strategically to advance the project through the education of public opinion.

By 1854, after more than twenty years of friendship, and three of civil marriage (Harriet's husband died in 1851) Mill was prepared to express in his diary, for Harriet's eyes only, a regret that the marriage vow should legally oblige; by 1855, he was communicating the same view privately in his correspondence with others:

> Nothing ought to be ultimately rested in, short of entire freedom on both sides to dissolve this like any other partnership. The only thing requiring legal regulation would be the maintenance of the children when the parents could not manage it amicably – and in that I do not see any considerable difficulty.[16]

Partners may part and call it freedom. Children must be expected not to mind.

Harriet had gained over Mill's earlier, more cautious self. By 1854 she and Mill were planning a series of Essays on questions of the day. She wrote to him:

> About the Essays, dear, would not religion, the utility of Religion, be one of the subjects you would have most to say on... to account for the existence nearly universal of some religion (superstition) by the instincts of fear, hope, and mystery etc., and throwing over all doctrines and theories, called religion as devices for

---

[14] Mill borrowed here from Robert Owen, just as from Coleridge he borrowed the idea of the 'clerisy'. *Ibid*: 16, for Owen.

[15] *Ibid*: 19.

[16] *Ibid*: 49.

power ... to show how religion and poetry fill the same want, the craving after higher objects, the consolation of suffering, the hope of heaven for the selfish, love of God for the tender and grateful – how all this must be superseded by morality deriving its power from sympathies and benevolence and its reward from the approbation of those we respect. There, what a long sentence ...[17]

One has the impression here of listening to a conversation, in which Mill has 'most to say' on 'the utility of Religion', and on 'fear, hope and mystery ... the hope of heaven [and] love of God' – a conversation in which Mill and Harriet discussed how best to replace these with a morality based on 'sympathies, benevolence and ... approbation'. Harriet's plea was for an open assault on Christianity. But Mill did not oblige. He hung on to the 'utility' of religion.

When his *Essay on Liberty* appeared in 1859, one year after Harriet's sudden death, he said, "None of my writings have been either so carefully composed, or so sedulously corrected as this."[18] He consecrated it to Harriet's memory. To her he attributed its authorship. The text was, so to speak, her 'room', everything in place just as she had left it. But it had been tidied by Mill. His emphatic attribution of the authorship to Harriet only underlines the absence, from the text itself, of any plea for the liquidation of the marriage vow. What there is in the text that bears on Christianity touches only on the Protestant Sunday – a plea for the pubs to be open for the sake of non-believers – and a striking passage arguing against "misapplied notions of liberty" enabling parents to regard children "as their peculiar property not thinking what a danger they might constitute to the State by their ignorance and poverty." Mill was throwing on the State the primary responsibility for the education of children. Compulsory education at school would compensate for 'ignorance' and 'poverty'. It would alter the condition in which "children ... are a real obstacle to the fulfilment by the State of its duties." Here we are tacitly in the presence of Mill's doctrine of the Stationary State, a world of zero population growth with an adequate supply of public parks and national reserves to protect the planet for the middle classes.[19] As

[17] Cowling cited this as the frontispiece to his *Mill and Liberalism*. He followed the citation with one from W. Somerset Maugham: "Philip thought this over for a moment, then he said: 'I don't see why things we believe absolutely now shouldn't be just as wrong as what they believed in the past.' 'Neither do I.' 'Then how can you believe anything at all?' 'I don't know.'" *Of Human Bondage*. London 1915: 121.

[18] *Autobiography*: 144.

[19] *Essay on Liberty*: Ed. S. Collini. Cambridge University Press 1989: 105–9. What Mill meant by the Stationary State is explained in his *Principles of Political Economy*: 128: "There is room in the world, no doubt, and even in old countries, for a great increase of population, supposing the arts of life to go on improving, and capital to increase. But even if innocuous, I confess I see very little reason for desiring it." He considered it "scarcely necessary to remark that a stationary condition of capital and population implies no stationary state of human improvement." He expressed a "hope, for the sake of posterity, that they will be content to be stationary, long before necessity compels them to it." *Ibid*: 129. Cowling considered that there was a hidden coercive agenda in Mill's strategy for mankind. Janice Carlisle in a subtle analysis of the People's Edition of the *Principles* (1865) confirms Cowling's view. Her work tends to remove any ground for Conrad Russell's confidence that Mill can be unambiguously claimed as a champion of the sexual revolution. Carlisle, *Mill*: 155.

we have seen, Mill had arrived at that before Harriet recognised its potential for 'raising the condition of women' so that she (through Mill) could thereby be 'Providence to the world'.

The Stationary State, as Mill was to argue in the *Principles of Political Economy*, would repose on full employment, attained by family limitation; the poor would be educated to comply, and Mill would educate the educators. "Read Mill" was Leslie Stephens' account of the advice given by Oxford and Cambridge Tutors to their charges, in the second half of the nineteenth century, in the years following the dissemination of Mill's *Logic*, which made its first appearance in 1843. It was an injunction more extensive than the book's title might lead us to imagine. Had the title accurately described its purpose, it would have sunk stone dead into the dustbin of history. But the real purpose of Mill's *Logic* was fully described in Leslie Stephens' words as "a Sacred Scripture for Liberal Intellectuals... a logical armoury for all assailants of established Dogmatism."[20] Established Dogmatism included traditional beliefs about matrimony and the procreation of children. Among Mill's disciples it became an axiom that "obedience to Malthus makes prosperous the French peasant, disobedience, the pauperised English labourer."[21] That became the doctrine of the new caste of professional administrators, professionally examined – teachers, architects, doctors, lawyers, engineers and not least civil servants – the makers of the Empire – issuing from the universities and conjoined by the work of 'the theological learned'. These were to be taken as "essential to the scheme" not as "priests whose office was to conciliate the invisible powers, and to superintend the interests that survive the grave."[22] Rather, the task of theology must be to promote the interests of humanity, to become an instrument of civilisation.

We should note that the clergy were to be regarded as 'essential to the scheme'. The sacerdotal idea was to be relegated and the clergy re-educated to subserve the 'principles' of Mill's 'political economy'. The Stationary State was to be advanced with the complicity of the clergy.

To Auguste Comte Mill wrote in 1844:

> The time has not yet arrived when, without compromising our cause, we can in England direct open attacks upon Christian theology. We can only by-pass it, peacefully eliminating it from all philosophical and social discussions, and ignoring all the questions proper to it as irrelevant to daily life.[23]

Here we see Mill as the master of the media, and the re-educator of the Church. Theology would be enlisted to promote the contraceptive State and the

---

[20] Quoted by Basil Willey, *Nineteenth Century Studies*. London: Penguin Books 1964: 161.
[21] *Ibid*: 172.
[22] Cowling, *Mill and Liberalism*: 16, quoting from Mill's *Three Essays on Religion*. London 1874: 82.
[23] Quoted by Philip Hughes in *The English Catholics 1850–1950: Essays to commemorate the centenary of the restoration of the Hierarchy of England and Wales*. Ed. G. A. Beck, London: Burns Oates 1950: 5 note 3.

universities would be transformed into purely secular academies of human development. Thus:

> The very first step should be to unsectarianise them ... by putting an end to sectarian teaching altogether. The principle itself of dogmatic religion, dogmatic morality, dogmatic philosophy, is what requires to be rooted out; not any particular manifestation of that principle.[24]

We may suppose that this essay of 1836 was well known to Newman. It throws clear light on what he was to write in his *Apologia Pro Vita Sua* in 1864, describing his life-long commitment to revealed truth enshrined in Christian Doctrine:

> First was the principle of dogma: my battle was with liberalism; by liberalism I mean the anti-dogmatic principle and its developments.[25]

In fighting the 'anti dogmatic principle' in religion Newman was fighting Mill, and through Mill, the ethos of the Stationary State. He was fighting the recruitment of the clergy to that enterprise. He was reaffirming the divine constitution of the Church, her apostolic vocation and her mission, in the face of a Christianity eviscerated from within, relativised, and serenely allocated a civilising role among the historical sciences. The clergy were to promote the creed of secularism. Thus Mill, in 1869, urged the students of St. Andrew's destined for holy orders to "use your influence to make the doctrines [regarded as essential to remaining in orders] as few as possible."[26] This was Mill speaking to the clergy and through the clergy. It clearly illuminates his strategy: convert the clergy and complete the indoctrination of humanity in the principles of the Stationary State.

As a matter of fact it was precisely this kind of influence which Mill had already found serviceable in the theologians of Oriel College, Oxford, as early as 1830. What Oriel promoted was a rejection of the appeal to authority in Theology, falling back on Logic to decide the application of Christianity to the new political economy. In that year Mill told a French correspondent, Gustave d'Eichtal, that if he wanted to promote his ideas in England, he should establish contact with two of the theologians of Oriel, Blanco White and Richard Whately: "Any impression made upon these two men", he wrote, "will spread far and wide."[27] Through such influences the poor would be encouraged by the clergy to follow the logic of the new Poor Law. The effect would be to discourage the poor from breeding. Fear of the workhouse would do by supposedly 'Christian' persuasion what Mill would elsewhere propose in his *Principles of Political Economy*.

Oriel was Newman's College. Whately was Newman's preceptor in Logic.

---

[24] Cowling, *Mill and Liberalism*: 20, quoting from Mill's 'Civilisation' (1836) in *Dissertations and Discussions*. London 1859, Volume I: 200–201.

[25] *Apologia Pro Vita Sua*. Ed. M. J. Svaglic, London: Oxford University Press 1967: 54.

[26] *Ibid*: 114.

[27] Quoted in Martin Murphy, *Blanco White: Self-banished Spaniard*. New Haven and London: Yale University Press 1989: 153–154.

In 1832 Newman resigned his tutorship at Oriel. He did so because he took his office as involving something more than a means merely of securing high examination results for his students. He took it as a pastoral office, involving the cure of minds as well as souls; a view now anathema to the University authorities and to the State which stood behind the new professional administrators. It is often said that Newman lacked a doctrine of State. That was far from being true. It was in opposition to the secularised political economy as promoted through the universities that Newman found his vocation, and founded it as an affirmation of the Church's teaching office to proclaim the Christian meaning of Holy Matrimony and love of the poor in the face of the subtraction of Christianity from marriage, education and what would come to be called 'welfare'. Thus, in later life he wrote, looking back on a century of de-Christianisation:

> For the last fifty years, since 1827, there has been a formidable movement among us towards assigning in the national life political or civil motives for social and personal duties, and thereby withdrawing matters of conduct from the jurisdiction of religion. Men are to be made virtuous, and to do good works, to become good members of society, good husbands and fathers, on purely secular motives. We are having a wedge thrust into us, which tends to the destruction of religion altogether; and this is our misery that there is no definite point at which we can logically take our stand, and resist encroachment on principle. Such is the workhouse system, such was the civil marriage act.[28]

Newman followed the resignation of his tutorship by leaving Oxford. He had a breakdown in Sicily. He returned to England in 1833. His prophetic ministry of the word from the pulpit of St. Mary the Virgin, all that became the Oxford Movement, dates from that moment, and should be seen in response to the unfolding of the Utilitarian State.

Towards the end of his life, in 1879, on the occasion of his Cardinalate, Newman made a speech recalling the course of his Christian life and ministry:

> For 30, 40, 50 years I have resisted to the best of my powers the spirit of liberalism in religion. Never did Holy Church need champions against it more sorely than now.[29]

He then explained his meaning:

> 'Liberalism in religion' is the doctrine that there is no positive truth in religion ... It is inconsistent with any recognition of any religion as *true*. Revealed Religion is not truth, but a sentiment and a taste ... Devotion is not necessarily founded in faith.[30]

---

[28] *The Letters and Diaries of John Henry Newman.* Volume XXVIII. Oxford: Clarendon Press 1975: Newman to Canon Thomas Longman, May 28, 1878.

[29] Newman's Biglietto Speech was printed in Wilfred Ward, *The Life of John Henry Cardinal Newman.* Volume II. London: Longmans 1913: 459–462.

[30] *Ibid.*

Was he thinking about Comte? Was he thinking about Mill? The word 'positive' in the above passage might lead us to think so – Logic, yielding Positivism, the conviction that for 'proof positive' you needed the relegation of all dogma, and the elevation of the experimental principle as the *only* principle in life. Auguste Comte's Religion of Humanity, promulgated through the Academy and promoting the apotheosis of Humanity, anglicised by Mill, shorn of its prescriptive character, transformed into an educational imperative – that was what Newman was talking about, and he knew it first as the doctrine of Oriel College, of Whately, Thomas Arnold and Rugby School – a broad, comprehensive, nationally based, useful religion, with few doctrines – yielding by 1859 to the attenuated Christianity of *Essays and Reviews*, introduced by the Chaplain of Rugby School, urging a religion which would go beyond that of the Apostles, to construct a future for humanity based on truly scientific credentials of historicity and progress. That was where the good and Christian intentions of Whately and Thomas Arnold had ended up by 1859 – in Rugby Chapel, whence Matthew Arnold would shortly mourn the demise of Christianity, on Dover Beach: "Where ignorant armies meet and clash by night."

The loss of Christianity in England: Newman knew that loss in his lifetime and in his own family. He knew it in his elder brother, Charles. He knew it in his younger brother, Francis, who helped to found the Secular Society. He knew it as a personal temptation while at Oriel College "to prefer intellectual to moral excellence". He knew it as a temptation of the mind and a *great* temptation, to decide the content of Christian teaching according to the logic of personal investigation, social policy and ecclesiastical promotion. From that logic he was rescued by grief. The death of his sister, Mary, in 1826 taught Newman the truths which he was to communicate to a generation intent on substituting political welfare for eternal welfare.[31] He knew the temptation as the cancer tearing out the life of Christianity in England. He knew it in the Froude family, especially in William, who married Catherine Holdsworth and became agnostic on the principle that he, as a naval engineer and scientist, could not but 'doubt', could never embrace 'dogma' or 'creed', while Catherine, his wife, and children followed Newman into the Catholic Church, after 1857.[32]

Newman's *Apologia* in 1864 gave expression to his view of the present age:

And in these latter days, outside the Catholic Church things are tending – with far greater rapidity . . . to atheism in one shape or another. What a scene, what a prospect, does the whole of Europe present at this day! And not only Europe, but every government and every civilisation through the world, which is under the influence of the European mind! Especially, how sorrowful, in the view of religion . . . is the spectacle presented to us by the educated intellect of England, France, and Germany!

[31] *Apologia Pro Vita Sua*: 26.
[32] Joyce Sugg, *Ever Yours Affly: John Henty Newman And His Female Circle*. Leominster: Gracewing, Fowler Wright Books 1996: 103–107, carries a fine account of William and Catherine Froude and their family.

And then an extraordinary passage:

> Lovers of their country and of their race, religious men, external to the Catholic Church, have attempted various expedients to arrest fierce wilful human nature in its onward course, and to bring it to subjection. The necessity of some form of religion for the interests of humanity, has been generally acknowledged: but where was the concrete representative of things invisible, which would have the force and the toughness necessary to be a breakwater against the deluge?[33]

Who did Newman refer to as the "lovers of their country and of their race, religious men, external to the Catholic Church"? Was Newman thinking about Whately and Thomas Arnold? No; I think we can detect a reference here to his closest friends in the Oxford Movement, Pusey and Keble. To Henry James Coleridge he wrote, immediately following the completion of the *Apologia* in 1864 (Fr. Coleridge had questioned him concerning Keble's views on certitude of faith):

> I believe I must say that I allude to Keble's conversation more than to anything he wrote ... He considered that religious truth came to us as from the mouth of Our Lord – and what would be called doubt was an imperfect hearing as if one heard from a distance. And, as we were at this time of the world at a distance from Him, of course we heard indistinctly – and faith was not a clear and confident knowledge or certainty, but a sort of loving guess.[34]

But 'indistinct hearing' and 'a sort of loving guess' would not do, to meet the challenge to Christianity in the coming age. Nothing would suffice except a certitude of faith:

> ... the very claim of the Catholic Church ... a provision adapted by the mercy of the Creator, to preserve religion in the world, and to restrain that freedom of thought, which of course in itself is one of our greatest natural gifts, and to rescue it from its own suicidal excesses.[35]

The word 'suicidal' carries a distinct resonance in a culture which has wanted to 'choose' death. That choice, the creation of a culture of death, would be attained by habituation. "I have often thought" wrote Newman in 1873:

> how soon I might get over the sense that murder, as such, is a sin ... after I have killed half a dozen persons. I suppose some nurses ... have not any great horror at the idea of killing children. And thus the idea of a God may go.[36]

---

[33] *Apologia*: 218–219.
[34] *The Letters and Diaries of John Henry Newman*. Volume XXI. London: Nelson 1971: Newman to Henry James Coleridge, June 24, 1864: 129.
[35] *Apologia*: 220.
[36] *The Letters and Diaries of John Henry Newman*. Volume XXVI. Oxford: Clarendon Press 1974: Newman to H. P. Liddon, March 2, 1873.

Against the suicidal freedoms of the modern age there must be no half measures:

> The initial doctrine of the infallible teacher must be an emphatic protest against the existing state of mankind. Man had rebelled against his Maker. The Church must denounce rebellion as of all possible evils the greatest. She must have no terms with it; if she would be true to her Master, she must ban and anathematise it . . . But in the next place she knows and she preaches that such a restoration, as she aims at effecting in it, must be brought about, not simply through outward provisions of preaching and teaching, even though they be her own, but from an inward spiritual power or grace imparted directly from above, and of which she is the channel. She has it in charge to rescue human nature from its misery, not simply by restoring it to its own level, but by lifting it up to a higher level than its own. She recognises in it real moral excellence though degraded, but she cannot set it free from earth except by exalting it towards heaven. It was for this end that a renovating grace was put into her hands and therefore . . . she goes on . . . to insist, that all true conversion must begin with the first springs of thought . . .

And then:

> Such truths as these she vigorously reiterates, and pertinaciously inflicts upon mankind; as to such she observes no half-measures, no economical reserve . . . 'Ye must be born again' is the simple, direct form of words which she uses after her Divine Master: 'Your whole nature must be reborn; your passions, and your affections, and your aims, and your conscience, and your will, must all be bathed in a new element, and reconsecrated to your Maker, – and the last not the least, your intellect.'[37]

Not least; and we should note also the words 'conscience' and 'affections' – each standing in need of re-consecration. This is the difference between Mill, Harriet and Newman – the conviction that 'affections' without re-consecration would simply destroy the capacity to love.

Newman, on entering the Oratorians, took as his patron St Philip Neri, who used to tap his brow and point to his intellect, saying: 'It is here, in the space of three fingers' that we must mortify ourselves. Newman, the theologian, knew what it was to suffer for that truth, to suffer in his intellect, from the decree of silence imposed upon him by the Church in 1859. He also knew where his Vindicator was to be found, in the Tabernacle. When, in 1879, he was elevated by Leo XIII to the College of Cardinals, his one concern was to urge upon the Church the just measure of the trial through which she was to pass. She must identify it for what it was. Newman did not call it secularisation. He called it apostasy:

> The general character of this great *apostasia* is one and the same everywhere . . .
> If a man puts on a new religion every morning, what is that to you? It is as

---

[37] *Ibid*: 222.

impertinent to think about a man's religion as about his sources of income or his management of his family. Religion is in no sense the bond of society.[38]

The question whether human wilfulness, human nature, intellectual pride, self-ishness, could in fact generate the 'benevolence' and 'sympathies' creative of a 'new' morality, also occurred to Mill. What Newman condemned, Mill had laboured lifelong to achieve. "You know", he told his daughter-in-law, Helen Taylor, on his deathbed in 1873 "You know that I have done my work."[39] Yet as the end approached it seems possible that Mill may have entertained a doubt. What would replace Christianity as the bond of society? Benevolence? Education?

Externally, Mill continued to sustain his creed and confidence to the end. Internally, a doubt, a caution, a voice, the same perhaps that spoke to him in 1826, may seem to have continued to put the question – Happiness?

Humanity, he wrote, in the *Utility of Religion*, composed between 1850 and 1858 – we seem to hear the other side, Mill's side, of his conversation with Harriet – humanity may find religion, without its dogmas, "morally useful without being intellectually sustainable"; but when mankind no longer needs "a future existence as a consolation", it will and can, even in the present "perfectly well do without the belief in heaven."[40] Indeed, in a better condition of human life "not annihilation but immortality may be the burdensome idea." Yet Mill did not publish these reflections. Then between 1868–70, he wrote on Theism, and concluded, against the creed of his childhood, that a creator there might be, after all. Mill's Creator was not, however, benevolent. He was not the Creator of Judaeo-Christian theism. Yet Mill, passing on to the person of Christ, could write:

> And whatever else may be taken away from us by rational criticism, Christ is still left; a unique figure . . .

Mill then allowed himself to reflect on the 'unique figure':

> as the ideal representative and guide of humanity . . . When to this we add . . . a possibility that Christ actually was what he supposed himself to be – not God . . . but a man charged with a special express and unique commission from God to lead mankind to truth and virtue . . .[41]

Here the Creator emerges as benevolent. Mill's Christ is not the Redeemer, the Son of God, the sacramental Christ. It is the ethical Christ of the Victorian agnostics. But it does seem to be a distinctly personal Christ; and that, in Mill, is surely remarkable.

---

[38] Biglietto Speech, Ward: 460–461.
[39] Carlisle, *Mill*: 229.
[40] Quoted in Willey, *Nineteenth Century Studies*: 193, from Mill, *Three Essays in Religion*. London 1873: 109
[41] *Ibid.*, quoting *Three Essays*: 255.

All his life, Mill had worked to deprive Christianity of its revealed and sacer-dotal character, to deprive its clergy of authority, to replace its authority by a professional civil administration. But he had never attacked Christ. And at the end of his life it seems that he may have begun to revere Him.

Something in Newman seemed to sense as much. He always held back from attacking Mill. In 1859, when Mill published his *Essay on Liberty*, the moment seemed opportune for a Catholic reply in *The Rambler*. Newman considered giving the review to Richard Simpson, an able controversialist. Yet he restrained himself, remarking how subtle Mill's doctrine was, and how considerable an opponent: he expressed a reluctance to see Mill and Simpson fighting 'like two Kilkenny cats' merely contributing to the ever growing tide of scepticism.[42] Then in 1876, three years after Mill's death, Newman wrote to thank his friend Frederic Rogers, Lord Blachford, for his review of Mill's *Autobiography*, which had been published posthumously. Newman expressed his keen apprecia-tion of Blachford's account of the Christian virtues, in implicit contrast to Mill's unchristian ones. He then added the remarkable sentence: "I wonder if I have made a great sbaglio in thus expressing myself" concerning "the delineation of poor Mill's ethos and history and his gradual shifts to maintain his first views and filial faith." Newman found Mill's account of his own views "as powerful as it is painfully interesting."[43] It is clear that Newman was moved to profound sympathy by the newly disclosed detail of Mill's childhood and upbringing.

To another correspondent Newman recognised in Mill's final reflections on Christianity, a feature of 'modern infidelity' – namely its inability to believe in itself.[44] It may be that he was thinking of Mill when he remarked, in his *Biglietto* speech as Cardinal in 1879:

> And thirdly, it must be borne in mind, that there is much in the liberalistic theory which is good and true; for example, not to say more, the precepts of justice, truthfulness, sobriety, self-command, benevolence... and the natural laws of society. It is not till we find that this array of principles is intended to supersede, to block out, religion that we pronounce it to be evil. There never was a device of the enemy, so cleverly framed, and with such promise of success. And already it has answered to the expectations which have been formed of it. It is sweeping into its own ranks great numbers of able, earnest virtuous men, elderly men of approved antecedents, young men with a career before them.[45]

[42] *The Letters and Diaries of John Henry Newman*. Volume XIX. London: Nelson 1969: Newman to Richard Simpson, July 6, 1859: 169.
[43] *Ibid*: Volume XXVIII. Oxford: Clarendon Press 1975: Newman to Lord Blachford, August 15, 1876: 102.
[44] *Ibid*: Volume XXIX. Newman to Lady Herbert of Lea, August 19, 1879: 169.
[45] Biglietto Speech, Ward: 462.

But had it, in the end, convinced Mill? Newman was aware of Mill's commitment to 'justice' and 'truthfulness' – Mill's courageous interventions in support of a just settlement of the land question in Ireland; his public declaration against brutalism in Jamaica; his concern to protect, by just inheritance laws, widows, and to promote among men a non-proprietorial attitude to women. This did not amount to Christianity. But it did amount to 'an array of principles' sincerely lived – an expression of real virtues which, only if intended to 'supersede' and 'block out' religion, could be identified as the form of a cleverly framed evil.

Mill has been hailed in the twentieth century as the patron saint of the emancipation of women. We have seen that it was Harriet who selected him for the task. How does Mill's doctrine compare with Newman's Christian understanding of the vocation of women to and in the Christian family? Clearly, the difference resides in Newman's appreciation of his own vocation to virginity and to fidelity rooted in God's revealed plan for humanity.[46]

Newman's understanding of the priesthood and the religion of the home earned him the lifelong gratitude of a succession of women converts. His appreciation of the vocation to domestic holiness, and the consecrated affections of Christian prayer and piety was something which Mill, through his immensely sad and emotionally deprived childhood, had never experienced. Contrast Newman's letter of thanks to Charlotte or Chattie Bowden, aged fifteen, who "showed her affection to him by baking him some cakes":

> Who is it that moulds and makes
> Round, and crisp, and fragrant cakes?
> .... One it is, for whom I pray,
> On St. Philip's festal day,
> With a loving heart that she
> Perfect as her cakes may be,
> Full and faithful in the round
> Of her duties ever found
> Where a trial comes, between
> Truth and falsehood cutting keen;
> Yet that keenness and completeness
> Tempering with a winning sweetness.
> Here's a rhyming letter Chat,
> Gift for gift, and tit for tat.[47]

One of William Froude's daughters, Isy, married Baron Anatole von Hügel, the younger brother of Friedrich. She became one of the foundresses of Newnham College Cambridge. In her later years, she would gather some students at her house, Croft Cottage, and read to them from Newman's works. As Joyce Sugg remarks "these clever young women, going out to live their lives amongst the

---

[46] 'Love of Relations and Friends'. *Parochial and Plain Sermon: Love of Relations and Friends*. Volume II. San Francisco: Ignatius Press 1987: 257–263.
[47] Sugg, *Ever Yours Affly*: 111.

uncertainties of the twentieth century, had the privilege and the challenge of a university education",[48] not untouched by the kindly voice of Newman. It is well to remark at this point what Newman stressed to his convert friends about the distinction between natural and supernatural talents:

> Samuel was disappointed when he saw Eliab, that 'the Lord's anointed was not before him.' I ever tell friends that they must look among Catholics, not for natural excellence, but supernatural. *But many Catholics do not like to allow this.*[49]

In those few italicised words, we can see summarised the history of the collapse of the Catholic Church in the twentieth century West. Religion as utility, education as the road to the top, in Manning's marvellous phrase, 'the key to Grosvenor Square'; Newman as the patron and exemplar of a worldly eminence: "they think" – Newman remarked in his sermons at the newly established Catholic University in Dublin – "we mean to spend our devotion upon a human cause, and that we toil for an object of human ambition."[50]

As a graduate of that university, I can verify the truth of Newman's prediction. Newman as the key to Grosvenor Square; the twentieth century seized on him as the promoter of an educated laity. This was Newman circulated to advantage. But Newman as the promoter of a supernatural excellence, rather than a purely natural one, of that – scarcely a word. Newman's vision tended to elude us. Perhaps I should say we eluded him.

That has been the great betrayal of the twentieth century. Its climax came in 1968, with the deployment of Newman as the supposed promoter of the rights of conscience in the reproductive act against *Humanae Vitae*. With no pretence of sincerity or love of truth, but with every appearance of plausibility, a conspicuously educated phalanx of Catholics made play of Newman's doctrine of conscience to appeal against the Pope. They quoted the famous words of his letter to the Duke of Norfolk:

---

[48] *Ibid*: 299.

[49] *Letters and Diaries*. Volume XX: Newman to J. Spencer Northcote, June 18, 1862: 209–210.

[50] "In truth, nobody cared for higher studies. Certain Catholic parents wished to get their sons into English society, and to have latch-keys to Grosvenor Square." Thus Manning, quoted in Edmund Sheridan Purcell, *Life of Cardinal Manning*. London: Macmillan 1896: 303. Newman, *Sermons Preached on Various Occasions*: Sermon IV, 'The Secret Power of Divine Grace', London: Longmans 1857: 57. "They think we mean to spend our devotion on a human cause..."; Newman was speaking of those who were outside the Church. But the application can be made to those inside it. Cp. "As early as the 1890s English political Nonconformity was being crushed by the weight of its own success; by the 1960s the same was true of the political Catholicism of countries like Belgium and the Netherlands. The various forms of discrimination and persecution had been overcome. Now the ghettos were beginning to feel claustrophobic. The secularising effect of a pluralist society lay primarily in the fact that the religious community was ceasing to be a necessary source of identity and support, and that neighbours who had once been regarded largely in terms of hostile stereotypes could now be seen as offering alternative ways of living." Hugh McLeod, *Religion and the People of Western Europe 1789–1970*. Oxford University Press 1981: 141.

> If I am obliged to bring religion into after-dinner toasts (which indeed does not seem quite the thing) I shall drink – to the Pope, if you please – still – to conscience first, and to the Pope afterwards.[51]

So disturbing was the construction placed upon these words that the then Archbishop of Birmingham, George Patrick Dwyer, made a personal visit to the Oratory to enquire as to their context. When it was brought home to him that Newman's appeal to conscience, 'the aboriginal Vicar of Christ', was to conscience as confirmed in matters of doubt by the certitude of faith and morals enunciated by Christ's living vicar the Pope, the Archbishop was confirmed in his agreement to advance the cause of Newman to the altar.

It was during the nineteen sixties that Newman's Cause began to gather pace worldwide, and shortly after the conclusion of the Council that *Humanae Vitae* was published. Now the restoration urged by *Humanae Vitae*, the restoration of the Creator to His creation, to return the sacramentality of the marriage act – that, of course, is the only remedy of the sexual revolution. But it is we who have to do it. We have to believe it. We have to teach it, and help people to put God back into the sacrament, not to contracept the sacrament. And when we do that we might then ask the question whether it is fair to the memory of John Stuart Mill to credit him with the patronage of the spiritual disasters of the sexual revolution of the twentieth century?

Yes, if you want to stick to the letter of the words he wrote; a qualified yes. Mill provided the state with the doctrine that it wanted for its new electorate – the doctrine that there are no doctrines, in faith or morals, that can survive Mill's vague criterion of 'harm to others'. It was not just Baroness Warnock and Lord Russell who credited Mill with the patronage of the sexual revolution. Keynes in 1924 attributed to Mill the decisive intellectual influence in removing from the educated mind the claim of theology, and of the clergy, to any authority whatsoever in matters of truth. Whitehead, in 1926, reflecting on the concluding chapter of Mill's *Logic*, saw in Mill what he considered causative in his own generation, the doctrine of necessity in yielding to emotional drives, the inner 'permission' accorded to Victorian and Edwardian England, to follow the compulsions of the libido where they lead.[52]

So there is no failure of logic in Conrad Russell's drawing the conclusion that Mill's understanding of Individuality extends to a 'right' to what St. Paul understands as fornication, and indeed to unnatural vice. Lord Russell considers that the promotion of homosexuality as morally equivalent to matrimony is something which schoolteachers should adopt as protective of the liberty of minorities.[53]

---

[51] John Henry Newman. 'A letter to the Duke of Norfolk', *Newman and Gladstone: The Vatican Decrees*. Ed. Alvan S. Ryan, Notre Dame: University of Notre Dame Press 1962: 138.
[52] J. M. Keynes, *Essays in Biography*. London: Rupert Hart-Davis 1961: 135. A. N. Whitehead, *Science and the Modern World*. Harmondsworth, Middlesex: Penguin Books 1926: 97.
[53] Letter to *The Times*, June 1, 2000.

All this was within the logic of Mill's doctrine of necessity. But I should think it doubtful that he would have been pleased with the consequences of that logic. Mill was not a libertarian.

I think we should regard Harriet Taylor, not Mill, as the patron saint of secular feminism – and Mill as her chosen spokesman, to lend what, by the close of the nineteenth century, had become his 'Pontifical Authority' to the secularism of a society which had not yet quite decided that Harriet's vision, more than Mill's, was what was wanted. That happened in the wake of two World Wars, and it happened through the propaganda of Marie Stopes, Margaret Sanger and the doomed mentality of the post Hiroshima, post Suez, collapse of the Victorian ethos of living 'as if' Christianity were 'socially' true. The sexual revolution could and did adopt Mill as its patron saint. It seems unlikely that Mill would have adopted it.

Was Mill responsible for the holocaust of the unborn? No, if you consult his meaning. What he did was to supply a philosophical framework for a century which wished to promote abortion as the continuation of contraception by other means. That is why the author of the Abortion Law Reform Society's report on its victory of 1967 invoked Mill – to the surprise of the Abortion Act's promoter in Parliament, David Steel. He seems to have believed that *he* was promoting, not abortion on demand, but 'just a few' abortions.[54]

Was abortion Mill's business? I think not. But the really important thing about the Abortion Law Reform Report is what it revealed about the testing of Catholic opinion in England. The Prime Minister of the day, Harold Wilson, was reluctant to introduce abortion because he feared the loss of the Catholic – largely Irish Labour – vote. So a private poll was organised. The poll revealed that there would be no Catholic opposition. The Act went ahead. The poll was verified. Catholic silence was the one thing requisite.

Since then, the real question for the Church has been to name our problem. The problem is what Newman called it – not secularism, but apostasy, *our* apostasy, the apostasy which has converted the Stationary State into the Stationary Church, in which parents have put their teenage daughters on the pill thereby effecting the contraception of the Church. This has happened in the silence created by the refusal of *Humanae Vitae*. The question is how should the Church conduct her mission in a time of apostasy? What Professor Finnis calls, in his contribution to this volume, 'secularism by default' is a temptation which Newman invites us to address with the assurance that we know how to recognise the voice of Christ teaching, in his aboriginal vicar, the voice of conscience, and in His living, earthly vicar confirming that voice and calling it to consecration.

"If it be inquired" wrote Newman, "what is the proper conduct of the Church in a time of apostasy?" Let us give the last word to Newman himself:

---

[54] Hindell and Simms, *Abortion Law Reformed:* see foreword by David Steel.

46

Christianity has been too often in what seemed deadly peril that we should fear for it any new trial now. So far is certain; on the other hand, what is uncertain, and in these great contests commonly *is* uncertain, and what is commonly a great surprise, when it is witnessed, is the particular mode by which, in the event, Providence rescues and saves His elect inheritance. Sometimes our enemy is turned into a friend; sometimes he is despoiled of that special virulence of evil which was so threatening; sometimes he does so much as is beneficial, and then is removed. Commonly the Church has nothing more to do than to go on in her own proper duties, in confidence and peace; to stand still and to see the salvation of God.

> *Mansueti hereditabunt terram,*
> *Et delectabuntur in multitudine pacis*
> The meek shall inherit the earth
> And shall delight in abundance of peace.[55]

'To go on in her own proper duties, in confidence and peace': what does that mean for us? It means, I think, that we should not blame Mill (or much less something impersonal called 'secularisation') for the evils of the age; but that we identify apostasy for what it is, and adhere in all confidence to the duty of the Church to preach, to pray, and to provide; such providence, for example, as the Liverpool Life Hospital offers to little children who would otherwise be aborted because born 'defective'. We need to fund such initiatives. We need more such, many more: hospices of hope, for the weak.

We do not have to blame Mill for the failure of Christianity. We have to blame ourselves. We do not have to be beguiled by the desperate attempts of people like Mill who sought to promote a world order which they had inherited as a bequest of the eighteenth century, without having any basis in reality, in human nature, or in the interior life of the soul – Mill's soul, as we have seen, rebelled against what he had received from the secular tradition. He was wounded by the taunt that he was 'a manufactured man', a 'mere reasoning machine'.[56] How many other 'manufactured' children have suffered likewise? Are they to be treated as 'enemies' of Christ? Mill looked for feeling, and Harriet supplied his need – on her own terms. But Mill's need was for Christian feeling. His tragedy was that first his father, and then Harriet, constructed and re-constructed his 'mission' and his 'feeling'. It was Harriet who reconstructed in Mill the mission and the feeling – that there was nothing more to life, to marriage, to human relations, *than* feelings. Change the feelings, substitute feeling for religion, and happiness is all.

But something in Mill was unconvinced – unconvinced by his father's refusal of the question 'Who made me?' and unconvinced by Harriet's confidence in the 'provision' of happiness by 'benevolence' and 'education' in contraceptive 'affections'. Something in Mill spoke of the 'unique figure': Christ. And that

---

[55] Biglietto Speech, Ward: 462.
[56] *Autobiography*: 66, 93.

unique figure, speaking in the soul, has commanded us to preach the Gospel, to souls like Mill. How? By preaching it first among our own congregations.

Humanae Vitae, *Evangelium Vitae*, the Gospel of Life; *Familiaris Consortio*, the gathering together of the families – every week in Church, when we assemble, would it not be possible, say four times a year to preach the Gospel of Life? To urge the simplicity of morning and night prayer, of Grace before and after meals, of regular sacramental confession – of *Evangelium Vitae* as matter of confession?

Mill's *Essay on Liberty* rested on a single criterion that actions which do not harm others are to be permitted. But the criterion of 'harm' was ill defined. It came in the end to signify the 'duty' not to 'harm' other people's feelings. That is what we have today; and *that* is what is so harmful, so destructive socially, spiritually, morally, of human happiness. But it is only harmful because we surrender to it.

So if we ask the promoters of the permissive society who invoke Mill, whether they have not merely a literal, but a sufficient account of Mill, the answer is 'No', in my opinion. It is insufficient to human need. Mill's own inner voice, the voice of Christ within, needed the outer echo of the Gospel, preached. So does the society which hails him as its authority on life and death.

Mill's *Essay on Liberty* proposed and successfully transmitted a doctrine that there can be no doctrines and, hence, no moral consensus. But that was a rhetorical strategy concealing the imperative of the Stationary State. That is the imperative today all-pervasive in our legislatures. Today, the doctrine *proposes*, as Mill did not, a 'right' to fornication, to abortion, and an 'equivalence' between matrimonial bonding and homosexual 'affectivity'. That is what Mill's Individualism is now taken to mean.

Mill was concerned to adapt into English the perspective of Tocqueville on the possible corruption of democracy. He was aware of the real danger of democracy imposing majority tenets on minority consciences. On that basis of course, once you go behind Mill to Tocqueville, you arrive at John Paul II – the doctrine of *Evangelium Vitae*, which warns against the strong imposing their tyranny of power over the weak, the unborn and the defenceless.

To conclude. Who's to blame? Not Mill. The problem is much deeper. The issue is the Catholic Church. Everybody knows it. The issue is our fidelity to the sacramental meaning of matrimony, and our willingness to teach it to our own congregations, and in seminaries. If we are faithful to the gift of God, He will do everything else. But if we are not, we are guilty of contracepting God.[57]

---

[57] My thanks are particularly due to Gerard Tracey for his generous help in enabling me to investigate the question of Newman's attitude to Mill. I also wish to thank David Allen, Luke Gormally, Philip Trower and Tom Ward for help in various phases of this paper.

5

The political theory of the culture of death

ROBERT P. GEORGE

'Choices for Death'

CONTEMPORARY LIBERALISM is the political theory of the culture of death.

My point in so bluntly saying so is not to be polemical or even provocative; rather, it is to be soberly descriptive. Self-described liberal political theorists in the United States and elsewhere have, over the past two decades or so, quite explicitly set for themselves the task of justifying and defending the regime of abortion, euthanasia, and, increasingly, infanticide that constitutes the culture of death in the contemporary world. Indeed, six of the most prominent liberal theorists in the United States – John Rawls, Ronald Dworkin, Thomas Nagel, Robert Nozick, Tim Scanlon, and Judith Jarvis Thomson – have taken their attack on traditional sanctity of life principles out of the common room and the classroom and into the courts, filing with the Supreme Court of the United States in 1997 a much acclaimed *amicus curiae* brief urging the justices (unsuccessfully, as it turned out) to declare a federal constitutional right to physician assisted suicide.[1]

Now, I am not saying (nor do I wish to be heard to say) that the political-theorists of the culture of death are moral monsters. They are not Nazis or hatemongers. They are our colleagues and very often our friends. Many of them are doing their level best to think through the moral issues at the heart of our cultural struggle and arrive at conclusions that are right and just. In most cases, they carefully and honestly *argue* for those *choices for death* whose moral worthiness they proclaim and whose legal permission and constitutional protection they defend. As a matter of reciprocity, it is, in my view, incumbent upon us, as their opponents, to engage them in debate, to answer their arguments, to say why they are wrong.[2] While we must oppose them with resolution and, indeed, determination to win, we cannot content ourselves merely to denounce them, as we would rightly denounce the moral monsters who created a different culture of death on the European continent in the 1930s and 40s.

---

[1] The Supreme Court unanimously rejected claims to a constitutional right to assisted suicide in *Washington v. Glucksberg* and *Quill v. Vacco*.

[2] On the application of the principle of reciprocity in these cirucmstances, see R. P. George, 'Law, Democracy, and Moral Disagreement'. 110 (1997) *Harvard Law Review*: 1388–1406, at 1397–1400.

A moment ago, I said that contemporary liberal political theorists defend 'choices for death.' The phrase is not my own, nor have I foisted it upon liberal theorists. It is Ronald Dworkin's description of abortion and euthanasia in the opening sentence of his book *Life's Dominion* – a book devoted in its entirety to defending abortion and euthanasia and their immunization from legal prohibition. "Abortion," Dworkin says "which means killing a human embryo, and euthanasia, which means killing a person out of kindness, are both choices for death."[3]

Of course, when Dworkin and other liberal theorists talk this way, they place the accent on the idea of 'choice.' They understand and present their view, not as the political theory of the culture of death, but rather as the political theory of 'the republic of choice,' or, if you will, 'the culture of freedom.' The subtitle of Dworkin's book clearly signals the author's ideological bent, to wit, "an Argument About Abortion, Euthanasia, and Individual Freedom." And the sentence immediately following his candid acknowledgment of the death-dealing nature of the choices he proposes to defend is already in ideological spin mode: "Abortion," he declares, "chooses death before life *in earnest* has begun; euthanasia chooses death after it has ended."[4] Well, as that master of sentence parsing – and of spin – Bill Clinton might say, it all depends on what the meaning of 'in earnest' is. Those two little words foreshadow Dworkin's vast argumentative effort to show that the lives of very young and very old or infirm human beings are not valuable in a way that makes it wrong to kill them or makes it right for the law to protect them against being killed.

That effort in its details needn't long detain us here. Its political theoretical apparatus was plainly gotten up for the occasion and has been thoroughly explored and decisively rebutted in the submission made by the Linacre Centre to the House of Lords Select Committee on Medical Ethics which considered the introduction of euthanasia in Britain and, in 1994, unanimously rejected it. As the Linacre Centre's submission demonstrated, Dworkin's central claim that liberals and those whom he dubs 'conservatives' – that is, people who oppose abortion and euthanasia – actually *share* a belief in the intrinsic and, indeed, 'sacred' value of human life, and disagree merely over the *interpretation* of this shared value is utterly fallacious. Dworkin's proposal was that law rightly treats human life as a central, protected value, but must maintain strict neutrality as between the views of those who 'interpret' life's value as existing in merely 'biological life' – i.e., the life of an unborn child or comatose or demented person – and those who see life's intrinsic and sacred value as consisting in "exercisable abilities, especially for rational control of one's life, in virtue of which people can give the shape and significance they wish to their lives." Dworkin's talk about the 'shared' ideal of the sanctity of life is, as the Linacre Centre's submission observed, 'practically empty.' The differences Dworkin

---

[3] R. Dworkin, *Life's Dominion: An Argument About Abortion, Euthanasia, and Individual Freedom.* New York: Knopf 1993: 3.
[4] *Ibid.*

describes as differences of *interpretation* of an allegedly shared fundamental value are, in truth, themselves fundamental, precisely in the sense of being basic. Neutrality between them is literally impossible. Law must come down on one side or the other, and what is at stake is not freedom versus authority, but, as the House of Lords Select Committee plainly saw when considering the question of euthanasia, the basic principle of the equality-in-dignity of all human beings – without regard to age, size, stage of development, or condition of dependency – a principle at the heart of our laws against homicide, and which the Select Committee expressly declined to abandon.

Its abandonment would have required a decision, at least implicitly, to embrace an essentially dualistic understanding of the human being as a non-bodily person (that is, the self-aware, conscious, and desiring 'self') who inhabits and uses as a mere instrument a non-personal body. Indeed, Dworkin himself more or less explicitly adopts this dualistic view in defending euthanasia. But it is simply untenable philosophically, for the very reason identified in the Linacre Centre's submission:

> It renders inexplicable the unity in complexity which one experiences in everything one consciously does. It speaks as if there were two things … a non-bodily person and a non-personal living body. But neither of these can one recognize as oneself. One's living body is intrinsic, not merely instrumental to one's personal life. Each of us has a human life (not a vegetable life plus an animal life plus a human life); when it is flourishing that life includes all one's vital functions including speech, deliberation, and choice; when gravely impaired it lacks some of those functions without ceasing to be the life of the person so impaired.[5]

Traditional ethics is on solid ground then in refusing to distinguish between, on the one hand, a class of human beings who are to count as 'persons', and, on the other, 'pre-' or 'post-personal' human beings who are relegated to the status of "merely biologically human non-persons." And the tradition of our homicide laws is on equally firm footing in treating the lives of all human beings – all persons – as equal in worth and dignity. Dworkin's argument – gotten up, as I say, specifically to justify abortion and euthanasia – casts no real doubt on the sanctity of life principles of traditional western law and ethics or the prohibitions of deliberate feticide and other forms of homicide which they ground.

But there is a more general liberal strategy – a strategy of theorizing that is general precisely in the sense that it is not gotten up to justify (or, at least, merely to justify) the liberal position on life issues – though, in the end, it purports to do that – but to respond to a more general problem or set of social conditions. This strategy does not *directly* attack traditional sanctity of life principles or

---

[5] *Submission to the Select Committee of the House of Lords on Medical Ethics by The Linacre Centre for Healthcare Ethics.* Reprinted in L. Gormally (ed) *Euthanasia, Clinical Practice and the Law.* London: The Linacre Centre 1994: 111–165; quotation at p.125.

understandings or cast doubt on their reasonableness or truth. What it does, rather, is to rule out as illegitimate for public-policy making these and other principles, their reasonableness and even their truth notwithstanding. It leaves them in place as quite possibly good reasons for certain forms of *private* action and restraint (such as not having an abortion or taking one's own life), but it excludes them from the class of 'public reasons' – that is, reasons justifying the restriction of liberty in certain contexts.

Moral pluralism

I said that this strategy responds to a general problem or set of social conditions. This is the problem of moral pluralism. Liberal political theory's preoccupation with the problem of pluralism reflects an important social fact about Great Britain, the United States, and other Western nations: People no longer disagree merely about the proper or most effective means of protecting public goods and combating public evils. People today disagree – reasonably or otherwise – about what is a public good and what is a public evil. And this disagreement is not merely about what is to count as a *public*, as opposed to a purely *private*, good or evil; it is about what is *morally* good or evil in itself.

Consider, for example, the question of homosexuality. No longer are people divided merely over the question whether the criminalization of sodomy is a proper or effective means of discouraging homosexual conduct. Their disagreement goes beyond the question whether such conduct implicates a legitimate *public* interest justifying legal restriction or is merely a *private* vice which the state has a duty to tolerate. The old consensus about the immorality of homosexual conduct and relationships integrated around such conduct has broken down. Although many people, particularly those who profess traditional Catholic, Protestant, or Jewish religious faith, continue to believe that homosexual acts and relationships are morally bad, many other people, notably including a great many journalists, intellectuals, and other opinion-shaping elites, have adopted the belief that homosexual conduct is no vice at all. 'Gay is good,' they say. So the debate has shifted from whether or not the state is justified in prohibiting sodomy to the question whether it is justified in refusing to honor homosexual relationships by, for example, declining to issue marriage licenses to same-sex couples.

And, of course, fundamental disagreement also characterizes the issue of abortion. I don't know the situation in the U.K. or in Canada or Australia or on the Continent. However, in the U.S., polling consistently reveals that a majority of citizens continue to believe that, except in certain rare and exceptional cases (i.e., where pregnancy threatens the life of the mother or would cause her severe and irreparable physical harm, or where it is the result of rape), abortion is morally evil. And something approaching a majority of Americans believe that abortion is a moral evil indistinguishable from infanticide and other forms of homicide. At the same time, a substantial number of Americans support legal abortion and even its public funding for indigent women, not merely on the ground that abortion is a 'private' immorality which, as such, the state has a duty to tolerate, but in the belief that abortion is, or can be, a morally good choice.

A similar moral pluralism obtains when it comes to physician-assisted suicide and euthanasia, the recreational use of drugs, and a host of other issues. Some disputed moral issues – particularly, I think, the issue of abortion – bring to mind the moral disagreement over slavery in the United States in the middle third of the nineteenth century. By then, supporters of slavery were no longer content to argue, as they had been in the late eighteenth century, that the 'peculiar institution' was a 'necessary evil' whose toleration was required under circumstances in which abolition would produce disastrous, and therefore morally unacceptable, social and economic consequences. Instead, they argued that slavery was morally good and right, and that the position of their abolitionist opponents represented, not a practically unattainable – albeit noble – moral ideal, but, rather, a morally repulsive religious fanaticism. Despite repeated efforts at political compromise, the moral disagreement over slavery proved, in the end, incompatible with peace and social stability. The issue had to be resolved finally by civil war which cost something approaching three-quarters of a million lives.

Reflection on the carnage of the American Civil War inclines me to think that contemporary political theory is right to take seriously the problem of moral pluralism. I am, however, skeptical about the mainstream of, if you will, liberal political theory whose ambitions are to identify basic principles of 'political' justice which can be agreed upon by all reasonable people and which promise to provide social stability by constraining the grounds of political advocacy and action when it comes to fundamental moral issues (such as abortion and euthanasia) upon which people today disagree. The most notable – and ambitious – example of philosophical work of this type is the 'political liberalism' of John Rawls. In the remainder of my remarks, I shall describe Rawls's effort to identify basic principles of justice which, as the fruit of an 'overlapping consensus' among people who otherwise differ over fundamental moral and religious issues, promise to make possible social stability for morally good reasons. Then I shall give my reasons for rejecting Rawls's political liberalism. In particular, I shall argue that Rawls's conception of 'public reason(s),' i.e., reasons which may legitimately be introduced in political advocacy and acted upon legislatively, is unreasonably narrow and restrictive.

Public reason and liberal legitimacy

In his influential 1971 book *A Theory of Justice*, Rawls defended a liberal conception of justice, which he called 'justice as fairness,' whose basic principles for a well-ordered society were identified as those that would be chosen by free and equal persons in what he called 'the original position.' Parties in 'the original position' select principles of justice in a state of ignorance regarding their personal moral and religious convictions, social and economic status, and related factors that will distinguish them from many of their fellow citizens when they emerge from behind 'the veil of ignorance' to live in a society governed in accordance with the principles they had selected.

In 1993, Rawls published a new book, *Political Liberalism*, which amends certain features of the theory of justice he had advanced in 1971. Most importantly, he now says that the argument for 'justice as fairness' as adumbrated in *A Theory of Justice* relied on a premise which was inconsistent with the theory itself, namely, the belief that "in the well-ordered society of justice as fairness, citizens hold the same comprehensive doctrine, and this includes aspects of Kant's comprehensive liberalism, to which the principles of justice as fairness might belong."[6] The problem with this belief is that neither liberalism, considered as what he calls a 'comprehensive' (as opposed to a merely 'political') doctrine, nor any other comprehensive view (e.g., Catholicism, Judaism, Platonism, Aristotelianism, communism), is held by citizens generally in contemporary pluralistic societies. And a plurality of comprehensive views is, Rawls suggests, natural and unavoidable in the circumstances of political freedom that characterize constitutional democratic regimes. Political theorizing which accepts the legitimacy of such regimes must begin, therefore, by acknowledging what Rawls calls "the fact of reasonable pluralism."

Recognition of "the fact of reasonable pluralism," according to Rawls, rules out the possibility of legitimately defending principles of justice for constitutional democratic regimes by appealing to comprehensive doctrines – including comprehensive forms of liberalism. Some alternative must, therefore, be found. Otherwise, the social stability of such regimes would be in constant jeopardy. Everything would depend on the capacity and willingness of people with fundamentally different moral views – including radically different conceptions of justice and human rights – to reach and preserve a *modus vivendi*. The alternative Rawls proposes is 'political liberalism.' Its ideal is that "citizens are to conduct their public political discusssions of constitutional essentials and matters of basic justice within the framework of what each sincerely regards as a reasonable political conception of justice, a conception that expresses political values that others as free and equal also might reasonably be expected to endorse."[7]

In such a framework, "deeply opposed though reasonable comprehensive doctrines may live together and all affirm the political conception of a constitutional regime."[8] Where constitutional essentials and matters of basic justice are at issue, public discussion and debate must be conducted – for moral reasons and not as a mere *modus vivendi* – in terms of a "strictly political conception of justice,"[9] and not in terms of moral doctrines of justice associated with the various comprehensive views about which reasonable people disagree. The common affirmation of a 'political conception' by adherents of competing comprehensive views enables

---

[6] J. Rawls, *Political Liberalism*, paperback edition. New York: Columbia University Press, 1996: xlii.

[7] *Op.cit.*, 1.

[8] *Op.cit.*, xx.

[9] *Op.cit.*, xvii.

them to participate in what Rawls refers to as "an overlapping consensus" on basic principles of justice. It is this consensus which makes social stability in the face of moral pluralism not only possible, but possible "for the right reasons."[10]

The core of 'political liberalism' is the idea that whenever constitutional essentials and matters of basic justice are at stake political actors, including citizens as voters and insofar as they engage in public advocacy of candidates and causes, must refrain from acting on the basis of principles drawn from their comprehensive views (as Kantians, Catholics, communists, or whatever) except to the extent that "public reasons, given by a reasonable political conception, are presented sufficient to support whatever the comprehensive doctrines are introduced to support."[11] Thus, citizens are constrained from appealing to and acting upon beliefs drawn from their most fundamental moral understandings and commitments precisely at the most fundamental political level, viz., the level of constitutional essentials and matters of basic justice. And they are so constrained on grounds entirely separate from the putative falsity, unreasonableness, or unsoundness of those understandings and commitments or the beliefs drawn therefrom.[12]

Rawls insists that "political liberalism is not a form of Enlightenment liberalism, that is, a comprehensive liberal and often secular doctrine founded on reason and suitable for the modern age now that the religious authority of Christian ages is said to be no longer dominant."[13] It is, rather,

> a political conception of political justice for a constitutional democratic regime that a plurality of reasonable doctrines, both religious and nonreligious, liberal and nonliberal, may freely endorse, and so freely live by and come to understand its virtues. Emphatically, it does not aim to replace comprehensive doctrines, religious or nonreligious, but intends to be equally distinct from both and, it hopes, acceptable to both.[14]

'Political liberalism' aspires, then, to be impartial with respect to the viewpoints represented by the various reasonable doctrines which compete for the allegiance of citizens. It "does not attack or criticize any reasonable [comprehensive] view."[15] Rawls says that "rather than confronting religious and nonliberal

---

[10] *Op.cit.*, xlii, 388, 390, and 392. Rawls's emphasis on the need for social stability in the face of moral pluralism should not lead the reader to suppose that his argument for 'political liberalism' is merely pragmatic. A 'strictly political' conception of justice is, he maintains, the *fairest* and *most reasonable* way of resolving questions of constitutional essentials and matters of basic justice.

[11] Rawls introduces this 'wide view' of public reason in the Introduction to the Paperback Edition of *Political Liberalism*: lii. It represents a broadening of the more restrictive view set forth in the text, pp. 247–252.

[12] Rawls says that appeals to comprehensive doctrines are never legitimate in legislative assemblies or in the public acts and pronouncements of executive officers. Nor may judges in interpreting the Constitution or justifying their interpretations rely upon or invoke principles drawn from comprehensive doctrines. See *Political Liberalism*: 215.

[13] *Op.cit.*, xl.

[14] *Ibid.*

[15] *Op.cit.*, xxi.

doctrines with a comprehensive liberal philosophical doctrine, the thought is to formulate a liberal political conception that those nonliberal doctrines might be able to endorse."[16] Hence, the crucial idea of an 'overlapping consensus' among comprehensive views which, inasmuch as they accept the fundaments of constitutional democracy, are 'reasonable.'

So 'political liberalism' is a doctrine that is not just for liberals. If Rawls is correct, not only proponents of Kant's or Mill's liberalism, but also faithful Catholics, evangelical Protestants, and observant Jews – assuming the reasonableness of Catholicism, Protestantism, and Judaism (something Rawls suggests he is willing to assume) – ought to be able to join the 'overlapping consensus' by reasonably embracing 'political liberalism' without compromising their basic religious and moral convictions.[17]

Although Rawls observes that a mere political compromise or *modus vivendi* might, under propitious circumstances, develop into an 'overlapping consensus,' he carefully distinguishes an 'overlapping consensus' from a mere *modus vivendi*. Unlike a *modus vivendi*, an 'overlapping consensus' is constituted by a certain level of *moral agreement* about what constitute fair terms of social cooperation among people who, being reasonable, view each other as free and equal citizens. So, although Rawls presents the liberal 'political conception' of justice as standing independent of any particular comprehensive doctrine (in that sense it is, he says, a "freestanding" conception), it is nevertheless a *moral* conception, containing "its own intrinsic normative and moral ideal."[18]

Rawls maintains that terms of cooperation offered by citizens to their fellow citizens are fair only insofar as "citizens offering them ... reasonably think that those citizens to whom such terms are offered might also reasonably accept them."[19] This 'criterion of reciprocity' is the core of what Rawls labels "the liberal principle of legitimacy," viz., that "our exercise of political power is fully proper only when it is exercised in accordance with a constitution the essentials of which all citizens as free and equal may be expected to endorse in the light of principles and ideals acceptable to their common human reason."[20] When, and only when, political power is exercised in accordance with such a constitution

---

[16] *Ibid.*

[17] In what has become a famous footnote in *Political Liberalism*, Rawls defends what he describes as a 'duly qualified' right to abortion in the first trimester (and possibly beyond). See n. 32, pp. 243–244. He treats the matter as falling within the category of constitutional essentials and matters of basic justice to which his doctrine of 'public reason' applies, concluding that "we would go against the ideal of public reason if we voted from a comprehensive doctrine that denied this right." This by itself should raise doubts in the minds of serious Catholics, Protestants, and Jews who consider whether their views have a place in Rawls's 'overlapping consensus.' For a detailed critique of Rawls on abortion, see R. P. George, 'Public Reason and Political Conflict: Abortion and Homosexuality'. 106 (1997) *Yale Law Journal*: 2475–2504, pages from which are reproduced below as the appendix to the present essay.

[18] *Op.cit.*, xliv.

[19] *Ibid.*

[20] *Op.cit.*, 137.

do political actors – including voters – maintain fidelity to the ideal of 'public reason'.

The challenge of natural law theory

The 'liberal principle of legitimacy' and ideal of 'public reason' exclude as illegitimate in political discourse and in the exercise of public authority, at least insofar as basic matters of justice – including constitutional rights – are concerned, appeal to principles and propositions drawn from comprehensive doctrines even though they are, or may well be, *true*. It would be one thing to argue that in certain circumstances *prudence* requires such an exclusion, at least temporarily, as part of a *modus vivendi*. It is quite another thing, however, to claim, as Rawls does, that such an exclusion is *morally* required by virtue of 'the fact of reasonable pluralism' even in circumstances in which people are not restrained by prudence from acting on principles they reasonably believe to be true, and which are not ruled out as reasons for political action by their reasonable comprehensive doctrines of justice and political morality. So, we must examine the justification Rawls offers for this exclusion. To that end, let us consider what Rawls has in mind in demanding, as a matter of reciprocity, that citizens offer to their fellow citizens with whom they disagree about basic moral, metaphysical, and religious matters terms of social cooperation which they reasonably think their fellow citizens may reasonably accept.

If Rawls's 'criterion of reciprocity' and 'liberal principle of legitimacy' are interpreted narrowly, then citizens offering terms of cooperation to their fellow citizens who happen to disagree with them about a matter in dispute must merely think that they are presenting to their fellow citizens sound reasons, accessible to them as reasonable people of goodwill, for changing their minds. The scope of 'public reason' under this narrow interpretation of reciprocity and legitimacy would be wide. It would, to be sure, rule out as illegitimate claims based on the allegedly 'secret knowledge' of a gnostic elite or the putative truths revealed only to a select few and not accessible to reasonable persons as such, but it would not exclude any principle or proposition, however controversial, that is put forward for acceptance on the basis of rational argumentation.

Now, even on this narrow interpretation, some religious believers would object that their views would be unfairly excluded from public political discourse. Others, however, would have no objection to a principle of reciprocity which demands only that they offer 'public reasons' in this very wide sense. They would have no interest in restraining the liberty of their fellow citizens, or in disfavoring them or their preferred ways of life or modes of behavior, on the basis of claims they could not defend by rational argumentation. They would accept the claim that to do so would be unfair. It seems clear, however, that Rawls himself cannot accept the narrow interpretation of reciprocity and the correspondingly very wide conception of public reason. His goal, after all, is to limit the range of morally acceptable doctrines of political morality in circumstances of moral pluralism to a single doctrine: viz., 'political liberalism.' The very wide conception of public reason simply will not accomplish that goal. It will not, for example, rule out appeals to principles and propositions drawn from comprehensive forms of liberalism. More importantly, it will not exclude appeals to principles and propositions drawn from nonliberal comprehensive doctrines which content themselves with appeals to 'our common human reason.'

Notable among such doctrines is the broad tradition of natural law thinking about morality, justice, and human rights. This tradition poses an especially interesting problem for Rawls's theory of public reason because of its integration into Roman Catholic teaching. So it is, at once, a nonliberal comprehensive philosophical doctrine *and* part of a larger religious tradition which, in effect, proposes its own principle of public reason, viz., that questions of law and policy (including what Rawls has in mind when he refers to "constitutional essentials and matters of basic justice") ought to be decided in accordance with natural law, natural right and/or natural justice (where, as in Aquinas's natural law theory, something is good, or right or just 'by nature' insofar as it is *reasonable*).[21]

If Rawls is to successfully defend a conception of 'public reason' narrow enough to exclude appeals to natural law theory, he must show that there is something unfair about such appeals. And he must, of course, demonstrate this unfairness without appeal to comprehensive liberalism or any other comprehensive conception of justice which competes with the natural law conception. In other words, he must avoid smuggling into the defense of his claim that "*only* a political conception of justice ... can serve as a basis of public reason and justification"[22] principles or propositions which are themselves in dispute among adherents to reasonable comprehensive doctrines (including, of course, Catholicism and natural law theory). This, it seems to me, he has not done and, I believe, cannot do.

Rawls does not explicitly address the claims of natural law theorists – Catholic or otherwise. He seems, however, to have something like their beliefs in mind in his critique of what he calls "rationalist believers who contend that [their] beliefs are open to and can be fully established by reason."[23] Rawls's argument against the so-called 'rationalist believers' rests entirely on the claim that they unreasonably deny 'the fact of reasonable pluralism.' But do they? I am myself something of a 'rationalist believer,' at least according to Rawls's definition, and I certainly do not deny the fact that people in our culture, including reasonable people, disagree about fundamental moral questions, including questions pertaining to euthanasia, abortion, homosexuality, and the recreational use of drugs. Nor do I deny that some measure of moral disagreement – though not necessarily moral disagreement on the scale of what we find today in the United States or Great

---

[21] See St. Thomas Aquinas, *Summa theologiae* 1–2, 71, 2c: "The good of the human being is in accord with reason, and human evil is being outside the order of reasonableness." On the proper interpretation of Aquinas on this point, see J. Finnis, *Natural Law and Natural Rights*. Oxford: Clarendon Press 1980: 36. See also Finnis's more detailed account in his *Aquinas. Moral, Political and Legal Theory*. Oxford: Oxford University Press 1998.

[22] Rawls, *Political Liberalism*: 137 (emphasis supplied).

[23] *Op.cit.*, 152–153.

58

Britain, for example – is inevitable under circumstances of political and religious liberty. So I do not see how Rawls can justify his claim that "rationalist believers" deny "the fact of reasonable pluralism."

Rawls own methodological and moral commitments require him to avoid denying the soundness, reasonableness, or truth of the reasonable, if controversial, moral, metaphysical, and religious claims that his 'political' conception of justice would exclude from political discourse and as grounds for political action. So he cannot rule out the views of natural law theorists or 'rationalist believers' on issues such as homosexuality, abortion, euthanasia, and drugs on the grounds that their views are unsound, unreasonable, or false. If he is reduced to arguing for the unsoundness, unreasonableness, or falsity of these views, then his *political* liberalism' will have collapsed into *comprehensive* liberalism.' And we are left with the conflict of comprehensive views to which 'political liberalism' is meant to provide an alternative.

Understandably, then, Rawls seeks to avoid engaging the specific claims and arguments of the 'rationalist believers.' He limits himself to a simple denial that their claims "can be publicly and fully established by reason."[24] But how can this denial be sustained independently of some engagement 'on the merits' with the specific arguments they advance in their public political advocacy – arguments which Rawls's idea of 'public reason' is meant to exclude in advance without the need to address their soundness and reasonableness or the truth or falsity of the principles and propositions in support of which they are offered?

It will not do for Rawls to claim that he is not denying the truth of 'rationalist believer's' claims but merely their assertion that these claims can be publicly and fully established by reason. What makes a 'rationalist believer' a 'rationalist' is precisely his belief that his principles can be justified by *rational argument* and his willingness to provide just such *rational argumentation*. The arguments he offers by way of justifying his principles and their applications to specific political issues will either be sound or unsound. If they are sound, then Rawls can give no reason for excluding the principles they vindicate on the ground that they are illegitimate reasons for political action; if they are unsound, then they ought to be rejected precisely on that basis, and not because the principles in support of which they are offered are, in Rawls's sense, 'nonpublic.'

Let us return, though, to Rawls's claim that 'rationalist believers' deny "the fact of reasonable pluralism." He states that "[i]t is unrealistic – or worse, it arouses mutual suspicion and hostility – to suppose that all our differences are rooted in ignorance and perversity, or else in the rivalries for power, status, and economic gain."[25] Natural law theorists and (other?) 'rationalist believers' do not deny this. Indeed, they recognize that differences of opinion and commitment often arise from factors which reason does not control – matters of taste and sentiment, for example. Moreover, matters can sometimes be rationally underdetermined even where reason guides reflection by excluding

---

[24] *Op.cit.*, 153.
[25] *Ibid.*

as unreasonable certain possibilities, but leaving more than one possibility open and, in that sense, rationally available. On some issues, there is a variety of unreasonable opinions, but no uniquely reasonable or correct one.

Natural law theorists (and others) maintain, however, that on certain other issues, including certain fundamental moral and political issues, there are uniquely correct answers. The question whether there is a human right against being enslaved, for example, or being punished for one's religious beliefs, admits of a uniquely correct answer which is available in principle to every rational person. We pro-life advocates assert that there is similarly a human right against deliberate feticide and other forms of direct killing of innocent persons. Differences over such issues as slavery, religious freedom, abortion, and euthanasia may be 'reasonable' in the sense that reasonable persons can err in their judgments and arrive at morally incorrect positions. But, assuming there is a truth of these matters – something Rawls cannot deny and, one would think, has no desire to deny – errors of reason must be responsible for anyone's failure to arrive at the morally correct positions. There are many possible roots of such errors, not all of which involve culpability or subjective guilt on the part of individuals who make them. Ignorance of, or inattention to, certain relevant facts or values may be the source of a particular error. Prejudice or other subrational influences – which may be pervasive in a culture or subculture making it difficult for any of its individual members to reason well about certain issues – may block insights which are critical to sound moral judgments. And, of course, logical failures or other errors in the reasoning process can deflect judgment in the moral field as they can in all other fields of inquiry. Nothing in the position of natural law theorists (or 'rationalist believers') entails the proposition that we can always easily arrive at correct moral positions or that we will not sometimes (perhaps often) get things wrong.

Is anything in their view *unreasonable*? Rawls certainly cannot declare their view unreasonable because they maintain that on certain morally-charged and highly disputed political questions – including questions of human rights – there are uniquely morally correct answers. The fact that 'reasonable people' can be found on competing sides of such questions in no way implies that the competing views are equally reasonable. Reasonable people can be wrong – as Rawls himself implicitly acknowledges in his claims against the 'rationalist believers' who are, after all, reasonable people even if their claim that their beliefs can be fully and publicly justified by reason is unreasonable. There is simply no unreasonableness in maintaining that otherwise reasonable people can be less than fully reasonable (sometimes culpably, other times not) in their judgments of particular issues.[26]

---

[26] In fairness to Rawls, I should acknowledge here his treatment of the sources of moral disagreement in connection with what he calls "the burdens of judgment." *Political Liberalism*, p. 58. However, to preserve the integrity of his political liberalism, we must read his account of the sources of disagreement in such a way as to avoid its collapse into relativism. If we do, then Rawls's idea of 'fully reasonable,' and even 'perfectly reasonable,' though erroneous, views refers to false beliefs which are formed without subjective fault. I think that this is what people generally have in mind when, though fully persuaded of the truth of a certain view,

In *A Theory of Justice*, Rawls identified the two basic principles of 'justice as fairness' by the method of 'political constructivism' which asked what substantive principles would be chosen by parties in the 'original position' behind the 'veil of ignorance' which hides from them (among other things) what Rawls now calls their 'comprehensive views.' In a key passage of *Political Liberalism*, he says that the "liberal principle of legitimacy" and the ideal of "public reason" have "the same basis as the substantive principles of justice."[27] It seems to me, however, that this basis was, and remains, insecure. Over more than twenty-five years, Rawls and his followers have failed to provide any reason to suppose that 'perfectionist' principles – principles of justice or political morality more generally drawn from 'comprehensive views' about what is humanly valuable and morally upright – which would not be selected under conditions of artificial ignorance by the unnaturally risk-averse parties in the 'original position' are *unjust* (or cannot be valid principles of justice). Rawlsians seem to suppose that from the proposition that principles which would be selected *by such parties under such conditions* are just (i.e., involve no injustice), it follows that perfectionist principles – which might very well be chosen by reasonable and well-informed persons outside the original position – are unjust. *Non sequitur*.

Conclusion

Contemporary liberalism, the liberalism of Dworkin, Rawls, and Thomson, cannot withstand intellectual scrutiny. Its efforts to identify sound reasons to exclude sanctity of life ideals as illegitimate reason for political action by Catholics and others to protect the basic right to life of every human being – every person – not to be directly killed, and to the equal protection of the laws against killing, utterly and manifestly fails. Its failure is identifiable by rational critical inquiry and dialectical argumentation. The effective critique of liberalism as the political theory of the culture of death in no way relies on esoteric information, private revelation, or any other non-public reasons.

There is, however, another liberalism. And, as my friend and co-author William L. Saunders and I have argued, this old-fashioned liberalism is a liberalism that is not only consistent with Catholic faith and the culture of life, but demanded by it.[28] This is not the liberalism of abortion, euthanasia, and the sexual revolution. It is the liberalism, rather, of the rule of law, democratic self-government, subsidiarity, social solidarity, private property, limited government,

---

they allow nevertheless that 'reasonable people' can disagree with them. The fact of 'reasonable disagreement' in this sense is certainly not a valid warrant for ruling out argument as to the truth of matters in dispute on the ground that reasons adduced in any argument 'on the merits' cannot qualify as 'public reasons.'

[27] Rawls, *Political Liberalism*: 225.

[28] See R. P. George (with W. L. Saunders), 'Religious Values in Politics: A Liberal Perspective', in F. Eigo (ed) *Religious Values at the Threshold of the Third Millennium*. Villanova: Villanova University Press 1999: 103–133.

equal protection, and basic human freedoms, such as those of speech, press, assembly, and, above all, religion. This, as I say, is a decidedly old-fashioned liberalism – if you will, a 'conservative liberalism.' It is the liberalism of Lincoln and the American founders, of Newman and Chesterton, of the Second Vatican Council and John Paul II: a liberalism of life.

Appendix: Abortion and public reason

Although the defense of political liberalism requires Rawls to resist the very wide view of public reason which could be endorsed by so-called rationalist believers, he is nevertheless eager to show that the scope of his doctrine of public reason is not excessively narrow. For example, his 'political liberalism' allows people to have resort to beliefs drawn from their comprehensive doctrines in a variety of areas which do not touch upon constitutional essentials and matters of basic justice.[29] And even in areas that do touch upon such matters it allows appeals to comprehensive doctrines subject to the proviso that citizens making such appeals "in due course" show that their position can be justified in terms of public reason(s).[30]

In *Political Liberalism*, Rawls offers the following explanation of the demands of public reason:

> What public reason asks is that citizens be able to explain their vote to one another in terms of a reasonable balance of public values, it being understood by everyone that of course the plurality of reasonable comprehensive doctrines held by citizens is thought by them to provide further and often transcendent backing for those values. In each case, which doctrine is affirmed is a matter of conscience for the individual citizen. It is true that the balance of political values a citizens holds must be reasonable, and one that can be seen to be reasonable by other citizens; but not all reasonable balances are the same. The only comprehensive doctrines that run afoul of public reason are those that cannot support a reasonable balance of political values.[31]

Precisely at this point, Rawls inserts a footnote (32) which, "as an illustration," takes up what he describes as "the troubled question of abortion." After stipulating that "we are dealing with the normal case of mature adult women," he asks the reader to "consider the question in terms of three important political values: the due respect for human life, the ordered reproduction of political society over time, including the family, in some form, and finally the equality of women as equal citizens." After acknowledging, parenthetically, that these are not the only important political values, he declares flatly that "any reasonable balance

[29] Rawls, *Political Liberalism*: 214–215.
[30] *Op.cit.*, lii.
[31] *Op.cit.*, 243.

of these three values will give a woman a duly qualified right to decide whether or not to end her pregnancy during the first trimester."[32]

How, one may ask, could this bold conclusion be justified without appeal to moral or metaphysical views widely in dispute about the status of embryonic and fetal human beings and the justice or injustice of choices to bring about their deaths, or to perform acts which include among their foreseeable side effects the bringing about of their deaths?

Here is Rawls's entire account of himself: "at this early stage of pregnancy the political value of the equality of women is overriding, and this right is required to give it substance and force." Why does the value of women's equality override the value of fetal life? Rawls does not say. The absence of argument for this claim is especially remarkable in view of the fact that opponents of abortion contend that the right to life, which, in their view, the unborn share with all other human beings, is fundamental and inviolable and, as such, cannot be 'balanced' against other considerations. Rawls goes on to comment that he doesn't think that the introduction of other political values into the calculation would alter his conclusion, and, indeed, that a reasonable balance of political values might allow a right to abortion even beyond the first trimester, "at least in certain circumstances." He explicitly declines to argue the point further, however, stating that his purpose in raising the question of a right to abortion at all is simply "to illustrate the point of the text by saying that any comprehensive doctrine that leads to a balance of political values excluding that duly qualified right in the first trimester is to that extent unreasonable."[33]

Needless to say, Rawls's footnote has elicited vigorous criticism.[34] As an argument for a right to abortion, it does worse than beg centrally important questions – it ignores them altogether. Moreover, it seems plainly, if silently, to import into the analysis of the question a range of undefended beliefs of precisely the sort that 'political liberalism' is supposed to exclude. This smuggling in of controversial moral and metaphysical beliefs is especially egregious in view of the fact that abortion is often put forward as a question that simply cannot be resolved, one way or the other, without introducing such beliefs into the deliberations.[35] As such, it presents a particular challenge to Rawls's central argument that constitutional essentials and matters of basic justice (assuming, as Rawls does, that we treat abortion as falling within these categories) ought to be resolved by appeal to a purely 'political' conception of justice, rather than to general doctrines of justice as parts of reasonable comprehensive views.

---

[32] *Op.cit.*, 32.
[33] *Ibid.*
[34] See especially T. McCarthy, 'Kantian Constructivism and Reconstructivism: Rawls and Habermas in Dialogue'. 105 (1994) *Ethics*: 44, 53 n. 16.
[35] See, for example, K. Greenawalt, *Religious Convictions and Political Choice*. Oxford: Oxford University Press 1988.

In a footnote to the Introduction to the new paperback edition of *Political Liberalism*,[36] Rawls acknowledges the force of some of these criticisms and offers a brief reply:

> Some have quite naturally read the [original] footnote as an argument for the right to abortion in the first trimester. I do not intend it to be one. (It does express my opinion, but an opinion is not an argument.) I was in error in leaving it in doubt that the aim of the footnote was only to illustrate and confirm the following statement in the text to which the footnote is attached: "The only comprehensive doctrines that run afoul of public reason are those that cannot support a reasonable balance [or ordering] of political values [on the issue]." To try to explain what I meant, I used three political values (of course, there are more) for the troubled issue of the right to abortion, to which it might seem improbable that political values could apply at all. I believe a more detailed interpretation of those values may, when properly developed as public reason, yield a reasonable argument. I don't say the most reasonable or decisive argument; I don't know what that would be, or even if it exists.

At this point Rawls cites with approval – noting only that he would add several (unspecified) 'addenda' to it – Judith Jarvis Thomson's argument for a right to abortion in her then recent article 'Abortion: Whose Right?'[37] Here is Thomson's summation of her argument:

> First, restrictive regulation [of abortion] severely constrains women's liberty. Second, severe constraints on liberty may not be imposed in the name of considerations that the constrained are not unreasonable in rejecting. And third, the many women who reject the claim that the fetus has a right to life from the moment of conception are not unreasonable in doing so.[38]

The affinities of Thomson's approach with Rawlsian political liberalism are, I trust, obvious. The central pro-life claims are that (a) human beings in the embryonic and fetal stages, like innocent human beings at all other stages of life, have a right not to be directly (or otherwise unjustly) killed, and (b) they, like all other human beings, are entitled to the equal protection of the laws against homicide. Thomson defends the right to abortion, not by claiming that the central pro-life claims are false, but, rather, by arguing that their truth or falsity are irrelevant to the political resolution of the question of abortion. What matters is that people are 'not unreasonable' in judging the central pro-life claims to be false. Therefore, even those who judge them to be true should refrain from taking political action which would restrict women's freedom based on their judgment. They should join those who consider the central pro-life claims to be

---

[36] Rawls, *Political Liberalism*: lv–lvi, n. 31.

[37] The article to which Rawls plainly is referring appeared under the title 'Abortion' in 20 (1995) *Boston Review*: 11–15.

[38] *Op.cit.*, 15.

false in a sort of Rawlsian overlapping consensus which recognizes a woman's right to abortion.

Here, I submit, we have fully on display all the equivocations, ambiguities, and weaknesses of the Rawlsian criterion of reciprocity, liberal principle of legitimacy, and doctrine of public reason. Immediately after offering the summary of her argument I quoted a moment ago, Thomson, evidently struggling to be generous, says that "[t]here is of course room for those who accept Catholic doctrine on abortion to declare it in the public forum."[39] But, she adds, "those who accept the doctrine ought not say that reason requires us to accept it, for that assertion is false."[40] What is Thomson claiming here? Is it that the central pro-life claims should be rejected because they are untrue or, even if true, somehow unreasonable? To establish that, she would have to engage pro-life arguments on the merits and refute them. This, however, she makes no serious effort to do. To have done so would, in any event, have shifted the ground of the argument for a right to abortion from the sphere of Rawlsian public reason to unrestricted debate of a sort which would engage, in violation of Rawlsian scruples, principles connected with competing comprehensive doctrines.[41]

What Thomson seems to mean is that not all 'reasonable people' accept pro-life claims or that the rejection of pro-life claims does not mark a person as 'unreasonable.' There are, as I suggested earlier, important senses in which assertions like these are true. But, contrary to what Thomson supposes, from the senses in which they are true nothing follows for the question whether women have a right to abortion or the unborn have a right not to be aborted. If, in truth, the latter right obtains – if, that is to say, it is true that the unborn have a right not to be aborted and, thus, that the pro-life position is more reasonable than its alternative – then the fact that reasonable people, perhaps without culpability, hold the contrary view in no way vitiates the human right of the unborn not to be killed, or confers upon women a moral right to the more or less unrestricted legal freedom to bring about their deaths. What matters, from the moral point of view, is that basic human rights be identified where they obtain and, to the extent possible, protected.

In the end, Thomson's argument that people are 'not unreasonable' in rejecting the pro-life position boils down to an assertion that the argument over

[39] *Ibid.* Thomson's rhetoric here, referring to 'Catholic doctrine' on abortion, helps her case along by presenting the prolife position, at least as it figures as part of Catholic moral teaching, as a sectarian matter which relies on religious premises which are somehow unavailable to nonCatholics. The 'Catholic doctrine' on the subject, however, condemns abortion as homicidal and unjust as a matter of publicly accessible scientific fact and rational (natural law) morality.
[40] *Ibid.*
[41] Moreover, it would undercut the support Thomson's argument supplies to what many find to be the politically attractive (though obviously questionable) idea that people can accept prolife claims as a basis for being 'personally opposed to abortion,' yet affirm at the same time support for a legal right to abortion on the ground that the *truth* of prolife claims is not relevant to (or, at least, is not determinative of) the question whether women are morally entitled to the legal freedom to abort.

the moral status of the human conceptus and early embryo ends in a sort of stalemate: "While I know of no conclusive reason for denying that fertilized eggs have a right to life, I also know of no conclusive reason for asserting that they do have a right to life."[42] But one is entitled to this conclusion about the moral status of newly conceived human beings (Thomson's 'fertilized eggs') only if one can make an argument sufficient to support it. And such an argument would have to rebut the arguments put forward to show that the unborn have a right to life even in the earliest stages of their existence. There is all the difference in the world between rebutting these arguments and ruling them out in advance on the ground that they implicate deep moral and metaphysical questions in dispute among reasonable people subscribing to competing comprehensive doctrines.

But what are the arguments that need to be rebutted if Thomson is to show that there is nothing unreasonable in rejecting the central pro-life claims? Perhaps these arguments are so tendentious or obscure or otherwise lacking in rational force that she is justified in ruling them out in advance as legitimate grounds for political action on pro-life principles. In considering the claim that "a human being's life begins at conception," Thomson observes parenthetically, and without further comment, that "[w]e are invited to accept that premise on the ground that the conceptus – a fertilized human egg – contains a biological code that will govern its entire future physical development, and therefore is already a human being."[43] Her suggestion, it seems, is not that the ground adduced for accepting the premise is false, but rather that it is inadequate. But let us here pause to consider the implications of the genetic coding and completeness of the human conceptus and early embryo. A human being is conceived when a human sperm containing twenty-three chromosomes fuses with a human egg also containing twenty-three chromosomes (albeit of a different kind) producing a single cell human zygote containing, in the normal case, forty-six chromosomes which are mixed differently from the forty-six chromosomes as found in the mother or father. Unlike the gametes (that is, the sperm and egg), the zygote is genetically unique and distinct from its parents. Biologically, it is a separate organism. It produces, as the gametes do not, specifically human enzymes and proteins. It possesses, as they do not, the active capacity or potency to develop itself into a human embryo, fetus, infant, child, adolescent, and adult.

Assuming that it is not conceived *in vitro*, the zygote is, of course, in a state of dependence on its mother. But independence should not be confused with distinctness. From the beginning, the newly conceived human being directs its own integral organic functioning. It takes in nourishment and converts it to energy. Given an hospitable environment, it will "develop continuously without any biological interruptions, or gaps, throughout the embryonic, fetal, neonatal,

---

[42] *Op.cit.*, 13.
[43] *Op.cit.*, 11.

childhood, and adult stages – until the death of the organism."[44] Thus, according to Dianne Nutwell Irving,

> The biological facts demonstrate that at conception we have a truly human nature. It is not that he or she [for sex is determined from the beginning] will become a human being – he or she already is a human being.... A human zygote or embryo is not a possible human being; nor is he or she a potential human being; he or she is a human being.[45]

Jed Rubenfeld, in an influential article entitled 'On the Legal Status of the Proposition that "Life Beings at Conception",' asserts the contrary. He claims that arguments that life begins at conception are "virtually unintelligible."[46] If this were true, then Thomson would seem to be justified in effectively ruling such arguments out in advance as reasons for legal restrictions on abortion. The trouble with Rubenfeld's assertion is that he engages no serious scholarly argument in favor of the proposition he claims to be not merely false or inadequate but "virtually unintelligible." Although he cites serious scholarly work in his analyses of claims that "life begins" at various biological marker events in prenatal development (such as the point in brain development at which interneural connections within the cerebral cortex make possible higher mental functioning), he fails to engage a single serious scholarly defense of the proposition whose legal status the title of his article promises to explore. The sole citation he gives for "these arguments" before declaring them to be "virtually unintelligible" is "a well-known antiabortion pamphlet written by Dr. John Willke of the National Right to Life Committee." And, to make matters worse, it is unclear whether Rubenfeld has even read this source, since he refers to it only parenthetically as having been discussed by Frances Olsen (a pro-choice scholar) in a 1989 *Harvard Law Review* article.

Rubenfeld should have examined the scholarly literature. It would have prevented his imagining, as Thomson seems to imagine, that the ground of the belief that the lives of new human individuals begin at conception is the bare proposition that "fertilization may be said to represent the moment of genetic completeness" (which is what Thomson seems to have in mind in referring to the "biological code that will govern its entire future physical development"). In response to the argument that life begins at conception, as he imagines it, Rubenfeld says that "every cell in our bodies is genetically complete,"[47] yet nobody supposes that every human cell is a distinct human being with a right to life. But, of course, this misses the point of the argument which establishes that there comes into being at conception, not a mere clump of human cells,

[44] D. N. Irving, 'Scientific and Philosophical Expertise: An Evaluation of the Arguments on "Personhood".' 60 (1993) *Linacre Quarterly*: 18–47, at 23.
[45] *Op.cit.*, 24.
[46] J. Rubenfeld, 'On the Legal Status of the Proposition that "Life Begins at Conception".' 43 *Stanford Law Review*: 599–635, at 625.
[47] *Op.cit.*, 625.

but a distinct, unified self-integrating organism, which develops itself, truly himself or herself, in accord with its own genetic blueprint. The significance of genetic completeness for the status of newly conceived human beings is that no outside genetic material is required to enable the zygote to mature into an embryo, the embryo into a fetus, the fetus into an infant, the infant into a child, the child into an adolescent, the adolescent into an adult. What the zygote needs to function as a distinct self-integrating human organism – a human being – it already possesses.

At no point in embryogenesis does the distinct organism that came into being when it was conceived undergo substantial change, that is, a change of natures. It is human and will remain human. This was the point of Justice Byron White's remark in his dissenting opinion in *Thornburgh v. American College of Obstetricians and Gynecologists* that "there is no nonarbitrary line separating a fetus from a child."[48] Rubenfeld quotes White's observation and then purports to demolish what he takes to be "the argument based on the gradualness of gestation," by pointing out that

> No nonarbitrary line separates the hues of green and red. Shall we conclude that green is red? That night is day?

But, again, Rubenfeld misses the point of the argument, which is not that development is 'gradual,' but, rather, that it is *continuous*. The human zygote that actively develops itself is, as I have pointed out, a genetically complete organism directing its own integral organic functioning. As it matures, *in utero* and *ex utero*, it does not 'become' a human being, for it is a human being already, albeit an immature human being, just as a newborn infant is an immature human being, who will undergo quite dramatic growth and development over time.

These considerations undermine the familiar argument, recited by Rubenfeld, that "an unfertilized ovum also has the potential to develop into a whole human being, but that does not make it a person."[49] The ovum is not a whole human being. It is, rather, a part of another human being. Unlike the zygote, it lacks genetic distinctness and the active capacity to develop into an adult member of the human species. It is living human material, part of the whole human being whose ovum it is, but, left to itself, however hospitable its environment, it will not mature as a human being. It will die as a human ovum. If successfully fertilized by a human sperm, which, like the ovum (but dramatically unlike the zygote), lacks the active potential to develop into an adult member of the human species, then substantial change, a change of natures, will occur. There will no longer be an egg, which was part of the mother, sharing her genetic composition, and a sperm, which was part of the father, sharing his genetic composition; there will be a genetically complete, distinct, unified, self-integrating human organism whose nature differs from that of the gametes – not mere human material, but a human being.

---

[48] 476 U.S. 747, 792 (1986) (White, J., dissenting).
[49] Rubenfeld, 'On the Legal Status of the Proposition that "Life Begins at Conception"': 625.

These considerations also make it clear, I believe, that Michael Lockwood, who takes a line on these issues similar to Rubenfeld's, is quite incorrect to say that "we were never week-old embryos, any more than we were sperm or ova."[50] Indeed, it makes no sense to say that I was a sperm that matured into an adult. Conception was the occasion of substantial change that brought into being a distinct self-integrating organism with a specifically human nature. Without itself undergoing any change of substance, this organism matured into a week-old embryo, a fetus, an infant, a child, an adolescent, and, finally, an adult.

But Rubenfeld has another argument: Cloning processes give to non-zygotic cells the potential for development into distinct, self-integrating human beings; so to recognize the zygote as a human being is to recognize all human cells as human beings, which is absurd. It is true that a distinct, self-integrating human organism which came into being by a process of cloning would be, like a human organism that comes into being as a monozygotic twin, a human being. That being, no less than human beings conceived by the union of sperm and egg, possesses a human nature and the active potential to mature as a human being. However, even assuming the possibility of cloning human beings from non-zygotic human cells, the non-zygotic cell must be activated by a process which effects substantial change and not mere development or maturation. Left to itself, apart from an activation process capable of effecting a change of substance or natures, the cell will mature and die as a human cell, not as a human being.

When, speaking of the conceptus, Thomson refers to the biological code that will govern "*its* entire future physical development," her syntax reveals the truth that each of us is the human being, i.e., the distinct, self-integrating organism, we were as an adolescent, a child, an infant, a fetus, an embryo, a zygote. Each of us is the *it* who has now experienced the physical development that was in *its* future when, at conception, *it* was coded for that development.

I have set forth in some detail the argument that the life of a human being begins at conception, and considered some (though by no means all) of the counterarguments, not to show that the unborn have a right to life (though I believe that they do) or that there is no general right to abortion (though I believe there isn't), but to show that the case for the right to life cannot be easily rebutted, nor can the case for a right to abortion – even a 'duly qualified' right to abortion 'in the first trimester' – be established without engaging the deep moral and metaphysical questions on the basis of which people divide over the question of abortion. If I am correct, then, Rawlsian 'political liberalism' does not offer a way of resolving the social and political conflict surrounding the issue on the basis of principles of justice which can be identified and applied independently of any particular view on these questions. Neither the arguments adduced by Rawls himself nor those advanced by Thomson give people on the pro-life side anything approaching a compelling reason to surrender in their political struggle

---

[50] M. Lockwood, 'When Does Human Life Begin?' in M. Lockwood (ed) *Moral Dilemmas and Modern Medicine*. Oxford: Oxford University Press, 1985: 29.

for legal protection of the unborn against abortion. They, like their opponents on the pro-choice side, may have good reasons to seek political compromises with their opponents on legislative proposals for the restriction or regulation of abortion, or even to seek a *modus vivendi* at the constitutional level on the best terms they can obtain; but nothing in the idea of 'public reason' gives them good grounds to suppose that justice itself requires them to shift from being 'politically pro-life' to being merely 'personally opposed to abortion, but pro-choice.'

6

Population control:
the global contours of the culture of death

KATERYNA FEDORYKA CUDDEBACK

[The] truths about the human person are the measure of any response to the findings which emerge from the consideration of demographic data.... No goal or policy will bring positive results for people if it does not respect the unique dignity and objective needs of those same people.[1]

CHARACTERISTIC of this era of post-modernity and deconstruction, the movement to promote population control around the world has benefitted as much from semantic sleight-of-hand as it has from the billions of dollars and the efforts of countless individuals, governments and non-governmental agencies. Indeed, the term 'population control' is hardly a term in use today, least of all by its proponents, who prefer to speak in terms of 'family planning'. While past involvement with population control cannot be denied, the terminological shift to 'family planning', these proponents claim, reflects a shift in priorities, in mode of operation, indeed in the maturity of our understanding about so-called population pressures, and the best ways to address these pressures.[2] As a matter of fact, however, the population control movement has done nothing more than engineer a verbal transition, in which 'population control' has become synonymous with 'family planning', and is to be understood according to whatever vague, non-threatening sense we may have about what it means to 'plan a family'.

In reality, 'population control' and 'family planning' are fundamentally different from each other, and we cannot attempt to understand one in terms of the other without a radical re-definition of one or the other term. Robert Whelan very succinctly formulates this difference when he writes that "Family planning is the decision taken by couples in the light of their own beliefs and circumstances, as to the number and spacing of their own children", while "population control is the decision taken by governments or other agencies that couples should have no more than a certain number of children, followed by measures to enforce this."[3]

---

[1] His Holiness John Paul II, 'Message to Mrs Nafis Sadik Secretary General of the 1994 International Conference on Population and Development and Executive Director of the United Nations Population Fund, 18 March 1994', in *Serving the Human Family: The Holy See at the Major United Nations Conferences*. New York: The Path to Peace Foundation 1997: 192.
[2] Cf. D. Hodgson and Susan Cotts Watkins, 'Feminists and Neo-Malthusians. Past and Present Alliances.' 23/3 (1997) *Population and Development Review*: 469–473.
[3] R. Whelan, *Whose Choice: Population Controllers' or Yours?* London: Committee on Population and the Economy 1992: 2.

The semantic transformation of population control into family planning was calculated to free the enterprise of limiting world population growth from the stigma of coercion, human rights abuse and governmental interference into personal lives, and to give this enterprise personal resonance with the vast majority of persons who, while rarely thinking about the birth, life or death of peoples on the other side of the planet, are passionately vested in their own so-called right to contracept, sterilize or abort their own fertility. The success of this transformation is demonstrated by the way any attempt to denounce population control is automatically understood as an attack upon the methods and liberty of practising fertility control that are predominant in the Western world today.

Ironically, while the public now hears the words 'population control' and understands 'family planning', the real transformation – the non-semantic change – has occurred in what 'family planning' now in fact is in ever increasing parts of the world. More and more, what should be private decisions of couples are being deliberately influenced – either more or less overtly – by governments that have very explicit plans for engineering the demographic profile of their populations to meet a specific – and limited – configuration.

It is valuable to look behind the formal definition of the term 'population control' to focus on what is an historical, continually evolving phenomenon. Knowing the origin of this phenomenon is invaluable in understanding what it is today, and how it will continue to evolve. In this essay, I would like to provide a brief outline of the history of population control, sketch out its main proponents today, and then discuss in more detail the ideologies it employs and the activity it undertakes to promote its agenda. It should become manifest, after a review of its activities and its objectives, how population control not only promotes the culture of death, but can in many ways be considered a summation, or an embodiment, of the culture of death itself.

The early days of population control: Malthusian and eugenic roots

The increase or forced decrease of population is partly the result of deficiencies in social institutions. ... Despite the fact that the world produces enough food for everyone, hundreds of millions of people are suffering from hunger, while elsewhere enormous quantitites of food go to waste.[4]

Just over 200 years ago (1798), the British mathematician and clergyman Thomas Malthus introduced a pamphlet simply entitled *Population*.[5] The core proposition of the essay functioned as a syllogism: (1) Population, when unchecked, increases in a geometical ratio, (2) Subsistence increases only in

---

[4] Pope John Paul II, *Address to the Pontifical Academy of Science*, 22 November 1991, par 4–6, as cited in *Ethical and Pastoral Dimensions of Population Trends*. Vatican: Libreria Editrice Vaticana 1994: par 56.
[5] T. R. Malthus, *Population: The First Essay*. Ann Arbor: The University of Michigan Press 1959.

arithmetical ratio, hence (3) the power of population is indefinitely greater than the power in the earth to produce subsistence for man.[6] Because our nature makes food necessary for our existence, subsistence exerts a continuous and ultimately inexorable check on the growth of population. The effects of this check, Malthus concludes, are misery and vice: misery as an absolutely necessary consequence once population growth has exceeded available food supply, and vice as a probable consequence, as people adjust their behavior to reduce fertility rates.[7]

According to Malthus, therefore, there are two dynamisms directing the course of human population growth: abundance, which stimulates population growth, and scarcity, which then halts population growth by the hunger, pestilence, and death which result when consumption has outstripped supply. Two of his other theses call for our attention in this context. The first is the assertion that the dynamism of scarcity is ultimately decisive for the course of human history. Any amelioration in the human condition, or improvement in production, can only be temporary, according to the fundamental syllogistic conclusion that the power of population is indefinitely greater than the power in the earth to produce the means of subsistence. Indeed, according to Malthus, any attempts to improve the human condition are rather to be condemned than promoted, since they only increase the magnitude of the misery that will eventually bring the inequality between population and production into balance.

The second thesis of interest to us is Malthus' observation that the oscillation between distress and comfort occur mainly among the poor, who are not only the first to suffer when population begins to exceed production, but are in fact primarily to blame for the fertility which creates this imbalance.[8] This pessimism about the capability of human resourcefulness to keep production in step with human consumption, and the singling out of the poor as the cause of over-population, figure as primary characteristics of contemporary population control ideology. Together, they are the key to understanding 'why' and 'how' the population control movement exists.

> It is the poorest of the poor which suffer such mistreatment, and this sometimes leads to a tendency towards a form of racism, or the promotion of equally racist forms of eugenics.[9]

The Malthusian conception of scarcity as a dynamism directing the process of human history reappears some fifty years later as an essential component of Darwin's theory of the evolutionary progress of man.[10] Darwin's work, elaborated upon by thinkers such as Sir Francis Galton, Julian Huxley, and Theodosius Dobzhansky, took Malthus' principle of scarcity in nature and turned it into the

---

[6] Malthus, *Population*: 5.

[7] Malthus, *Population*: 6.

[8] Malthus, *Population*: 11.

[9] Pope John Paul II, *Sollicitudo rei socialis* (1987): 25.

[10] Cf. R. Messal, 'The Evolution of Genocide'. 26/2 (2000) *The Human Life Review*: 48.

determinant of genetic supremacy.[11] At the turn of the century, Sir Francis Galton coined the term 'eugenics'[12] for this concretization of the Darwinian principle, bought this pseudo-science respectability by endowing an academic chair for its study, and launched it on the path to universal recognition.

Population control gained its ascendancy as a modern force for political and social design through the eugenics movement. By 1922, Eugenics Societies had sprung up all over the world, dedicated to furthering the study of eugenics and to financially supporting its implementation. The leadership of the movement sat in the United States, England, and Germany, and many of its members assumed influential positions in the scientific community, in non-governmental organizations and in national governments.[13] Those early enamored of the eugenic dream include Adolf Hitler, Margaret Sanger, Alan Guttmacher, billionaires John D. Rockefeller Senior and Junior, Eastman Kodak founder George Eastman, early UNESCO director Julian Huxley, economist John Maynard Keynes and ethicist Joseph Fletcher. They or other members of the Eugenics Society went on to found organizations such as the Population Council, the American Association for the Advancement of Science, SEICUS, Planned Parenthood Federation of America and the International Planned Parenthood Federation, Marie Stopes International, Negative Population Growth and the World Conservation Union.[14]

The early promoters of eugenics saw the need for clothing their agenda in humanitarian garb if it were to succeed in those places of the world where overt coercion was unacceptable. Hence, they introduced their plan to limit births among the 'unfit' as a campaign to liberate women from the burdens of childbearing, improve the quality of life for parents and existing children, improve marriages, and abolish poverty.[15] Peer-promoted programs such as Margaret Sanger's 'Negro Project' used African Americans to spread birth control among the black communities,[16] and welfare programs, such as Clarence Gamble's introduction of contraceptive subsidies for the 'indigent' of North Carolina, spread population control among the impoverished white populations of the American Southeast.[17]

---

[11] G. Greer, *Sex and Destiny. The Politics of Human Fertility*. New York: Harper and Row 1984: 302ff; Messall, 'The Evolution of Genocide': 66–67.

[12] Cf. C. P. Blacker, 'Eugenics in Retrospect and Prospect', in *Occasional Papers on Eugenics*, No. 1, The Galton Lecture 1945 at Manson House, London. London: The Eugenic Society and Cassell and Company Ltd. 1950, as cited in Messal, 'The Evolution of Genocide': 51 (fn. 31).

[13] J. Cavanaugh-O'Keefe, *Introduction to Eugenics*. Stafford, VA: American Life League, Inc. 1995: 3–5; Greer, *Sex and Destiny*: 306–309.

[14] M. Meehan, 'The Road to Abortion (I)'. 24/4 (1998) *The Human Life Review*; Cavanaugh-O'Keefe, *Introduction to Eugenics*; Greer, *Sex and Destiny*: 302–347; Messall, 'The Evolution of Genocide': 53, 62, 64; J. Kasun, *The War Against Population*. San Francisco: St. Ignatius Press 1999: 274.

[15] Cf. 'Ten good reasons for birth control'. 12/1–13/1 (1928–29) *Birth Control Review*.

[16] Meehan, 'The Road to Abortion (I)': 82–84; J. Miller, 'Betting with Lives: Clarence Gamble and the Pathfinder International'. 6/4 (1996) *PRI Review*: 6–7.

[17] Miller, 'Betting with Lives': 5–6.

Eugenics did not limit itself to proceeding according to democratic process if it could spare itself the trouble. Hitler's racial cleansing and eugenic elimination of the handicapped are the most notorious examples of eugenics unfettered by a need to preserve respectability. But other countries had similar programs. The US first, and then Switzerland, Denmark and Sweden enacted eugenic sterilization laws. Sweden's sterilization program in one year sterilized as many as did the American program in all years combined. Britain narrowly voted down similar eugenic legislation when it was brought before Parliament in 1935.[18]

Today's players in population control

Aside from intentions, which can be varied and perhaps can seem convincing at times, especially if presented in the name of solidarity, we are in fact faced by an objective *'conspiracy against life'*, involving even international institutions, engaged in encouraging and carrying out actual campaigns to make contraception, sterilization and abortion widely available.[19]

World War II and its horrors cast eugenics into disrepute, and the movement fell silent for a time. After a period of re-grouping in the 1950s, it reemerged in the 1960s as the 'Campaign to Check the Population Explosion'.[20] During this regrouping period, promoters of population control had successfully worked their way into positions of influence in academic and public policy circles.[21] By founding research organizations such as the Population Council, service organizations such as the International Planned Parenthood Federation or Pathfinder International, and cultivating close ties with governments and government interests, the eugenicists used these transitional years to set up the structure according to which, with very little change, the population control movement operates today.

Governments

The 'transitional' eugenicists worked diligently and ultimately successfully to introduce national governments to the idea of population control as a political concern. Today, untold sums of money are dedicated by the governments of developed, underpopulated countries to controlling the population growth in less developed, predominantly dark-skinned, and still reproducing parts of the

---

[18] Greer, *Sex and Destiny*: 310–320; Kasun, *The War Against Population*: 159–161.

[19] Pope John Paul II, *Evangelium Vitae* (1995): 17.

[20] Kasun, *The War Against Population*: 214–217; Greer, *Sex and Destiny*: 379 ff.

[21] Kasun, *The War Against Population*: 217 ff.; Meehan 1998b; Hodgson, 'Feminists and Neo-Malthusians': 478–479.

world.[22] Countries such as the US, Canada, Japan, Sweden and the UK are particularly aggressive in their promotion of international population control, often forcing it onto aid-dependent countries by making desperately needed assistance in areas such as food and health contingent upon the implementation of population reduction programs.

The divide between exporters and importers of population control generally corresponds to the North/South divide, and most population control programs in the developing world are instigated and funded by the wealthy countries of the developed North. Many developing countries, however, have embraced the goal of reducing population as a solution to their countries economic and social woes. Countries such as China, India,[23] Vietnam,[24] Peru,[25] Costa Rica,[26] Venezuela,[27] Kenya,[28] and Mexico[29] have drafted and are implementing their own population reduction programs. However, the majority, if not all, of the developing world countries that have adopted population programs have done so under pressure from or the direct influence of the developed world.[30]

Non-governmental organizations

This influence takes many forms. To avoid the appearance of inappropriate involvement in another country's affairs, population planners were careful to establish non-governmental organizations (NGOs) to promote their population

[22] For example, Kasun has calculated that in 1995, the United States government alone spent $1,295 million on foreign population control and 'related' expenditures, a six-fold increase over the amount spent in 1982. See *The War Against Population*: 221, table 7-1. See also M. Meehan, 'The Road to Abortion (II): How Government Got Hooked'. 25/1 (1999) *The Human Life Review*.

[23] Cf. Whelan, *Whose Choice?*: 28–29; J. Miller, 'The disassembly lines. Indian women sterilized under industrial conditions (I)'. 7/4 (1997) *PRI Review*: 1; J. Miller, 'The disassembly lines. Indian women sterilized under industrial conditions (II)'. 7/5 (1997): 3. CWNews, 'Indian Law Would Penalize Large Families', (7 Sept 1999) *Daily News Briefs*.

[24] Cf. Population Research Institute, 'UNFPA Awards Vietnam for Aping China's One-Child Policy'. 1/7 (1999) *Weekly Briefing*.

[25] Cf. D. Morrison, 'With honor aborted. A closer look at Peruvian President Alberto Fujimori'. 6/1 and 6/2 (1996) *PRI Review*: 10; D. Morrison, 'Cutting the poor. Peruvian sterilization program targets society's weakest'. 7/2 (1998) *PRI Review*: 1; D. Morrison, 'Tiahrt Violations? USAID continues to fund family planning programs in Peru, despite verifiable abuses'. 10/1 (2000) *PRI Review*: 1.

[26] Cf. ZENIT News Agency, 'Sterilization an attack against dignity of poor. Costa Rican Archbishop Clarifies Campaigns' Sophisms'. (12 July 1999) *Daily Dispatch*.

[27] Cf. Catholic World News Service, 'Venezuela Bishops oppose sterilization campaign'. (24 May 1999) *Daily News Briefs*.

[28] Cf. 'Government's perpetual grapples with population'. (10 July 1999) *Daily Nation*.

[29] Cf. Catholic World News Service, 'Mexican bishop confirms massive sterilizations of Indians'. (2 May 98) *Daily News Briefs*.

[30] Meehan, 'The Road to Abortion (II)': 71–72; Kasun, *The War Against Population*: 102–131.

agendas.[31] These NGOs are almost too many to be counted, and new ones are created almost daily: the *International Planned Parenthood Federation* and its affiliates, *Marie Stopes International, Care,* AVSC (*Access to Voluntary and Safe Contraception* formerly *Association for Voluntary Surgical Contraception*), *Program for Appropriate Technology in Health* (PATH), *Pathfinder International*.[32] All of these are heavily subsidized by developed world governments, and particularly by the United States, the UK, Sweden and Japan.

Organizing and financing these NGOs serves the goals of the population lobby in many ways. Once it became clear that pursuit of these goals by the early eugenic movement alienated popular opinion, their pursuit through NGOs facilitated 'crypto-eugenic' programs, the eugenic character of which was hidden under the cloak of humanitarianism and social service. Governments seeking to promote population control in foreign countries are able to deflect suspicion of their elitist and colonialist motives by working through indigenous branches of the various NGOs, giving the population reduction programs a home-grown appearance and circumventing accusations of racist genocide. Moreover, through contracting out programs to NGOs, governments are able to distance themselves from the population reduction activities they fund, 'laundering' billions of dollars in this manner. Money is fungible, and the millions of dollars that the US government, for instance, has given for the non-contraceptive or non-abortive programs of family planning organizations has freed up equal amounts of money for contracepting, sterilizing, and aborting the unfortunate beneficiaries of US foreign assistance.

International agencies

International agencies such as the International Monetary Fund, (IMF), the World Bank, and the United Nations (UN) have proven equally effective in lending population control a respectable face. They have, moreover, thrown the enormous authority and financial leverage of these powerful institutions behind the efforts of the population lobby. The specter of population growth has become an over-riding focus in UN conferences and UN-sponsored programs.[33] While lacking legal authority, UN resolutions and programs of action serve to justify the population reduction activities of any individual country, and in reality act as politically binding on any country that wishes to remain in good standing within the international community. Both the World Bank and the IMF use their power as lending institutions to pressure resisting countries into compliance with

---

[31] US Government Document, National Security Study Memorandum 200, *Implications of Worldwide Population Growth for US Security and Overseas Interests.* 10 December 1974; declassified 31 December 1980. Available on-line at http://www.pop.org/students/nssm200.html; Meehan, 'The Road to Abortion (II)': 72; Kasun, *The War Against Population:* 102–131, *passim.*

[32] For more comprehensive, yet still partial, listing of population control NGOs, see Kasun, *The War Against Population:* 234ff. See also Greer, *Sex and Destiny:* 348–387.

[33] Meehan, 'The Road to Abortion (II)': 74.

UN targets and resolutions.[34] The World Bank has moreover stated that it is prepared not only to give loans, but to directly fund non-governmental organizations working to promote its social mandates within a country or a society.[35]

Private individuals and foundations

Despite the sheltering web of non-governmental and inter-governmental organizations, governments remain in principle accountable to their tax-payers and to the international community. At times this accountability has resulted in the reduction of population funding, or the suspension or reform of programs. Private individuals and foundations, on the other hand, are not threatened by such accountability. As in the earliest days of the eugenics movement, the population control lobby continues to attract many of the world's richest and most powerful men and women, including names such as Gates, Turner, Buffet, Pew, Rockefeller and Ford. These proponents of population reduction serve the cause not only by placing their vast fortunes at its disposal, but also by personally championing this cause. Shielded by their wealth and its attendant celebrity status, many of them push for ever more radical forms of anti-population sentiment. Ted Turner's unapologetic call for the adoption of a 'voluntary one-child policy' in the United States is an example of how these individuals, protected by their wealth and status, are effective in broadening the sphere of acceptable discourse in population matters.

The small number of eugenicists remaining in the 1950s successfully secured for their connections and interests the support of the richest and most powerful institutions of the day, and a roster of supporters that for the most part is the same almost five decades later. This roster includes the governments of the developed world, the international and non-governmental organizations, and individuals who have vast sums of money to throw behind their convictions. The strategic value of establishing commitment to population control on such various levels and entrenching it within a wide variety of interest groups and geographical regions cannot be underestimated. It has given the population control movement a pool of resources and a fund of influence that is virtually

---

[34] D. Morrison, 'Weaving a Wider Net'. 7/1 (1997) PRI Review: 6–7. Morrison writes that according to World Bank president James Wolfenson, "the business of the World Bank will not be primarily economic reform, or governmental reform. The business of the World Bank will primarily be social reform", and that population control activities are an essential component of 'sensible' social policy. J. Kasun reports that the World Bank spent $2 billion directly on population control between 1970 and 1996, but considers the entire $20 billion of the World Bank's annual budget as part of the world population control effort, because of the conditions the World Bank places on its loans. Kasun, The War Against Population: 277. In 'World Bank Banks on Population Control,' the Catholic Family and Human Rights Institute reports that the lending agency has "adopted 'an overall mandate in reducing fertility rates' as part of its commitment to 'alleviate poverty' in developing countries." 1/8 (1997) Friday Fax.
[35] Morrison, 'Weaving a Wider Net': 7.

inexhaustible. Moreover, this global dispersion of pro-population control senti-ment among key individuals and organizations gives it the appearance of a majority that the movement in fact does not have.

Alliances

A significant addition to the roster of players set up in the 1950s is the later alliance of population control enthusiasts with two very significant interest groups: the feminists and the radical environmentalists.

Turning the concern for nature into an attack against population

> While population growth is often blamed for environmental problems, we know that the matter is more complex. Patterns of consumption and waste, especially in developed nations, depletion of natural resources, the absence of restrictions or safeguards in some industrial or production processes, all endanger the natural environment.[36]

The alliance between radical environmentalism and population control is a natural match. What population control seeks as its end, radical environment-alism embraces as a means in its quest to preserve the natural world from its most dangerous enemy: the human person. Groups such as the Sierra Club or the Audubon Society actively lobby to promote population control within their membership and in local and national policy. Authors such as Al Gore[37] or Bill McKibben[38] target the popular audience with factually flawed but emotively powerful arguments for 'stabilizing human population' for the sake of saving the natural environment. It is practically impossible to visit an aquarium, zoo, or museum of natural history without being confronted with some exhibit or narrative of how human population growth is the greatest threat to the beauties of nature we have come to enjoy.

This alliance has been tremendously beneficial to the cause of population control. Most people would not embrace population control in itself, or for eugenic reasons. And yet several generations now have accepted a supposed need for population reduction out of a genuine, albeit misguided, concern for the natural world.[39]

[36] His Holiness John Paul II, 'Message to Mrs Nafis Sadik ': 195.
[37] Cf. *Earth in the Balance*. New York: Houghton Mifflin 1992: in particular 307–317.
[38] Cf. *Maybe One: A Personal and Environmental Argument for Single-child Families*. New York: Simon & Schuster 1998.
[39] Cf. also Hodgson, 'Feminists and Neo-Malthusians': 496.

The cause of women's rights as a basis for opposition to population growth

> [T]o formulate population issues in terms of individual 'sexual and reproductive rights', or even in terms of 'women's rights' is to change the focus which should be the proper concern of governments and international agencies.[40]

The alliance between population control and feminism is less natural, and yet has proved tremendously advantageous for both partners.[41] Despite the inherent contradiction between the notion of womens' liberation on the one hand and that of centralized social control of reproduction on the other, the two movements have coalesced into one virtually identical machine that fights for sexual liberation, unlimited access to contraceptive methods, an unconditional right to abortion, and the dissolution of the traditional family. The present cast of international population policy is almost exclusively formulated in terms of the feminist and human rights rhetoric of 'reproductive choice'. In return, the feminists receive financial backing from the vast sums of money dedicated to population control, and access to the processes of national and international policy formation.

The conflict between the crusade for women's freedoms and the campaign to control population does not remain on the purely theoretical plane, and the programs of 'reproductive health' which this alliance spawned have resulted in repeated violations of women's dignity and rights, in the developing world in particular. Feminist denunciation of these violations, voices such as those of Betsy Hartmann, Farida Akhter and Germaine Greer are relatively rare, and receive little echo in the feminist community at large. The alliance, cemented definitively at the 1994 UN Summit on Population and Development (Cairo), proved so advantageous to the radical feminist agenda as a whole, that the suffering of individual women around the world is not tolerated as a reason for its termination.[42]

'Control' as the heart of population control and the importance of artificial contraception

> Would anyone blame those in the highest offices of the state for employing a solution [contraception] considered morally permissible for spouses seeking to solve a family difficulty, when they strive to solve certain difficulties affecting the whole nation? Who will prevent public authorities from favoring what they believe to be the most effective contraceptive methods and from mandating that everyone must use them, whenever they consider it necessary?[43]

[40] His Holiness John Paul II, 'Message to Mrs Nafis Sadik': 193.
[41] For an excellent historical survey of the development of this relationship, see Hodgson, 'Feminists and Neo-Malthusians'.
[42] Cf. Whelan, *Whose Choice?*: 40–41.
[43] Pope Paul VI, Encyclical Letter *Humanae Vitae* (1968): 17.

Equipped with a world-wide network of governmental and non-governmental supporters, the promoters of population control adapt their programs and their *modus operandi* to the specific political and cultural context in which they operate. Control 'is fundamental to the very concept of population control', and the natural logic of its implementation demands predictability and the certitude of reaching its objectives. It is no accident that today population control advocates consistently overlook or commend the use of dictatorial force in the implementation of population programs, and avail themselves of every opportunity to by-pass human freedom in the reproductive sphere.[44] Before anything else, the nature of a population control program is determined by one fundamental characteristic of the society in which it operates: the level of freedom this society affords its members.

In democratic settings, population planners cannot directly act against freedoms and rights, and must induce population-limiting behavior by changing popular attitudes and mores. The typical approach has been a combination of expanding the so-called 'right' to abortion, promoting birth control, encouraging sexual promiscuity by disparaging the traditional ideals of fidelity, monogamy and abstinence as outdated and oppressive, destroying the traditional family, and encouraging a standard of 'quality of life' that conflicts with the sacrifices that undeniably arise with each additional child. These changes in attitude are pursued through aggressive publicity campaigns that harness the news media and the entertainment industry, through legislation that fosters a political and economic climate inimical to the traditional structures of marriage and the family, through a saturation of the educational system with an anti-population bias,[45] and through a linking of social assistance to fertility reduction initiatives.[46]

Attitude change certainly accounts for a significant portion of the fall in fertility that invariably follows such concerted social engineering. However, it is important to recognize that although these changes in attitude in the so-called free world are not engendered through explicit coercion, they are nonetheless engineered, achieved by weaving anti-natal policy into the social and economic

---

[44] The UNFPA has repeatedly given its highest population award to flagrant violators of human rights, such as China (1983) and Vietnam (1999); in 1989, the IPPF dedicated an issue of its *People* magazine to praising the Chinese family planning program. According to John Cavanaugh-O'Keefe (*Introduction to Eugenics*: 15–16) when the Reagan administration cut off funds for the UNFPA because of its involvement in the coercive Chinese family planning program, feminist leaders Eleanor Smeal and Molly Yard spoke out strongly in defence of the UNFPA and its involvement in this coercive program.

[45] Cf. Kasun, *The War Against Population*: particularly chapters 5 and 6; Meehan, 'The Road to Abortion (II)': 76–80.

[46] Examples of such linking of social assistance with fertility control initiatives in the US include an Oregon initiative subsidizing vasectomy for low-income men (see Population Research Institute, 'Let them all have vasectomy. State seeks to cut social spending by cutting poor men'. 7/3 (1997) *PRI Review*: 1); and a 1997 discussion in the Arkansas State Legislature considering passage of a bill that required all females using state assistance to receive Norplant (Population Research Institute, 'Correspondence'. 10/2 (2000): *PRI Review*: 4).

structures of societies. The legislated 'right' to abortion, unwarranted tax burdens for married couples and couples with children, societal stigma against stay-at-home mothers, or against families with more than one or two children, are all examples of the indirect force that is turned against the bearing of children in free societies. It is significant to note that in the United States, for example, desired fertility is higher than actual fertility.[47] Many couples do not feel 'free' to have the number of children they want.

Countries with minimal or no respect for fundamental freedoms and human rights have a tragic record of population control. China's one-child policy is infamous, and hardly needs elaboration. But it is certainly not alone. In the past, Indonesia, Bangladesh and India have implemented harsh punitive measures and mobilized special cadres to ensure the achievement of their demographic targets.[48] Vietnam today implements a mandatory one- or two-child policy that dictates maximum number of children; minimum age of childbearing; minimum years between children; mandatory contraceptive usage (preferably sterilization or intra-uterine devices), and prescribes punitive measures for compliance failures on any of these points.[49] The Indian Parliament launched an incentive program in February of 2000 encouraging parents to become sterilized after two children, and narrowly avoided passing legislation that would have blocked parents of three or more children from holding public office.[50]

The use of force in the implementation of population policy today can easily be attributed to a dictatorial regime, rather than to population policy itself. Yet the use of force is not limited to totalitarian governments. It emerges in any situation where an individual or a community lack the power to avail themselves of the legal or societal safeguards against violations. Throughout the world, the poor, the minorities, the ignorant and the weak suffer gross violations of their dignity, of their physical integrity and of their right to be parents.

Whether carried out in a more or less totalitarian setting, modern population programs depend for their effectiveness on the development of ever more effective and permanent methods of contraception. One of the characteristics of artificial contraception, the one that makes it particularly central for any program of population control, is that it requires little or no user participation. Hence, it is uniquely suited as a means in those cases where contraceptive practice is imposed upon an unwilling populace, as is so often the case in population control programs. Indeed, population control as we know it would not have been possible without the development of artificial birth control methods.

---

[47] In his 1997 documentary 'The Grandchild Gap' (*Think Tank, Public Broadcasting Service* 4 April), demographer Ben Wattenberg notes that while desired fertility in the US is 2.5 children per woman, actual fertility stands at 1.98 children per woman.

[48] Whelan, *Whose Choice?*: chapter 4, 6, and 7; Kasun, *The War Against Population*: 109 ff.

[49] D. Goodkind, 'Vietnam's One-or-Two-Child Policy in Action'. 21/1 (1995) *Population and Development Review*: 85–111; Population Research Institute, ' UNFPA Awards Vietnam'.

[50] 'India's New Population Policy Raises Concerns'. *CNS News* 16 Feb 2000, as cited in 'India Launches Controversial Population Policy'. 10/2 (2000) *PRI Review*: 14–15.

Modern forms of artificial contraception depend as much on the development of modern technology as on the formation of the eugenics and then the population control movements. And certainly the prevalence of contraceptive use and its hold on the modern mentality cannot be explained solely with reference to these two movements. The active promotion of contraception among the working classes had begun in the early 1800s, by members of the Freethought movement. Once the eugenicists seized upon contraception as the heart of their program, their message fell upon an audience that had heard, and to a large extent already responded to, several decades of birth control propaganda. Attempts of public authorities to the contrary, the propaganda had enjoyed widespread success among the masses, appealing to motives as varied as women's liberation, 'marital prudence', freedom from the burdens of rearing a large family, and the fear of overpopulation.[51]

Nevertheless, one cannot fail to note the conspicuous presence of the eugenicists and Malthusians within the history of the development and promotion of modern contraceptives.[52] Almost from the beginning, population control proponents have been at the forefront of contraceptive research, pioneering devices and methods such as the IUD, spermicides, subdermal implants such as Norplant, RU 486, surgical and non-surgical sterilization, and anti-fertility vaccines.[53]

This ongoing development of contraceptive technology is rooted in a very practical problem: demographic study has demonstrated that parental preference, rather than contraceptive access, is the determining factor in actual fertility.[54] In other words, it is impossible to predict the outcome of any population program simply by maximizing contraceptive availability and leaving actual contraceptive use up to the decision of individuals and couples. Moreover, precisely those populations targeted by a Malthusian/eugenic program of population control – the poor, the illiterate, the dark-skinned – are those who value and desire their children. The history of contraceptive development and marketing is conspicuous for the predominance of permanent and semi-permanent methods, requiring little or no user-participation: surgical and non-surgical sterilization, implants, vaccines, and intra-uterine devices.

---

[51] Greer, *Sex and Destiny*: 348–378.

[52] For instance, one of the early contraceptive 'how to' manuals, *The Wife's Handbook*, was published in 1882 and made widely available by the Malthusian League, which also widely promoted contraceptive usage among the working class. See Greer, *Sex and Destiny*: 353–357. For a study of how population control interests were responsible for the widespread acceptance of artificial contraception in the United States, see D. Critchlow. *Intended Consequences. Birth Control, Abortion, and the Federal Government in Modern America*. New York & Oxford: Oxford University Press 1999.

[53] Greer, *Sex and Destiny*: 348–387; Population Council, *Annual Report 1995*: 22, as cited in Kasun *The War Against Population*: 261–262; J. Miller, 'Betting with Lives': 5, 7; J. Miller, 'Money for Mischief. USAID and Pathfinder tag-team women in the developing world'. 6/5 (1996) *PRI Review*: 3 ff.

[54] L. Pritchett, 'Desired Fertility and the Impact of Population Policies'. 20/1 (1994) *Population and Development Review*: 1–55.

How population control promotes and embodies the culture of death

> In discovering the family as the '*sanctuary of life*' and the '*heart of the culture of life*', men and women can be freed from the 'culture of death'. This latter culture begin with the '*anti-baby mentality*', so widely developed in the ideology of coercive population control.[55]

The worldwide network of promoters on the governmental and non-governmental levels is crucial for the advance of population control. Equally as crucial, however, is the creation of first the appearance, and then if possible the reality, of grassroots conviction about the need to curb population. Such conviction, however, was slow in the making. As a first step, the American eugenicists, and then the English, adopted a program of 'crypto-eugenics', which involved turning the eugenics societies into grant-giving and promotional organizations, increasing financial support to family planning organizations, and promoting the cause of 'biosocial science', the new name for eugenics[56] within the academic community. But more was needed.

It took a propaganda campaign masterminded by the American marketing genius and millionaire, Hugh Moore, to motivate the groundswell of popular outrage and conviction which has carried the population control movement for the last 40 years. Moore had made his fortune marketing disposable paper cups by creating a panic about the health threat posed by common, reusable drinking cups. The first step in 'marketing' the curb on population growth was like the first step in creating a demand for paper cups: scaring the public into an interest in the product. In 1960, the World Population Emergency Campaign was launched, and on June 9 readers of the *New York Times* were confronted with a full-page advertisement, depicting the US taxpayer struggling under a heavy burden identified as 'foreign aid'. The ad gave personal relevance to the perhaps worrisome but ultimately distant specter of overseas overpopulation. It little mattered that foreign aid at that time consisted predominantly of military assistance. The public was misled into believing that the high fertility of the world's poorest peoples was being subsidized by the hard work of the American taxpayer, and was given a reason to become deeply interested in promoting the ends of population control.[57]

This beginning is emblematic of the population control movement's need to distort and manipulate in order to grow and exercise influence. The scientific argument for eugenics had already been discredited when its proponents renewed their efforts to secure its goals by transforming it into a campaign to save the world from overpopulation. While the demographic transition from rising birth rates to falling birth rates worldwide was yet to occur in 1970, there was

---

[55] Pontifical Council for the Family, *Ethical and Pastoral Dimensions of Population Trends*, in *Serving the Human Family. The Holy See at the Major UN Conferences*. New York: The Path to Peace Foundation 1997: 753 (par 89).
[56] Greer, *Sex and Destiny*: 328–329.
[57] Greer, *Sex and Destiny*: 378–381.

certainly no sign even then that the earth was close to reaching depletion of its carrying capacity. Today, there is even less reason than in 1970 to believe that population growth will outstrip the earth's ability to feed and clothe coming generations, and yet the panic is as fresh and if anything more urgent than before.[58] Through a distortion of science, half truths and outright lies, the myth that more people necessarily means less for every individual person, continues misleading the minds, manipulating the emotions and warping the consciences of the vast majority of the public today. As a result, the unconscionable has become commonplace, as the masses accept as necessary the violation of human rights and the redefinition of fundamental freedoms and traditional morality.

It is impossible to circumscribe the cost of population control in the scope of this or of a much larger presentation. However, I would like to identify, however briefly, the main areas in which population controllers are focussing their efforts today.

Population control and the violation of rights

> Indeed, there is a tendency to promote an internationally recognized right to access to abortion on demand, without any restriction, *with no regard to the rights of the unborn*, in a manner which goes beyond what even now is unfortunately accepted by the laws of some nations.[59]

Essential to the population control enterprise is the destruction of an authentic understanding of human rights. Population control presupposes the belief that individual persons do not have the right to control their own destiny about one of the most personal and intimate aspects of their lives: their decision as to when and how often to bear a child. To those convinced of the necessity of population control, there is no such right to procreation; to those who believe in such a right, the history of population control is one long series of human rights violations, as governments and non-governmental agencies labor to meet, in one way or another, their demographic targets.

These abuses include not only explicit coercion, but also the implicit force which exploits ignorance and dependence, mocking the dignity and innate worth of the people it violates. Population programs exploit ignorance about the full effects of the family planning services being offered, about the safety, permanence, or side-effects of the procedures. And the programs exploit the

---

[58] For comprehensive considerations of the evidence supporting this statement, see the work of the late Julian Simon, in particular *The State of Humanity*. Oxford & Cambridge, Mass.: Blackwell, 1995 and *The Ultimate Resource 2*. Princeton: Princeton University Press 1996. See also Ronald Bailey, ed., *The True State of the Planet*. New York: The Free Press 1995 and Kasun, *The War Against Population*: chapters 1 & 2.

[59] His Holiness John Paul II, 'Message to Mrs Nafis Sadik': 193.

poverty of their targets, using the leverage that comes when the agency so urgently recommending some form of birth control also holds the power to enroll individuals or their family members in food or medical assistance programs, or to provide them with educational or economic opportunities.

Warping the very notion of rights, the population control movement works incessantly to establish access to abortion and contraception as uncontested human rights, such that restrictions placed upon abortion or contraception, or even the failure to provide them when they are desired, constitute human rights violations prosecutable by international criminal law.[60] Were this attempt to enshrine the new understanding of 'reproductive rights' as a basic human right to succeed, countries would be obligated to legalize and subsidize their provision, medical personnel could no longer invoke conscience clauses as a defense against performing services such as sterilization and abortion,[61] and any legal defense of the unborn would be rendered contrary to international accord and a crime against humanity.

Added to the violation of individual rights is the gross violation of the rights of nations to determine their own political and social policies. As was baldly stated in a 1970 US government memorandum, the primary purpose of US population policy overseas is to secure US economic and political interests by inhibiting the full economic and social maturation of the developing world.[62] That the US and other aid-supplying countries care as little now for the sovereignty and right to self-determination of other nations as they did when this memorandum was written is made abundantly clear by the way in which recalcitrant nations are threatened with a withdrawal of foreign assistance if they fail to implement the required population reduction programs.[63]

---

[60] Cf. Catholic Family and Human Rights Institute, 'Geneva Human Rights Panel Provides Glimpse Inside UN NGO Establishment'. 1/30 *Friday Fax* (1998); 'Broad New Rights Introduced at Geneva Meeting of UN Commission on Human Rights'. 1/27 (1998) *Friday Fax.*

[61] The Convention for the Elimination of Discrimination against Women (CEDAW) and the International Criminal Court (ICC) are perhaps the two most infamous entities striving for ratification of this understanding of reproductive rights and its codification into international criminal law. Cf. S. Dateno, 'UN Committee Presses Chile, Nepal to Loosen Abortion Restrictions'. 9/4 (2000) *PRI Review*: 15; Catholic Family and Human Rights Institute, 'New International Court nears Reality/Pro-lifers Claim Small Victories'. 3/31 (2000) *Friday Fax*; 'Feminist Coalition Urges Naming Catholic Teaching on Abortion a "Crime Against Humanity" in New World Court'. 3/18 (2000) *Friday Fax*; 'UN Committee Directs Reinterpretation of Religion Along UN Guidelines'. 2/36 (1999) *Friday Fax*; 'Feminists refuse to define their "Gender Agenda" for the International Criminal Court'. 1/37 (1998) *Friday Fax.*

[62] US Government Document, NSSM 200, *Implications of Worldwide Population Growth for US Security and Overseas Interests* (see footnote 31 above).

[63] Cf. F. Sai and Lauren Chester, 'The role of the World Bank in shaping third world population policy,' in Godfrey Roberts (ed.), *Population Policy: Contemporary Issues*. New York: Praeger 1990 and 22 U.S. Code, sec. 2151-1; 22 U.S. Code, sec. 2151(b), both cited in Jacqueline Kasun, 'The High Cost of Population Control'. 9/2 (1999) *PRI Review*: p. 10.

Population control and the destruction of the family

> Among the most important ... rights, mention must be made of the right to life, an integral part of which is the right of the child to develop in the mother's womb from the moment of conception; the right to live in a united family and in a moral environment conducive to the growth of the child's personality; the right to develop one's intelligence and freedom in seeking and knowing the truth ... and the right to have and to rear children through the responsible exercise of one's sexuality.[64]

The traditional family has long been recognized as perhaps the greatest obstacle to establishing a long-term trend of zero or negative population growth. Consistent with this realization, the family has also been the target of population engineering the world over. Already postponing the age of marriage has a considerable effect on fertility rates; avoiding marriage altogether an even greater effect. The ways of achieving either a postponing or complete avoidance of marriage are many: propaganda advocating this postponement, active attempts to alter the ideal image of the family and the encouragement of homosexuality; economic and legislated deterrents to marriage and stay-at-home parenting; social controls such as the public stigmatization of larger families and the creation of a society that has no room for children or those caring for children.[65]

The attempt to create a social and economic climate inimical to starting a family has enjoyed considerable success. Couples nonetheless choose to have families, despite the difficulties, and those that do pose a particular challenge to the project of population control. The population control lobby has become conspicuous in its efforts to destroy the very notion of the nuclear family by creating legal and cultural divisions among its members.

First, it identified the bond between husband and wife as a target for destruction. In this vein, the very decision to have a child and start a family has been appropriated as the exclusive domain of women, completely excluding husbands and fathers from the realm of either choice or right in this sphere. Indeed, the traditional, male-headed family has been almost completely banished from public policy discourse or consideration. UN summit and conference discussions are emblematic of this trend. Preparatory documents for these meetings are drafted without a single mention of the traditional, two-parent family. Female-headed households alone are discussed or considered as candidates for social recognition and assistance.

The destructive effect of contraception on marriage has also been harnessed in this attempt to sever the bond between husband and wife. The never-ending search for newer and more effective forms of contraceptives explicitly aims at developing contraception which can be used by married women without the

---

[64] Pope John Paul II, Encyclical Letter *Centesimus Annus* (1991): 47.

[65] Cf. Frederick Jaffee, 'Activities Relevant to the Study of Population Policy for the US,' October (1970) *Family Planning Perspectives*: chart of proposed measures to reduce US fertility, as reprinted in Whelan, *Whose Choice?*: 54–55; see also Greer, *Sex and Destiny*: chapter 1.

knowledge or consent of their husbands, and population control promoters explicitly encourage such use. This aspect of the feminist revolution – its hatred and destruction of the marriage bond and the male-headed household – has been fully absorbed by the population control effort as a means of promoting its own ends.

Searching out the bond between family members that is potentially the weakest, the population planners are now placing particular emphasis on destroying the relationship between parents and children. The rights of parents to exercise authority over their children and to be the primary influence in the education of their children have in particular come under consistent attack. Children and adolescents are now being endowed with a new-found right of privacy, a right which in principle prevents parents from exercising parental authority, but which also frees other adults from an obligation to disclose to parents any involvement with their children. So, for instance, UN conference discussions have included attempts to guarantee minors "confidentiality in family planning services", as well as attempts to lower the age at which an adult is criminally liable for engaging in sexual activity with a minor.[66]

This adolescent rights movement is conspicuously geared towards winning the freedom to propagandize children in sexual immorality and encouraging them in lifestyles of permissiveness, if not promiscuity. The need for sex education and sexual freedom is continually being discovered at ever younger ages: not long ago it began to be passionately promoted as a right for all adolescents, adolescents defined as children between the ages of 10 and 18. Most recently, it was decided that teaching four year olds about sex will prevent unwanted pregnancies and the spread of AIDS.[67] As Jacqueline Kasun has thoroughly documented,[68] this focus on the young is intended to encourage reckless behavior, the consequences of which then will be remedied by abortion, contraception and sterilization. Such an approach has successfully delivered a reduction in the rates of marriage and of births.

Population control and the attack on religion

Are countries more sensitive to the vales of nature, morality and religion going to accept such a vision of man and society without protest?[69]

---

[66] Cf. Catholic Family and Human Rights Institute, 'Abortion and Contraception for Pre-Teens Promoted at Key UN Meeting'. 2/20 (1999) *Friday Fax*.

[67] United Nations Foundation, 'Sex Education used as AIDS prevention tool in Brazil and China'. *UN Wire*, 21 June 1999, as cited in *PRI Review* 9/4 (1999): 14.

[68] Kasun, *The War Against Population*: 160–211.

[69] His Holiness Pope John Paul II, 'Letter to the World's Heads of State' in *Serving the Human Family. The Holy See at the Major United Nations Conferences*. New York: The Path to Peace Foundation 1997: 201.

Two hundred years ago, Malthus wrote that only two things can curb the otherwise uncontrollable growth of population: misery and vice. The vice he speaks of is sexual activity without marriage and hence without children – whatever the means used to ensure this childlessness. The population control movement spends countless dollars to turn this vice into what Jacqueline Kasun calls 'the new orthodoxy', not just among the young, but throughout every stratum of society, and throughout every society.

Perhaps the greatest obstacle to the spread of this new orthodoxy has been the orthodoxy of traditional religion, Judeo-Christian and Islamic in particular. It is no accident, then, that traditional religion has also become a target for the promoters of population control. Population programs, for example, include explicit components directed towards 'reconciling' the practices they promote with the religious beliefs of the target population, or towards overcoming what they call religiously-motivated prejudices or inhibitions towards contraception, abortion and sexual activity outside of marriage. Apologists for population reduction are recruited to spread the message of family limitation and make it acceptable within the various religions and Christian denominations.[70]

On the policy level, traditional religious groups are marginalized at national and international conferences and policy discussions. The role of religion in public life is continually eroded, and the right of religious bodies to participate in international meetings aggressively attacked.[71] In the meantime, alternatives to traditional religion, such as neo-paganism, witchcraft, animism, or New Age pantheism are given special prominence, singled out for virtues such as eco-friendliness, non-patriarchalism, globality, or woman-centeredness. As environmentalist and population controller Herman Daly elaborates in *For the Common Good*, the population planners' Utopia calls for a religion that would be transformed under the "influence of ecological and feminist sensitivities," so that humanity would no longer take their moral direction from "ancient religious texts that came out of a very different social and demographic situation."[72] In other words, it calls for the destruction of religion understood as man's relationship with a transcendent God, Who is both Creator and Judge of the world and of each individual and their actions.

[70] Cf. Kasun, *The War Against Population*: 149–150; Catholic Family and Human Rights Institute, 'Liberal and New Age Religious Groups Gather to Effect International Affairs'. 3/34 (2000) *Friday Fax*; 'New International Criminal Court may Revoke Priest-Penitent Privilege'. 2/39 (1999) *Friday Fax*; 'Islamic Conference Agrees to Cooperate with UN Population Controllers'. 2/1 (1998) *Friday Fax*.

[71] Most recently, the Holy See's position as a Permanent Observer at the UN has come under fire by a coalition of pro-abortion and feminist groups, led by Catholics for a Free Choice. Cf. Catholic Family and Human Rights Institute, 'Campaign to Kick the Vatican out of the UN Grows to 400 Organizations'. 3/10 (2000) *Friday Fax*.

[72] Herman Daly, *For the Common Good: Redirecting the Economy Towards Community, the Environment and a Sustainable Future*. London: Green Print 1990: 377, 250, as cited in J. Kasun, 'The High Price of Pop Control'. 9/2 (1999) *PRI Review*: 7.

Conclusion

> The ultimate reason for these mentalities is the absence in people's hearts of God, whose love alone is stronger than all the world's fears and can conquer them.[73]

Throughout this paper, I have been discussing population control as a movement or an ideology. Such generalization is a useful exercise if we are seeking to understand what the Holy Father has called 'the culture of death'. For us engaged in fighting this culture of death, the understanding of population control as a movement and as a dynamism driving so much of the evil in our culture today is vital, since it enables us to separate often hidden causes from their more obvious effects, and shows us the interconnectedness of what may otherwise appear as random casualties of a world gone astray. The apparent irrationality of evil is certainly a component of its oppressive power. Simply understanding the influence of population control for evil in the world today starts lifting the burden of this oppression.

Generalizations are less useful in understanding individuals, particularly if we try to understand the motivations of those actively promoting population control today. The historical evolution of the population control movement does provide us with a wide range of possible motives for promoting population control: racism, eugenic chauvinism, desire for power, greed, fear of hardship, fear of losing the comforts already possessed, genuine confusion about the possibility of solving the world's problems through population control. Certainly, a large number of people are misguided about the beneficiality of population control; a large number of people certainly are not. Between these two poles there is an infinity of possible combinations of motives, in various degrees of purity and consistency.

Ultimately, this question of what motivates population control is as difficult to answer as the question 'why do men choose to do evil rather than good?' And ultimately, all issues of responsibility, causality or psychology aside, I believe that we must look to the father of all evil as the final explanation for the sway that the population control mentality has over our culture today. This particular ideology arguably encompasses the most comprehensive attack on the two things that the devil hates the most: God and man.

As did many other ideologies before it, population control injures and defiles the human person in a multitude of ways: corrupting his knowledge, destroying his innocence, violating his dignity, rights and freedoms, and taking the life of those most vulnerable. But unlike other ideologies, population control has assumed as one of its primary goals the very denial of existence to human persons. Contraception, more than anything else, is the hallmark of population control, and, I would argue, its greatest blow to humanity. For whether its proponents operate with such a transcendent purpose in mind or not, the primary end of population control in effect denies human persons even the possibility of their greatest happiness and fulfillment: eternal union with God.

[73] Pope John Paul II, Apostolic Exhortation *Familiaris Consortio* (1981): 30.

In similar vein, population control strikes at God as has no other ideology before it. Population control is not the first movement to attack God and religion, directly or indirectly, by visiting suffering and destruction on humanity and tempting it from its vocation to beatitude. It seems, however, that population control has uniquely targeted the very sovereignty of God as Lord of creation, by reaching out to thwart the only act of creation in which God has made Himself dependent upon the cooperation of his creatures: the creation of human persons. It takes the promise of the Serpent – "ye shall be like gods" – and makes this promise a reality, as it delivers into human hands power over creation itself, and a rationale for exercising this power as a rejection of life. Population control is truly the apex of the culture of death.

Population control must be recognized for what it is, and must be fought at its roots, not only in its manifestations. And yet, precisely because it so comprehensively embodies the culture of death, any struggle to promote the culture of life strikes a blow at the dominion and the strength of this movement. Its very comprehensiveness, while certainly a great strength, is also ironically an unanticipated weakness. Any effort to teach chastity to the young, protect the lives of the unborn and the elderly, or dispel the economic, environmental or demographic myths justifying population control, any act of generosity within our own marriages, or encouragement of the same kind of generosity in others, any act of faith in the providence of the Creator and His ability to provide for His creatures, builds up the culture of life and frustrates the spread of population control on every level.

Population control is ultimately grounded in a vision of despair, and understands only the logic of desperation. In light of this, the eminent wisdom and insight of the man who decades ago took as his motto the words "Be not afraid" shine in their full brilliance. We must not be afraid, not only in our confrontation with the culture of death, which at times certainly seems overwhelming, but also in our own relationships with ourselves, our families, our communities and our God. For without fear, the threatening predictions of the Malthusians, the eugenicists and the population controllers have no plausibility, their arguments have no ground. Without fear, we find the courage to follow our original vocation to be fruitful and multiply. And if we live this vocation, then we will succeed in building a true and lasting culture of life.

The Culture of Life

1. Theology and the Culture of Life

7

Faith in the incarnation, death and resurrection of Jesus, and the culture of life

LIVIO MELINA

The heart of the bioethics debate: what is life?

THE QUESTION of life is at the heart of bioethics. Yet it is often neglected – where it is not censored – as if it were entirely straightforward. Bioethics is, indeed, born out of an urgent practical need: to establish ethical criteria, publicly shared, to regulate the interventions of medical science on life. New and ever-more extraordinary powers over life itself allow interventions not only on its beginning and end, but even on its biological form and genetic structure, which it is now proposed to refashion. A profound unease over the unusual scenarios envisaged has crystallised in a demand for ethical criteria to limit these powers. In face of the pluralism of our Western societies it has been thought that such criteria must be found in terms of the formal features of justice; that is, according to procedural rules of fairness in arriving at a majority view, leaving aside the substantive perspective of the good of the acting subject, which is relegated to the private sphere. In this way, the fundamental question, that of the objective value of the good of life for the acting subject, is removed.

As a consequence, bioethics sets aside the question of what life is, taking for granted that it is for biological science to define life, while ethics has only the subsequent task of prescribing rules and limits to the power of science.[1] Thus ethics is inevitably estranged from the life of which it wants to speak. It always arrives too late, when the party is already over. And it arrives as an unwanted, petulant guest. There is here a combination of two factors: the excessive influence of scientific knowledge, which marginalizes as not objective every other form of knowledge; and the lack of critical reflection on science, and on ethics itself, which is reduced to problems of the formal logical features of argumentation.[2]

If, then, we should want to introduce into the bioethical debate reference to the Christian faith and its specific contents, as the theme assigned to me requires, we note that the censorship becomes still more far-reaching. The proposal of

---

[1] In the context of italian bioethics, one should mention two collections of essays which have recently questioned this censorship and reproposed the fundamental question: A. Scola (ed), *Quale vita? La bioetica in questione*. Milan: Mondadori 1998; G. Angelini (ed), *La bioetica. Questione civile e problemi teorici sottesi*. Milan: Glossa 1998.

[2] Cf. G. Angelini, 'La questione radicale: quale idea di "vita"?', in G. Angelini (ed), *La bioetica*: 177–206.

possible religious foundations for bioethics certainly does not find favour in discussions taking place in the context of our democratic societies; it meets rather with suspicion and mistrust. Any such proposal must reckon with the objection that it is fundamentally irrelevant, an objection which would tend to exclude religion from public debate on ethics. Respect for social pluralism is held to imply an unquestionable assumption of 'secularism' in the foundations chosen. Any reference to absolute and indisputable truths – not only religious, but also philosophical ones – would generate intolerance and rigidity. Only uncompelling proposals, lacking truth claims, could guarantee at the same time respect for the autonomy of every subject and flexibility in the solutions adopted. It is clear that what is contested here is not only the public value of religion, but the very capacity of reason to arrive at universal truths which are valid for all.

This confrontation therefore demands that we free ourselves from the very concept of reason as it relates to the truth about the good of life and the conditions which allow for an authentic and just society. My reflection will address in the first place the epistemological question just mentioned. The theological question will then be addressed: how the mystery of Jesus, in his incarnation, death and resurrection, illuminates life. It will thus be possible to show how faith in this mystery can generate a publicly valid culture, corresponding to the demands of universality and relevance to our times.

The epistemological question: bioethics and theology

We have already seen the strong ideological component that has characterised the introduction of bioethics into the field of human knowledge. Some maintain that bioethics arises in fact from a conscious break with every religious principle that affirms the inviolable 'sanctity of human life'.[3] Bioethics, with the inescapable novelty of its problems, can only be thought of in 'secular' terms, accepting the new 'quality of life' approach, according to which human life is only a relative good, to be valued according to a balanced calculation of the advantages it brings to the individual (in terms of pleasure and well-being) and to others or to society (in terms of utility or productivity). The response of authors on the Catholic side of the debate has been characterised by their refusal of the description 'Catholic' for the bioethics they propose. They have rightly defended the rational character and universal defensibility of an ethic which recognises absolute norms with regard to human life, to be respected always and in every case, without exceptions. Only by grounding ethics in the truth and developing a common dialogue on the *humanum* can we avoid arbitrariness, abuse of power and domination by the most powerful. In this sense many 'Catholic' bioethicists do not believe it is appropriate to use theological arguments in bioethics, but are willing to speak

---

[3] Cf. M. Mori, 'Bioetica. Nuova scienza o riflessione morale?' 11 (1990) *Mondoperaio*: 120–128. See also the debate which arose over the *Manifesto of secular bioethics* published by C. Flamigni, A. Massarenti, M. Mori, and A. Petroni in *Il Sole/24 Ore* of 9 and 16 June 1996.

solely on a rational and human level, without, however, falling into relativism and without renouncing the metaphysical truth about man.

Nonetheless, on close examination, even the principle of 'quality of life', which is clear in its theoretical opposition to the principle of the sanctity of life, straight away appears insufficient in its concrete applications. How is one to value the quality of a human life? Who can value it adequately? So it is evident, in fact, that the real problem is not simply one of morality. It cannot find a satisfying response solely in the field of normative ethics, while avoiding the fundamental question, which pertains to anthropology. Ethical responses are insufficient in themselves: they make sense only if located in a broader horizon of meaning.

There is need for that wisdom about man without which moral solutions cannot satisfy. It is at this point that religious concepts, and in particular the Christian vision of man, can make a valuable contribution. In this sense the suppression of the full horizon of Christian anthropology exacts a heavy price. The exclusion of theology from the public domain implicitly presupposes that theology is extraneous to rational understanding. The formal delimitation of bioethics as philosophical ethics, grounded in anthropology and metaphysics, but separate from theology, presupposes a 'rationalistic' view of reason, in which the question of truth is assumed in advance to be separate from that of freedom.[4] In this view faith, not only as a theological virtue, but in the first place as a human trait, has nothing to do with access to the truth, which is guaranteed in its objectivity precisely by bracketing the subject, with his aspirations and his search for meaning. But one cannot grasp the truth about life, with which bioethics is concerned, with a conceptual purchase which is univocal and 'scientifically' neutral. Life is not an object which is separate from ourselves, on which to carry out investigations. If we see it in this way, it escapes us. The convictions on which conscience draws in order to judge and to act concern the ultimate meaning of life and the dignity of the human person. In a radical way they call into play freedom, and the certainties they require cannot avoid the risk of faith; that is, belief placed in what is proposed as a reasonable foundation for hope in life.[5]

In this way, the current opposition between faith and reason can be overcome, with the rediscovery of a 'non-rationalistic' concept of reason and a non-fideistic concept of faith. Reason is not, in fact, separate from the act through which the human conscience in its integral operation refers to truth in the first place. Faith, before it is a theological virtue, is, in the Augustinian tradition, a universal anthropological pattern of access to the truth[6]: only faith, as a free and reasonable response to being, which is revealed through a sign, can know that which is beyond the limited grasp of the concept. In the rationalistic view of the modern

---

[4] On this see G. Angelini, 'Il dibatto teorico sull'embrione. Riflessioni per una diversa impostazione', in 16 (1991) *Teologia*: 147–166.

[5] Angelini, 'Il dibattito teorico sull'embrione': 151.

[6] On this point, see F. Chiereghin, *Fede e ricerca filosofica nel pensiero di S. Agostino* Padova: Cedam 1965; Idem, *Saggi di filosofia della religione* Padova: Cusl 1988.

era reason is the sole and autonomous source of the norms of public law. The model of scientific knowledge constructed so as to prescind from the subject and in this way rendered technically powerful, becomes, as it dominates, a factor in the marginalisation of theology. But the end of the modern era brings also a crisis for this type of rationality, and therefore renewed discussion of this exclusion.[7] The amplification of the concept of reason, understood as openness to reality in all its aspects, also allows for the possibility of a new consideration of the contribution from the theological perspective. If 'faith', understood as a human attitude, is not extraneous to 'reason' in its dynamism towards truth, then an input from a superior source of enlightenment, received through the freely chosen risk of theological faith, cannot be ruled out. Hence, also, theology, as a critical and systematic reflection on revelation, cannot be assumed from the outset to be extrinsic and out of place in discussions concerning the mystery of human life.

The assertion of H. T. Engelhardt that "Even if theology cannot make a contribution of moral theory to the endeavours of bioethics, it can contribute aesthetic suggestions of purpose and meaning"[8] can and should be countered. On the one hand this view decries the limits of a rationalistic formalism in moral theory, which in order to be purely rational and universal can say nothing about the meaning and purpose of human life and must leave this topic – which nonetheless needs to be considered – to theology. On the other hand this view would relegate theology to the domain of aesthetics; that is, subjective taste, which must remain confined to the private sphere, in as much as it does not have the status of knowledge which can be publicly debated and defended. If the presupposition of theology is an act of faith in revelation, it does not thereby renounce its claim to rationality, or exclude itself from dialogue. Rather, theology aims at rational argument starting from revelation, which for its part makes an indefeasible claim to tell *the truth* about man: a truth to be proposed for consideration in the public domain.[9]

"He brought to light life" (2 *Tim* 1:10)

"...our Saviour Jesus Christ...abolished death and through the gospel brought to light life and immortality" (2 *Tim* 1:10). This is the faith of the Church: life shines through the gospel of Jesus Christ. The Encyclical of John Paul II,

---

[7] See R. Guardini, *La fine dell'epoca moderna. Il Potere*. Brescia: Morcelliana 1984. (See R. Guardini, *The end of the modern world: a search for orientation*; translated by J. Theman and H. Burke, and edited with an introduction by F. Wilhelmsen. London: Sheed & Ward 1957.)

[8] H. T. Englehardt, 'Looking for God and finding the abyss: bioethics and natural theology'. In E. E. Shelp (ed), *Theology and Bioethics. Exploring the Foundations and Frontiers* (Series: *Philosophy and Medicine*, Volume 20), Dordrecht & Boston: D. Reidel 1985: 79–91, at p. 90.

[9] This is the essential meaning of the Encyclical *Fides et ratio*: see the lecture given in Madrid by Cardinal Ratzinger, 'Fede, verità e cultura. Reflessioni in relazione all'Enciclica *Fides et ratio*' (Madrid, 16 February 2000), in *Tracce* n. 3, March 2000.

Evangelium vitae[10], although it does not cite this biblical passage, elaborates the characteristics of an authentic 'theology of life', centred on Christ and the mysteries of his life, death and resurrection. We will follow the Encyclical in this, although we will not be able to exhaust the riches it provides.

The import of the question 'Why is human life a good?' is practical and existential (*EV* 34). Why is it always a good? Why should it warrant an absolute and unconditional respect, rather than being subjected to a balanced evaluation of the advantages and disadvantages that are actually involved for a given life and for others? Why does human life have primacy over other, plant and animal, forms of life, and what relationship should men have with these other forms of life? And the reply is distinctly christocentric: "Through the words, the actions and the very person of Jesus, man is given the possibility of 'knowing' *the complete truth* concerning the value of human life." In Him indeed "life was made manifest" (1 *Jn* 1:2).

Christ Jesus, in the mystery of his incarnation, death and resurrection, is the reference point needed to understand the value of human life. Thus the essential epistemological principle is laid down, taking up and applying to the theology of life the central thesis of christocentric anthropology from the Constitution *Gaudium et spes* of the Second Vatican Council: "In reality it is only in the mystery of the Word made flesh that the mystery of man truly becomes clear. For Adam, the first man, was a type of him who was to come, Christ the Lord. Christ the new Adam, in the very revelation of the mystery of the Father and of his love, fully reveals man to man and brings to light his most sublime calling."[11] But the epistemological aspect is founded on the protological-eschatological: man can know the full truth about his life only because in Christ both the eternal primordial word about man and his definitive destiny are revealed.[12]

Here we find the two great pillars supporting the theology of life, in the two christological titles which Sacred Scripture attributes to Jesus in reference to life: He is in fact the "Word of life" (ὁ λόγος τῆς ζωῆς: 1 *Jn* 1:1) and the "Archegos" [prince/leader] of life (ὁ ἀρχγός τῆς ζωῆς: *Ac* 3:15).[13] The first title refers to the beginning: "In Him was life" (*Jn* 1:4), and to the initial gift of creation. The second conveys instead the sense of an eschatological orientation of life: a fulness to which the Risen One brings us.

In the light of Christ, the Word of Life, the eternal plan of the Father for human beings is revealed: that they become "conformed to the image of His Son" (*Rm* 8:29, cited in *EV* 36). God freely created men out of love, giving them their

---

[10] References to the Encyclical internal to the text employ the abbreviation *EV*, followed by the number of the section of the Encyclical referred to.

[11] Vatican Council II, *Pastoral Constitution on the Church in the Modern World (Gaudium et spes)* 22; cf. J. Ratzinger, 'Kommentar zum I Kapitel', in *LThK. Das Zweite vatikanische Konzil*, III. Freiburg im B: Herder 1968: 706.

[12] On this see G. del Pozo Abejón, 'Dios Creador y Señor de la vida humana', in R. Lucas Lucas (ed), *Comentario Interdisciplinar a la 'Evangelium Vitae'*. Madrid: BAC 1996: 315–332.

[13] See A. Izquierdo, 'En Cristo se cumple la Escritura de la vida', in R. Lucas Lucas (ed), *Comentario Interdisciplinar*: 333–344.

present earthly life, so that they might welcome and freely participate in the divine life itself through faith in His Son by the action of the Holy Spirit (cf. *EV* 1–2, 37). The mystery of the Incarnation of the Son of God reveals the incomparable value of every human person, since He is thereby "united in a certain way to every man".[14] Contemplating the mystery of redemption, the Church grasps with ever-new amazement the Gospel of the dignity of every human person, which is "a single and indivisible Gospel" with that of God's love for man (*EV* 2).

The recognition of the unique dignity of the personal life of man, the patrimony of every authentic culture, has its starting point and its firm foundation in biblical revelation with the doctrine of the image. This doctrine constitutes, as John Paul II stated in his Apostolic Letter *Mulieris dignitatem*, "the immutable basis of all Christian anthropology".[15] The Encyclical *Evangelium vitae* also exhibits that approach to a dynamic and christologically oriented theology of the image, finding a theological rationale for the value of human life in that "specific and particular bond with the Creator", which is established in His original deliberation: "Let us make man in our own image, in our own likeness" (*Gn* 1:26; *EV* 34). If every creature exists by virtue of a relationship with the Creator and if, in particular, every form of life manifests something of the richness of the life of God, there is nonetheless a clear distinction between human life and the life of other creatures. This distinction is captured in the theology of the image: the human person is in a unique and individual relationship with God. While all other living beings are in a generic and mediated relationship with the Creator, the human being, every human being, is in a *relationship of personal immediacy* with Him.

In the first place, this is a relationship of *origin*. In the second, Yahwistic, account of creation (*Gn* 2:7), the life of man, although he is formed from clay, does not come about in continuity with a lower biological dynamism, but through a new and extraordinary intervention of God, who breathes into man His divine breath. Traditional Catholic doctrine, set out by Pope Pius XII in *Humani generis*[16], states that the immortal soul of each person is created immediately by God and that with it is transmitted His image and likeness. The great Christian thinker Romano Guardini has expressed in transparent and incisive terms this perception of the value of life, which is native to all human beings:

> Man is not inviolable by virtue of the fact that he lives. Such a right would belong also to an animal, in as much as the animal also lives ... The life of man is inviolable because *he is a person* ... Being a person is not a psychological, but an existential phenomenon: fundamentally it does not depend on age, nor on psychological condition, nor on the gifts of nature which the subject enjoys. Personhood can even remain hidden, as in the embryo, but it

[14] Vatican Council II, Pastoral Constitution on the Church in the Modern World *Gaudium et spes*: 22.
[15] John Paul II, Apostolic Letter *Mulieris dignitatem* (15 August 1988) 16.
[16] Pius XII, Encyclical Letter *Humani generis* (12 August 1950). 42 (1950) *Acta Apostolicae Sedis*: 575: "Animas enim a Deo immediate creari catholica fides nos retinere iubet".

is present from the beginning in the embryo, and has its own rights. It is this personhood which gives men their dignity. It distinguishes them from *things*, and makes them *subjects*... An entity is treated as a thing when it is possessed, used and, in the end, destroyed, or, in the case of human beings, when it is killed. *The prohibition on killing a human being expresses in its most pointed form the prohibition on treating him as if he were a thing.*[17]

Secondly, a relationship of *finality* is established with God. Every man is created with a view to personal communion with God, in knowledge and in love. It is this vocation to eternal life (*EV* 38) that gives us further insight into the significance of our origin 'in the image and likeness' of God. The specific creaturely 'givenness' of man is with a view to a free and supernatural gift: participation in the life of God himself as a 'son in the Son'. Indeed, "this is eternal life: that they know You, the only true God, and Jesus Christ whom you have sent." (*Jn* 17:3) The full value of human life, from its first stages and in its humble biological dimension, can only be properly grasped in relation to the supernatural end to which it is destined. If only God can take the initiative of calling a creature to participate in His own divine life, and if every human being created by God is in fact predestined to this supreme vocation, in the Son through the Holy Spirit, then it must be said that from the inception of a human life God Himself, through his Trinitarian and personal initiative, is involved in a unique and unrepeatable vocational bond with that human being.

Christ is therefore the 'archegos' of life in his three-fold role as 'hero', 'author' and 'head': Through his resurrection Christians have the certainty that they too participate in the destiny of their 'hero-saviour'[18], earned through his passion and death. Their citizenship from that point on is no longer of this world. Christ is the 'archegos' who leads many brothers to the beatific vision, namely the fullness of life in God (*Heb* 2:10). He rose from the dead precisely because he is life (cf. *Jn* 11:25).[19] He reveals that life which he receives from the Father in abundance, because it has its source in the Father. Because of this Jesus is not afraid to lose his life: he gives it for his friends so that they too may participate in the fullness of life and love which is his relation with the Father. Thus Jesus also unveils the secret of life: only he who is willing to lose it in giving himself can find it forever (cf. *Jn* 12:25). His death on the cross is the sign of a freedom in giving which is already a triumph over death and a manifestation of the abundance of divine life, to which the Son alone has access. On the cross he is also the source of life for men. Through the salvific action of Christ the very same life of the Son remains in us to this day (cf. *2 Cor* 4:10), and achieves a transformation of love and joy that is already an anticipation of glory. The life of the believer is therefore subject to the law of love (ἐντολή τῆς ἀγάπης): fraternal love becomes the criterion that demonstrates the passage from death to life (cf. *1 Jn* 3:14). Thus in the life of the

---

[17] R. Guardini, 'I diritti del nascituro', in May/June 1974 *Studi Cattolici*.

[18] Cf. G. Delling, ἀρχω, in G. Kittel and G. Friedrich (eds), *Theologisches Wörterbuch zum Neuen Testament*, vol. 1, Stuttgart 1932.

[19] Cf. R. Bultmann, ζάω, in Kittel-Friedrich, *op.cit.*, vol. 3.

disciple the agapic fullness of Trinitarian life is made manifest.

Faith in Christ and the culture of life

We here arrive at the final part of our reflection, concerning the opportunity and means we have whereby faith in Christ becomes the source of an authentic culture of life. To begin with, what do we mean by 'culture'? In his famous speech to UNESCO, John Paul II proposed the following definition: "Culture is that by which man as man becomes more man, he 'is' more, he enters further into being".[20] To pursue our analysis and demonstrate what a culture of life consists in, we need at this point a definition that will highlight the elements which make up that culture which allows 'man to be more man'. In general but sufficiently precise terms, Cardinal Josef Ratzinger speaks of culture as follows: "we can say that culture is the historically developed, common form of expression of the convictions and values that characterize the life of a community".[21]

This definition names the essential features of what we mean by 'culture'. It has to do with knowledge and values, above all, but is not something purely theoretical; rather, it concerns the fundamental interests of human existence. Moreover, it has to do with a communal affair that involves people in their search for the meaning of life and in mutual dialogue on what is important in life, on the fundamental values on which the human city is to be built, on how to respond to the challenges that life inevitably poses to everyone. The bearer of culture is social, which on the one hand benefits from the experiences of particular individuals, but on the other hand contributes to giving these experiences a definite form. Furthermore, culture is not a phenomenon closed in upon itself and fixed once and for all, but grows dynamically in history through the impact of events that stimulate its life and through encounter with other cultures. The sign of greatness in a culture is its openness, its capacity to receive and to give, to develop, and to allow itself to be purified and, therefore, to be more conformed to the truth about man.[22]

As an essential human phenomenon, culture answers to a fundamental need of human beings: the need for truth, value and purpose in life. Culture includes going beyond the visible and beyond apparent causes to search for the ultimate foundation of existence and reality. For this reason, as John Paul II observes, "at the centre of every culture is the attitude that man assumes before the greatest mystery, the mystery of God".[23] Now Christian faith, which welcomes the Gospel of life which is Jesus in person, is itself a source of culture. Faith, to the extent that it reveals to man who he is and how he can begin to be a human being in his encounter with Jesus, Son of God made man, is itself the origin of culture. If

[20] John Paul II, Allocution to UNESCO, 2 June 1980.
[21] J. Ratzinger, 'Christ, Faith and the Challenge of Cultures'. 24 (1995) *Origins*: 679–686.
[22] Ratzinger, *op.cit.*
[23] Pope John Paul II, Encyclical Letter *Centesimus annus* (1991) 24.

every culture is, at its core, a search for and openness to the mystery of God, Christian faith proposes as a new centre of culture the revelation of God made man, the definitive truth about man. It sets itself up as the genesis of culture and offers to every human culture the definitive key to understanding who man is and what is the value of his life. Christianity shows the foundation of her claim to be the complete truth about man precisely in her 'catholic' or 'ecumenical' nature: that is, her knowledge of how to pass into the secret heart of human cultures, entering into dialogue, converting and saving what is true in those cultures. In particular, the challenge of promoting a culture of life, animated from within by the light of faith in the Lord Jesus, 'who has made life shine through the Gospel', is to show its universal value, and counter the claims of the scientific culture which is dominant at present.

Accordingly, we would indicate the lines along which a dialogue can be carred out with the scientific culture, and the related elements of a possible cultural integration. An epistemological critique of the biological sciences reveals, in fact, the limitations and the *a priori* nature of a reductionist approach to the phenomenon of 'life'. According to Michael Polanyi[24], a living organism can be seen as a system that functions under the control of two distinct principles: its biological structure, which, as the higher principle, serves as a limiting condition for the proper deployment of the resources provided by physico-chemical processes; the latter in their turn, as the lower principle, permit the various organs to perform their functions. In this sense the structure of living things is extraneous to the laws of physics and chemistry which the organism makes use of: we are concerned here with irreducibly higher principles which add a regulative function. Or, in the words of Hans Jonas, the identity of a living organism is the identity of a form in time and not the identity of matter: this living form is ontologically "the general structural and dynamic order of a multiplicity".[25] Information is not reducible to matter, nor to energy, even if its conservation, transmission, and conversion depend physically on both matter and energy. Genetics itself impels us towards the adoption of a multi-level analysis and an informational paradigm as the most suitable for interpreting the phenomenon of 'life'.[26]

In this way biological knowledge is opened up to different and higher-level understandings of the phenomenon of life and can be integrated into such understandings. Scientific objectification is a way of interpreting reality, but it does not exhaust the possibilities of reason, understood as openness to the reality of a living

---

[24] M. Polanyi, 'Life's Irreducible Structure'. 160 (1968) *Science*: 1308–1312.

[25] H. Jonas, *Philosophical Essays: From Ancient Creed to Technological Man*. Englewood Cliffs, New Jersey: Prentice Hall 1974. See also, H. Jonas, *The Phenomenon of Life: Toward a Philosophical Biology*. New York: Harper & Row 1966. The biological phenomenon of 'life' involves two factors which are irreducible to chemistry and physics: the capacity for self-control of the living organism, which guarantees its identity, and its intrinsic goal-directedness. See Ph. Caspar, 'Génération: enracinement biologique et enjeux spirituels'. 14/2 (1998) *Anthropotes*: 287–358.

[26] See R. Colombo, 'Vita: dalla biologia all'etica', in A. Scola (ed), *Quale vita?*: 169–195.

being in all its aspects.[27] Life is not an object to be investigated but the basis for every activity. It is, then, clear that the higher form of life is that which is given to and with the consciousness of man. Consciousness and life cannot be contrasted as subject and object: intellectual consciousness is the most perfect level of living. "Quis non intellegit non habet perfecta vita".[28] The conscious life of man is the place where it becomes apparent what life is, where its origin from God and destination in God comes to light. The concept of life seems therefore fundamentally analogical: it is applied to an ascending scale which reaches from the most elementary levels all the way up to God, Who has life as His essence, Who possesses life in its fullness and Who creates it. Here the strictly theological dimension finds its place, the dimension in which we perceive the supernatural call to participate in the divine life itself in Christ.

In the light of this christocentric theological anthropology, the good of human life can be clarified in terms of its fundamental dimensions, avoiding either materialistic undervaluations or unwarranted idolisations. In fact the concept of life, though in itself simple and immediate, carries with it great semantic complexity. The physical life of man will be found to be ordered to the value of the person who is called in Christ to participate in the divine life. A 'boundary' phenomenon, located between the lower levels of matter, from which it emerges, and the higher level of the spirit, in which it participates, human life has ambiguous and even paradoxical features. As von Balthasar noted, the position that Sacred Scripture assigns to man on the stage of the created universe is highly and dramatically ambiguous: between heaven and earth, "above the earth" but "under the heavens".[29] If this ambiguous position refers to human life, one should note that other forms of life simultaneously exhibit dimensions of continuity and transcendence. On the one hand man appears as the crowning of an urge towards fulfilment 'from below' of the vital forces, peculiar to the evolution of matter. On the other hand, man's ability to reflect on himself implies a distance from the immediacy of living reality. What appears from below as a goal of evolution, looked at from the vantage point of the end achieved, is revealed 'from above' as the meaning which moves the whole dynamism towards its end.[30]

Guided by Johannine theology concerning life[31], and making use of terminological distinctions to be found in this theology, we can recognise three fundamental distinctions. (1) At the basic level one finds βίος – which

---

[27] Colombo, 'Vita: dalla biologia all'etica': 193–195.

[28] St Thomas Aquinas, *Summa theologiae* 1, q. 18, art. 3. See R. Spaemann, 'On the anthropology of the Encyclical *Evangelium Vitae*', in J. Vial Correa and E. Sgreccia (eds) *Evangelium Vitae. Five Years of Confrontation with the Society*. Vatican City: Libreria Editrice Vaticana 2001: 437–451.

[29] H. U. von Balthasar, *Le persone del dramma: l'uomo in Dio*, volume II of *Teodrammatica*. Milan: Jaca Books 1982: 170. English translation in *Theo-Drama, Vol 2: Dramatis Personae: The Person in Christ*. San Francisco: Ignatius Press 1992.

[30] von Balthasar, *Le persone del dramma*: 336.

[31] On this, see F. Mussner, *Zôè. Die Anschauung von 'Leben' in vierten Evangelium*. Munich 1952; R. W. Thomas, 'The meaning of the terms "Life" and "Death" in the Fourth Gospel and in Paul'. 21 (1968) *Scottish Journal of Theology*: 199–212.

man fundamentally shares with other living things. It is that dynamic organicity which spontaneously tends to establish itself and keep itself alive through exchanges with the environment, but which inevitably declines, falling back into the inorganic. (2) At a higher level of nature we find the spiritual dimension of life which is human (ψυχή). This dimension derives in man from the spiritual principle of the soul and makes him a free and conscious person. The dignity proper to the soul is that of reaching out towards the infinite, of being *capax Dei*. (3) Finally, at the level of grace, we find an event which is new in kind and cannot be derived from lower levels (whether it be constitutively, or essentially, or as an exigence): the divine, supernatural life (ζωή).[32] Here we are concerned with a gift which is totally dependent on the freely bestowed love of God, who calls man to participation in the intimate life of God Himself. The distinctive character of man consists precisely in the fact that these three levels are related to each other and united to each other, so that the biological dimension participates in the other two and vice versa. The distinctive purpose of redemption is 'eternal life' (ζωή), which sanctifies and makes inviolable even the biological dimension (βίος), without this implying an identification of the two.

As can be seen from this schematic overview, the structured unity of the different dimensions of human life requires a reference point with hierarchical primacy which draws together the other subordinate levels without erasing their value. In this framework one can also grasp the value of the body and of bodily life (*EV* 47). In Christian anthropology, the body is not an appendage of purely instrumental significance in relation to the soul. St Thomas Aquinas goes so far as to say that the body is an essential component of the perfection of the person as such, and that without the body the person in the true sense is not present.[33] The life of the body is therefore not to be idolised as an absolute to be preserved at all costs. One should be ready to sacrifice this life in the name of higher spiritual goods, as so many martyrs have testified in the history of the Church and of humanity. Bodily life is not, however, an instrumental good which is disposable at will: it is not a possession but a gift to be cared for.

To the three-part division just described, organically structured, is linked the distinction of two phases in the life of man: the temporal and the final. It would nonetheless be a serious error to relegate eternal life to the beyond. On the contrary, eternal life begins already in the temporal phase and serves as the initial seed of the final phase and as a pole which in the end attracts and gives significance to every other expression of life. Earthly life is at once *relative* and *sacred* (*EV* 2); it is not the ultimate good to which all else must be sacrificed or which should be preserved at all costs; nor is it an instrumental good which is totally at our disposal. "The absolute master ... is the Creator alone" (*EV* 47), to whom alone belongs the choice of bringing it to an end, since to Him belonged the initiative of having given it a beginning.

[32] H. de Lubac, *Petite Catechèse sur nature et grâce*. Paris: Communio-Fayard 1980: 18–25. [English translation: *A Brief Catechesis on Nature and Grace*. San Francisco: Ignatius Press 1984].
[33] St Thomas Aquinas, *De Potentia* q. 5, a. 10: "Corpus etiam hominis ordinatur ad hominem non secundum animalem vitam tantum, sed ad perfectionem naturae ipsius."

Charity, as total dedication of the self to God, Who is loved above all else, and to one's neighbour, who is the bearer of His image, realises the ultimate meaning of life and anticipates the final destination of the blessed. In fact, "the deepest and most authentic meaning of life [is] that of being *a gift which is realised in the giving of self*" (*EV* 49). Demonstrating the summit of love on the Cross, Christ testifies that "A man can have no greater love than to lay down his life for his friends" (*Jn* 15:13) and proclaims in this way "that *life finds its centre, its meaning and its fulfilment when it is given up*" (*EV* 51).

With regard to other, lower forms of life, a Christian culture of life will avoid both the arbitrary exercise of an undiscriminating technological power and an ecological sacralisation of nature. "Everything in nature is ordered to man and everything is made subject to him" (*EV* 34). Human beings are called, then, to exercise a "lordship... not absolute, but ministerial", a reflection of the unique and infinite lordship of God (*EV* 52). It is a matter of caring for and preserving creation and also bringing its potential to fulfilment, letting human action be guided by the knowledge of the original plan of God inscribed in creation and revealed, in its ultimate destination, in Christ, the principle of the future world.[34]

The comprehensive light which enables us to value in a full and harmonious way human personal life, in its different dimensions, in relation to other forms of life is, then, the light which comes to us from the divine life, revealed to us in Christ. For this reason, we will conclude with a wonderful patristic testimony in celebration of life: a text of Pseudo-Dionysius, which is also cited in *Evangelium Vitae*:

> We must celebrate Eternal Life, from which every other life proceeds. From this, in proportion to its capacities, every being, which in any way participates in life, receives life. This Divine Life, which is above every other life, gives and preserves life. Every life and every living movement proceed from this Life which transcends all life and every principle of life. It to this that souls owe their incorruptibility; and because of this all animals and plants live, which receive only the faintest glimmer of life. To men, beings made of spirit and matter, Life grants life. Even if we should abandon Life, because of its overflowing love for man, it converts us and call us back to itself. Not only this: it promises to bring us, soul and body, to perfect life, to immortality. It is too little to say that this Life is alive: it is the Principle of life, the Cause and sole Wellspring of life. Every living thing must contemplate it and give it praise; it is Life which overflows with life.[35]

---

[34] J. J. Walter, 'Theological issues in genetics'. 60 (1999) *Theological Studies*: 124–134.
[35] Pseudo-Dionysius the Areopagite, *De divinis nominibus* VI, 1–3. *Patrologia Graeca* 3: 856–857.

8

What does it mean for a Christian to be "against the world but for the world"?

CARLO LORENZO ROSSETTI

Introduction: The Ambiguity of the World

"He was in the world that had its being through him, and the world did not know him" (*Jn* 1:10)

IN HIS FIRST encyclical, Paul VI proposed a balanced and prophetic discernment regarding the relationship between the Church and the world by saying:

> The fascination of worldly life today is very powerful indeed, and many people regard conformity to it as an inescapable and indeed a wise course to take. Hence, those who are not deeply rooted in the faith and in the observance of the Church's laws, readily imagine that the time is ripe to adjust themselves to worldly standards of living, on the assumption that these are the best and only possible ones for a Christian to adopt. This craving for uniformity is observable even in the realm of philosophy [...] It is observable also in the realm of ethics, making it more and more perplexing and difficult to define moral rectitude and the right conduct of life. 49. [...] We must be in the world, but not of it (cf. *Jn* 17:14,16). These important words of Christ are especially relevant at the present time, difficult though they may be to put into practice. It will be well for us if Christ, who lives always to make intercession for us, (Heb 7:25) includes us moderns in the wonderful prayer He addressed to His heavenly Father: "I pray not that thou should take them out of the world, but that thou should keep them from evil" (*Jn* 17:15)[1].

Paul VI continues by urging us to live in the world but not to belong to it:

> The fact that we are distinct from the world does not mean that we are entirely separated from it. Nor does it mean that we are indifferent to it, afraid of it, or contemptuous of it. When the Church distinguishes itself from humanity, it does so not in order to oppose it, but to come closer to it. A physician who realizes the danger of disease, protects himself and others from it, but at the same time he strives to cure those who have contracted it. The Church does the same thing. It does not regard God's mercy as an exclusive privilege, nor does the greatness of the privilege it enjoys make it feel unconcerned for

[1] *Ecclesiam suam* (hereafter *ES*, 1964), 48–49.

those who do not share it. On the contrary, it finds in its own salvation an argument for showing more concern and more love for those who live close at hand, or to whom it can go in its endeavor to make all alike share the blessing of salvation (ES 61).

Here is how Pope Montini put across the terms of our theme: a Christian, like the Church, must be in the world, for the world, but conscious of carrying out an unavoidable therapeutic and saving mission. St John's warning to beware of the world is also an invitation to establish a healthy relationship with it, which could be defined as an "Apostolic Dialogue"[2]. This kind of "spiritual contact" has to balance two evangelical requirements: on the one hand respect for faith's radicality and the uniqueness of Truth[3]; on the other hand the sympathetic missionary zeal that urges us "to approach all men and bring salvation to all, after the example of the Apostle Paul being *all things to all men*, that all may be saved".[4]

At times we forget the eminently biblical and apostolic prospective of this 'dialogue'. To Paul VI, to dialogue means to engage with the other in a credible and delicate manner, with the objective of communicating the unique saving truth. We are poles apart from the *'irenic'* relativism of some post-conciliar misinterpretations. It is not a matter of communicating in order to converge on

[2] Cf. *ES* 78: "it seems to Us that the sort of relationship for the Church to establish with the world should be more in the nature of a *dialogue* [...] We do not mean unrealistic dialogue. It must be adapted to the intelligences of those to whom it is addressed, and it must take account of the circumstances [...] 79. ....If, in our desire to respect a man's freedom and dignity, his conversion to the true faith is not the immediate object of our dialogue with him, we nevertheless try to help him and to dispose him for a fuller sharing of ideas and convictions. 80. Our dialogue, therefore, presupposes that there exists in us a state of mind which we wish to communicate and to foster in those around us. It is the state of mind which characterizes the man who realizes the seriousness of the apostolic mission and who sees his own salvation as inseparable from the salvation of others. His constant endeavor is to get everyone talking about the message which it has been given to him to communicate".

[3] Cf. *ES* 61 that quotes 2 *Cor* 6:14–15: "Bear not the yoke with unbelievers. For what partnership has justice with injustice? Or what fellowship has light with darkness? [...] Or what has a believer in common with an unbeliever?". See also *ES* 88: "... the danger remains. Indeed, the worker in the apostolate is under constant fire. The desire to come together as brothers must not lead to a watering down or whittling away of truth. Our dialogue must not weaken our attachment to our faith. Our apostolate must not make vague compromises concerning the principles which regulate and govern the profession of the Christian faith both in theory and in practice. An immoderate desire to make peace and sink differences at all costs (irenism and syncretism) is ultimately nothing more than skepticism about the power and content of the Word of God which we desire to preach. The effective apostle is the man who is completely faithful to Christ's teaching. He alone can remain unaffected by the errors of the world around him, the man who lives his Christian life to the full".

[4] 1*Cor* 9:22 quoted in *ES* 87 which goes on to say: "Since the world cannot be saved from the outside, we must first of all identify ourselves with those to whom we would bring the Christian message – like the Word of God who Himself became a man". That is why dialogue should always have the following characteristics: clarity, meekness, confidence and prudence (*ES* 81). See also *ES* 87: "Furthermore, if we want to be men's pastors, fathers and teachers, we must also behave as their brothers".

a truth to be found. For the Church, this dialogue is not so much a way of searching for the truth, but rather a way of transmitting it. Dialogue involves a difficult journey which follows the logic of divine accommodation and of Incarnation. The Truth came into the world, for the world, but accepted refusal by the world. This is the challenge that the 'ambiguity' of the world poses.

Council documents confirm this analysis, which truly fits the biblical vision in which the 'kosmos' is both good and blessed by the Lord (cf. *Gn* 1:21–22.28) *and* a place of evil, sin and death and therefore bearing also God's curse (*Gn* 3:17)[5]. The world is regarded as good and worthy of glorification, through God's incarnation and eschatological redemption, but at the same time as so evil and corrupt as to have induced divine love to pass through the extremely bloody and painful trial of the Cross.

The Christian's, and the Church's, mission in the world is nothing but a reflection of Christ's own mission[6]. The response to Jesus, the Sun of Justice (cf. *Lk* 1:78, *Mal* 3:20), is the light of the Church–'Moon' which lights up the darkness of the night in the world, until the fullness of the eschatological sunrise finally appears[7]. The splendour of the revealed truth illuminates man and allows him to "walk in this world", but this truth also reveals the darkness that envelopes a world governed by evil (1 *Jn* 5:19), even though this darkness is dissipating (cf. 1 *Jn* 2:8; *Rm* 13:12). As long as this 'Eon' continues to exist, the Church must face the world's mysterious lack of understanding, hostility and even persecution[8].

Our thesis can be stated as follows: "in order for a Christian to really be *for* the world, he must also be *against* it". First of all this means that our mission in the world is not positive on the one hand and negative on the other. The Christian is fully for the world. His mission is entirely in favour of it, wholly for its salvation: *pro salute mundi*. On the other hand, for the sake of this positive mandate for salvation, the disciple of Christ must also irrefutably assume a role of opposition, of contestation and denunciation. Nevertheless, this is not, nor can it ever be, the

---

[5] Recall, for example, *Gaudium et spes* [hereafter GS, 1964] 2,2: "The Council focuses its attention on the world of men, the whole human family along with the sum of those realities in the midst of which it lives; that world which is the theatre of man's history, and the heir of his energies, his tragedies and his triumphs; that world which the Christian sees as created and sustained by its Maker's love, fallen indeed into the bondage of sin, yet emancipated now by Christ, Who was crucified and rose again to break the stranglehold of the evil one, so that the world might be fashioned anew according to God's design and reach its fulfillment"; see also GS 9,5: "The modern world shows itself at once powerful and weak, capable of the noblest deeds or the foulest; before it lies the path to freedom or to slavery, to progress or retreat, to brotherhood or hatred. Moreover, man is becoming aware that it is his responsibility to guide aright the forces which he has unleashed and which can enslave him or minister to him".

[6] Cf. John Paul II, *Redemptoris missio* [hereafter RM; 1990], part I.

[7] On the *Mysterium lunae* cf. H. Rahner, *Symbole der Kirche*. Salzburg: Müller 1964: 91–173; B. Forte, *Sui sentieri dell'Uno. Saggi di storia della teologia*. Cinisello Balsamo: San Paolo 1992: 65–92.

[8] "Inter persecutiones mundi et consolationes Dei peregrinando procurrit Ecclesia". (Augustine, *De civitate Dei* XVIII, 51, quoted also in *Lumen Gentium* [hereafter LG] 8.)

last word of a Christian. He must be prepared to take prophecy (Proclamation-Judgment) to its furthest extreme: the testimony of Martyrdom. Relying principally on the Scriptures and on contemporary documents of the Magisterium, I will organise the exposition of my thesis around three main themes: Proclamation (*Kerygma*), Judgment (*Krisis*), and Witness (*Martyria*).

In the first part we will look at what constitutes the germinal centre of the Christian's relationship with the world: the prophetic proclamation of the Good News (1). In the second part, which is almost a corollary of the first, it will be necessary to see in what way this Proclamation intrinsically leads to an extraordinary Judgment. At this point we will reflect on the *mysterium iniquitatis* (2). Finally, we will say to what extent all Christian life is a prophetic witnessing against the presence of evil in the world and why martyrdom represents the culmination and synthesis of the Christian mission (3).

The first theme has already been widely studied and discussed; we will therefore limit ourselves to briefly recalling some of the main points. The focus of my paper will be on the more uncomfortable theme of 'being against the world'.

1. 'Kerygma': 'Mysterium Salutis' and human advancement

"Yes, God loved the world so much that he gave his only Son, so that everyone who believes in him may not be lost but may have eternal life. For God sent his Son into the world not to condemn the world, but so that through him the world might be saved." (*Jn* 3:16–17)

The world is the scene of the coming of God's Kingdom (cf. *Mt* 13:38). Christ's mission was that of being the last prophet, foretold in the Mosaic Law[9]. The core of Christ's message is the Kingdom of God: the eschatological event of the Father's offer of salvation made present in him. This is the announcement the Church has to proclaim all over the world, as well as being called on to incarnate this proclamation through her testimony:

The Kingdom is clearly visible in the very Person of Christ, the Son of God and the Son of Man, who came "to serve and to give His life as a ransom for many" (*Mk* 10:45). When Jesus, who had suffered the death of the Cross for mankind, had risen, He appeared as the one constituted as Lord, Christ and eternal Priest (cf. *Ac* 2:36; *Heb* 5:6; 7:17–21) and He poured out on His disciples the Spirit promised by the Father (cf. *Ac* 2:33). From this source the Church, equipped with the gifts of its Founder and faithfully guarding His precepts of charity, humility and self-sacrifice, receives the mission to proclaim and to spread among all peoples the Kingdom of Christ and of God and to be, on earth, the initial budding forth of that kingdom. While it slowly grows, the Church strains

[9] Cf. *Dt* 18:18–19.

toward the completed Kingdom and, with all its strength, hopes and desires to be united in glory with its King[10].

The 'Kerygma' or Gospel means that God loves the world. The coming of his Kingdom into the world (even if it does not belong to it) further testifies to the preciousness of the world in God's eyes.

As is well known, the Christian's 'pro-existence' for the world has been one of a number of ideas given particular emphasis in conciliar and post-conciliar theology. After centuries of misunderstanding, the Catholic Church appeared to widen her doors to the modern world in all its positive aspects, and to do so without a trace of condemnation or anathema. The most celebrated and famous example of the Council's 'optimism' can be found in the Pastoral Constitution on the Church in the Modern World, *Gaudium et spes* (see especially §§ 40–44), to which we have already referred.

If we were to summarize in a single concept what is basically at issue in this conciliar text it would surely be 'human advancement'. Armed with the treasure of grace given to it by Christ, the Church is the greatest defender of man's dignity, of human work and of social action for peace and justice. *Gratia non tollit naturam sed eam elevat et perficit*[11]. This famous scholastic dictum seems to have influenced the engaging perspective of the entire magisterial document. Man finds himself in Christ, and through the Church he discovers his vocation to universal fraternity. Heaven does not dominate the earth but makes it more human and liveable. Rarely has the Church ever before expressed with such clarity and beauty what radically contradicts the perverse dilemma of modern ideology: 'either God or man'. The biblical logic of the Covenant "God *and* man, God with and for man" shines in all its splendour. A dissertation on the 'being-for-the-world' of the Christian can take the form of commenting on and illustrating the main points of the Constitution[12].

We shall limit ourselves to highlighting three 'arguments' which bring out why it is that the world is a positive reality and worthy of love, given the involvement of the Divine Persons in the plan of salvation (*mysterion*).

---

[10] *LG* 5; cf. also John Paul II, *RM* 7: "The salvation in Christ is *self-communication* of God"; 11: "Integral salvation, which invests all of man and all men, opening the horizons of divine sonship"; 12: "Salvation consists in believing and welcoming the mystery and love of the Father which manifests itself and is given in Christ through the Spirit. So the Kingdom of God is fulfilled"; 13: "The kingdom will grow in the same measure in which each man learns to turn to God in the intimacy of prayer as to a father and try with all his might to fulfil his will".

[11] St Thomas Aquinas, *Summa Theologiae* I,1,9.

[12] See J. de Fabrègues, *L'église esclave ou espoir du monde?* Paris: Aubier Montaigne 1971 (preface by card. J. Daniélou); R. Coste, *L'Eglise et les défis du monde*, Paris: Nouvelle Cité, 1986; *Gaudium et spes*. Bilan de trente années. Lorette '95, in 39 (1996) *Laics aujourd'hui*.

1.1 Theo-logical and proto-logical argument

God said, God saw, God rested (cf. *Gn* 1). These three verbs express why it is that the world and all of creation, generated from God's thoughts, are in His eyes "good" and "very good". The biblical account, contrary to any dualism or nihilism, constitutes the basis of the imperative which every believer should submit to: You shall love the world! Because the world is entirely produced by God and only by God, everything that exists is the result of a liberal, sovereign and wise decision made by God who is Almighty and good[13]. In New Testament and patristic texts *Eudokia* is attributed to the Father: that is, goodwill, good purpose, the liberal and wise decision to create in order to save[14]. The Christian needs to love the world and to be for the world, which primarily originates from God's goodwill in creating it. What is already inherent here is the plan for incarnation and redemption through which the 'philanthropy' of God is fully manifested (*Tt* 3:4).

1.2 Christological and soteriological argument

For the Son, the *pro mundo et pro homine* is total and personal. All is created in Christ and for his coming (cf. *Jn* 1:1–3; *Col* 1:15; *Eph* 1:1–13). God's dominant thought has been Christ (the Son of God made man) since the beginning of creation. The Church has always considered the mystery of the *Verbum caro* to be the culmination of the divine 'condescension' (*synkatabasis*) as well as the unsurpassable summit of the revelation of human dignity. Amongst the many texts belonging to the Tradition, we can once again refer to *Gaudium et spes* (much of which we owe to the then Bishop Wojtyla, and to which he has constantly referred during his pontificate).

> Christ, the new Adam, in the very revelation of the mystery of the Father and of his love, fully reveals man to himself and brings to light his most high calling [...] He Who is *the image of the invisible God* (*Col* 1:15), is Himself the perfect man who has restored in the children of Adam that likeness to God which had been disfigured ever since the first sin. Human nature, by the very fact that it was assumed, not absorbed, in him, has been raised in us also to a dignity beyond compare. For, by his incarnation, He, the Son of God, has in a certain

---

[13] "Deus bonitate sua et omnipotenti virtute non ad augendam suam beatitudinem nec ad acquirendam, sed ad manifestandam perfectionem suam per bona, quae creaturis impertitur, liberrimo consilio 'simul ab initio temporis utramque de nihilo condidit creaturam, spiritualem et corporalem'" (*Dei Filius*, Vatican Council I [quoting Lateran Council IV], H. Denzinger, A. Schönmetzer, *Enchiridion symbolorum, definitionum et declarationum de rebus fidei et morum*, Barcelona – Freiburg – Roma: Herder 1976[36] [hereafter *DS*] 3002).

[14] Amongst the Fathers of the Church it is St. Ireneus in particular who developed this theme: "In the end, not for the will of the flesh nor for the will of man, but for the purpose of the Father (*ex placito Patris*), his hands (sc. the Word and the Spirit) made living man, so that Adam could become God's image and resemblance" (*Adversus Haereses* V,1,3; see also *ibid.* I,9,43; III,9,3; 23,1; IV,7,3; 20,2).

way united himself with every man (*Filius Dei incarnatione sua cum omni homine quodammodo Se univit*)[15]. [...] Born of the Virgin Mary, He has truly been made one of us, like us in all things except sin. As an innocent lamb He merited for us life by his blood which he freely shed. In Him God reconciled us to Himself and to one another, freeing us from bondage to the devil and sin, so that each one of us can say with the Apostle: "The Son of God loved me and gave Himself for me" (*Gal* 2:20). By suffering for us He not only gave us an example so that we might follow in His footsteps, but He also opened up a way. If we follow this path, life and death are made holy and acquire a new meaning. Conformed to the image of that Son Who is the firstborn of many brothers, the Christian man receives "the first-fruits of the Spirit" (*Rm* 8:23) by which he is able to fulfil the new law of love. By this Spirit, who is "the pledge of our inheritance" (*Eph* 1:14), the whole man is inwardly renewed, even to the achievement of "the redemption of the body" (*Rm* 8:23 [the text than quotes *Rm* 8:11]) (*GS* 22).

"You shall love the world and man, every man". This command of the Christian faith has such a strong force because nothing can suppress its link to the mystery of the union between the Word of God and humanity, and the final act of redemption. From the time of His only Son becoming human, God has looked at every human creature through the eyes of a loving father. In every person God seeks out the traits of his Son, even in the greatest sinner. This is because Jesus himself took the last place and even identified himself with 'sin' (cf. *Rm* 8:3; *2 Cor* 5:21) and through the love for His crucified and resurrected Son, there burns within the Father – for every man – a fire of love, resurrection and adoption (cf. *Ac* 13:33). As the Father raised Jesus in the flesh proclaiming him 'Son of God in all his power' (*Rm* 1:4), He sees in every man a potential candidate for His adoption, in his grace and glory. Any kind of scorn for the world or misanthropy has become blasphemy. Pope John Paul II's *magisterium* has even identified 'Gospel' and 'Christianity' with amazement at man's true dignity[16].

---

[15] John Paul II stressed this theme from his first encyclical *Redemptor hominis* [hereafter *RH*; 1979], n.13.

[16] Cf. "In reality, the name for that deep amazement at man's worth and dignity is the Gospel, that is to say: the Good News. It is also called Christianity. This amazement determines the Church's mission in the world and, perhaps even more so 'in the modern world'. This amazement, which is also a conviction and a certitude – at its deepest root it is the certainty of faith, but in a hidden and mysterious way it vivifies every aspect of authentic humanism – is closely connected with Christ. It also fixes Christ's place – so to speak, his particular right of citizenship – in the history of man and mankind. Unceasingly contemplating the whole of Christ's mystery, the Church knows with all the certainty of faith that the Redemption that took place through the Cross has definitively restored his dignity to man and given back meaning to his life in the world, a meaning that was lost to a considerable extent because of sin. And for that reason, the Redemption was accomplished in the paschal mystery, leading through the Cross and death to Resurrection. The Church's fundamental function in every age and particularly in ours is to direct man's gaze, to point the awareness and experience of the whole of humanity towards the mystery of God, to help all men to be familiar with the profundity of the Redemption taking place in Christ Jesus. At the same time man's deepest sphere is involved – we mean the sphere of human hearts, consciences and events" (*RH* 10,2).

1.3 Pneumatological and eschatological argument

The Son's mission of salvation is followed by His celestial intercession and by the Spirit's mission on earth. Breathed upon the disciples by the glorified Christ (cf. *Jn* 20:22; *Lk* 24:49), the Holy Spirit inhabits the Church and uses it as a privileged instrument to testify to Christ's lordship and God's paternity (cf. *I Cor* 12:3; *Gal* 4:5). But God is not bound in any way to use his own ordinary instruments. The Holy Spirit is free and blows where He wills (cf. *Jn* 3:8). The same Spirit which hovered over the waters in the beginning to give life to the universe and renew the face of the earth (cf. *Gn* 1:4; *Ps* 104:30) is the same Spirit which communicates the resurrected Christ's immortal life. The primitive Church's experience was one of docility towards the Spirit's action, which is present in the world and eschatologically poured out, working within the hearts of men even before they formally belong to the ecclesial community.[17]

Paragraph 22 of *Gaudium et Spes* includes a statement on what the Church considers to be a most important feature of the Holy Spirit's saving action, namely, that it does not apply to Christians alone but to all men of good will, in whose hearts grace acts invisibly. In fact, Christ died for all of us and man has simply one ultimate vocation, a divine one. Therefore, we must believe that the Holy Spirit gives everyone the opportunity to be associated, in ways known only to God, with the mystery of the Passover.[18]

Christian doctrine moves from pneumatology to eschatology. The sanctifying action of the Holy Spirit will find its outlet through history in the final fullness where God will be all in all[19]. The destiny of glorification, of human beings assumed and redeemed in the Son's incarnation, will spread and envelope the whole of creation. The dogma of the resurrection of the flesh cannot be separated from the dogma of the eschatological transfiguration of the universe. Modern theology has rightly warned us of an excessive emphasis on the 'spiritual', characteristic of certain Christian mentalities and deriving from a dualistic contrast of 'worldly' and 'otherworldly'. As the first Fathers of the Church had to defend the truth of incarnation, resurrection and the restoration of the cosmos against the spiritualism of the ignorant (*gnosis*), we also need to strongly reassert the whole

---

[17] Recall the paradigmatic episode of Cornelius, *Ac* 10:44–48.

[18] "All this holds true not only for Christians, but for all men of good will in whose hearts grace works in an unseen way. For, since Christ died for all men, and since the ultimate vocation of man is in fact one, and divine, we ought to believe that the Holy Spirit in a manner known only to God offers to every man the possibility of being associated with this paschal mystery" ("*Spiritum Sanctum cunctis possibilitatem offerre ut, modo Deo cognito, huic paschali mysterio consocientur*"; GS 22,5). See also Commissio theologica internationalis (hereafter: CTI), *Christianity and religions* (1997) nn.71–73. The certainty that the Spirit precedes evangelization and mysteriously acts in men's hearts instead of diminishing missionary zeal should stimulate it (cf. on this John Paul II, *RM* 28–29).

[19] The famous expression of St. Paul "*omnia in omnibus*" (*ta panta en pasin*, *I Cor* 15:28) admits of alternative translations depending on whether one reads '*en pasin*' as masculine (all in everyone) and neuter (all in all). The latter translation was recently preferred by Cardinal J. Ratzinger, 'L'ecclesiologia della Costituzione *Lumen Gentium*', *L'Osservatore romano* (4 March 2000): 6.

of creation's involvement in the process of salvation begun with the resurrection of Christ. The idea that justice will reign in the new heavens and earth is certainly unimaginable, as is the glorified body (cf. 1 *Cor* 15:35ff; 2 *Pt* 3:13). Nevertheless, these must be considered by the Christian to be a real and concrete *vita venturi saeculi*. What is at stake here is the assumption of the body and the 'worldly' dimension of the human being. God loved man so much that he assumed a human nature in the incarnation of his only Son and glorifies the whole cosmos for him.

In this connection the Council insists on the idea that "eschatological hope does not diminish the importance of earthly duties, but rather supports fulfilment of those duties with fresh motives" (*GS* 21:3).

> We do not know the time for the consummation of the earth and of humanity, nor do we know how all things will be transformed. As deformed by sin, the shape of this world will pass away; but we are taught that God is preparing a new dwelling place and a new earth where justice will abide, and whose blessedness will answer and surpass all the longings for peace which spring up in the human heart. Then, with death overcome, the sons of God will be raised up in Christ, and what was sown in weakness and corruption will be invested with incorruptibility. And with charity and its fruits remaining, all that creation which God made on man's account will be freed from the bondage of vanity. Therefore, while we are warned that it profits a man nothing if he gain the whole world and lose himself, the expectation of a new earth must not weaken but rather stimulate our concern for cultivating this one (*extenuare non debet sed potius excitare sollicitudinem hanc terram excolendi*). For it is here that the body of a new human family grows, a body which even now is able to give some kind of foreshadowing of the new age. Hence, while earthly progress must be carefully distinguished from the growth of Christ's kingdom, to the extent that the former can contribute to the better ordering of human society, it is of vital concern to the Kingdom of God. For after we have obeyed the Lord, and in His Spirit nurtured on earth the values of human dignity, brotherhood and freedom, and indeed all the good fruits of our nature and enterprise, we will find them again, but freed of stain, burnished and transfigured, when Christ hands over to the Father: "a kingdom eternal and universal, a kingdom of truth and life, of holiness and grace, of justice, love and peace". On this earth that Kingdom is already present in mystery. When the Lord returns it will be brought into full flower (*GS* 39).[20]

To summarize: the Christian Gospel for the world identifies itself with the real and highest advancement of man, society and cosmos. This advancement is rooted in

---

[20] After quoting from this passage, the *Catechism of the Catholic Church* (hereafter: *CCC*; 1993) at n.1050 adds, quoting St. Paul and St. Cyril of Jerusalem: "God will then be all in all in eternal life (cf. 1 *Cor* 15:28). True and subsistent life consists in this: the Father, through the Son and in the Holy Spirit, pouring out his heavenly gifts on all things without exception. Thanks to his mercy, we too, men that we are, have received the inalienable promise of eternal life." See also *GS* 43 and 57,1.

the supernatural destiny which God has desired for human beings since creation, is fulfilled in the Passover of the incarnate Word, and is communicated by the life-giving force of the Spirit. There does not exist, nor can there ever exist, a more elevated or more remarkable message than the Christian one: the divinization of the human being in all his dimensions, including body and social being; the eschatological glorification of humanity and the redemption of the universe in the freedom of God's children (cf. *Rm* 8:21).

2. 'Krisis': 'Mysterium iniquitatis – Mysterium Crucis'

"No one who believes in him will be condemned; but whoever refuses to believe is condemned already, because he has refused to believe in the name of God's only Son. On these grounds is sentence (*krisis*) pronounced: that though the light has come into the world men have shown they prefer darkness to the light because their deeds were evil" (*Jn* 3:18–19).

We cannot confuse Christian hope and human optimism. The former is a gift of the Spirit which inspires a trusting and active openness towards the future already imbued with Christ's victory. The latter is a positive human attitude, which always runs the risk of naivety.[21] In order to ensure that we do not lose touch with reality, we need to acknowledge, for example, that the healthy 'secularity' and autonomy of temporal realities, recognized and approved of by the Council (cf. e.g. *GS* 36) has turned into 'secularism': the openness towards other confessions, religions and ways of thinking (cf. *Unitatis redintegratio* and *Nostrae aetate*) has given way to a loss of conviction in most Christians and to the diffusion of relativism. All this leads us to reflect upon the second character-ization of the world the Bible offers us. In almost all the New Testament (especially in the writings of John and Paul) the *kosmos* is not only God's creation, loved and saved by Him, but also a place inhabited mysteriously by evil and the sinful rejection of God[22]. We can summarize this in the striking statement: "the

---

[21] As G. K. Chesterton cautioned, in characteristically paradoxical fashion: "One could be at peace with the universe and yet be at war with the world...One must somehow find a way of loving the world without trusting it". "All the optimism of the age had been false and disheartening for this reason, that it had always been trying to prove that we fit in to the world. The christian optimism is based on the fact that we do *not* fit in to the world". (Quotations from *Orthodoxy*, in *A Chesterton Anthology*. San Francisco-London: Ignatius Press-The Bodley Head 1985: 280, 281).

[22] Christ is not of this world (*Jn* 8:23); the world cannot receive the Spirit of truth (*Jn* 14:17); it hates Christ and his disciples (*Jn* 15:18ff; 17:14–16), but the spirit will convince it of sin (*Jn* 16:8ff). And Christ overcame sin with the cross (*Jn* 16:28). In St. Paul, the world is inhabited by sin (*Rm* 5:12); its knowledge and wisdom is confused by the Kerygma (1 *Cor* 1:20). Christians have not received a spirit of the world (1 *Cor* 2:12) and do not have to conform to it (*Rm* 12:2). Life "according to the world" indicates sinfulness and atheism (cf. *Eph* 2:2,12). The Catholic letters also encourage man to be averse to the *kosmos* and its mentality (*Jm* 4:4; 2 *Pt* 1:4). Love for the world cannot co-exist with the love of God (1 *Jn* 2:15–17); only faith which comes from God can win over the world which is a victim of evil. (1 *Jn* 5:4–5).

whole world lies in the power of the evil one" (1 *Jn* 5:19). In order to understand why a Christian is inevitably also "against the world" we should rediscover what is designated as the 'mystery of iniquity'. To do so we shall start by looking at a reading of original sin (2.1.1) which will lead us to discuss the uncomfortable but inescapable theme of the Evil One (2.1.2). Both realities have been brought to light and overturned by Christ's Cross (2.1.3); the 'mystery of iniquity' (2 *Th* 2:7) is only illuminated by the light of the 'mystery of godliness' (1 *Tm* 3:16). The revelation of divine love in Christ has manifested at one and the same time the growth of evil and the superabundance of grace. We must, therefore, face the question of the origin of evil, looking fixedly through the eyes of faith to the only One who can claim the victory[23].

2.1 Sin as Anarchy and Idolatry

2.1.1 Original sin[24]

As we know, theology makes the distinction between original sin as *originating* (i.e. Adam's personal and 'corporate' trespass) and original sin as *originated* (the consequence in us of the first sin). The Fathers of the Church distinguished between the image (*eikon*) and resemblance (*homoiosis*)[25]. Sin has reduced human nature, hurt and weakened it, but has not destroyed it. It distorted the image sufficiently to make it different to Christ, its prototype, but has not eliminated it completely. Human dignity is preserved in the possession of free will. Free will – the power together with the tendency to choose to do good – remains even after sin, even if it is "*attenuatum et inclinatum*"[26].

A speculative reflection on the concept of original sin in this perspective (i.e. understood as distortion of the image exhibited in the Son) leads us to define it as *a rejection of God's paternity*. This active setback already present in Adam (as the proud explicit decision to break the filial bond with God) exists passively in us, as

---

[23] Cf. *CCC*: "It is precisely in the Passion when the mercy of Christ is about to vanquish it, that sin most clearly manifests its violence and its many forms: unbelief, murderous hate, shunning and mockery by the leaders and the people, Pilate's cowardice and the cruelty of the soldiers, Judas's betrayal – so bitter to Jesus, Peter's denial and the disciples' flight. However, at the very hour of darkness, the hour of the prince of this world, the sacrifice of Christ secretly becomes the source from which the forgiveness of our sins will pour forth inexhaustibly" (n. 1851). See also n. 385.

[24] For the following interpretation of original sin, see C. L. Rossetti, ' "Perché diano gloria al Padre vostro celeste". Paternita divina e missione della Chiesa.' 66 (2000) *Lateranum*: 235–258, especially 242–245.

[25] Cf. e.g. Origen, *Peri Archon*, III,6,1.

[26] The transmission of original sin occurs through generation and propagation; Pelagianism is therefore rejected (along with the doctrine of transmission via imitation). So the Council of Trent, following Augustine (*DS* 1512–1513; 1521; 1525; 1555).

forgetfulness and ignorance of the Father[27]. We can define original sin as *originated* as: the existential ignorance of God's paternity, which results in an egocentric self-constituting life and therefore mortal slavery to lust (cf. *Eph* 2:1–3).

The 'I' of the human person has been created to correspond to the image of the ineffable divine person of the Son which recognizes Himself as the 'You' loved by the Father. The eternal Son's 'I' is totally centred in the Father (*Jn* 1:18). It is an infinite Abyss which is forever overflowing with the richness of the Father who constitutes it as the 'I' distinct from Himself, addressing it as 'You': *tu es filius meus*. Fullness of personality and life consists in letting oneself be loved, begotten as filial interlocutor of the Father. The human 'I' is called to fulfilment, in Jesus, as the Father's desired and loved 'you': to become the receptacle of His fullness. *Haec vita in Filio eius est* (1 *Jn* 5:11).

Original sin is, therefore, an attack on the divine 'an-arché'. Christians can and must interpret *Genesis* 3 in a Trinitarian perspective. The text speaks about two trees: the Tree of Life and the Tree of the Knowledge of good and evil. Though the two terms are different in sense, the reference of the terms points to a fundamental identity. Some Jewish traditions see these two trees as symbols of divine prerogatives[28]. Let us look into the identity-distinction of the trees to find two possibilities that describe the relationship between man and God founded on two notions of the Holy Trinity. The Tree of Life, which Adam and Eve could eat from[29], represents for us 'sonship'. Man has been created in this filial bond for sonship and has not been excluded from this full relationship, which is fulfilled in Christ. The Christian tradition will go on to see this tree in the crucifixion of the Son Christ, in the Cross made accessible to humanity. The Tree of the Knowledge of good and evil, on the other hand, represents the notion of 'An-arché', of 'Principle', of the Lord God's absolute primacy. The Great commandment in *Gn* 2: 17 more than being a "test", is, like every divine command, a word of love, truth and life[30]. It amounts to saying: "All is yours, everything has been given to you,

---

[27] Evocative is the thought of Clement of Alexandria who sees original sin as man's disobedience to the Father (*parakoê Patrós*), when man is son-child-servant (*pais*) of God. For K. Rahner originated original sin is the "existential 'no' " said to God, against God's self-communication and holiness, by human personal transcendence. In us original sin is a condition described as a lack or absence (cf. *Foundations of Christian Faith*. London: Longman & Todd 1984: 106–115).

[28] See C. Giraudo, *Eucaristia per la Chiesa*. Roma-Brescia: Morcelliana-Gregorian University Press 1989: 41ff. "L'Albero della Vita designa Dio in quanto origine fontale del soffio di vita e perciò stesso il solo immortale; l'altro, L'*Albero della scienza del bene e del male*, ancora designa Dio come il solo cui compete disporre, regolare, normare la vita che da lui procede, e ciò in forza di quella assoluta conoscenza esperienziale che egli ha delle creature" (p. 41). For the Jewish tradition on this interpretation see p.42, n.17.

[29] On this we do not follow Giraudo, *Eucaristia per la Chiesa*: 41, n.14.

[30] The theme of the test of obedience is taken up again in *CCC* 396, where the perspective is slightly more positive: "man can live this friendship only in free submission to God". The forbidden tree "symbolically evokes the insurmountable limits that man, being a creature, must feely recognize and respect with trust". We must also remember that Gen 2: 17 "is not an order, but a warning of a destiny" (cf. P. Evdokimov, *La novità dello Spirito*. Milano: Ancora 1997: 27). See also John Paul II, *Dominum et Vivificantem* (hereafter: *DeV*) 36,2.

all you possess is a gift for you to enjoy. Recognise your role of divine beneficiary. Acknowledge yourself to be a filial and privileged creature. Accept that you are a creature and become a son. You have been made to be fully adopted as my son. I ask just one thing of you: do not forget that the truth is your filial bond with me, your sonship. Do not make yourself the Father. This is a lie, this is falseness and slavery. This is death. Do not seek to lay claim to what is uniquely my prerogative: being without a father, without origins, without 'principles'. If ever you were to reject or forget the fact that Life exists in Me and that you can only really enjoy it if you remain in Me, you would deprive yourself of that life, you would die". 'An-arché' only befits the Lord God, the Father. Not even the eternal Son is 'an-archic' but is eternally in God's embrace, in the Principle (we could almost call it 'En-Arché'[31]).

Man's truth and life is to dwell in the Father, to receive life from Him. Sin is, on the other hand, 'an-arché', a demand for independence, for 'aut-archia'. This is the tragedy of sin: it is not primarily a moral evil but an 'ontological error'[32], that is, like missing the target (*hamartia*). The nudity that man discovers after sinning, his death, is nothing other than an entering within the Lie, disconnection from the very Source of Life. By becoming 'an-archic', man has no other 'arché' but himself, no other source of life but his fragile life as creature. What arises here is an internal dichotomy: the desire to love but without the capacity to do so, brilliantly described by St. Paul in *Rm* 7. By breaking away from the Source of Life, man is left with no life within himself. Wanting to love and give life, he realises he cannot do this because no one can give something he does not have. Man remains profoundly filial, the divine image – the image of the Son – is permanently imprinted in his heart, that is, the image of the loved who knows how to love. But this image is disfigured, living in a kind of 'orphaned filial relationship'. Adam grew away from the Light, so his children will be born in darkness[33]. The sense of the Real Father is lost and so one needs to find other 'fathers' (idols), at the school of the father-usurper, the pseudo-father.

Original sin is the refusal of filial achievement in the Other, in the Father. The inevitable consequence of this rejection is the anxious search for self-fulfilment, which is in substance an illusion because the human being is "*ens finitum capax infiniti*". In trying to find realization in oneself and in the limited world, man is condemned to existential alienation and moral idolatry (cf. *Jr* 2:27).

---

[31] According to an intuition of Alexandrine theology; cf. Athanasius, *Contra Arianos*, IV, 1 and Cyril, *In Ioannem* 1,1.

[32] An expression to be found in S. Bulgakov (*La sposa dell'Agnello*. Bologna: Edizioni Dehoniane 1991: 239). Cf. also John Paul II, *Veritatis Splendor* (hereafter: *VS*) 102,2: "What is the ultimate source of this inner division of man? His history of sin begins when he no longer acknowledges the Lord as his Creator and himself wishes to be the one who determines, with complete independence, what is good and what is evil".

[33] See the beautiful text of St. Gregory the Great, *Dialogues* 4,1.

2.1.2 Idolatry

Idolatry, therefore, is the practical carrying out of a perverse worldliness determined by personal sin and provoked by the 'Prince of this world' (*Jn* 12:31). The 'Lustfulness of this world' (*epithymia*; cf. 1 *Jn* 2:16–17) leads to the 'absolutization' of a series of realities which are believed to secure human happiness, such as politics, success, pleasure, health, money etc. Such realities are capable of being good or morally neutral, but they may also become dangerous instruments of evil when proposed as remedies against human 'anxiety and restlessness' (cf. *CCC* 2113). Biblically, idols or the false gods of pagan nations have a double connotation: they are illusory on the one hand but require human sacrifice on the other. Idols always promise but never deliver ("they have mouths, but never speak, eyes, but never see...", cf. *Ps* 115:4ff). They appear as powerful as the Kingdom of Nebuchadnezzar (*Dn* 2:34ff) or the Beast of the Apocalypse (*Rev* 13), but in reality they have feet like clay and at the end they will fall (cf. *Rev* 19:21). They are deceptive because they cannot provide an answer to man's ultimate question: death. And yet they are powerfully seductive (*planan*), so much so that they demand a bloody cult-following by man. There is a Moloch in every era who is thirsty for human lives[34]. How much blood has been spilt for these idols, for idols of race, for the class struggle, but also for a rigid religious system? How many bodies of women and children have been put to the pyre of immoral pleasure and filthy profit! How many embryos have been sacrificed in order to obtain the 'child at all costs'! How many families have been destroyed as a result of gambling, alcohol or drugs! For as long as the world is governed by "principalities and powers, by the world rulers of this present darkness, by evil spirits which inhabit the heavenly regions", the Christian will have to be against the world, wearing an "armour of light" (cf. *Eph* 6:12ff).

2.2 Demonology

As regards evil, it has been asserted that "speaking of the devil will not solve a thing, or perhaps lessen the difficulty. If we do not want to fall into the trap of dualism.... We must explain why God allowed these [devils] to act, why the Lord of the world let the great assassin free. We must ask ourselves first how the devil came to become evil, without there being a devil to make him become so"[35]. This is quite an incisive challenge which forces us to reflect

[34] Cf. Lv 18:21: "And you shall not let any of your children pass through the fire to Moloch, neither shall you profane the name of your God: I am Yhwh". Cf. also the painful refrain put in the mouth of the Lord in Jeremiah "And they have built the high places of Tophet, which is in the valley of the son of Hinnom, to burn their sons and their daughters in the fire; which I commanded them not, neither came it into my heart" (*Jer* 7:31; 19:5; 32:35; see also *Ez* 16:21).

[35] A. Torres Queiruga, *Credo in Dio Padre*. Casale Monferrato: Piemme 1999: 130.

upon the radical question: Why has God, who is only goodness and light (cf. 1 *Jn* 1:5), wanted to allow the existence of the prince of darkness and the deadly enemy?

The 20th century, with its array of slaughter and genocide, forces us to reflect on the diabolical. The silence which reigns over most contemporary theology on the subject of the devil – after the Shoah! – insults God's Truth and Justice. Human beings are victims of this silence, as it is only by affirming the existence of Satan that we can continue to hope in humanity[36]. After years of timid silence the need to re-open this difficult point of Christian doctrine is emerging[37].

A theologian of Catholic faith who faces the problem of evil without resorting to demonology would be like a man trying to learn a language with a seriously defective dictionary.

If we dwell on this troublesome and almost 'taboo' subject it is because we are convinced that, like any point of faith and theology, demonology also contributes to illuminating the mystery, to instilling superior knowledge and to moving us to glorify God.

A simple reading of the Bible confirms quite an amazing fact: the New Testament, compared to the Old Testament which prepares for it, focuses in an extraordinary and powerful way on the resplendent fatherly love of God, but also on an evil power whose presence is progressively revealed[38].

The data of Tradition on the devil lead us to assume that he was the first of the Angels, an intelligent and free spirit originally created not only like all other spirits '*prope Deum*' but also par excellence '*prope Filium*'. We accept the hypothesis that Lucifer, the 'bearer of light', was the one who was able liberally and freely to praise the Father at the image of his Son, more than any other creature. This closeness to the Son can help us to understand his double sin: pride and envy. *Corruptio optimi pessima.* We must consider that, with an act of extreme liberty (much superior to ours), the one who more than anyone resembled the Logos, loving and praising the Father with an entirely filial and free dependence, totally moved away from this state, radically rejecting the loving acknowledgement of divine paternity. The divine plan of the Son's incarnation (which would have lifted the humble and earthy creature to a dignity far superior to an angel's) was the reason for envy and for the fall of the angel. Satan's sin consists in breaking the filial bond with the Father and in his claim to

[36] Along these lines, cf. A. Gesché, *Il male*. Milano: San Paolo 1996: 74.

[37] Cf. what is clearly said in *CCC* 391–395 and 677; in the documents of the Council see mainly *LG* 16; 17; 35,1; 48,5; *Ad gentes* (hereafter: *AG*) 3; 9,2; *GS* 13,2; 22,3; 37,2. Cf. also Bulgakov, *La sposa dell'Agnello*, 222–241; Gesché, *Il male*, 73–76; W. Kasper, K. Lehmann, *Diavoli, demoni, possessione. Sulla realtà del* male. Brescia: Queriniana 1985 and principally the good and complete synthesis of R. Lavatori, *Satana. Un caso serio*. Bologna: EDB 1996.

[38] The word 'devil' occurs 34 times compared with one occurrence in the OT (*Wis* 2:24); 'Satan' occurs 40 times compared with 14 occurrences in the OT; 'demon/demoniacal' 26 compared with 7. It is as if the apparition of Light (Christ) provoked a contrasted reaction.

'an-arché'[39]. This is, therefore, the prototype of original sin. The bearer of light, of liberal and free (*dôrean*) praise, transformed himself into the prince of darkness, the one who brings into the world the totally incomprehensible *odium Dei*[40] and the worst of moral evils: cruelty. Unknown in the animal kingdom, this enters the human world as a distinguishing mark of moral evil through the father of lies, the anti-God, the anti-Son, the pseudo Father, the devil. To proclaim the presence of radical evil, of the demonic, is the only valid answer to the question of "Why?" when referring to totally irrational and unjustified evil.

We can no longer be content with an answer like: evil exists because the world is 'finite' and therefore, imperfect in itself. Evil is not only and simply an absence of good, it can take on (and has already tragically done so) the particularly depraved form of cruelty and sadism. To assert the existence of the devil as pseudo-Father and anti-Son, that is as 'the beginning of the gratuitousness of evil', is the only thing which can allow us to understand intellectually this kind of evil. The orthodox doctrine of the eternity of hell as the fate of the devil is also the only valid response to the need for justice which cries out to God from the depths of human pain and suffering[41].

2.3 The Cross as Unveiling and Victory

"The world cannot hate you, but it does hate me because I give evidence (*martyrô*) that its deeds are evil" (*Jn* 7:7).

"Now sentence (*krisis*) is being passed on this world; now the prince of this world is to be overthrown. And when I am lifted up from the earth, I shall draw all men to myself" (*Jn* 12:31–32).

---

[39] St. Thomas, heir to St. Augustine, says that the devil aspired to final beatitude in virtue of his own nature and not through the grace of someone superior, i.e. he claimed what is God's prerogative. He desired likeness to God. We could almost assert that what Thomas called *proprium Deo* is *proprium Patri*. The sin of the devil is an attack on divine paternity, the exact opposite of the filial being of the only Son. Maritain says very clearly that the devil "wanted in his own way to enjoy that divine privilege which is the sovereign autarkeia" (cf. Ch. Journet, J. Maritain, Philippe de la Trinité, *Le Péché de l'Ange*. Paris: Beauchesne 1961: 80–81, n.5). Bulgakov spoke of "self-deification" (*La sposa dell'Agnello*: 228).

[40] John Paul II explains: "Here we find ourselves at the very centre of what could be called the 'anti-Word,' that is to say the 'anti-truth:' For the truth about man becomes falsified: who man is and what are the impassable limits of his being and freedom. This "anti-truth" is possible because at the same time there is a complete falsification of the truth about who God is. God the Creator is placed in a state of suspicion, indeed of accusation, in the mind of the creature. For the first time in human history there appears the perverse 'genius of suspicion'. He seeks to 'falsify' Good itself; the absolute Good, which precisely in the work of creation has manifested itself as the Good which gives in an inexpressible way: as *bonum diffusivum sui*, as creative love. Who can completely 'convince concerning sin,' or concerning this motivation of man's original disobedience, except the one who alone is the gift and the source of all giving of gifts, except the Spirit, who 'searches the depths of God' and is the love of the Father and the Son?" (*DeV* 37,3).

[41] On this cf. C. L. Rossetti, 'Speranza universale e possibilità dell'inferno'. 45 (1999) *Lateranum*: 131–137.

"If I had not performed such works among them as no one else has ever done, they would be blameless; but as it is, they have seen all this, and still they hate both me and my Father. But all this was only to fulfil the words written in their law: 'They hated me for no reason' (*dôrean*)" (*Jn* 15:24–25).

What is revealed through the Cross is the Truth, the mystery hidden throughout the ages (cf. *Eph* 3:8). The death of Jesus encapsulates the godly wisdom that reveals the Glory of God as well as the Sin of the World; man's wretchedness and divine mercy. The Cross represents all of this: God's absolute love for humanity as well as Jesus' utter love for the Father and humanity, but also the depths of abjection and of the diabolical rejection of God. In the Cross we can also catch a glimpse of an answer to the question of the drama of human suffering, especially of the innocent. The mystery of the Cross cannot be understood in its reality unless seen in the light of the Resurrection. It is faith in the Resurrection which makes sense of death. The Cross seen through the eyes of the flesh can appear to be nothing but condemnation and execution. The eyes of faith see in the Cross the highest revelation of God and of man itself.

The Cross reveals the *Hour of darkness* (cf. *Jn* 19:11), the results of the workings of evil (cf. *Lk* 4:13) and the sinful freedom of men (cf. *Ac* 5:30) – all the evil and sin of the world – as a rejection of God and of Love. Sin in the world is nothing other than the rejection of Christ. Every sin committed by us is like "re-crucifying" Jesus (cf. *Heb* 6:6). The Cross, therefore, reveals the time of the Prince of this world, who hates Jesus, his word of truth and his love. But it is through the revelation of the abyss of iniquity that the sin of the world can be taken away (*Jn* 1:29) and the "Prince of this world can be cast out" (*Jn* 12:31).

On the other hand, the Cross also manifests the *Hour of Christ* because it originates from the liberty of God (*Ac* 2:23; 4:28) and of Jesus himself (*Jn* 10:17–18). In the Cross shines the highest form of God's love towards man, which is manifested in the most precious and total Gift of the Son (*Rm* 8:32), as Mercy and Compassion. The *mercy of God* shines from the Cross like the sun which shines on everyone, good and bad[42]. In Jesus' silence throughout his trial (cf. *Jn* 19) we find the echo of the silence of the father who accepts being mortified by his ungrateful son (cf. *Lk* 15:12). The *compassionate God* is not indifferent to human suffering, but wants to make it his, fully sense its weight, share it completely. This is the sense given to Jesus' cry "My God, my God why have you abandoned me?" (*Mt* 27:40). On the cross, Jesus, the Son of God, experiences the worst kind of suffering: God's distance, His silence. In this way he associates his suffering with every human suffering. "Because he himself has been through temptation he is able to help others who are tempted" (*Heb* 2:18)[43].

[42] In the hymn of the sixth hour, the liturgical tradition expresses the paradox of the light of divine love that shines on the cross in the following way: "In the light of His glory even the Sun will darken" (*cuius luce clarissima tenebricat meridies*) cf. *Mt* 27:45.

[43] H. U. von Balthasar was very insistent on the claim that divine love in Christ wants to console all human suffering, to the point of sharing the worst kind of solitude (*Miteinsamkeit*: Co-solitude), cf. e.g. *Epilogo*. Milano: Jaca Book 1995: 165. See also F. X. Durrwell, *Le Père. Dieu en son mystère*. Paris: Cerf 1988: 68ff; 161ff.

By putting himself completely in the Father's hands (*Lk* 23:46) and forgiving his enemies (*Lk* 23:34), on the Cross Jesus *perfectly fulfils the divine law* (Torah) expressed in the two commandments of Love towards God and towards others (cf. *Mk* 12:30–31). The highest form of love man has towards God is manifested as obedient trust, (*Phil* 2:8), contempt for ignominy (*Heb* 12:2), faithfulness (*Wis* 2:18–20) and filial docility (*Heb* 5:18). The highest form of man's love towards others is manifested through giving himself over completely (*Eph* 5:2; *Gal* 2:20) and through forgiveness (*Lk* 23:34); the *victory of love over violence*. The infernal cycle of sin, which is energized by responding to evil with evil, is shattered by the cross. By dying, Jesus fulfils the supreme act of forgiveness, which is expiation: the taking on of others' sins, offering God his own suffering and asking him to accept it in the place of the punishment, which would be the rightful fate of sinners[44].

In a word: the Glorious Cross of the resurrected Lord is the '*Victory over Death*', because Christ has come "so that by his death he could take away all the power of the devil, who had power over death, and set free all those who had been held in slavery all their lives long by the fear of death" (*Heb* 2:14–15). By dying with love, Christ has overcome the spiritual death of sin, selfishness and hate and through his Resurrection has triumphed over physical death. The Cross is the absolute Anti-Idol; it has nothing attractive, but it confronts and solves the deepest human quest: to overcome death. *Stat crux dum volvitur orbis*.

3. Martyria: the Christian's struggle against evil

The Cross is the Christian's criterion of discernment and action with regard to evil in the world. The Spirit of the Risen Christ gives life to the Church so that she can talk to the world in the light of the judgement of truth and mercy of Christ Crucified.

3.1 Prophecy

3.1.1 '*Elenkein*': *Denouncing every kind of sin in the light of the Spirit*

> I tell you the truth: it is to your advantage that I go away, for if I do not go away, the Counselor will not come to you; but if I go, I will send him to you. And when he comes, he will convince the world concerning sin and righteousness and judgment: concerning sin, because they do not believe in me; concerning righteousness, because I go to the Father, and you will see me no more; concerning judgment, because the prince of this world is judged (*Jn* 16:7–11).

In his encyclical on the Holy Spirit, *Dominum et Vivificantem*, John Paul II interprets these verses as follows:

---

[44] This is the mission of the Servant of Yhwh, cf. *Is* 53; 2 *Cor* 5:21; *Rm* 3:25; *Gal* 3:13; *Heb* 7:22; I *Pt* 2:24.

"Sin" in this passage, means the incredulity that Jesus encountered among *his own*, beginning with the people of his own town of Nazareth. Sin means the rejection of his mission, a rejection that will cause people to condemn him to death. When he speaks next of *"righteousness"*, Jesus seems to have in mind that definitive justice, which the Father will restore to him when he grants him the glory of the Resurrection and Ascension into heaven: "I go to the Father". In its turn, and in the context of *sin* and *righteousness* thus understood, *"judgment"* means that the Spirit of truth will show the guilt of the *world* in condemning Jesus to death on the Cross. Nevertheless, Christ did not come into the world only to judge it and condemn it: *he came to save it* (cf. *Jn* 3:17; 12:47). Convincing about sin and righteousness has as its purpose the salvation of the world, the salvation of men. Precisely this truth seems to be emphasized by the assertion that *"judgment"* concerns only the *"prince of this world"*, Satan, the one who from the beginning has been exploiting the work of creation against salvation, against the covenant and the union of man with God: he is "already judged" from the start. If the Spirit-Counselor is to convince the world precisely concerning judgment, it is in order to continue in the world the salvific work of Christ (*DeV* 27,4).

Because he knows that Christ came into the world to redeem it, the believer proclaims emphatically that this very world radically needs salvation and redemption. Jesus came not to condemn but to save, yet the indispensable condition for obtaining this gratuitous salvation is to be aware that you need it. The unpardonable and most insidious sin is that of self-justification, of alleged self-sufficiency[45]. By contrast, in face of the mentality of this world, the prophetic mission of Christians stems from their docility to the Spirit. The Spirit of truth ("light of consciences", *DeV* 45,2) bears witness *simultaneously* to man's baseness and to the even greater mercy of God, and convinces the world concerning sin, revealing its malice but (at the same time) placing it in the divine context of redemption brought about on the Cross. In this sense: "convincing the world concerning sin" also means bringing it to believe in the forgiveness of sins, in the power of the Holy Spirit" (*DeV* 31,2)[46]. So convincing the world concerning sin is a means of bringing about its conversion:

[45] " 'It is for judgement (*krima*) that I have come into this world, so that those without sight may see and those with sight turn blind'. Hearing this, some Pharisees who were present said to him: 'We are not blind, surely?'. Jesus replied: 'If you were blind, you would not be guilty, but since you say: We see, your guilt remains' " (*Jn* 9:39–41).

[46] "By convincing the 'world' concerning the sin of Golgotha, concerning the death of the innocent Lamb, as happens on the day of Pentecost, the Holy Spirit also convinces of every sin, committed in any place and at any moment in human history: for *he demonstrates its relationship with the Cross of Christ*. The 'convincing' is the demonstration of the evil of sin, of every sin, in relation to the Cross of Christ. Sin, shown in this relationship, is *recognized in the entire dimension of evil* proper to it, through the '*mysterium iniquitatis*' (cf. *2 Th* 2:7) which is hidden within it. Man does not know this dimension – he is absolutely ignorant of it apart from the Cross of Christ. So he cannot be 'convinced' of it except by the Holy Spirit: the Spirit of truth, but who is also the Counselor" (*DeV* 32,2).

The Spirit of truth who helps human beings, human consciences, to know the truth concerning sin, at the same time enables them to know the truth about that righteousness which entered human history in Jesus Christ. In this way, those who are "convinced concerning sin" and who are converted through the action of the Counselor are, in a sense, led out of the range of the "judgment", that "judgment" by which "the ruler of this world is judged" (cf. *Jn* 16:11). In the depths of its divine-human mystery, conversion means the breaking of every fetter by which sin binds man to the whole of the mystery of iniquity (*DeV* 48,2).

Since the Spirit of truth – which proceeds from the one and unique Father, who alone is good – lives in her, the Church, like Christ, can denounce evil and error:

At that point, awareness of the common fatherhood of God, of the brotherhood of all in Christ – "children in the Son" – and of the presence and life-giving action of the Holy Spirit will bring to our vision of the world a new criterion for interpreting it. Beyond human and natural bonds, already so close and strong, there is discerned in the light of faith a new model of the unity of the human race, which must ultimately inspire our solidarity. This supreme model of unity, which is a reflection of the intimate life of God, one God in three Persons, is what we Christians mean by the word 'communion'. This specifically Christian communion, jealously preserved, extended and enriched with the Lord's help, is the soul of the Church's vocation to be a "sacrament" (*Sollicitudo rei socialis* [hereafter: *SRS*; 1987] 40,2).

The *No* which the Church says loud and clear follows like a shadow the powerful and glorious *Yes* which she addresses to the world to save it. As she is the bearer of light and salvation, she cannot refrain from condemning everything which goes against Communion. We cannot dwell on this basic theme, but we need to mention the unavoidable task of denunciation which the Church has to carry out, precisely because she is the handmaid and temple of the Spirit of truth and freedom. Since she contemplates everything in the light of this Spirit, which radiates the truth of man as son of God, of the community as a brotherhood and of the cosmos as destined for glory, the Church becomes the voice of the conscience of the world and of contemporary man. Fortified by the light, she can dissipate the darkness of sin and error and so must rise up against all the violations of the "rights of God"[47], of the rights of man and of the rights of society and nations[48]. But she must also denounce the sophistical disguises designed to hide the malice of actions which are intrinsically perverse[49]. Today the Church is the clearest and most authoritative voice against every kind of sin: from

---

[47] Cf. Cl. Bruarie's famous and penetrating essay, *Le droit de Dieu*. Paris: Montaigne 1974.

[48] On this theme see Pope John Paul II's speech to the U.N. 1995, §6.

[49] In France, for instance, some 'innocent' initials like 'IVG' are normally used to mean abortion, which make it seem something trivial; think also of the term 'genetic therapy' used indiscriminately.

personal sin against God and one's neighbour to the sin that has long-term consequences for the community, becoming social sin or structures of sin[50]. "Have nothing to do with the unfruitful works of darkness, but rather expose (*elenkete*) them" (*Eph* 5:11).

3.1.2 Discernment in a world in the balance

3.1.2.1 A world in the balance

Today's more and more united and 'globalized' world is characterized by two conflicting tendencies: on the one hand the materialism of the secularised and liberal West and on the other the violently hostile extremism of a certain religious world (especially the Islamic). It is easy to foresee that in the 21st century this phenomenon, which can be summed up as the contest between Nihilism and Fundamentalism, will grow rapidly. Situated between the two, the Church will have to be the bulwark of authentic liberty and dignity.

Only the Spirit of Christ helps consciences to "call good and evil by name" (*DeV* 43,4). Currently, in the Western world at least, the *mysterium iniquitatis* is not yet emerging in its tragic and radical form of anti-theism and anti-Christianity[51]. We seem to have an intermediate phase: the spreading of a very insidious 'soft-paganism', which aims at dismantling the fabric of commonly acknowledged values which had their roots in Christianity. It takes on the appearance of 'tolerance', of 'democracy', and leads progressively to the relativization of all truths, and thus to the denial of the actual possibility of an authentic communion between people. Disguised as an 'angel of light' (cf. 2 *Cor* 11:14), the 'liar' undermines from within the foundations of human society.

---

[50] Cf. John Paul II, *SRS* 36, 1–2: "The sum total of the negative factors working against a true awareness of the universal common good, and the need to further it, gives the impression of creating, in persons and institutions, an obstacle which is difficult to overcome. If the present situation can be attributed to difficulties of various kinds, it is not out of place to speak of 'structures of sin', which [...] are rooted in personal sin".

[51] The theses of Romano Guardini (1950) on the process of dechristianization are well known: first, the positive content of Revelation is rejected, whilst the values which it transmitted are preserved (cf. the French Revolution); then, these too are rejected (98). The 'unfairness' of the modern world consists in trying to affirm the values of the person (human rights) while rejecting their natural Christian foundation (100). He predicted the advent of a "radical denial of Christianity" (101), of a Neo-paganism worse than the old one, which in some ways was "youthfully naïve" (102). There will be a purification from ambiguities: "secularized Christian values will be considered sentimentalism and the atmosphere will be purified. It will be full of hostility and danger, but clean and open" (105). Christians will be called on to have an attitude marked by strength and trust (105); by pure obedience to God, whose Holiness is absolute (107). Trust and courage will characterize the end of time (108). "Perhaps there will be a totally new experience of charity; of its absolute originality, of its independence from the world, of the mystery of its supreme why and wherefore" (108). (Quoted from R. Guardini, *La fine dell'epoca moderna. Il potere*. Brescia: Morcelliana 1993.) Among other "prophetic" voices of the 20th century there are those of Solove'ev in Russia (cf. *The legend of the Antichrist*); of G. Papini (*The Devil*) and S. Quinzio (*Mysterium Iniquitatis*) in Italy; of Ch. Péguy, L. Bloy and G. Bernanos in France.

3.1.2.2 *"Do not conform to the mentality of the world around you"* (Rm 12:2)

I offer now a simple synthesis – largely inspired by *Veritatis Splendor* chapter 2 – of the main 'half-truths' advocated by the World, comparing them with the message of the Church. The various worldly or antichristian concepts – which seduce the minds and hearts of our contemporaries – have in common the rejection of God's paternity and of the divine-human covenant revealed in Christ; on the other hand they have very different origins: liberalism, materialism, communism, Islam, spiritualism, ecologism, etc. Clearly, they are often mutually contradictory.

WORLD	CHURCH
(I) – The *truth* does not exist; everyone has their own truth (nihilism, subjectivism, tolerance as an end in itself) ↔ there is only one truth that must be imposed socially (religious fundamentalism, ideological totalitarianism).	(I) – There exists an *absolute Truth*: God, who is Love and has revealed himself in Jesus. This Truth must be *proposed* to free persons.
– everyone can live as they like as long as they don't hurt others. A supreme moral *Law* valid for all men does not exist (relativism).	– God has revealed how Man should live to be happy (*Decalogue*). This corresponds to the dictates of the *natural Law* that can be perceived by the moral conscience.
– the supreme norm for human society is the opinion of the *Majority* (spurious democracy – positivism – conventionalism).	– you must conform to an *upright conscience* rather than to the majority (cf. *VS* 99–101).
(II) – The important thing is this *Life on Earth*; even if God and an afterlife exist, they are not relevant (secularism-immanentism). Life is considered as an absolute but without sacredness (cf. genetic manipulations).	(II) – *Life on Earth* is very important and decisive, but it is only a passageway, a preparation for true life, for Eternity. Earthly Life is *not absolute* but is *sacred*.
(III) –Freedom is the power to do what you want (libertarianism);	(III) –True *Freedom* is the ability to aim at and accomplish Good spontaneously;
– the morality of our acts depend basically on their consequences and/or on our motives and goals (teleologism-proportionalism).	– the fundamental criterion in concrete choices is the *object* of our acts and their capability of being ordered to God (cf. *VS* 73–78).

WORLD	CHURCH
(IV) – *Nature* is only physical material so it can be exploited and manipulated at will by man (technicism); ↔ Nature as such is Sacred. Plants, animals and human beings all have an analogous value which is subordinate to that of Nature (ecologism).	(IV) – *Nature* and the Earth are neither only physical material nor sacred in themselves. They are entrusted by God to Man, for him to use and take care of, with dignity and responsibility, as God's deputy, according to God's plan as Creator.
(V) – The absolute value is individual well-being (individualism); ↔ the absolute value is the good of society (collectivism).	(V) – Neither the individual nor society hold the primacy, which belongs instead to the *Person*, a unique, relational and transcendent being.
(VI) – *The Body* and *sexuality* are a possession belonging to each single subject who uses them as he/she likes (hedonism-individualism).	(VI) – *The Body* and *sexuality* are entrusted to man by God to be the place and opportunity for a real and personal love between a man and a woman.
– Sexual love is a matter of erotic feeling to be enjoyed as an end in itself (eroticism)	– *True Love* is the sincere gift of oneself (to which erotic feeling is subordinate) and it reaches its fulfilment thanks to the Holy Spirit.
In man–woman relationship total equality, and parity must prevail (Western world); ↔ the unquestioned supremacy of men and the subordination of woman is in force (Islam).	– In the man–woman relationship there is a 'communion in difference' deeply-rooted in the Trinitarian and Christological mystery and paradox, by which the husband has a primacy in the marriage, but the wife is not his inferior.
(VII) – *Happiness* is reached through *having*: material well-being (materialism), ↔ through ascetic-meditative disciplines which despise the body (spiritualism).	(VII) – *Happiness* consists in communion with God (the Father) and with others (brothers and sisters) in the Spirit of Christ. It begins with the life of faith on earth and will be complete with the resurrection of the body at the eschaton.

The prophetic mission of the Church is obviously first of all the positive preaching of the Truth of Christ in all its radiant splendor (*kerygma*). Its 'negative' mission is firmly to contest the assertions made by the world, by revealing their aporias and irrationality – through dialogue and philosophical reflection – and by showing, by contrast, the reasonableness of Christian doctrine[52]. Moreover, it is the mission of Christians, especially of lay people[53], to help to reduce the gap which exists between the Church and the world by bringing the values of the Catholic Faith to the shaping of culture. This is the core of the temporal mission of the Church, as the salt, light and leaven of society, as well as being the christian's commitment in philosophy, politics, economics and related disciplines.

3.2 Action in Hope

The mission of the Church, as well as being one of prophecy, discernment and judgment, also involves a real praxis which aims at opposing the evil in the world in a positive way. If it is true that *"there is not a single aspect of the Christian message that is not also in part an answer to the question of evil"* (CCC 309), it is also the case that there is no truth of Christian ethics which is not, in some respect, concretely opposed to the presence of evil[54]. In this regard, we should note the practical consequence of the Christian's eschatological faith in the presence of Christ (the Son of God, God Himself) in the suffering (cf. *Mt* 25:40). This consequence can be summed up in two absolutely inseperable notions: hope and love.

3.2.1 Hope: the Father will incorporate the suffering into Christ's glory

The Christian gives an amazing answer to evil in the eschatological revelation of Christ as Judge: Christ is present in those often reckoned of least account, in the victims of pain and injustice. They are the least of his brothers and they will be together with him in his glory just as they were near him in suffering. This is the only, the truest and deepest consolation for all innocent suffering. Without this hope of redemption, deeply-rooted in the Risen Christ, who is "in the throes of death until the end of the world" (Pascal)[55], life, after the first torture in history, after the first tears shed by a tortured child, would be absurd and it would be absolutely legitimate to refuse the entrance ticket to it (Dostoievski)[56].

---

[52] Cf. John Paul II, *Fides et ratio* (1998), chap. V.

[53] Cf. *GS* 43, 2.

[54] From many points of view it is recognized that, in face of the mystery of evil, it is more important to put forward effective ways of fighting it than it is to discuss the theoretical question of its origin. Cf. for example, P. Ricoeur, *Il male*. Brescia: Morcelliana 1993 (French original 1986): 48–50; V. Possenti, *Dio e il male*. Milano: SEI 1996: 57–61.

[55] Cf. D. Leduc Fayette, *Pascal et le mystère du mal*. Paris: Cerf 1996: 261ff; 273ff.

[56] Cf. "If the suffering of children has served to complete the sum of the sufferings necessary to pay for the truth, I declare from now that no truth is worth this price ... so I'm hurrying to give my ticket back" (*I fratelli Karamazov*. [II, l. V, 4] Cinisello Balsamo: San Paolo 1995: 315 (English translation: *The Brothers Karamazov*); see P. Evdokimov, *Dostoievsky e il problema del male*. Roma: Città Nuova, 1995).

Unredeemed, suffering crushes the just man who is condemned to religious resignation (cf. Judaism and Islam) or to anxiously and *desperately* trying to oppose the spread of evil[57]. The message of the healing and consoling power of God, which is so clear in biblical revelation[58], must be believed and proclaimed, uncontaminated by protests inspired by a Marxist or materialistic mentality. This message is an irreplaceable element in the Christian answer to the problem of evil and provides that spiritual support which saves us from plunging into despair. The Christian elevates pain and suffering because he knows that *there will be* a final healing, given to us by the One who became a man of sorrows and whom the God of life filled with joy in his presence. It is also true, however, that you cannot refer to this message of consolation and hope without at the same time reaffirming equally vigorously the second and more concrete element of the Christian protest against the challenge of evil and suffering.

3.2.2 Love. Helping the poor as a duty towards God

Matthew 25 does not only affirm the significance of justice and hope, but it also suggests the decisive element of the *struggle* against evil, suffering, and pain: love. To love and help those in need has become a necessity for those who love God. From the moment of his Son's Incarnation, the Father sees in each person, especially in the most downtrodden, a living image of his Only-Begotten Son. Not to help one of them is tantamount to blaspheming, apostatising, not recognizing the Son made flesh. It is tantamount to being the Antichrist (1 *Jn* 2:22). So the same reply which filled us with consolation, stops us from being inactive in the face of pain. This element of the Christian reply to evil is the greatest incentive there is to solidarity and to the struggle, including the social struggle, against evil and injustice. The historical examples, from the first Mercedarian Fathers to Mother Teresa of Calcutta, from St. John of God to Padre Pio, are the clearest testimonies to the dynamic power which this reply to evil can introduce into praxis. This reply includes the creation of what we could call 'concrete structures of the Culture of Life'.

3.3 Martyrdom as the synthesis of the Christian mission

In the Bull inaugurating the Jubilee Year, *Incarnationis Mysterium* (hereafter: *IM*; 1999), John Paul II writes:

> A sign of the truth of Christian love, ageless but especially powerful today, is *the memory of the martyrs*. Their witness must not be forgotten. They are the ones

---

[57] This is the "drama of atheist humanism", like that of Camus who declared: "until the day I die I will refuse to love this creation where children are tortured", and: "the only concrete problem I know of is whether one can be a saint without God" (*La Peste*. Milan: Bompiani 1997: 169; 197). See P. Miccoli, *The Problem of Evil in Albert Camus*. Alba: ed. Paoline, 1971.

[58] Think in particular of the third Gospel (*Lk* 6:20ff; 16:19–31), but also of the Book of Revelation (*Rev* 21:1ff).

who have proclaimed the Gospel by giving their lives for love. The martyr, especially in our own days, is a sign of that greater love which sums up all other values. The martyr's life reflects the extraordinary words uttered by Christ on the Cross: "Father, forgive them, for they know not that they do" (*Lk* 23:34). The believer who has seriously pondered his Christian vocation, including what Revelation has to say about the possibility of martyrdom, cannot exclude it from his own life's horizon. The two thousand years since the birth of Christ are marked by the ever-present witness of the martyrs [...] May the People of God, confirmed in faith by the example of these true champions of every age, language and nation, cross with full confidence the threshold of the Third Millennium. In the hearts of the faithful, may admiration for their martyrdom be matched by the desire to follow their example, with God's grace, should circumstances require it (*IM* 13).

The Pope, echoing a text of the Council and taking up a *topos* of his own teaching[59], proposes the testimony of the martyr as the horizon of ultimate significance in the life of every Christian who is seriously aware of his Christian identity. It is in martyrdom in fact that we glimpse the synthesis and summation of the Christian's mission for and against the world[60].

Martyrdom in a Christian sense implies a frankly Trinitarian dimension and consists of the non-violent affirmation of the Truth which becomes free intercession and expiation. These are signs which denote the supreme testimony given by a fragile human being, through the powerful action of the Holy Spirit. It appears to us like the apex of the prophetic, which becomes 'liturgy': sacrificial and priestly intercession (cf. *Ac* 7:60).

3.3.1 *The theological dimension of witness*

The force of martyrdom proceeds from the incontrovertible evidence of the Truth. The Apostles declared that they could not keep quiet about what they had seen and heard (cf. *Ac* 4:20 and *Rm* 11). The power (*dynamis*) that the Spirit infuses into the hearts of the believers (cf. *Ac* 1:8) is an inner witness to the Truth (in the Hebrew sense of *emeth*: reliability and perpetuity) of the Paschal event of

---

[59] See *LG* 42,2; John Paul II, *VS* 93,2: "Although martyrdom represents the high point of the witness to moral truth, and one to which relatively few people are called, there is nonetheless a consistent witness which all Christians must daily be ready to make, even at the cost of suffering and grave sacrifice. Indeed, faced with the many difficulties which fidelity to the moral order can demand, even in the most ordinary circumstances, the Christian is called, with the grace of God invoked in prayer, to a sometimes heroic commitment. In this he or she is sustained by the virtue of fortitude, whereby – as Gregory the Great teaches – one can actually 'love the difficulties of this world for the sake of eternal rewards' [cf. *Moralia* VII, 21,24]"; see also *Tertio Millennio adveniente* (hereafter: *TMA* 1994) 37 and the ecumenical celebration of the Memory of the New Martyrs held at the Colosseum on the 14 May 2000.

[60] Cf. e.g. M. Naro (ed) *Martirio e vita cristiana*. Caltanissetta-Roma: Sciascia Editore 1997; D. Wood (ed) *Martyrs and Martyrologies. Papers read at the 1992 Summer Meeting & the 1993 Winter Meeting of the Ecclesiastical History Society*. Oxford: Blackwell Publishers 1993; A. Riccardi, *Il secolo del martirio*. Milano: Mondadori 2000.

Jesus. The Spirit of Truth who proceeds from the Father (*Jn* 15:26) bears witness in the hearts of the believers that the Jesus, who died like a cursed man hanging from the cross, has risen from death through the glory of the Father, that he is indeed the supreme revelation of God's action among men. The Spirit, author and first witness of the Resurrection (cf. *Rm* 1:4; *Ac* 5:32), gives rise to the cry of faith: "Jesus is *kyrios*" (1*Cor* 12:3). It is the Spirit who knows and announces the things to come (*Jn* 16:13), who, in the Church-Bride, gives rise to the call of hope: "Come, Lord! Maranà tha!" (*Rev* 22:20; 1*Cor* 16:22). It is the Spirit of the Son (cf. *Gal* 4:5–6), Spirit of love and filial obedience, who evokes the cry "Abbà Father!" (cf. *Rm* 8:15; *Mk* 14:36). This pneumatological and theological dimension is the basis of Christian martyrdom. The Spirit envelops and transfigures the conscience of the believer; He floods and inflames it with tranquil certainty (faith), with blessed desire (hope) and with the power of self-giving (charity). Martyrdom is a putting of one's steps in the footprints of Christ, the faithful Witness (*ho martys ho pistos*; *Rev* 1:5) who came into the world to bear witness to the Truth (*Jn* 18:37; 1 *Tim* 6:13). Jesus's witness was based on the human-divine evidence which he received (by listening/seeing) from the Father (cf. *Jn* 5:19; 7:26; 10:18; 15:15). The testimony of the apostles and saints of all ages is based on the Spirit who makes men participate in the consciousness and filial love of Jesus towards the Father (cf. 1 *Tim* 1:7–8). The *martyria* of the Spirit makes men conform to the Christ-Martyr and brings them to offer themselves as a living sacrifice of love to the Father[61].

3.3.2 *Liberty and Intercession*

An outstanding characteristic of martyrdom is the liberty with which the martyr faces the suffering of the final testimony. The Master has freed his followers with the word of truth and "offering Himself freely to His passion", he loved them "until the end", giving up His life of his own accord, without anyone taking it from Him[62]. Following him, the martyr "does not die, he gives up and offers his life instead, in the full liberty which he has acquired"[63]. So the martyr is the freest and most responsible of men. He can reply, with Christ and after Christ: "I am he, arrest me", when the guard come to capture him (cf. *Jn* 18:4ff). In this sense he witnesses, to the world and for the world, to the highest and most ennobling message there is: the true man (*ecce homo!*) is the one who has met Christ-the-Truth, who has been freed by Christ from every kind of fear, from every kind of slavery, from all rancour and spirit of revenge. He is the one who is penetrated by the Spirit of the Father, and, strong with the pledge of

---

[61] Cf. for Christ: *Eph* 5,2; *Heb* 9,24. For the martyrs, cf. e.g. Ignatius of Antioch: "don't have Jesus on your lips and the world in your hearts ... inside me a living water murmurs to my heart: 'Come to the Father'" (*Ad Romanos*. VII:1.2).

[62] Cf. Canon of the Mass, introduction to the consecration (cf. *Jn* 8:32; 13:1; 10:17–18). On the sequence Truth, Liberty, Love cf. *VS* 87.

[63] R. Fisichella, 'Martirio', in *Dizionario di Teologia fondamentale*. Casale Monferrato: Piemme 1993: 680.

eternal life, can despise the ignominy of death and offer himself for those who are killing him while interceding for them. Martyrdom denounces sin and evil and therefore has the ultimate custody of moral truth in society[64], but it is also the incontrovertible sign of the fullness of humanity which can be reached in total communion with God. Martyrdom is the courageous (*parrhêsia*) testimony in persecution to the freedom and dignity of human beings and to the universal need for Jesus as unique Saviour[65].

3.3.3 *"So that the world may believe"*

Martyrdom sums up the whole of the mission of the Christian towards the world. It is all 'responsorial' i.e. theo-logical, determined by the anticipating and cooperating action of the grace of the Spirit of Christ[66]. It speaks first of all of absolute fidelity to the Truth which has "captured" (cf. *Phil* 3:12) the believer and inspires him to reply to God's infinite love with total love. It also speaks of the radical contradiction and condemnation of sin and the unmasking of its diabolical inspiration. But on an even deeper level, it becomes intercession of the greatest value to the world. Prophecy becomes royal priesthood, contention becomes supplication, the sacrifice of life becomes eucharist and epiclesis over the world[67]. Martyrdom is not only personal testimony to victory over death, it also reveals the deepest communion. The martyr is the one who breaks the isolation of selfishness and is completely at union with God and with his brothers and sisters in the communion of saints[68]. In this lies the ecclesial reality of martyrdom.

---

[64] John Paul II, *VS* 93,1: "Martyrdom is an *outstanding sign of the holiness of the Church.* Fidelity to God's holy law, witnessed to by death, is a solemn proclamation and missionary commitment *usque ad sanguinem*, so that the splendour of moral truth may be undimmed in the behaviour and thinking of individuals and society. This witness makes an extraordinarily valuable contribution to warding off, in civil society and within the ecclesial communities themselves, a headlong plunge into the most dangerous crisis which can afflict man: the *confusion between good and evil*, which makes it impossible to build up and to preserve the moral order of individuals and communities. By their eloquent and attractive example of a life completely transfigured by the splendour of moral truth, the martyrs and, in general, all the Church's Saints, light up every period of history by reawakening its moral sense. By witnessing fully to the good, they are a living reproof to those who transgress the law (cf. *Wis* 2:12), and they make the words of the Prophet echo ever afresh: 'Woe to those who call evil good and good evil, who put darkness for light and light for darkness, who put bitter for sweet and sweet for bitter!' (*Is* 5:20)".

[65] Cf. *VS* 92,2: "martyrdom is also the exaltation of a person's perfect 'humanity' and of true 'life', as is attested by Saint Ignatius of Antioch, addressing the Christians of Rome, the place of his own martyrdom: 'Have mercy on me, brethren: do not hold me back from living; do not wish that I die... Let me arrive at the pure light; once there *I will be truly a man* [*paragenomenos anthropos*]. Let me imitate the passion of my God' [*Ad Rom.* VI,2]". Analogous reflections can be found in *DeV* 60,2 and *RM* 11,1.

[66] Proceeding from grace, animated by charity (cf. *VS* 89,2), it draws its strength from hope in the Resurrection (cf. CTI, *Questions on eschatology* [1991], n.1).

[67] Cf. Ignatius of Antioch again, *Ad Ephesios VIII*, 1; X, 1–2.

[68] This is Chesterton's intuition: "A martyr is a man who cares so much for something outside him, that he forgets his own personal life. A suicide is a man who cares so little for anything outside him, that he wants to see the last of everything" (*Orthodoxy*, ed. cit. 276).

In our days, we feel more and more the need to expand the notion of martyrdom, and recover its connection with the fundamental witness which the believer undertakes to bring to the world in virtue of his Baptism[69]. In this regard it is urgently necessary to rediscover Christian initiation as an "exodus", as a passage "from the power of darkness to the kingdom of the Son of Love" (cf. *Col* 1:13). Radical conversion – *metanoia* – (and the witness which results from it) is the concern of all Christians[70]; it comes about in Baptism, becomes mission in Confirmation and is celebrated in the Eucharist. It is only in recovering the awareness of being foreigners and pilgrims in this world (cf. 1 *Pt* 2:11) that a true spirituality of martyrdom can be infused into the hearts of Christians so that they will consider themselves to be in the world but not of the world, for the world but also against the world.

I would like to conclude with the justly famous text of the *Letter to Diognetus* (2nd century)[71]:

> For the Christians are distinguished from other men neither by country, nor language, nor the customs which they observe. For they neither inhabit cities of their own, nor employ a peculiar form of speech, nor lead a life which is marked out by any singularity. The course of conduct which they follow has not been devised by any *speculation* or deliberation of inquisitive men; nor do they, like some, proclaim themselves the advocates of any merely human doctrines. But, inhabiting Greek as well as barbarian cities, according as the lot of each of them has determined, and following the customs of the natives in respect to clothing, food, and the rest of their ordinary conduct, they display to us their wonderful and confessedly striking method of life. They dwell in their own countries, but simply as sojourners (*paroikoi*). As citizens, they share in all things with others, and yet endure all things as if foreigners. Every foreign land is to them as their native country, and every land of their birth as a land of strangers. They marry, as do all [others]; they beget children; but they do not destroy their offspring. They have a common table, but not a common bed. They are in the flesh, but they do not live after the flesh. They pass their days on earth, but they are citizens of heaven (*en ourano politeuontai*). They obey the prescribed laws, and at the same time surpass the laws by their lives. They love all men, and are persecuted by all. They are unknown and condemned; they are put to death, and restored to life. They are poor, yet make many rich; they are in lack of all things, and yet abound in all; they are dishonoured, and yet in their very dishonour are glorified. They are ill spoken of, and yet are justified; they are reviled, and

---

[69] Cf. e.g. H.U. von Balthasar, *Cordula ovverosia il caso serio*. Brescia: Morcelliana 1993: 132.

[70] Thinking of Christian couples, John Paul II wrote: "There is a need to foster the recognition of the heroic virtues of men and women who have lived their Christian vocation *in marriage*. Precisely because we are convinced of the abundant fruits of holiness in the married state, we need to find the most appropriate means for discerning them and proposing them to the whole Church as a model and encouragement for other Christian spouses" (*TMA* 37,4).

[71] *Letter to Diognetus*, 5–6. Quoted also by *LG* 38.

bless; they are insulted, and repay the insult with honour; they do good, yet are punished as evil-doers. When punished, they rejoice as if quickened into life; they are assailed by the Jews as foreigners, and are persecuted by the Greeks; yet those who hate them are unable to assign any reason for their hatred. [6] To sum up all in one word: what the soul is in the body (*hoper estin en somati psychê*), that are Christians in the world. The soul is dispersed through all the members of the body, and Christians are scattered through all the cities of the world. The soul dwells in the body, yet is not of the body; and Christians dwell in the world, yet are not of the world. The invisible soul is guarded by the visible body, and Christians are known indeed to be in the world, but their godliness remains invisible. The flesh hates the soul, and wars against it, though itself suffering no injury, because it is prevented from enjoying pleasures; the world also hates the Christians, though in nowise injured, because they abjure pleasures. The soul loves the flesh that hates it, and [loves also] the members; Christians likewise love those that hate them. The soul is imprisoned in the body, yet preserves that very body; and Christians are confined in the world as in a prison, and yet they are the preservers of the world. The immortal soul dwells in a mortal tabernacle; and Christians dwell as sojourners in corruptible [bodies], looking for an incorruptible dwelling in the heavens. The soul, when but ill-provided with food and drink, becomes better; in like manner, the Christians, though subjected day by day to punishment, increase the more in number. God has assigned them this illustrious position (*taxin*), which it were unlawful for them to forsake.

9

The Church as a community of hope in face of the culture of death

BISHOP DONAL MURRAY

IN HIS FIRST ENCYCLICAL, which already looked forward to the Great Jubilee of the Year 2000[1], Pope John Paul spoke of how God's love frees us from the fear that life may be senseless. In Christ the infinite God gave us his only Son who died and rose for us so that we would have eternal life. That realisation gives rise to adoration of God and to wonder at ourselves:

> In reality, the name for that deep amazement at human worth and dignity is the Gospel, that is to say: the Good News. It is also called Christianity[2].

The Church is a community of hope first of all because it believes that Jesus Christ has called humanity to abundant life (*Jn* 10:10) which is an endless sharing in the life of the Triune God. It is precisely in this eternal life "that all the aspects and stages of human life achieve their full significance"[3]. In other words, it is because the Church is a community of hope that it is, as Pope John Paul often puts it, "an expert in humanity"[4].

This does not, however, imply that the Church's hope can be communicated only to those who share the Christian faith:

> The Church knows that this Gospel of life, which she has received from her Lord, has a profound and persuasive echo in the heart of every person – believer and non-believer alike – because it marvellously fulfils all the heart's expectations while infinitely surpassing them[5].

The communication of that hope occurs not just in words but in a life lived by individuals and by a community – a life that can attract and fascinate when it is lived to the full.

In this paper I wish to reflect particularly on some fundamental truths about human life and about morality which are expressed in the encyclicals *Veritatis Splendor* and *Evangelium Vitae*.

---

[1] John Paul II, *Redemptor Hominis* (hereafter *RH*). 1979: 1.
[2] *RH*: 10.
[3] John Paul II, *Evangelium Vitae* (hereafter: *EV*). 1995: 1.
[4] John Paul II, *Sollicitudo Rei Socialis* (hereafter: *SRS*). 1987: 41.
[5] John Paul II, *EV*: 2.

The Gospel of Life is Good News about the incomparable dignity and worth of the human person. It is "the source of invincible hope and true joy for every period of history"[6]. It speaks to every human being, even those who do not share Christian faith, because it touches the deepest truth of our being; it responds to the most fundamental questions about the meaning of life. It tells us who we are and what our freedom means.

The Church is a community of hope at the service of this Gospel of life, "sustained by the awareness that we have received it as a gift and are sent to preach it to all humanity"[7].

The full meaning of life

The first element in being a community of hope is, paradoxically, to recognise the utter inadequacy of all our hopes. The human person is an unsatisfied quest. Every human being, in his or her deepest being, experiences a longing which seems incapable of being satisfied. Nothing that I can possess or control or achieve or imagine could satisfy all my aspirations. Everything I experience is fragile, imperfect, passing. The things I hope for will not make me permanently happy; some of the things I hope for may well be incompatible with what other people hope for; even my most splendid schemes may prove to be flawed or unworkable.

The best art and culture reveal the human paradox – a tension between the greatness of our longings and the limitations of our condition. Our life span is short, yet we declare our love to be undying; our hopes for a better world are fulfilled, if at all, only in partial and defective ways; our thirst for knowledge and beauty and freedom remains always incompletely quenched. We journey towards boundless happiness, which we seek "with sighs too deep for words" (*Rom* 8:26), but only through faltering steps along an often unpromising road.

Art, poetry, music – especially the great cultural heritage in which the Christian faith has been expressed – can be an important voice, capable of opening up the human depths in which the Gospel echoes.

Once one glimpses the restlessness of the human heart there are only two possibilities – either to accept that the restlessness cannot be fulfilled and that the road really goes nowhere, or to believe that we are restless until we reach our journey's end in God.

When Pope John Paul set out to address the fundamental elements of moral teaching, he began his reflection with the question asked by the rich young man; "What good must I do to have eternal life?" (*Mt* 19:16). This question is the starting point precisely because it links moral behaviour with the question of meaning.

[6] John Paul II, *EV*: 2.
[7] John Paul II, *EV*: 78.

For the young man, the *question* is not so much about rules to be followed, but *about the full meaning of life*. This is in fact the aspiration at the heart of every human decision and action, the quiet searching and interior prompting which sets freedom in motion. This question is ultimately an appeal to the absolute Good which attracts us and beckons us; it is the echo of a call from God who is the origin and goal of human life[8].

St Thomas Aquinas said something very similar about how the ultimate purpose of life is present in every exercise of our freedom: "The last end moves the desires in a way similar to the action of the First Mover in other movements"[9].

Both imply that unless one begins by asking what human life is for, and where it leads, it is hard to see how any serious understanding of human actions can be reached. The meaning of human actions depends on the ultimate purpose of human life.

One may conclude that there is no final goal and seek to live with the ensuing sense of pointlessness. Like Sartre, one may describe the human being as *'une passion inutile'*. Whatever meaning one can create for oneself in such a context can never overcome the ultimate bleakness of the vision:

> If all human activity is simply one form or another of a fruitless attempt to be *ens causa sui* then it matters little which form we adopt[10].

Alternatively, one may recognise the unimaginable greatness of a destiny that would satisfy all the deepest longings of the people of every generation and culture and believe that a fulfilment greater than we can construct or imagine is given to us as a gift. One may, in other words, live in a world of hope and meaning, or one may try to live with fundamental absurdity.

That is not to say that only those who believe in eternal life can understand morality. But it does mean that only those who appreciate the profundity of the human quest for truth and meaning, and who pursue that quest, can understand the seriousness and the urgency of the moral question.

To believe that life has a meaning which fully responds to what human beings long for, but which we can neither imagine nor construct, is the beginning of hope. It is a hope which stretches us. That is why the encyclical *Evangelium Vitae* stresses that, in order to appreciate and celebrate the Gospel of Life, a contemplative outlook is needed:

> It is the outlook of those who see life in its deeper meaning, who grasp its utter gratuitousness, its beauty and its invitation to freedom and responsibility. It is the outlook of those who do not presume to take possession of reality but instead accept it as a gift, discovering in all things the reflection of the Creator and seeing in every person his living image[11].

[8] John Paul II, *Veritatis Splendor* (hereafter: *VS*). 1993: 7.
[9] "...ultimus finis hoc modo se habet in movendo appetitum, sicut se habet in aliis motionibus primum movens." Aquinas, *Summa Theologiae* 1–2, 1, 6c.
[10] I. Murdoch, *Sartre*. London: Fontana Press 1967: 66.
[11] John Paul II, *EV*: 83.

Relationships

Christian hope is concerned with relationship. In calling each human person into existence, God enters into a personal relationship with each, addressing each by name, inviting him or her into friendship with him:

> The invisible God, from the fullness of his love, addresses men and women as his friends, and lives among them, in order to invite and receive them into his own company[12].

That is why it is possible to believe in a fulfilment which answers all the yearnings of the human heart. Our destiny is to belong to the new creation where God will make his home with us, where there will be no mourning or weeping, where the former things will have passed away (*Rev* 21:1–8).

Our hope is not, in the last analysis, a belief that things will turn out as we would wish. It is not so much a 'hope that' as a 'hope in'. The hoper "anticipates nothing; he holds himself in readiness for a fulfilment still to come, although he is aware that he knows neither its dimensions nor its time"[13].

The person who hopes in God has:

> ...the inner disposition of one who, setting no condition or limit and abandoning himself in absolute confidence, would thus transcend all possible disappointment and would experience a security of his being, or in his being, which is contrary to the radical insecurity of *Having*[14].

That hope is at the foundation of Christian morality. The opening words of the section on moral living in the *Catechism of the Catholic Church* are a quotation from St Leo the Great:

> Christian, recognise your dignity and, now that you share in God's own nature, do not return to your former base condition by sinning. Remember who is your head and of whose body you are a member. Never forget that you have been rescued from the power of darkness and brought into the light of the Kingdom of God[15].

The imperative nature of moral obligation springs from this truth. We were made and redeemed for a destiny which responds to our deepest longings in a way beyond what human eye has seen or ear heard or mind conceived (I *Cor* 2:9).

The Is/Ought debate asks how it is possible to pass from statements of fact to statements of obligation. Faced with the promise of the superabundant fulfilment of the most profound human hunger for what is true and good and beautiful, faced with the loving invitation of the God who is the source of human life and

---

[12] Vatican II, *Dei Verbum*. 1965: 3.
[13] J. Pieper, *Hope and History*. London: Burns and Oates 1969: 28.
[14] G. Marcel, *Homo Viator* (translated by E. Craufurd). New York: Harper Torchbooks 1962: 46.
[15] *Catechism of the Catholic Church* (hereafter: *CCC*). Dublin: Veritas 1994: 1691.

of the universe, it hardly seems logical or sensible, to ask, 'Does it follow from these facts that we have an obligation to accept that promise and invitation?'

To reject that invitation would be to reject who we are. It would mean using our freedom – which is ultimately a search for the only destiny which can satisfy us – to refuse that destiny, to choose not to be what I am, to betray myself[16].

The young man's question was not so much about rules but about meaning. The first response of Jesus to his question, before speaking about the commandments, was: "There is only one who is good" (*Mt* 19:17). The beginning of a Christian moral response is to recognise God as God. That means recognising him not as one person among many but as the source of all meaning and all love. The only appropriate response to God is to love with all one's heart, soul and strength (*Dt* 6:5). The whole meaning of life is found in him. Rules, even the Ten Commandments, come in the second place. Above all else, "Moral existence is a response to the Lord's loving initiative"[17].

There is a further important implication of the recognition that morality is ultimately a response to God. "If God loved us so much, we too should love each other" (I *Jn* 4:11). At the beginning of this Jubilee Year, looking to the uncertainties of a new century, Pope John Paul made an obvious yet vital point:

> We cannot of course foresee the future. But we can set forth one certain principle: *there will be peace only to the extent that humanity as a whole rediscovers its fundamental calling to be one family*, a family in which the dignity and rights of individuals – whatever their status, race or religion – are accepted as prior and superior to any kind of difference or distinction[18].

When Jesus begins to list some of the commandments for the rich young man, they are all taken from the second part of the Decalogue, that is, they are all concerned with how we treat our neighbour.

Each human person in being brought into existence is addressed by God with the same promise. The promise is made explicit in the preaching of the Gospel and then in Baptism. In being created, however, the human being is made capable of hearing that invitation and, therefore, capable of accepting it. Each human being is brought into existence by a particular act of God's creation. To put it more personally, the creation of the human soul, of human life, is the act in which God addresses a being chosen for his or her own sake and called into a personal relationship with God.

That is the most fundamental truth to which human freedom responds. It does not invent its own goals; it does not arbitrarily determine its own road; it does not possess the resources to construct a fully satisfying destiny for itself. It seeks to recognise a truth, which it does not create, and to live it.

Human dignity 'in the light of the Gospel' does not, therefore, depend on abilities and achievements. It depends on being addressed by God, which is

---

[16] Cf. G. Marcel, *Being and Having*. London, Fontana: 1965: 116.

[17] *CCC*: 2062.

[18] John Paul II, *Message for the World Day of Peace*: 2000: 5.

what happens in the creation of each new human life. Being addressed by God, being human, means having the radical ability to respond, an ability which will be fully realised in an existence free from the limitations of time and space, of weakness and disability. Even the most severe disability does not nullify that invitation and the radical capacity to respond which is implicit in the invitation itself.

The culture of life recognises the value and irreplaceable dignity of every human life. Policies, actions and attitudes which marginalise or exclude others far more fundamentally marginalise and exclude those who adopt and implement them. This is so because the hope that is adequate to human longings is found together with the whole human family, or not at all. It is in the name of the frail elderly, the unborn child, the AIDS sufferers, the women and men deprived of basic medical care, that Christ will say, 'I was hungry, thirsty, sick, and you did, or did not, come to my help'.

The hope at the heart of the Gospel of Life is not simply a hope for individuals; it is a hope for the whole human family. The fulfilment of God's promise exceeds our expectations because it is a new act of the Creator. It is unimaginable because it is the fulfilment not just of our own hope but of the deepest hope of people who have lived in cultures and times unimaginably different from our own; it will gather what is good in each human culture, each human life, and free it from every imperfection and limitation; it will vindicate all those who have suffered, bringing about "a finally perfect justice for the living and the dead, for people of all times and places, a justice which Jesus Christ, installed as supreme Judge, will establish"[19].

The various aspects of hope are summed up in the words proposed by Gabriel Marcel as the most adequate formulation of hope: "*I hope in Thee for us*". This expresses what he calls, 'the remedy of communion, the remedy of hope'. The human tragedy takes many forms, but it can only be resolved in a communion which exceeds anything we know, a communion which hope foreshadows. Marcel's formula recognises an intimate link between 'Thee' and 'us':

> ... 'Thou' is in some way the guarantee of the union which holds us together, myself to myself, or the one to the other, or these beings to those other beings. More than a guarantee which secures or confirms from outside a union which already exists, it is the very cement which binds the whole into one. If this is the case, to despair of myself, or to despair of us, is essentially to despair of the Thou[20].

The Church is a community of hope, first of all because it believes in God's promise. The Gospel of life, which is the Gospel of hope, "exceeds every human expectation and reveals the sublime heights to which the dignity of the human person is raised through grace"[21].

[19] Congregation for the Doctrine of the Faith, *Instruction on Christian Freedom and Liberation*. 1986: 60.
[20] Marcel, *Homo Viator*: 60f.
[21] John Paul II, EV: 80.

Solidarity

The rich young man's question was "really a religious question" because the goodness that attracts us and obliges us "has its source in God and indeed is God himself"[22].

If the goal of life is seen in terms of achievements and possessions and status and power, it is perceived as being made up of commodities in limited supply. The pursuit of the goal becomes a matter of competition in which the interests of me and mine are opposed to the interests of others.

If, on the other hand, the unimaginable goal of life is understood to be God's creative and renewing gift offered to every human being, then it is a goal to be shared. The more richly and fully the human family shares in that gift, the more richly it will reflect the variety of God's creation. Life is not fundamentally competitive because its goal is an unlimited gift.

The response to the loving invitation of God cannot be separated from a response to one's fellow human beings:

> The Gospel of God's love for man, the Gospel of the dignity of the person and the Gospel of life are a single and indivisible Gospel[23].

One of the primary characteristics of what Pope John Paul has called the culture of death is that it "despairs of 'us'". It is "a culture which denies solidarity"[24]. In *Sollicitudo Rei Socialis*, he described solidarity, which is "undoubtedly a Christian virtue"[25], in terms which anticipated the concerns of his later encyclicals, especially of *Evangelium Vitae*:

> *Solidarity* helps us to see the 'other' – whether a *person, people, or nation* – not just as some kind of instrument, with a work capacity and physical strength to be exploited at low cost and then discarded when no longer useful, but as our 'neighbour', a 'helper', to be made a sharer, on a par with ourselves, in the banquet of life to which all are equally invited by God. Hence the importance of reawakening the *religious awareness* of individuals and peoples.[26]

Any relationship, any social structure or policy, which does not recognise and foster that fundamental equality in hope, is to a greater or lesser extent a 'culture of death'. It fails to recognise the promise of life to which one's neighbour is invited and which is equally one's own hope. To deny another person's hope is to deny one's own.

The encyclicals of Pope John Paul are full of that vision. The 'other' is called to share on a par with ourselves in the eternal banquet. In a perspective that looks to

---

[22] John Paul II, *VS*: 9.
[23] John Paul II, *EV*: 2.
[24] John Paul II, *EV*: 12.
[25] John Paul II, *SRS*: 40.
[26] John Paul II, *SRS*: 39.

the lesser and utterly inadequate goal of possessions and influence and so on, hope is deprived of its real meaning:

> What is in question is the advancement of persons, not just the multiplying of things that people can use. It is a matter – as a contemporary philosopher has said and as the Council has stated – not so much of 'having more' as of 'being more'[27].

That is why *Evangelium Vitae* points to the dangers of a society which is "excessively concerned with efficiency"[28]. We are well aware of the importance of efficiency in the use of resources in health care and in society generally. But the concept of efficiency becomes excessive when it is in conflict with solidarity:

> A life which would require greater acceptance, love and care is considered useless, or held to be an intolerable burden, and is therefore rejected in one way or another. A person who, because of illness, handicap, or more simply, just by existing, compromises the well-being or life-style of those who are more favoured tends to be looked on as an enemy to be resisted or eliminated.[29]

This can also happen in the world of work, destroying the workers' sense of their own dignity and of the importance of their work by making them feel that they are mere instruments, cogs "in a huge machine moved from above"[30].

The gift of self

The recognition of the dignity of each human being, invited on a par with ourselves to share in the banquet of life, points to the fundamental truth about human freedom. It is not in our own resources and possessions that our hope is based, but on opening ourselves to a gift which is to be shared.

Human beings, as Vatican II put it, "can fully find their true selves only in sincere self-giving"[31]. The hope which the Church tries to proclaim and live is a hope 'for us'. We are made for relationship with God and with each other. No purely individual hope can satisfy. Marcel states it well:

> Once again we are led to draw attention to the indissoluble connection which binds together hope and love. The more egoistical love is, the more the allur- ingly prophetic declarations it inspires should be regarded with caution as likely to be literally contradicted by experience; on the other hand, the nearer it approaches to true charity, the more the meaning of its declarations is inflected and tends to become full of an unconditional quality which is the very sign of a presence. This presence is incarnated in the 'us' for whom 'I

---

[27] John Paul II, *RH*: 16.
[28] John Paul II, *EV*: 12.
[29] John Paul II, *EV*: 12.
[30] John Paul II, *Laborem Exercens*: 1981: 15
[31] Vatican II, *Gaudium et Spes* (hereafter: *GS*): 24.

hope in Thee', that is to say in a communion of which I proclaim the indestructibility.[32]

The various commandments of the Decalogue are really reflections on what it means to be a person in the light of that hope. They express the implications of belonging, through the Covenant, to the indestructible communion of God with his people.

They point to the conditions of a life lived in that communion and to the conditions of any genuinely human relationship with others and with the world:

> The Decalogue must first be understood in the context of the Exodus, God's great liberating event at the centre of the Old Covenant... The 'ten words' point out the conditions of a life freed from the slavery of sin. The Decalogue is a path of life.[33]

Human freedom

The promise of God and the perfect solidarity to which it leads are beyond anything in our experience. But Christian hope does not look to a world unrelated to this one. The Gospel of life does not see our present, bodily existence as a mere preliminary:

> Life in time, in fact, is the fundamental condition, the initial stage and an integral part of the entire unified process of human existence. It is a process which, unexpectedly and undeservedly, is enlightened by the promise and renewed by the gift of divine life, which will reach its full realisation in eternity.[34]

Our freedom could never create the conditions that would permanently and completely satisfy us. The freedom which we have is human not divine. Human freedom is situated. It has an intrinsic relationship to time and space and matter. It does not create its own universe either physically or morally.

The beginning of freedom is to consent to reality. Refusal to do so, refusal to accept that human freedom is situated, would be the real slavery, since it would trap us in the illusion that our freedom was omnipotent:

> To consent is not to capitulate if, in spite of appearances, the world is the possible theatre of liberty. I say: this is my place, I adopt it, I do not surrender, I acquiesce, it is well thus...[35]

---

[32] Marcel, *Homo Viator*: 66.
[33] *CCC*: 2057.
[34] John Paul II, *VS*: 2.
[35] "Consentir n'est point capituler si malgré les apparences le monde est le theâtre possible de la liberté. Je dis: voici mon lieu, je l'adopte; je ne cède pas, j'acquiesce; cela est bien ainsi." P. Ricoeur, *Le Volontaire et L'Involuntaire (Philosophie de la Volonté I)*: Paris: Aubier 1949: 439.

Every free decision is made by choosing among possibilities which present themselves, with abilities that the person has or can acquire, for reasons which suggest themselves. None of these possibilities, abilities or reasons is created out of nothing. On the other hand, to choose a possibility which does not exist, or to try to exercise an ability one does not have, or to act for a reason that does not correspond to reality would be to deceive oneself.

Our free decisions do not float in some kind of featureless ocean; they are carried out in the real world, in a physical world which is shared with other people. They have, therefore, to be measured ultimately against reality, against the truth. Human freedom does not enable us to escape from reality but to deal with it. From one point of view what matters is that people should sincerely try to respond to reality, to one another and to God as truly, as generously, as justly as they can. Mistakes may occur in all sincerity, and these may be entirely blameless. But a choice which is based on a misreading of the situation is nevertheless out of harmony with reality and may, therefore, singularly fail to achieve what one had imagined and hoped it would – and it may do an unanticipated wrong to somebody. The fact that a decision is sincere, for instance, does not ensure that it properly respects the rights of others.

Besides, sincerity is not as easy at it may look. There is a story in the Gospel about a man who was completely at peace with his conscience and one who was not. It begins, "Two men went up to the temple to pray" (*Lk* 18:10). The one whose conscience was troubled went home justified. The Pharisee did not. One may be contented in one's conscience because one has long suppressed the unease which warned that one was not being true to one's deepest reality:

> The fault, therefore, is found elsewhere, deeper: not in the act of this moment, not in the present judgement of conscience, but in that disregarding of my own being which has deafened me to the voice of truth and its inner promptings[36].

It is important that we do not presume insincerity and malice on the part of those with whom we disagree. I was struck by the efforts made by many of the speakers at this conference to understand what had led people to the conclusions and attitudes they had reached. It is an essential step in addressing their positions effectively. In this they are following the headline set by Pope John Paul in *Veritatis Splendor*. Before pointing out where some efforts to rethink moral theology have gone astray, he recognises at the root of that rethinking "certain positive concerns which to a great extent belong to the best tradition of Catholic thought"[37].

[36] "La colpa quindi si trova altrove, più in profondità: non nell' atto del momentoi, non nel presente guidizio della coscienza, ma in quella trascuratezza verso il mio stesso essere, she me ha reso sordo alla voce della verità e ai suoi suggerimenti interiori." J. Ratzinger, 'Elogio della Coscienza', in *Il Sabato*: Rome 16 March 1991: 92.
[37] John Paul II, *VS*: 36.

Every free decision is a response to the invitation of God. "Their conscience is people's most secret core and their sanctuary. There they are alone with God whose voice echoes in their depths"[38]. That promise is addressed to the human being in his or her full reality, not to a spiritual soul but to an embodied person.

"Christ Jesus our hope" (I *Tim* 1:1) was made flesh and lived among us. The Christian creeds express belief in the resurrection of the body. This is not a hope that bypasses the human condition. It is in continuity with it because the fruits of human nature, enterprise, dignity, solidarity and freedom – all the fruits of our life in this world – will be found again in the eternal kingdom, illuminated and transfigured[39].

This world is filled with hope not as something alien but as its deepest purpose. The fact that we are situated in time and space can be seen as a limitation on our freedom. More fundamentally, if we understand what human freedom is, this world is the place where we meet and respond to the promise of God:

> Creation is the foundation of 'all God's saving plans', the 'beginning of the history of salvation' that culminates in Christ. Conversely, the mystery of Christ casts conclusive light on the mystery of creation and reveals the end for which 'in the beginning God created the heavens and the earth': from the beginning, God envisaged the glory of the new creation in Christ.[40]

The freest human acts, the acts of great artistry, the great achievements, are often not those in which a person appears to be battling against hostile and unresponsive material; they are frequently acts in which the person seems to be utterly in harmony with the material through which his or her intention is faithfully expressed. The person who is morally virtuous, like the artist who is skilled in the use of his or her material, does with a certain ease what others would find extremely difficult. The material world is not simply an inert and resistant mass which human freedom struggles to control and direct. It is the range of possibilities and potential within which freedom expresses itself, and can learn to express itself more fully.

The human body can be considered as a physical object like any other. It can be analysed chemically or measured physically; but one could never deduce from a list of chemical components what it means to be human. Neither can an understanding of human freedom be built on the foundation of the body conceived simply as a thing, a mass of matter, manipulated by a disembodied freedom. It is the human being, at once spiritual and embodied, who is addressed by God's promise and it is the whole human being who responds in freedom.

The human body involved in the exercise of freedom is not the body I possess or use, not the body as physically or chemically analysed, but the body *I am*. A free action is not simply a physical event being manipulated or controlled by a disembodied consciousness; it is the expression of my freedom:

[38] Vatican II, *GS*: 16.
[39] Vatican II, *GS*: 39.
[40] *CCC*: 280.

...it is of the essence of the act that it cannot be objectively recognised or understood; it is not thinkable without a personal reference, the reference to an 'it is I who...' This amounts to saying that an act shows itself in its aspect of act only to the agent or to someone who adopts ideally, by sympathy, the agent's perspective.[41]

Responding to hope

The Church, the community of hope, is founded on the realisation that the ultimate purpose of human freedom is to respond to the promise of God. In the perspective of the Gospel of Life, every free human action ultimately has to be understood in the light of the community's "hope in Thee for us". Reflecting on that vision and purpose leads Christians to a deeper understanding

- of human dignity and destiny,
- of the universal communion offered to humanity, and
- of the unity of the human person as situated or embodied.

All of that has important implications for how seriously we take the exercise of human freedom, and for how we understand and approach moral questions.

The deepest meaning of our free decisions is that they are meant to be expressions of our longing for and steps on our journey towards the promise of God. That is why morality makes absolute claims on us. That is why *Psalm* 119, the magnificent hymn of praise to God's law as the psalmists delight, and as "a joy beyond all wealth" (*Ps* 119:14), is a truer approach to morality than one which sees it as a heavy and perhaps arbitrary burden.

The community of hope expresses itself most fully when it assembles to celebrate the Eucharist. This is perhaps the only context where human beings gather explicitly recognising our mortality, our fallibility and sinfulness, our utter dependence on God for the fulfilment of our hope. We join in Christ's unreserved entrustment of himself to the Father – his body given up, his blood poured out.

So, the community of hope looks to the *dignity and destiny* that God gives us in Christ. That hope is not of our making; the path that leads towards it is not something to be invented by each individual. The Way is Christ, to be followed in a giving of self which is without limit, as his was. In the Eucharist we are in the presence of the goal of our journey.

The community of hope looks to the *communion* God offers to all humanity, vindicating all injustices, healing all wounds, perfecting all that is good, the

---

[41] "...il est de l'essence de l'acte de ne pas pouvoir être constaté ou appréhendé objectivement; il n'est pas pensable sans une référence personnelle, la référence à un 'c'est moi qui...' Ceci revient à dire que l'acte ne se présente par son côte acte qu'á l'agent ou à quiconque épouse idéalement, par sympathie, la perspective de l'agent." G. Marcel, *Essai de Philosophie Concrète*. Paris: Gallimard 1967: 165.

fulfilment of every genuinely human longing. It is a fulfilment for all people, living and dead. In the Eucharist we are in the presence of the Risen Christ who calls people of every race and language, of every culture and historical epoch. Indeed the Eucharist is "a foretaste of that heavenly liturgy which is celebrated in the holy city of Jerusalem toward which we journey as pilgrims"[42].

Our hope differs from the utopias which offer perfect peace only to some future generation. Such utopias lack the note of infinity and mystery which would be necessary if they were to be the foundation of moral obligations which make inescapable demands on us: "This is all too finite, we say; we see too well the vacuum beyond"[43].

The community of hope looks to the *resurrection of the body*; it is hope for the whole person. In the Eucharist we are in the presence of Christ, raised body and soul from the dead. Human nature and the human body are not extrinsic to the person; otherwise one would be left with an inadequate picture of human freedom. Freedom would then be regarded as existing in a different, non-physical dimension, using and manipulating the raw datum of the physical body and of the natural world.

This is a crucial point. It was remarked during the conference that God's holiness does not loom large in Proportionalism. This is not surprising. The full meaning of our actions is not found simply in the results which they bring about in the physical world.

To put it another way: the philosophical framework we use to evaluate human actions has to take account of the full richness of what is happening when we exercise our freedom. *An adequate ethics can only be developed on the basis of an adequate philosophy of human existence. That is why Christian Anthropology is fundamental both to the community of hope and to a response to the moral challenge of the culture of death.*

Any assessment that views human action solely, or even primarily, as a mechanism for producing results fails to do it justice. This is one of the basic concerns at the root of the encyclical *Veritatis Splendor*. That is why the encyclical begins by recognising that the question is not primarily about rules to be followed but about the full meaning of life – the full meaning to which the whole person is called to respond.

The encyclical insists that certain kinds of choice are intrinsically wrong. It is not that any particular physical event can always be labelled immoral. Rather it is that the *choice* to behave in certain ways is incapable of being reconciled with the ultimate purpose of human life. Certain kinds of choice deny human dignity, reject universal communion, refuse the truth of one's own being.

If a rock falls, crushing a person to death, one cannot say that his fundamental rights have been violated. If, however, the rock was deliberately made to fall and crush him to death, then he has been deliberately, or directly, killed. In other words, somebody has chosen to kill him. It is the *choice*, either as a means or

---

[42] Vatican II, *Sacrosanctum Concilium*: 1963: 8.
[43] W. James, *Essays on Faith and Morals*. New York: Meridian 1962: 212.

as an end, deliberately to kill a person that is always morally wrong, not the simple fact that someone has died:

> The object of the act of willing is in fact a freely chosen kind of behaviour... By the object of a given moral act, then, one cannot mean a process or an event of the merely physical order, to be assessed on the basis of its ability to bring about a given state of affairs in the outside world.[44]

The consequences of our choices are clearly important and no one is acting morally who ignores the consequences of what he or she chooses to do. But the purpose of our free action goes beyond the changes we may make in the 'outside world'. The purpose is to respond to the promise, to express our "hope in Thee for us".

Actions which imply a denial of someone's place among the 'us' are morally wrong. In relation to the fundamental demands of morality "we are all absolutely equal"[45]. A refusal to accept that equality is in contradiction with the meaning of the Eucharistic celebration[46].

The community of hope must, therefore, regard human freedom with absolute seriousness. But, and perhaps it is this more than anything else that we need to recover, it should regard human freedom as a gift which responds to *the Gift* which fulfils and surpasses our most ambitious hopes for ourselves and for the human race. That is the meaning of human freedom and action. Our reflection on it has to do justice to that meaning. Our free acts express who we are and who we would wish to be. They shape us. They express our acceptance or rejection of the invitation of God, the Absolute 'Thou', and our acceptance or rejection of the 'us', which is the communion of humanity with God:

> It has been rightly pointed out that freedom is not only the choice of one or another particular action; it is also, within that choice, *a decision about oneself* and a setting of one's own life for or against the Good, for or against the Truth, and ultimately for or against God.

> Human acts are moral acts because they express and determine the goodness or evil of the individual who performs them. They do not produce a change merely in the state of affairs outside of man but, to the extent that they are deliberate choices, they give moral definition to the very person who performs them, determining his *profound spiritual traits*.[47]

---

[44] John Paul II, *VS*: 78.
[45] John Paul II, *VS*: 98.
[46] Cf. Jn 13: 1–15; Jm 2: 1–9.
[47] John Paul II, *VS*: 65, 71. cf. Vatican II, *GS*: 35. Cf. also G. McCool, 'The Philosophy of the Human Person in Karl Rahner's Theology', in W. Meissner (ed) *Foundations for a Psychology of Grace*. London: Paulist Press 1966: 168: "What is most precious and important in a free act is not what the agent brings into being in the external world by means of it. Rather it is the attitude which the agent imprints on his own spirit in its fulfilment."

Morality is not an arbitrary, alien imposition. As we try to find our way through the labyrinths of bioethics, we need to remember that we are not negotiating a maze into which we have been placed by some god who is toying with us. We are trying to discover the implications of our own humanity and to respond to the Creator who made us so that we could be happy with him forever. We need to hear the words of Moses at the end of his life in which he shows the law of God, not as something alien but as being within our deepest selves. He also, incidentally, points to the contradiction we can find in the modern use of the phrase 'pro-choice'. It is the very meaning and purpose of choice, of human freedom, to be *for life*:

> This law which I am laying down for you today is neither obscure for you nor beyond your reach... No the word is very near to you, it is in your mouth and in your heart for you to put into practice... Today I call heaven and earth to witness against you: I am offering you life or death, blessing or curse. Choose life, then, so that you and your descendants may live, in the love of Yahweh your God, obeying his voice, holding fast to him; for in this your life consists... (*Dt* 30: 11, 14, 19, 20).

The Culture of Life

2. Promoting the Culture of Life

10

The role of the Bishop in promoting the Gospel of Life

ARCHBISHOP GEORGE PELL

Declining birth rates

OSHIMA IS A small Japanese island, 32 kilometres long, cradled between the large islands of Honshu, Shikoku and Kyushu. There we can confront the future. With Germany, Japan has the most quickly ageing population in the world, because the Japanese are living longer and having fewer and fewer children. Their fertility rate has fallen to 1.39; a rate of 2.1 children per woman is necessary to keep the population stable.

Oshima is the Island of the Old, with the oldest population in the oldest country. The barber with the cutthroat razor is 84 years of age, as is the papergirl. The taxi driver is only 83 years old and the policeman a sprightly 60 year old. In the town of Towa, at the eastern end of the island, octogenarians outnumber teenagers by more than three to one, septuagenarians by seven to one, half the population is over 65. Towa had a population of 20,600 in 1945; 55 years later the population is 5,500.[1]

Although the trends in Oshima have been worsened by youth emigration for work, Oshima is not a social aberration, a development which goes against the current. Following present patterns Japan's population will be halved by the end of the twenty-first century – and so will Western Europe's!

Thirty years ago, when fears of uncontrollable population growth were at their height, the world's population had already commenced its long and steady slide to zero population growth and to the negative population growth – that is, depopulation – that lies beyond that point. In the decade from 1965 to 1975, world birth rates decreased by 13 percent, with decline occurring in 127 countries.[2] In 1996, the United Nations forecast zero population growth for the world as a whole by 2040, with population peaking at 7.7 billion, an increase of less than two billion people on the current world population of 5.9 billion. Thereafter population will decline by 25 percent in each successive generation, giving an expected world population in 2100 of 5.6 billion. This anticipated

---

[1] R. L. Parry, 'Old World Order'. *The Australian Magazine, Weekend Australian*, January 8–9, 2000.

[2] R. Brunton, *The End of the Overpopulation Crisis?* (IPA Backgrounder Series). Melbourne: Institute of Public Affairs 1998: 16.

decline in population does not factor in the results of war, famine, environmental disaster or epidemics such as AIDS.[3] It is a product of a drastic decline in fertility which will unfold, to use the optimistic language of the UN document, "under conditions of orderly progress".[4]

This dramatic fall in birthrates is occurring in a context where people are living longer and longer, a corollary of the 'health explosion' modern people are so fortunate to enjoy.[5] The combination of low fertility and longer lives will mean "a radical ageing of the human population – a shift whose magnitude would be without historical precedent." In 1900, the global median age was about 20 years, not much more than what it had been in all other eras. By 2040 it will be over 42 years. Germany and Japan have the oldest populations in the world today with a median age just under 40. By 2050, however, the population of the developing world will have a median age of 41, while Japan's median age will be 53, Germany's 55 and Italy's 58.[6]

As recently as the late 1960s, the total fertility rate – that is, the number of births per woman per lifetime[7] – was 5.0. Today it has fallen to 2.7. In some developing countries, this decline has been more spectacular still. Mexico has dropped from 6.8 to 2.8; India from 5.7 to 3.1, and China (with its brutally enforced "one-child norm"), from 6.1 to 1.8.[8] In the developed world the fall in total fertility rates has occurred over a longer period, and today every developed nation has a total fertility rate below the replacement rate of 2.1. Ireland's fertility rate is now 1.93. With a total fertility rate of 2.0 the USA is at the high end of the

---

[3] Since 1980 16.3 million have died from AIDS. In sub-Saharan Africa life expectancy is seven years less because of AIDS. This region has 70 percent of those infected with HIV, and 13.7 million dead from the disease. In Asia there were 1.4 million new infections in 1999 and it is spreading into Papua New Guinea. World Health Organisation & UNAIDS, *Epidemic Update*. December, 1999.

[4] United Nations (Department of Economic and Social Affairs, Population Division) *World Population Prospects: The 1996 Revision*. In these UN studies, projections are always given in the form of 'low', 'medium' and 'high' variants. I have cited the low variants throughout, following the practice adopted in the expert commentary consulted in preparing this paper. The UN itself recommends the use of the medium variants, but describes each of the variants offered as "provid[ing] reasonable and plausible future trends." For the sake of completeness, the low, medium and high variants offered in the 1994 Revision and the 1996 Revision of *World Population Prospects*, together with the variants in the as yet (at the time of writing) unpublished 1998 Revision (available at www.undp.org/popin) for world population in 2050 are as follows:

1994	7.9 billion	9.8 billion	11.9 billion
1996	7.7 billion	9.4 billion	11.2 billion
1998	7.3 billion	8.9 billion	10.7 billion

[5] P. G. Peterson, *Gray Dawn*. New York: Times Books, 1999: 41.

[6] N. Eberstadt 'Research: Too Few People?' (December 1997) *Prospect*: 52.

[7] The total fertility rate is generally considered a more reliable indicator than simple birth rates – numbers of children per 1,000 women – because the latter can be skewed by changes in the age distribution of women.

[8] Peterson, *Gray Dawn*: 47.

scale for the developed world, while in Japan the rate is 1.4, Germany 1.3, and Italy 1.2.[9] In 1993, the rate in Bologna was 0.9.

As couples have only one or two children – or none at all[10] – the family itself will be drastically narrowed and lengthened in its shape. If the trends in those countries with the lowest fertility rates – Italy for example – continue, then within two generations more than three in every five children will have "neither brothers nor sisters, nor uncles nor aunts, nor cousins." Projecting the fertility rates of the European Union over two generations only slightly alters this scenario: "about 40 percent of European children would have no collateral blood relatives [and] less than one sixth would have a brother or a sister and a cousin."[11] The genealogical tree "will be all stem and no branch".[12]

Contrary to some expectations, the economic and social problems caused by these enormous demographic changes are not ones that can be easily offset by increased immigration. A report of the United Nations Population Division earlier this year makes it very clear that while the numbers of immigrants required to offset general population decline in most Western countries in the short term is comparable to or less than the levels of the past, significantly larger numbers are required to offset the decline in the working-age population in the longer term. The level of migration needed to offset population ageing is extremely large, "and in all cases entails vastly more immigration than occurred in the past."[13] I do not think I need to spell out the political problems that immigration at these sorts of levels will create even in the most enlightened and liberal Western countries.

In its 1998 Declaration on the fall in fertility, the Pontifical Council for the Family raised the question of how an increase in a population's mean age might affect "its psychological profile." "Moroseness," which the Declaration describes as "the lack of intellectual, economic, scientific and social dynamism and reduced creativity," is likely to be a conspicuous feature of elderly societies, and may "already be at work" in those countries leading the trend.[14] In Australia depression is already a significant problem costing $5 billion a year nationally. The main author of a UN report on which the Declaration draws, Jean-Claude Chesnais, Director of Research at the French National Institute for the Study of Demography, puts this point simply: "You cannot have a successful world

[9] Ibid. 48.

[10] Latest (at the time of writing) Australian figures indicate that 16 percent of women are having only one child, and 22 percent are having none at all (Australian Bureau of Statistics figures cited in the *Age*, October 12, 1999).

[11] Eberstadt, 'Research: Too Few People?': 55.

[12] Peterson, *Gray Dawn*: 57.

[13] United Nations (Department of Economic and Social Affairs, Population Division) *Replacement Migration*. March, 2000.

[14] Pontifical Council for the Family *Declaration on Decrease of Fertility in the World*. Rome, February 27, 1998. Published in *L'Osservatore Romano* (English language weekly edition), April 16–22, 1998.

without children in it."[15] This point is dramatically illustrated in P. D. James' novel *The Children of Men* (1993), which is set in 2021 in a world where universal male sterility has not seen a child born for over a generation.

The American social critic Gertrude Himmelfarb has also pointed out that, almost certainly, the family in the Western world will undergo a 'second' revolution to deepen the impoverishment it has suffered after the first revolution that is "reflected in the statistics of divorce, illegitimacy, single-parenthood and cohabitation." "In addition to the fatherless family," Himmelfarb writes, "we now have to worry about a family without peers."[16] The family "has been the primary and indispensable instrument for socializing people," but in a world where the vast majority of children find themselves without brothers and sisters, cousins, uncles or aunts, the "extended bonds of obligation and [the] reciprocal resources – including emotional resources" that play such an important part in a child's life and development will be enormously diminished. The nuclear family is sometimes criticized for its failings compared to earlier forms of family arrangement, but "the nuclear family does not begin to approach the limits of social atomization which may await us in a depopulating world."[17] Already in mainland China with its ruthless 'one child' policy, there is concern over the long-term behaviour of the 'little princes', the pampered single sons.

I have commenced with this thumbnail sketch of family life in the Western world because it is the overwhelmingly important context in which we conduct the struggle for life and battle against the culture of death.

In Australia at least, few people, even Catholics, realize that no country in the Western world is producing enough children to maintain a stable population. Even fewer realize that if present trends continue depopulation consequences will be drastic for the Western world, representing a colossal shift (ultimately) in the balance of power. This is the other side of the coin; an unspoken motive for the First World enthusiasm to limit population in the Third World. Like the upper middle classes in nineteenth century England, the rich Western countries do not want too many unruly poor, even at a distance! Our young people are well aware of the dangers of over-population, especially in Asia, and ignorant of what is happening at home. We too must not spend our time rearranging the deck chairs.

---

[15] Quoted in Peterson, *Gray Dawn*: 247 n19. James' novel provides an imaginative (and extreme) illustration of the moroseness that attends life in a world without children. The inescapable sense that the world is winding down and the effects this has on those remaining are well drawn, but zero or negative population growth do not quite mean a world without children. In contrast though, Eberstadt ('Research: Too Few People?': 55) has observed that as fertility in the modern world is falling, so too is childlessness. Although an increasing number of couples remain childless voluntarily, sub-replacement fertility primarily means that almost everyone will have a first or second baby if they can, but very few will seek a third.

[16] Gertrude Himmelfarb, 'The Ghost of Parson Malthus'. *Times Literary Supplement*, January 23, 1999.

[17] Eberstadt, 'Research: Too Few People?': 55.

The religious situation in Australia

This background might be of some interest to those of other countries and provides the context for the three suggestions I will make.

I now want to spend a little time on the religious situation in Australia and the state of pro-life sentiment there. Many, or most, pro-life activists have come from the ranks of practising Christians. Here our base is shrinking and anti-life attitudes are influencing even churchgoers and especially our young people. Christians are people of hope, champions of life for today and tomorrow, but none of us can choose the times in which we live and die. Apparently, a Chinese curse is that one should live in interesting times. We are on the brink of even more interesting times in the struggle for life, immersed in mighty forces of social, indeed global change, which are largely beyond our control.

One of the most important of these forces is the (in the Western world at least) apparent waning of religious belief and *commitment* – as opposed to religious *sentiment*, which as the burgeoning of new-age cults and fads shows, is probably as strong as ever. In Australia, which has a population of a little over 19 million, the religious situation is within the parameters for the West, somewhere between the situations in the USA and the UK. The number of Australians who believe in God is large but falling. In 1999, the figure was 74 percent, down from around 80 percent in the early 1990s.[18] In the USA, by contrast, the figure is closer to 94 percent. The most recent census (1996) put the total number of Christians in Australia at 70 percent, down from 74 percent in 1991. As one might expect, not all of these regularly practise their religion in a formal way.

Catholic religious practice in particular, as measured by regular Mass attendance, has declined from about 55–60 percent in the 1950s and early 1960s to 18 percent nationally.[19] Many 'R.Cs' are not retired Catholics, but resting, relaxed or reluctant Catholics. It is important to understand this practice rate comparatively. It means that every Sunday in the Melbourne Archdiocese, about 180,000 Catholics go to Mass.[20] The number of Anglicans worshipping each Sunday in Melbourne is probably not more than 30,000, a practice rate of under 5 percent.[21] In every Catholic parish there is a hard core of dedicated believers and it is these people who keep parish life alive

The major difference between the religious situation in Australia and that in the United States is the weakness of Protestantism in Australia. Catholics are now the largest religious denomination in the country, accounting for 27 percent of the population, and at the last census the number of people who said they were Catholics increased by over 4 percent. All the major non-Catholic but Christian denominations saw their number of affiliates decline, some by less than one

[18] National Church Life Survey figures published in the *Sydney Morning Herald*, March 30, 1999.
[19] H. Mol, *Religion in Australia*. Melbourne: Nelson, 1971: 13–14. In 1954, according to Mol, Gallup Poll estimated that 75 percent of Catholics attended Mass weekly.
[20] Catholic Research Office for Pastoral Planning, Archdiocese of Melbourne, *1996 Mass Count*.
[21] P. J. Hughes, *Religion in Australia: Facts and Figures*. Melbourne: Christian Research Association, 1997: 6–7.

percent (the Lutherans), some by almost 8 percent (the Presbyterians), most by 3–5 percent. The only growth was recorded by the Pentecostals and the Jehovah's Witnesses, but although the percentage increase was significant (16 and 11.6 percent respectively) the numbers involved are comparatively small.[22] I do not rejoice in this at all. Unlike the United States, Australia has no real equivalent to the Southern Baptists, the evangelicals and therefore no protestant basis for building something akin to Reagan's 'moral majority', or even a powerful, organized, minority mass movement.

One of the most significant developments is the growth in the number of those stating they had no religion. Between 1991 and 1996 this group grew from almost 13 percent of the population to 17 percent – an increase of 35.5 percent in five years. This group is larger than every protestant denomination, but not the Anglicans, and ranks number 3 in size after the Catholic and Anglican populations.[23]

The pro-life situation in Australia

At 19.7 abortions per 1,000 women aged 15–44 per year, Australia's abortion rate is at the higher end of First World abortion rates – three to four times the rate in Holland and Belgium, and around double the rate in Scotland, Finland, Canada and New Zealand.[24] The Australian abortion rate is significantly higher than that in England, Wales, Norway and Denmark, and is comparable with Sweden and the United States. With a total abortion rate of 584 per 1,000 women (conservatively), the prevalence of abortion in Australia, after taking into account the proportion who have more than one, is estimated at approximately one third of women at some stage in their life-time.[25] This means there is a huge emotional investment in these issues and often a grim determination not to hear the truth, especially from the Church.

Meanwhile the abortion industry is promoting a radical increase in the variety and quantity of abortion, at all stages of gestation. We are also amongst the world leaders in assisted reproductive technology, and therefore in embryo exploitation and destruction. The advent of cloning promises numerous further developments. Australia is also one of the few places in the world to have legally tolerated euthanasia at one time in one of its territories and there is a continuing campaign to legalize it throughout Australia. But the overturning of the euthanasia legislation of the Northern Territory by the Federal Parliament, with the support of the Prime Minister and Opposition Leader, was a stunning victory.

[22] Australian Bureau of Statistics, *Australia Now – A Statistical Profile.* 1999.
[23] Ibid.
[24] National Health and Medical Research Council, *Termination of Pregnancy Services in Australia.* 1995 (draft report) and 1996 (final report). While this report has proven unreliable in several places due to its advocacy of abortion, it is probably conservative on abortion rates because these figures do not include unreported surgical abortions and abortions induced by other means such as the IUD and the morning-after pill.
[25] Ibid.

Attitudes of Australians to life issues

There are three constituencies everywhere in the struggle for life, present to different degrees in different countries and at different times, i.e. the minority of committed people who oppose us; the majority who are often confused, sometimes hostile, sometimes indifferent, usually eclectic and at least partially open to persuasion; and the hard core of pro-life forces, preferably a coalition of people of all beliefs and no religious belief.

However, in Australia at least, it remains true that the strength of the pro-life forces comes from the Catholic community, where attitudes to moral questions are changing as moral uncertainty and confusion gather pace, especially among the young. To me, it is no coincidence that Holland, where Catholic faith and practice have collapsed so radically, is the euthanasia capital of the world. In Australia we have a lot of work to do to keep our home fires burning.

It has been established that one in three Australian women has an abortion in her lifetime. So everyone knows someone who has had an abortion, whether they realize it or not. And that means there is a huge emotional investment in these issues and often a grim determination not to hear the Church. Abortion also seems to be one of those issues on which catechesis has varied in quality and effectiveness.

The National Social Science Survey of 1993 and National Church Life Surveys of 1991 and 1996 found that the vast majority of Australian Church attenders think that human life is sacred and that access to abortion should be severely restricted. However, most church-attenders believe abortion is okay in the case of serious defect in the child, and a significant proportion think terminally ill people should be able to choose to die whatever that means precisely. The same studies have shown that practising Pentecostals and Baptists are much more anti-abortion and anti-euthanasia than Anglicans and members of the Uniting Church.

In the 1996 Catholic Church Life Survey many Catholic church-goers declared themselves at least partly at odds with Catholic teaching on abortion and euthanasia. Only 47 percent of Mass attenders said that they thought abortion is always wrong, and another 42 percent said it is justified (only) in extreme circumstances; only 51 percent of Mass attenders said they disagreed with voluntary euthanasia.[26]

While there is some comfort in finding that the more frequently one attends Mass the more likely it is that one will oppose abortion and euthanasia, and in the more general finding that Catholic and evangelical church-attenders are still much more pro-life than the general community, the churches clearly face

---

[26] M. C. Mason, *Confidential Report to the Australian Catholic Bishops Conference on the Catholic Church Life Survey.* Unpublished. 1996. This Report is one of a series by Fr Michael Mason CSSR, who is Principal Investigator of the Survey. A new survey was conducted in 2001, but results are not yet available. Selected results from the 2001 survey will be made available progressively at www.ncls.org.au

an enormous pastoral task of preaching the Gospel of Life even to their own members, and in offering people real alternatives to the culture of death and its supposed 'solutions'.

The capacity of a bishop to influence public opinion, as distinct from fostering the faith and moral beliefs of his community, depends on many things, but especially on the size and wealth and education of his own national faith community. A well-educated, prosperous Catholic community of 30, 40 or 50 percent of the population should be able to do more than a poor minority of 5 percent. Whether it will achieve more is another question!

We know grace builds on nature and the religious decline in so many places indicates not only a weakness of faith, but also that the traditional sociological forces of parish, school and family, supplemented by the activities of the religious orders, are being over-run and are no longer adequate. We need new sociological agents, new sociological defences, as well as interior faith renewal. One part of this response is to use the secular media more creatively.

Abortion research

We all know that political parties do extensive polling to investigate public opinion; sometimes, it is claimed cynically, to devise policies which suit public opinion and enhance the chances of election or re-election, rather than responding to a situation with unpopular measures.

My suggestion is not simply to discover public opinion through short questions on the whole range of life issues (results which we know to be heavily influenced by the wording of the question), but to do extensive polling through long interviews with different representative individuals, e.g. young, old; male, female; Christian or neo-pagan; pro-life, pro-choice or indifferent. Here we should be able to discover their individual points of view, why they hold them, and most importantly, what arguments they regard as persuasive, irrelevant or counterproductive.

There is a legion of particular issues which might be explored.

Are logical arguments or anecdotes more effective especially with the middle ground? In advertising how much of the message should be positive, how much negative?

In an age of individualism how strong is the reluctance to judge another person? Are men particularly reluctant to impose their views on women? How pervasive is the conviction that mitigating circumstances can undermine any position of principle? Is the invocation of church authority a help or a hindrance? How influential is medical advice?

Pro-life groups in Australia have traditionally emphasized the rights of the unborn child. Does this resonate with the general public or do they see the issue almost exclusively as belonging to the woman involved? Does this mean that arguments should be focused more on how bad abortion is for the woman rather than on the killing of the aborted?

Is it useful or counterproductive for pro-life forces to emphasize the grief and guilt of the woman involved in abortion, or would it be more effective with the middle ground we are attempting to convince, simply to acknowledge the intensely difficult situation of these mothers, building on the consensus that nearly everyone believes that fewer abortions would be better.

Does it help to compare abortions with the Holocaust? Does it help in opposing euthanasia to compare it with abortion? How frequently, if at all, should men or members of the Church hierarchy be used in advertising against abortion? Is it effective with public opinion, or counter-productive, for bishops to address street rallies on life issues?

At a different level, how effective is the argument that a woman has a right to keep her baby, to resist pressures for abortion? How should we approach the important question of the father's role in deciding the fate of his child?

Are pro-life supporters as confident in expressing their views in public as the supporters of abortion and euthanasia? Do Christians recognize that their faith brings important moral consequences for daily living, including life issues, or is their faith compartmentalized, isolated from many of the difficult life decisions?

The answers to these questions are important for any strategy to influence public opinion. After discovering these answers, where do we start? One fascinating suggestion is to insert paid advertisements onto the evening radio frequencies listened to by young adults.

Many of you here will be familiar with the article by Paul Swope which was published in *First Things* in 1998, outlining the strategy he uses.[27] It is woman-centred and designed to deter pregnant women from proceeding to an abortion, rather than influencing opinion more generally. His approach is also based on a series of in-depth one-on-one interviews with people, the results of which he claims can be accepted at a better than 95 percent confidence level.

These studies help us understand the contradiction in many people's thinking who simultaneously believe that abortion is killing and also believe that it should be legally available. Swope points out that many young women have developed a sense of identity that emphasizes control and which does not include being a mother – at least not until other priority goals have been reached. "The sudden intrusion of motherhood is perceived as a complete loss of control over their present and future selves." The possibility of accepting an unplanned pregnancy is seen to mean the end of all their other aspirations – university, travel, career. If the pregnancy is accepted, then their life is "over," a feeling often reinforced by family, friends and society at large. For a woman in such a crisis, there is felt to be no real choice. Abortion is a matter of survival.

Swope claims this is why the traditional approach emphasizing the humanity of the child in the womb and the evil of killing him has not made any decisive impression on opinion. It is seen by many as an unfeeling and judgmental response to women facing "death."

[27] P. Swope 'Abortion: A Failure to Communicate.' 82 (April, 1998) *First Things*. 31–35.

Swope suggests we need to reframe the debate to address the crisis of a woman with an unplanned pregnancy. She needs to be encouraged and reassured that going through with pregnancy will not mean the "end" of her life, and that she can regain control over her life by actually deciding to accept the baby. TV advertisements developing these themes seem to have enjoyed some success and although Swope's approach is regarded by some in the pro-life movement as controversial,[28] I think we need to look at it carefully if we are serious about making ground on abortion. It is not particularly useful to answer questions which people are not asking, even though a long-term strategy might be to encourage other questions.

Let me now conclude by mentioning three areas for foundational spiritual activity in the pro-life struggle, where a bishop might usefully be engaged.

Faith and reason

The recent Encyclical, *Fides et Ratio* (1998), was addressed to bishops. Even today for some, and certainly for the Enlightenment thinkers of the past, it would seem strange that a pope, even a philosopher pope, should be urging Catholic bishops to defend reason.

This is now an important human as well as religious task for bishops because truth is under attack; indeed the very idea that there is truth at all is hotly disputed. This is reflected not merely in an explicit post-modernism, but even in Christian circles where an incoherent relativism flourishes. "What is important is that you are comfortable with that." "It depends on how each person feels." The Church is a partner with the rest of humanity in service of truth and should be a voice for truth.

This is not suggesting that the defence of truth is important because it is a useful moral, political or therapeutic tool (although for our purposes in the struggle for life, it is certainly such). The systematic and intellectual search for truth develops from our sense of awe and wonder, which is rooted in our nature; such a search is also life enhancing. We are born to know and it is one of humanity's greatest achievements (and a blessing) that we know so much. Knowledge as such is no threat or insult to God our Creator; rather it is a tribute to God, reflecting the development and use of gifts he has given us.

The Holy Father in this Encyclical spoke of faith and reason as "two wings on which the human spirit rises to the contemplation of truth."[29] However, they do not have the balanced function of a pair of wings, because reason has a certain primacy and cannot be judged by anything other than itself.[30]

---

[28] See for example S. Klusendorf 'The Vanishing Pro-Life Activist.' 22:1 (nd) *Christian Research Journal.*

[29] *Fides et Ratio*, Preamble.

[30] H. Ramsay, 'The Philosophical Significance of *Fides et Ratio*'. XXXIV/100 (1999) *Philippiniana Sacra*: 79.

While the heart still can have its reasons which reason does not know, all those interested in the struggle for life, as well as our opponents who often stress adult autonomy, are interested in the reasons we adduce to support our claims. If the concept of truth, and especially moral truth, is removed from popular consciousness, the pro-life struggle becomes increasingly difficult and degenerates into a battle of personal preferences, even feelings.

Primacy of conscience

In England you have an intriguing writer and intellectual, Felipe Fernandez-Armesto, who writes extensively about the cultural hegemony of the United States, especially in small countries like Australia. He believes this culture of the United States is self-subverted by two genuine heresies, the Lone Ranger heresy and the Donald Duck heresy.

The Lone Ranger is the successful man, who claims that he did it all by himself, the outsider who does not need society, who owes nothing to anyone.

My concern is with the consequences of the second heresy, the Donald Duck heresy, in the wider community, but especially among Catholics. Donald Duck is warm-hearted and well disposed, believes in the natural goodness of man and has an unshakeable conviction of self-righteousness. He means well and he is likeable, despite his indulgence in all the vices of individualist excess; he knows it all, he is noisy, often bad-tempered at the incomprehension surrounding him. His activity is often disastrous, for himself and for others, but he means well. In the comic strips this is sufficient for all to be forgiven as we go to the next episode. But in real life this is a recipe for disaster.

Too many Donald Ducks produce the 'feel good' society, which works to remove personal guilt, anything that would make people feel uncomfortable so that complacent self-satisfaction is a virtue, confession is replaced by therapy and self-reproach by self-discovery.[31]

Let me translate the Donald Duck heresy into the terms of contemporary public debate on morality in Australia, where a goodly number of Catholics publicly espouse the primacy of conscience as a Catholic doctrine, which has been long taught by the Church.

It is of course one of the principal targets in Pope John Paul II's marvellous encyclical, *Veritatis Splendor* (1993). Only truth, or the Word of God has primacy, is the ultimate rule of action, while individual conscience is a proximate norm, necessary but insufficient. Even a genuine searcher for truth can be mistaken, sometimes with disastrous consequences.

In this encyclical the Holy Father rejected certain currents of modern thought that absolutize freedom of conscience, so that it becomes the supreme tribunal of moral judgement, where the claims of truth are displaced by the criteria of sincerity,

---

[31] F. Fernandez-Armesto, 'America can still save the world.' *Spectator*, January 8, 2000.

authenticity and being at peace with oneself. He rejects this quasi-idolatry of freedom and sincerity.[32]

This primacy of conscience and rejection of moral truth, this repudiation of an objective moral order is heavily influenced by secular intellectual currents, e.g. relativism and the deconstructionists as well as the imperatives of advertising in a consumer society. People often do not like being told what is right or wrong, or what to do, by authority figures, clerical or otherwise.

When Church leaders, clerical or lay, lapse into silence or are unable to argue convincingly for moral principles, even pro-life supporters who are pro-family and opposed to abortion and euthanasia, can be tempted to see their position as an individual one, which they would not want to force onto others, especially by public legislation. This is no basis for action.

Theology of the body

In his recent biography of John Paul II, George Weigel claims the Holy Father's theology of the body represents his most important theological contribution or development.[33] As Archbishop of Kracow, Karol Wojtyla served on the committee established in the late 1960s to reconsider the Church's teaching on artificial contraception. He was part of the minority whose advice was accepted by Pope Paul VI. Paul VI's reiteration of the traditional teaching on artificial contraception in 1968 after years of delay and rising expectations of change provoked a crisis of confidence like the Galileo case – one that has been compounded later by both pastoral and catechetical failure. Disagreement over this particular moral issue has played a major part in discrediting and casting doubt on the teaching capacity of the Church on moral matters especially on sexuality. However, what is in dispute now within the Catholic community is not only natural family planning, but the whole range of Christian teachings on life and sexuality.

There is very little understanding in the public mind, even within the Catholic community, of the connection between the Pill as the trigger of a contraceptive mentality and the evil consequences for society of this contraceptive and irresponsible mentality. So a major task for the Church is to encourage people more and more to see the wisdom, both human and divine, of this particular teaching. John Paul II's Theology of the Body is a powerful aid to this purpose.

John Paul developed his theology of the body over four years at 130 papal audiences, beginning on 4th September, 1979.[34] The central point is that human sexual love, with the Sacrament of Marriage, is an icon of the inner life of the Holy Trinity; that is, of God himself.

The cultural revolution of the 1960s and 70s saw the nature and limits of freedom hotly contested, especially in the area of sexuality. Modern mythology has it that the Pill freed women from the threat of pregnancy, although in fact

[32] *Veritatis Splendor*, §§32; 35; 52; 54–64.
[33] G. Weigel, *Witness to Hope*. New York: Harper Collins, 1999: 333–343.
[34] John Paul II, *The Theology of the Body*. Boston: Pauline Books, 1997.

it was not removed, but radically reduced. The intolerance of limits in the sexual realm, often taken as a given today, is relentlessly reinforced by advertising, popular music and films.

In this context it is increasingly difficult to get a hearing for Christian teaching on sexuality even among young Catholics, where incomprehension of such Catholic teaching is a major reason for disaffection and lapsing from practice, but I think that the hurts and harms caused by sexual freedom and its illusory promises offer us a unique long-term opportunity to offer healing, especially to those who have been wounded, and therefore to evangelize, initially with minorities, just as the Church grew in the Roman Empire. Church growth will only follow the faithful living and effective presentation of the fullness of Catholic teaching on life. No growth will follow from its dilution and deformation; or a tactful silence!

God created us male and female "from the beginning" (Mt 19:3–6). Our divine provenance imbues us with many wonderful privileges over other creatures. One is the human capacity to create "mirrors", to express and reflect God's creative power. Because we can think and choose freely we are also images of God.

It helps us to understand the nature of human sexuality by reflecting on Adam's original solitude – neither the company of God nor the animals could console him. It was only repaired through the creation of Eve. Man and woman become images of God in the act of communion together, which requires a radical giving of the self and receiving of the other. We can see the oneness of man and woman in their original nakedness in the Garden, in the original solitude that brought the one to the other and in the original unity that followed. The 'bodyliness' of this unity is part of God's scheme and it highlights that the body itself is not evil, despite tinea, piles and dandruff.

Original sin disrupts the unity between man and God and between man and woman. Human flourishing depends on self-giving, not self-assertion, and this is particularly true in sexual love. Original sin compromises our capacity for self-giving, inclining us to treat the other as an object. It also introduces shame into the equation. Genesis is very clear that prior to eating from the tree of knowledge Adam and Eve were quite comfortable in their nakedness with each other. The intrusion of sin disrupted the unity between them and led them to see themselves no longer as one together, but as two separate creatures, who felt ashamed of their nakedness before each other and before God. This separation of the one into two automatically opens the possibility of treating and regarding the other as an object rather than as part of one's self.

In his catechesis on the theology of the body John Paul provoked considerable controversy with his warning against adultery of the heart (Mt 5:27–8). This was possible, he said, even within marriage where otherwise faithful spouses treat each other as objects in their sexual relations. The lines from Matthew's Gospel where Our Lord warns against committing adultery in one's heart form a key reference for John Paul.

When love turns to lust male and female differences become a source of confrontation. The reality of sin makes the world a place of toil and fear and the human heart a battlefield between love and lust, self-mastery and self-assertion, freedom as giving and freedom as taking. Lust does not desire the good of the other – it uses the other as an object of pleasure. Christian ethics redeems sexuality from the trap of lust – just as purity of heart redeems the body.

Living the good life as created beings depends on living within the limits and according to the truths of the human condition. Purity of heart and the capacity to channel desires towards personal self-mastery in holiness and honour are part of the high calling of the Christian life. These remain necessities, despite the promises of a false humanism which claims that human nature has neither limits nor boundaries, being infinitely plastic and malleable; a vain and counter-productive attempt to liberate humans from guilt.

Marriage is the most ancient sacrament. In the twelfth chapter of Mark's Gospel Jesus is asked who the widow of seven brothers will be married to in heaven. He replies that there is no marriage in heaven (*Mk* 12:18–26). This is not because we lose our bodies in heaven, but because there self-giving and reciprocity are perfect, first of all with God and then with others. There we undergo a divinization in some form to become like the Risen Christ.

Celibacy in this context is an icon of heaven. It is lived in this life for the kingdom in anticipation of the heavenly state. It aspires to the perfect inter-subjectivity which constitutes the final communion of saints. Lived well it leads to a spiritual paternity and maternity.

This is also prefigured in the chasteness that marriage demands of spouses. Chastity, in the form of self-mastery, is essential to genuine self-giving. What does a man or a woman's "yes" mean if they are unable to say "no"? As self-giving, marriage is an icon of the union of God and his people Israel – the Church; and an icon of the inner life of the Trinity. It reveals God's purposes in creation and redemption. Proper sexual love is an act of worship.

There is a painful ignorance among our Catholic youth, and many older, on the rationale for the Christian teaching on life and sexuality. Often it is seen as an old-fashioned list of prohibitions, denying people their rights to sexual activity.

The theology of the body needs to be worked into our secondary school catechesis showing that the essential linkage of the love between a man and woman, sexual intercourse and new life is not only the best preparation for life-long marriage and children, but also something sacred and important reflecting the very life of the one true God.

Conclusion

Let me conclude on another note.

In Australia at least, we might have understated the religious dimension in our argumentation in the struggle for life. Everywhere in the English speaking world there is a majority of self-declared Christians; most of them and even the non-religious, especially outside the circle of the opinion makers, are not truly secularized, but open in a muddled way to transcendence, superstitious and sentimental, as well as sometimes exercising genuine religious insight. Certainly they are moved more by their heartstrings than their head, often as open to religion and generalized Christian aspirations, as they are to philosophical argumentation. I believe we do a disservice to God and probably to the pro-life cause, if God is never mentioned in our pro-life argumentation. But that might be another topic for another occasion, to be argued differently in different countries. It also goes without saying that prayer, conversion and Christian living, are mighty prerequisites for our struggle.

My task, as I saw it, was to suggest a few strategies from my Australian experience that might work in different contexts. We need grace and hope, but we also need ideas and confidence and strategies for our struggle, not as an alternative to our basic Christian calling, but as an essential dimension of our response to Christ's gospel message. We should all be grateful to the Linacre Centre for their help in this area.

II

The role of the priest in promoting the culture of life

RICHARD M. HOGAN

I WOULD LIKE to begin with a story.

It is not generally known, but Mikhail Gorbachev was not the first Soviet Premier to visit a Pope at the Vatican. Actually, one day in the early 1960s, Nikita Khruschev arrived in Rome and was taken secretly to the Papal apartments in the Vatican for a luncheon meeting with Pope John XXIII. The luncheon was far more elaborate than most luncheons. It was what the Italians call *Pranzo* – a feast. Seated at two ends of a very long Renaissance table with engraved woods, the head of the Soviet Union, dedicated to the destruction of the Church, and the Pope, the head of the Church to be destroyed, shared first the antipasti, then the soup course, followed by several varieties of pasta, the fish course, the meat course, dessert which consisted of bread, cheese and fruit. Of course, with all the courses, there were fine choices of Italian wines. With the coffee came a very wide assortment of brandies and chocolates. The 'luncheon' had been leisurely, taking over two hours with nothing of substance discussed. Finally, with the coffee, chocolates and brandies, Khruschev began to make his points. He told Pope John that it was useless to continue as head of the Church, that the Soviet Empire would certainly arrange for the destruction of the Church within ten years, that the Pope and his priests might as well give up now, surrender to the Soviet Empire, because otherwise there would be great difficulty and greater harshness. To emphasize his point, Khruschev began to raise his voice. He even took off his shoes and pounded them on the beautiful table.

At this point, Pope John rose and walked the full length of the table towards Khruschev. (This was contrary to protocol because the Pope never stood while others were seated, but John did it anyway.) Pope John reached the other end of the table and bent down over the seated Khruschev, putting one arm around the neck of the Soviet Premier. John said, "Niki! Oh, may I call you Niki?" Khruschev looked up rather quizzically into the smiling face of the Pope. (This is not the reaction he had expected!) Rather unsure how to respond, Khruschev said, "I guess so." "Niki," said John XXIII, "Don't try it. Don't try to destroy the Church. I am thinking only of you and your Empire, not the Church. You will not be able to destroy the Church and you and your Empire will be seriously harmed. You see, our priests have been trying to destroy the Church for two thousand years, and if they can't do it, no one can!"

Of course, the story is just that, a story. It never happened. But there is a certain truth in Pope John XXIII's supposed comment to Khruschev. At times in the Church's history, it has seemed that the priests (and we might add, the bishops as well) have been trying to destroy it. Many in the pro-life movement in the U.S. today believe that the Church's position on the sanctity of life, which to quote Pope John Paul II in the first line of the *Gospel Of Life* encyclical, is the Gospel of Jesus, continues to be put before the public in spite of the priests. In other words, members of the pro-life movement argue that the priests no longer preach the Gospel! In part, they are correct!

Preaching on life is at the heart of the priesthood because it is at the heart of the Gospel. But it is not being done as regularly or as often as it should be. On one occasion, a priest told me that in his parish he preferred to preach on the Scriptures rather than on the life issues. (Unfortunately, I thought of the proper and effective response to this only eight hours later while falling asleep!) The response to the remark is that from *Genesis* (the account of Creation – the gift of life to all human beings by God) to *Revelation* (the vision of St. John of the end times and the Second Coming when, God willing, we all will be brought to the fullness of the divine life in heaven) is about life. To preach on the Scriptures, to preach on the Gospels, is identical to preaching on life and vice-versa. If priests do not do it, they not only betray the Church, but they are false to their own calling, to their own vocation. They risk the warning of Paul, "Woe to me" if I do not preach the Gospel. (See I *Cor* 9:16.)

Our Lord Jesus Christ is the Gospel. But He is also Life. "I am the way and the truth and the life." (See *Jn* 14:6.) The priest stands in the place of Christ. He is an *alter Christus*. He is a living sign of the Gospel, of Christ and therefore of life. If the priest as an *alter Christus* fails to stand for life, he fails himself (as one who is called to stand in the place of Christ), the Church (because he does not fulfill the office given to him by the Church), and the world (because it does not receive the witness to the Gospel it desperately needs). It is not too much to say that there is a crisis in the priesthood. Part of that crisis (certainly not all of it) can be attributed to the widespread failure of priests to be faithful to themselves as other Christs in the full meaning of that very high and sacred calling.

Another way of saying the same thing is that a priest exists to offer the sacrifice of Christ to the Father. But before he offers the sacrifice of Christ, he should himself become a sacrifice. The priest is called to offer his life to the Lord. In return, he receives life from God in abundant graces through his priesthood. Through his self-sacrifice and the supernatural life-giving graces he receives from God in return, he is able to offer the sacrifice of Christ so that he receives from that sacrifice the sustaining strength of the Eucharist. In other words, the self-offering of the priest and the graces received from the priesthood are pre-requisite to the offering of the Eucharist in a way that brings to him the awesome graces of the Eucharist. But without standing for the sanctity of life, for its goodness, for its dignity, how can the priest presume to offer himself to God? Witnessing to life, preaching on life, is absolutely central, urgently central, to the very life of the priest. As St. Paul said, "Woe to me if I do not preach the Gospel!"

Not only is preaching on life, i.e., preaching the Gospel, absolutely central to the identity of the priest, to his service both to the Church and to the world, politically it is important in changing the culture of death to the culture of life. The organization I represent, Priests For Life, was founded in San Francisco in 1990 by Father Lee Kaylor and two other priests in response to a local pro-life political issue. They realized that if priests would promote the culture of life among their congregations consistently and repeatedly, the beginnings of a civilization of love could be established. The Church with its parishes gathers large groups of people together every Sunday of the year. It is (from a strictly political viewpoint) one of the most astounding grass roots organizations in the world. With the possibility of influencing so many people, the priests who founded Priests For Life ten years ago thought that priests by influencing their people could be the leaders of a true conversion of the culture from one of death to one of life.

The founders of Priests For Life are right. If priests consistently and repeatedly teach the principles of the faith to their people and are able to persuade their people (or, at least most of them) to act on those principles, the culture will change. In the United States, Catholics represent at least a fifth of all voters. Such a powerful force, if it acted together, could clearly change the political climate. Similarly, from a broader perspective, fifty million Catholics could be a significant catalyst of cultural development and change. In other words, the Catholic population in the U.S. could establish a political culture favorable to life and could influence the cultural institutions now favoring the culture of death towards a stance in favor of life. Similarly, Christian populations in many countries could have a similar impact. But why do we need an organization called Priests For Life? With the identity between the Gospel and life, with its centrality to the identity of the priest, and to his service to the Church and the world, why have priests not promoted the Gospel of Life? In fact, in the face of the numbers of Catholics and Christians in the U.S. and other countries, how could the culture of death gain a foothold in the first place? Catholics and other Christians, led by their priests and ministers, should have been formed in the Gospel and using their large numbers, should have long ago resisted those promoting death sufficiently to prevent the turn of the culture towards death. In fact, as we know, this did not happen. As it is, the culture of death not only has a foothold, it seems to be able to maintain even extreme positions, e.g., partial birth abortion. Why has the Gospel of life not taken hold sufficiently to counteract these tendencies so hostile to the Gospel itself?

The answer the founders of Priests For Life gave was that priests were not preaching on life often enough and consistently enough. In other words, Catholics and other Christians were not led by their pastors to take strong positions on the life issues. But the question arises: Why? Why do priests not preach on an issue so fundamental to their very priesthood? What is it about the life issues which causes the silence of the pastors? This is the question we at Priests For Life are asked repeatedly. If we could persuade pastors to speak to this issue on a regular basis, it does seem unassailable that they would be able to form a people in sufficient numbers to convert our culture to an affirmation of life. So, why do priests not speak out? If the premises that preaching on life is at the heart of the priesthood and that pastors are essential to persuading their people to influence the culture towards life (and I think these are obvious) are true, then the importance of discovering why they are reluctant to speak out on the life issues is vital.

I want to sketch a couple of reasons why I think some Catholic priests do not address the life issues as often as some of us would like. Of course, my remarks will reflect my experience in pro-life work in the U.S. Still, it seems to me that the U.S. experience is not so idiosyncratic as to be inapplicable to other parts of the world.

Many priests do not address abortion and even euthanasia because to do so is not politically correct. Another way of saying the same thing is that priests are sometimes disinclined to take on issues about which they believe their people do not wish to hear. One might argue that addressing unpopular issues is at the heart of preaching and that the Church has had a long history (beginning with its Founder) of addressing counter-cultural issues. And, of course, this is true. However, before standing before their people and challenging an accepted viewpoint or a lifestyle, priests need to be absolutely sure that they are speaking with the authority of the Church. It is too much to ask of any pastor that he challenge a culturally accepted norm or practice on his own authority. (In fact, such a stance is dangerous and can lead to excesses.) If the culture is to be confronted on a belief or practice, it has to be done with the full authority of the Church. But, therein lies the difficulty of today. Priests are not as sure of the moral authority of the Church as they were in the past. They do not perceive that they can rely on the Church for support when they challenge the culture. In part, this perceived lack of support from the teaching authority of the Church accounts for the reluctance of priests to speak on abortion and the other life issues (as well as many other areas of sexual morality).

An example might help. In the 1950s, no one would have dared to challenge the Church in the United States. Hollywood, for example, would have never presented priests or sisters, except in the most favorable light. It was too dangerous! Catholics would never have stood for an attack on their faith. The Catholic bishops would have launched a campaign against any perceived insult and most of the faithful would have followed the bishops. The cultural and political force of the Catholic Church was simply too strong to be challenged. The Church and its teaching was like the Rock of Gibraltar. When priests spoke on counter-cultural issues, that Rock was behind them. They could lean on it while they preached. The people could see the Rock towering over their pastor. It was crystal clear to everyone that Father was not speaking on his own, but only giving them a 'piece of the rock'. They could oppose the Rock, but only at their own peril. Unfortunately, that Rock is gone. It has been smashed. It sits now in pieces on the floor behind the pulpits. Or, at least, that is the perception of many priests. They do not see the Rock. They think it is not there and they do not perceive that they can lean against it. Furthermore, and most importantly, they do not perceive that when they take on the life issues, that they are giving the people a 'piece of the rock'. What happened? The Rock (to continue with the metaphor) was smashed – at least in the minds of many priests – with the arguments against *Humanae Vitae*, the so-called birth control encyclical. The four arguments questioning the Church's authority to teach definitively on contraception can be applied to any moral teaching of the Church. In other words, if even one out of the four objections to the teaching of Pope Paul VI on contraception is accepted, then any moral teaching of the Church is called into question. Since one or more of these four arguments against *Humanae Vitae* are widely accepted by many priests, their perception of the moral authority of the Church has been radically altered. In other words, the bombs that blew the Rock to smithereens were launched by the dissenters to *Humanae Vitae*. But, please notice, that it is not the teaching in *Humanae Vitae* that is the essential problem. From this perspective, it is the objections to the teaching. The objections to the teaching are the bombs that blew apart the Rock in the minds of many because once these objections are accepted, they (or any one of them) can apply to any moral teaching of the Church. In effect, the topic of *Humanae Vitae* is irrelevant to this discussion. Any teaching of the Church taught in the 1960s which occasioned the same or similar dissenting opinions would have caused the same result. What are the four objections to *Humanae Vitae* which question the moral authority of the Church?

Chronologically, the first objection to *Humanae Vitae* actually was made before the encyclical was promulgated on July 25, 1968. From about 1964 through 1968, there were many articles which argued that the Church did not have an official teaching on the question of the newly developed contraceptive pill. Although Pope Paul VI re-affirmed the traditional ban on contraception and asserted repeatedly that the Church actually did teach that it was immoral to employ contraceptives, several authors maintained that the newly developed pill required a new statement from the Church. In other words, the argument was that the teaching of Pius XI in *Casti Connubii* against contraception did not hold for the newly developed pill. Many priests, faced with 'hard' cases presented to them by their parishioners, followed the argument that there was a *vacatio legis*, a 'vacancy in the law'. In the case where the Church has not yet decided an issue, every Catholic is free to follow the best advice possible. If there is conflicting advice, one can choose among the legitimate opinions. Thus, if there were a 'vacancy in the law' and there were legitimate moral opinions allowing the use of the contraceptive pill, then it would be permissible for a couple to employ the pill. In the 1960s, there were moral theologians, some very prominent people, who accepted the moral legitimacy of contraception. So, if the 'vacancy in the law' argument prevailed, it would be morally permissible for couples to use contraception. Of course, once Pope Paul VI promulgated *Humanae Vitae*, the 'vacancy in the law' argument could not be maintained. But, for a while, people used it as a moral argument for the use of contraceptives.

In addition to the 'vacancy in the law' argument, there were three other arguments against the teaching of *Humanae Vitae* which were proposed by the dissenters after the encyclical appeared. For convenience, we might label these the infallibility, conscience, and parallel magisterium arguments. The argument from infallibility is familiar to most. Some argued that the teaching in *Humanae Vitae* was not issued with the theological note of infallibility. Since it did not have the theological certainty of the doctrines of the Immaculate Conception or the Assumption, some argued that the ban on contraceptives did not have to be accepted by Catholics. Implicitly, of course, this argument held that only infallible statements were matters which Catholics in faith were to believe and practise.

If the teaching on contraception did not have to be followed because it was not infallible, then the decision was left to the individual conscience. In fact, as some dissenters argued, since no one, not even the magisterium of the Church, can compel a conscience, even if a particular teaching of the Church was infallible, people still were obligated to follow their own consciences. At first, the conscience argument was seen as the final arbiter for moral decisions on non-infallible teachings of the Church. However, very soon, it was evident that the claim for the authority of conscience was absolute. In other words, everyone was free to decide for himself or herself in the mystery of his or her own conscience what acts were moral or immoral. The freedom of the individual conscience, said the dissenters, was absolute. Conscience had to take into account the teaching of the Church, but only as one statement, not as an authoritative guide for one's conscience. As is evident, with this claim for the absolute authority of the individual conscience, the teaching against contraception in *Humanae Vitae* would only be one voice which couples should at least hear before they determined for themselves how they would act regarding contraception. In other words, the claim for conscience, if accepted, vitiated the force of Pope Paul VI's teaching.

The dissenters to *Humanae Vitae* also offered the so-called parallel magisterium argument. They suggested that Popes and bishops were busy administrators of the institutions of the Church who had little time and resources to spend on the study of practical moral problems. On the other hand, there are moral theologians who have devoted their lives to the study of morality and proper conduct. The argument suggests that if one wants an adequate, studied answer to a moral question, a moral theologian should be approached, not an overworked administrator. If a car needs repair, the car is taken to an auto mechanic, not to a physician. If there is a moral question, a moral theologian should be asked, not a pope or bishop. Therefore, in the area of contraception, the ultimate authority is not an encyclical letter of a Pope, but rather the judicious and informed opinions of theologically trained and competent academics in the area of moral theology.

It should be noticed that all these arguments, or each one individually, can be applied to any moral teaching of the Church. For example, when was the last time the Church officially promulgated a teaching against stealing? Facetiously, it might be suggested that there is a 'vacancy in the law' on the question of stealing. Further, the teaching against stealing has certainly not been proclaimed infallibly by the extraordinary magisterium and therefore, some could suggest that people

175

are free to make up their own minds. The argument from conscience could also apply. Since every moral teaching of the Church is simply one voice among many which the individual considers, the teaching against stealing is subject to the judgment of conscience. If one's conscience, having considered the Church's position, rejects the Church's teaching against stealing at least in a particular instance, it would not be immoral for that person to steal on that occasion. In addition, the argument that moral questions should be referred to a moral theologian could also undermine the applicability of the Church's teaching. Given all the theologians available, is it not likely that one could be found who would agree with one's judgment of conscience?

Each of the four arguments presented by the dissenters to *Humanae Vitae*, the 'vacancy in the law' argument, infallibility, the appeal to conscience, as well as the parallel magisterium argument can be applied to any teaching of the Church. Since a great number of priests have not only heard these arguments, but accepted one or all of them, at least in particular cases, the teaching authority of the Church has been severely weakened. To use the previous metaphor, the 'Rock' – representing the teaching authority of the Church on moral questions – is in pieces. There is nothing for the priests to lean on when they attempt to preach on questions about which they believe people do not wish to hear. In addition to the perceived lack of support from the Church, there is the fear on the part of priests that a counter cultural message from the pulpit will lead to their parishioners abandoning the parish with a concomitant reduction in donations. Of course, if parishioners abandon a parish and income is reduced, it will not be long before most parish priests will receive a summons from the bishop asking why things are not going well! It is small wonder that priests are reluctant to preach on the life issues or sexual morality.

Of course, the arguments from the 'vacancy in the law', infallibility, conscience, and the parallel magisterium do not hold. There are numerous and weighty arguments against each and every one of them. Further, most Catholics attending Church regularly want to hear the Gospel – it is the Good News and they want it preached in its fullness. I know of several priests who have taken on some of the more difficult issues who have received applause for their homilies. In other words, the perception that the 'Rock' is in pieces is false, especially with the teaching of Pope John Paul II. Therefore, the perceptions of many priests about what their faithful want to hear and about the strength of the Church's authority are not valid. Nevertheless, the perceptions continue to determine what subjects are addressed in homilies, sermons, and talks. These perceptions need to be changed and they are changing, only it is happening gradually. If we want priests to lead their parishes to an active campaign to establish the culture of life, then addressing these misperceptions becomes essential.

While priests do not cite their perceptions about the moral authority of the Church when asked why they do not preach on the life issues more regularly, they will mention that many in their congregations do not want to hear these teachings. Even more emphatically and more often, they will mention that "they do not want to hurt people". Some will forcefully maintain that if the question of abortion is talked about from the pulpit that it opens wounds in the flock. Priests are not priests because they want to hurt people. Most of us want to help and assist. Since mentioning abortion is often very painful to those who have been involved in an abortion, many priests have decided not to mention the issue. It must be remembered that priests as a group are extremely well read. They know how many abortions are done every year. They also are well aware that each abortion affects many more people than the child and the mother. Knowing these figures, they also are well aware that at least some of the people listening to any given homily have probably had some direct involvement with a surgical abortion. Since mentioning the issue is painful and priests do not want to hurt people, they are most reluctant to address the subject.

This false compassion is almost more important a factor than the question of the Church's authority. While it is true that mentioning the subject of abortion can be painful to those who have been involved with an abortion, it is even more painful not to mention it. David Reardon's interviews with post-abortive women in the United States have shown that when they do return to the Church (usually after some years away after the abortion), they are shocked and hurt that no one mentions the cause of their pain. It is as though they walk into the parish Church bleeding from one of their legs. Imagine the scene, this young woman walks into Church one Sunday gushing blood from one of her legs. None of the ushers remark on her wound. They take her to a pew not even offering to help her as she leaves a trail of blood while walking up the aisle. Kneeling down, her leg continues to bleed leaving a pool of blood beneath the pew, but none of those around her mention it. Of course, since the wound of abortion is hidden from view, it is not like a bleeding leg. Yet, most women returning to Church after experiencing an abortion are not yet recovered from the event. They come to Church because they know they are spiritually hurting and they want the spiritual healing that only God can offer. But no one offers that spiritual healing. Interiorly, they continue to live in intense and searing spiritual and psychological pain. A physician treating a wound in a leg, first cleans the wound. This cleaning can be painful and so often a pain killer is administered, but even the giving of the pain killer can be painful. Should the physician not treat the leg because it will cause some pain to the patient? Obviously not. By the same token, the priest, the doctor of the soul, must treat the soul even if the treatment causes some pain to the patient. If the physician does not treat the wounded leg, eventually it will become infected and an amputation will have to be performed. If the priest does not treat the wounded soul, the soul can be lost. False compassion leads to even greater pain and difficulties.

Priests will sometimes argue that they have tried to preach on the issue and then been severely criticized for insensitivity by post-abortive women who have heard them preach. Of course, such complaints do happen. Why? Those who have suffered from an abortion (and women are also victims of abortion), and come back to Church usually are not completely healed. They need the spiritual healing of the Church. In other words, they are wounded. When that wound is touched, it hurts. Just as the needle administering the pain-killer hurts as it goes in, so the preacher lancing the wound of abortion in the soul causes some pain. But unless the physician treats the wound, the leg is lost. Unless the doctor of the soul treats the wound in the soul, it is lost. Sometimes, the pain caused by the lancing of the wound of the soul through preaching is vocalized: there is a cry of pain expressed to the one causing the pain, in this case, the priest. But it is simply that, the cry of pain. Once that pain is completely released, the cure can begin. The post-abortive woman, having released the pain, is ready to seek the forgiveness of God.

If you would permit a personal anecdote, I can illustrate this point. I was preaching on pro-life in a parish in the U.S. After I completed my homily, I strolled out to the grounds around the Church which were very beautiful on this particularly sunny day. Shortly after I began enjoying the sunshine and park-like atmosphere, a young woman appeared and approached another man sitting on a nearby bench. After a short time, she approached me and struck up a conversation. She was very angry with me for having discussed the whole issue of abortion. She admitted to being post-abortive and to having confessed the sin (she was Catholic). Still, she firmly maintained that she believed that she had not committed any sin in having an abortion. She also said that the other man had told her he was a priest and that I had not meant what I said in the homily, at least not in the way she understood me.

There were several things happening with this woman. First of all, she was clearly in pain and was reacting to the pain. In effect, I had touched the wound. In confessing her sin, she had not sufficiently dealt with it. Either she was not yet ready to discuss it or the confessor was unable to help her deal with the sin. She needed to vent the pain and then it would be possible for her to experience psychologically the forgiveness which God extended to her. However, the priest who had told her that I did not mean what I preached in my homily undid what I had tried to do. While trying to be compassionate, he had told her that the wound in her soul really was not there. He was denying reality and trying to hide the wound with a bandage. What I had done was to expose the wound and let her see it so she could realize it was there and that it had to be treated. If the young woman believed the other priest, she would need to have his bandage ripped off (by someone willing to tell her the truth) and then experience the pain all over again. Actually, the pain would be worse than she already had experienced because now there was a bandage over the wound which would have to be ripped off before she could be compelled to see the wound. The woman who approached me had not dealt with her wound, had denied its existence, was forced to acknowledge its presence, was hurt by seeing it (and therefore reacted to me) and then was allowed to return to her denial. The whole situation was tragic because having begun to deal with a real trauma in her life, the woman was allowed to believe it was not there. She suffered all the pain leading to a cure and then the cure was prevented by a return to denial which was possible because the other priest gave her permission to continue her denial.

178

Priests who do not preach on abortion allow those who are post-abortive to continue denying their pain. They refuse to act as doctors of souls because they do not want to cause pain. But, in the end, their refusal to practice their profession of spiritual healing causes even more pain. There is absolutely nothing comparable to the forgiving love of our merciful God. It is the most compassionate and most merciful act possible to bring people to the point where they willingly put themselves before God and experience the immense flow of His merciful love. The greater the sin, the greater the love offered by God for its forgiveness. This is truly the stuff saints are made of. But it does depend on priests doing their part, not shrinking from the 'hard' truths. Not preaching on abortion and the other life-issues for fear of offending someone is a terrible mistake because it is a refusal to treat the spiritual pain of abortion with the only medicine there is: God's forgiveness. It is false compassion which leads to even greater pain.

What is the role of the priest in promoting the culture of life? It is vital. He can shape and form his flock so that they resist by every legal means possible the march of the culture of death. It is to preach the truth of the sins of abortion and euthanasia so that those who are the living victims of these sins will be able to find relief from the spiritual pain caused by these sins. Even if the preaching of the truth about these sins may be painful for an individual from time to time, the results are truly unbelievable. It is only in the truth that we can be free of sin and its pain. Let us never fail to remember that fidelity to the Gospel is the calling and vocation of all of us. Even false compassion cannot be a motive for us to abandon this sacred calling!

12

The role of the family in promoting a culture of life

LAURA L. GARCIA

TODAY'S CHRISTIANS BEAR a grave responsibility toward the world community, given two features of the current scene: utter confusion about marriage and the meaning of family life combined with a silencing of many voices who used to support and publicize the truth about persons and families. Some of these voices now speak out on the side of falsehood, while some are simply weakened through discouragement or internal dissension. But the Church continues to address its message to every person of good will on the face of the earth. "Following Christ who 'came' into the world 'to serve' (*Mt* 20:28), the Church considers serving the family to be one of her essential duties. In this sense both man and the family constitute 'the way of the Church'."[1] The truth about persons and about love that is at the heart of the culture of life ideal has never been more timely or more necessary. But the world community, especially in the West and in cultures heavily influenced by the West, has grown hard of hearing so that the voices of truth are almost inaudible to it. If the Church is to continue to teach, it is the family which must prepare the world to hear its message.

Call for evangelical spirit

This explains why the call for a new evangelization addresses the laity especially, and looks to Christian families (that is, parents) to model the values and virtues so crucial to authentic human development. One of the earliest publications of John Paul II's pontificate is an apostolic exhortation on the family in which he emphasizes the critical importance of understanding the mystery of marriage and family in today's terms, interpreting it for our own times, drawing out its implications and coming up with strategies for solving its problems. "The Church does not accomplish this discernment only through the Pastors, who teach in the name and with the power of Christ, but also through the laity... Christian spouses and parents are qualified for this role by their charism or specific gift, the gift of the sacrament of matrimony."[2] Nor is this simply a matter of surveying the

[1] John Paul II, *Letter to Families* (hereafter: *LtF*) 2. Boston: St. Paul Books and Media 1994. The Letter was published on the occasion of the United Nations Year of the Family.
[2] John Paul II, *Familiaris Consortio* (hereafter: *FC*) 5. Boston: St. Paul Books and Media 1981. Also available via the Vatican website at www.vatican.va

faithful to find the most popular views on these issues. Rather, the Church "listens to conscience and not to power," even if that power comes from the vote of a majority, and even if that majority is inside the Church. Nor is it simply a matter of putting together the most recent research from the social sciences, as helpful as this may be in its place. Rather, there are gifts bestowed by the *Holy Spirit* for the needs of the Church – and since "the future of humanity passes by way of the family"[3] – we will find in the family the gifts it needs to build a better future for the human race.

The sacramental grace of marriage has many purposes, and perhaps we married persons are accustomed to thinking of it as a grace pertaining to our own marriage. We may feel we need all the grace we can get in dealing with our spouse and children and that we don't have any to spare. But just as the sacrament of holy orders bestows grace not simply for the benefit of the priest but for the sake of the people of God, the sacrament of marriage bestows a grace which is meant not only for the couple themselves, or even for the individual family, but for the whole community. The supernatural gift communicated in this sacrament is not given in a lump sum; it is an ongoing fountain of grace to enable the couple to fulfill this high and holy vocation to which God has called them.

Mission of the Family

The family's vocation follows from its origins in the plan of God. The family is formed as a community of life and love, so its mission is to *guard, reveal, and communicate love*. "Love is the fundamental vocation of every human being." This vocation takes different forms for those who are married and for those who are leading a celibate life. If you are not married, it doesn't mean that you have no one to love; rather, you have everyone to love. The world has never suffered from too much love, and there will always be those who are especially in need of our concern, our time and our strength. When it is lived for others, celibacy "liberates the human heart," making possible a truly selfless form of love for those around us. Of course, even those who are living out the vocation to love within marriage cannot assume that they have done enough simply by caring for those in their immediate family circle. We need to acquire a new enthusiasm for service, and a willingness to communicate love by our actions to the love-starved community around us.

Building a community of persons: husband and wife

For today's families, it is the marriage itself, the relationship between the spouses, that provides the key to this training in love. We hear often that the family is the

[3] *FC*: 86.

fundamental cell of society – or, in an even better image, the "cradle" of humanity[4] – but then it's also true that the marriage is the heart and soul of the family. As the marriage goes, so goes the family. With the help of the Holy Spirit, Christian spouses are to grow toward "an ever richer union with each other on all levels – of the body, of the character, of the heart, of the intelligence and will, of the soul."[5] This already calls for a major dose of selflessness on the part of each of the partners in marriage, since a union of wills must be created by surrendering one's own preferences on occasion for the sake of harmony.

Family life is sometimes described as "a school of deeper humanity"[6], and in this school of the family the parents are the teachers. How do we teach? In words, of course, but even more fundamentally, in deeds. If we don't know how to set aside our own desires and plans for the sake of the others, then our children will never learn the most important and most basic of all human truths – *we find ourselves by giving ourselves*. It should go without saying, then, that a husband and wife need to make that gift of themselves in a way which is *total, unconditional, exclusive, and permanent*. Where the marriage commitment is weakened – by divorce, by infidelity, by a contraceptive mentality – the children, the young men and women who 'graduate' from this school of the family, are afraid to give themselves as well.

What is at the root of the recent boom in the number of couples who are co-habiting without a marriage license? David Popenoe and Barbara Dafoe Whitehead sum up a number of studies of this phenomenon in a report called *Should We Live Together? What Young Adults Need to Know About Cohabitation Before Marriage*. They find that while in 1960 there were less than 500,000 such couples in the U.S., in 1997 there were four million of them.[7] About 25 percent of unmarried American women between 25 and 39 are living with a 'partner', and over half of first marriages today are preceded by cohabitation. Some of this surely has to do with the similarly skyrocketing rate of divorce. Young people are afraid to make a commitment that they don't believe anyone can seriously expect to be able to keep.

We can only teach fidelity by staying faithful in good times and bad. We can only teach love by loving, allowing the grace of the sacrament of marriage to soften our hearts and to teach us how to forgive one another seventy times seven. For some couples, and probably for every couple at some times, this can be difficult in the extreme. Our culture peddles such a sentimentalized view of love and marriage that when the man or woman of our dreams turns out to be a mere mortal, we can hardly believe it. Many college students voice the belief that there is a single 'right' person for them, and once they find that person

---

[4] *FC*: 15.

[5] *FC*: 19.

[6] *Gaudium et spes* 52. Cf. N. Tanner, S. J. *Decrees of the Ecumenical Councils*, vol.2. London: Sheed & Ward 1990: 1104.

[7] D. Popenoe and B. D. Whitehead, *Should We Live Together? What Young Adults Need to Know about Cohabitation Before Marriage*. The National Marriage Project 1999: 3.

married life will be heaven on earth – totally effortless. This is a tempting view, to be sure, but utterly false. One should not underestimate considerations of compatibility, of course, but it is wildly off the mark to suggest that some couples won't have to work hard at loving each other or at becoming more lovable themselves. G. K. Chesterton expressed surprise that making incompatibility grounds for divorce had not yet made divorce virtually inevitable. He claimed that although he knew many happily married couples, he had never met any who were compatible.

In addition to his insistence on being human, I've found that my husband persists in being, well, a man. There's that Mars/Venus phenomenon and we just have to accept that men and women will remain to some extent mysterious to each other. We can see these differences between the sexes as an advantage to the union or as an obstacle, especially an obstacle to our own desire to be fully understood. But since we cannot eliminate them, we would do well to understand and appreciate them, not expecting our spouses to feel exactly the same way we do about things or to share all our reactions to life's challenges.

Serving life

Another major lesson we teach in the family, for better or worse, comes from our attitude toward new life. A recent *Newsweek* article presented two views of marriage: either marriage is for love or marriage is for children. The truth, however, is that love and openness to children are really one thing. Love is a concern for the welfare of *others*. Genuine love wants to expand; it doesn't just *lead* to generosity; it *is* a form of generosity. Couples who rejoice in the children God sends them and who make themselves available to their children are increasingly rare, but by that very fact they become an amazing witness to the value of human life and a reflection of God's joy in his creatures.

What keeps us from welcoming life into our world, into our society, into our homes? There can be genuine grounds for anxiety about our ability to feed and clothe these little ones, but in Western societies it is much more likely to be either panic over the so-called population explosion or a consumer mentality that puts material things above persons. These days you don't have a baby; you have another threat to the rain forest. It is considered an ecological sin to have too many children. In fact, a popular bumper sticker in my neighborhood reads, "Thanks for not breeding". It's just *bad manners* to have a baby – or so some would have it.

Now the dangers of overpopulation have clearly been exaggerated, as research by Julian Simon and others has definitively shown. Even those ecological problems that remain are no excuse for depriving a husband and wife of their intrinsic right to determine the size of their own family by morally licit means. As for the value of persons over things, I know of none more eloquent on this subject than John Paul II. "Against the pessimism and selfishness which cast a shadow over the world," he writes, "the Church stands for life: in each human life she sees the splendor of that 'Yes', that 'Amen', who is Christ Himself."[8] Every human being, even when weak or suffering, is an image of the invisible God, an icon of the divine nature. C. S. Lewis reminds us that "Next to the Blessed Sacrament itself, your neighbour is the holiest object presented to your senses."[9]

How do we transmit to our children this amazing truth – a human life is more precious than any merely material thing, because the human soul partakes of the divine? We can only do so if we ourselves can say 'yes' to God's gift of life in our own families, and if we find ways to reach out to those in the community around us who are most needy or most difficult to love. There are many ways to work for an end to the abortion culture, to the enormous toll that millions of abortions a year are taking on us all. But one strategy within the reach of each one of us is to battle against our own selfishness and our own tendency to flee from those who will interfere with our so-called freedom. What is our attitude toward our own children? Toward our elderly parents and grandparents? Toward the weak and suffering members of our own communities?

Recent threats to the family

We're aware these days of so many discouraging statistics that indicate a serious pathology in Western families. At the root of these negative phenomena, according to John Paul II, is a *corruption of the idea of freedom*: "conceived not as a capacity for realizing the truth of God's plan for marriage and the family, but as an autonomous power of self-affirmation, often against others, for one's own selfish well-being."[10] Freedom must be at the service of love; it must be based on truth – about ourselves and what truly fulfills us, about others and their inviolable dignity, about God and his fatherly love for us.

Internal threats

Materialism is the view that human persons are nothing more than elaborate machines, organisms with enough brainpower to run the show, at least for the time being, but with no special claims or privileges. This false view of the person provides fuel for the out-of-control hedonism that is all around us and, thanks to original sin, within us as well. Hedonism urges us to seek freedom, but not freedom at the service of love, since we are just glorified animals after all. Rather, freedom exists to serve our desires and appetites, however excessive or base (or even perverse) these might be.

The advertising industry sinks ever lower in appealing to these desires, even encouraging them and making them seem legitimate. Cars are simply tools for

[8] FC: 30.
[9] C. S. Lewis, 'The Weight of Glory'. In *The Weight of Glory and Other Addresses*. New York: Collier Books 1980 (orig. 1949): 19.
[10] FC: 6.

stroking our egos. Obsession used to be a mental disorder; now it's a cologne. Commercials from The Gap imply that the joy of Christmas is largely about colorful name-brand clothes. In an image from the Greek philosopher Plato, we are making our souls into sieves – no matter how much pleasure or wealth we pour in, our appetites keep expanding. Like today's computers that become obsolete almost as soon as they leave the store, many of our possessions cease to satisfy in a very short time. Less just isn't more any more. Obviously, this emphasis on pleasure and material things interferes with our ability to recognize the value of life's intangibles – relationships, character, learning, cultivating the spirit.

External threats: our cultural context

The battle against consumerism would be hard enough without the added pressures created by today's economic realities. The first of these might be called the *Time Bomb*. In the United States, the average worker is now at work 163 hours a year more than in 1969. This adds up to an extra month of work every year.[11] For American parents, time with their children, which is critical to the ability to shape a child's values and sense of self, has declined about 13 percent over the past 30 years.[12] Parents increasingly feel that they are not providing their children's formation; it is being provided by the media, the schools, and the many other adults involved in after-school programs, coaching, dance classes, etc. Some of these benefit our children, of course, but the difficulty is that parents feel forced to find some such combination of such caregivers for the many hours that they are unavailable, and it can be impossible to keep a close eye on their quality.

Another relatively recent economic pressure for today's families is the phenomenon of the *Marketable Mother*. Two scholars of the family sum it up this way: "For generations women spent huge chunks of their lives making the nonmarket investments in family and community that underpin our nation. By nurturing children and by nourishing a web of care that included neighborhood and township, women created the competence and character upon which our democracy and our economy depended."[13] This work is no longer being performed, and our children and communities are suffering mightily because of it. What is the solution? Women may be able to find opportunities for occasional absences from the work force, or for a less intensive involvement in it, and men may rise to the occasion and begin doing more of this work alongside women; in fact, many already have. But for now, those who choose to drop out of the rat race often find themselves struggling financially and ostracized socially. After all, "In the late 1990s, what really counts in America is how much you

---

[11] S. A. Hewlett and C. West, *The War Against Parents*. New York: Houghton Mifflin 1998: 48.
[12] Hewlett and West, *The War Against Parents*: 48.
[13] Hewlett and West, *The War Against Parents*: 38.

get paid and what you can buy."[14] It's that consumer mentality again. Parents feel that they must make as much money as possible for the sake of the children, so that the children will not suffer a sense of deprivation when they don't have the same things as others at school or in the neighborhood.

A final and extremely serious component of today's family crisis is the *Missing Father*. Several recent books document this trend with distressing thoroughness.[15] One scholar reports that the percentage of children living with their biological fathers fell from 82 percent in 1960 to 62 percent in 1990. "In 1960, 15 percent of teenage girls who gave birth were unmarried; by 1996, this figure had reached 76 percent."[16] Between births to unwed mothers and the fallout from divorce, we are increasingly a society of families in which fathers are simply not in the picture.

One consequence of the fatherless society is that the meaning of masculinity and the meaning of fatherhood have sharply diverged. Since masculinity has long been associated with sexual prowess, casual and even predatory sex have become the sex code of many young males.[17] What generates the current plague of violence among young men? The politically correct answer accepted for years by many in the social science community is that traditional masculine values generate this rage and hostility. What the evidence increasingly shows, however, is that a young man raised by a traditionally masculine father is not the one who turns to crime. It is rather the young man raised with no father at all. He cannot discover the meaning of his manhood by learning to be his father's son and so safely separate from his mother.

One main reaction to this situation is rage: "rage against the mother, against women, against society."[18] Note the titles of some contemporary rap songs: "Beat That Bitch with a Bat," or "Momma's Gotta Die Tonight," a 1980s hit by Body Count that describes "setting the mother alight with lighter fluid, hitting her with a baseball bat, cutting her body up into pieces and stuffing them into a garbage bag. The chorus includes the lines 'Ha, ha ha/Burn momma, burn momma, burn bitch, burn, burn, burn."[19] Many young men who do not express such intense rage in an overt way still retain a deeply felt anger at the world. "In his book *Family and Nation*, Senator Daniel Patrick Moynihan draws one unmistakable lesson from American history: 'A community that allows a large number of young men to grow up in broken families ... never acquiring any stable relationship to male authority ... asks for and gets chaos.' "[20]

---

[14] Hewlett and West, *The War Against Parents*: 30.

[15] See especially D. Popenoe, *Life Without Father: Compelling New Evidence That Fatherhood and Marriage Are Indispensable for the Good of Children and Society*. New York: Free Press 1996; D. Blankenhorn, *Fatherless America: Confronting Our Most Urgent Social Problem*. New York: Basic Books 1995.

[16] Hewlett and West, *The War Against Parents*: 163.

[17] Blankenhorn, *Fatherless America*: 17, quoting E. Anderson, *Streetwise: Race, Class, and Change in an Urban Community*. Chicago: University of Illinois Press 1990: 112–137.

[18] Blankenhorn, *Fatherless America*: 30.

[19] Hewlett and West, *The War Against Parents*: 133.

[20] Hewlett and West, *The War Against Parents*: 167. Cf. Daniel Patrick Moynihan, *Family and Nation*. New York: Harcourt Brace Jovanovich 1986: 168.

Equally disturbing are the number of children who fall into despair and hopelessness because of the absence of their father's love and support in their lives. Eighty percent of adolescents in psychiatric hospitals come from broken homes, and three out of four teen suicides occur in single-parent families, which are almost exclusively families minus a father.[21] Pope John Paul II speaks straightforwardly of the dangers for today's families when their unity and stability is destroyed. "As a result of these dangers families cease to be witnesses of the civilization of love and can even become a negation of it, a kind of *counter-sign*. A broken family can, for its part, consolidate a specific form of 'anti-civilization' [chaos], destroying love in its various expressions, with inevitable consequences for the whole of life in society."[22]

Faced with these serious consequences, what is today's father to do? The first priority for men today has to be to love their wives; we must turn the divorce culture into a marriage culture. As the Holy Father reminds us, love is demanding. Citing the famous passage from *1 Corinthians 13*, he explains that: "Nowadays people need to rediscover this demanding love, for it is truly the firm foundation of the family, a foundation able to 'endure all things.' ... At work within it is the power and strength of God himself, who 'is love' (*1 Jn* 4:8,16)."[23] Even when fidelity to the marriage commitment becomes difficult, even when the paths of this vocation are uphill and the obstacles "seemingly insuperable," John Paul II prays that married couples will continue to love their vocation and remain faithful to their covenant with God. The love of the spouses in marriage, this kind of stubborn, enduring, unselfish love, stands as the model of all other loves within the family – a sign that must not become, for the children and others, a counter-sign.

In addition to protecting and building up their marriage relationship, there are several things men can do to ensure that their children's father-hunger is satisfied. First among these is availability. Fathers cannot allow their work to become an end in itself, crowding out family life and consuming all their attention and energies. Work is a vocation to be sure, and it is also a path to holiness, but this does not make it more than it is: *a means to an end*, a way of serving God and others. Even with today's constraints on working parents and the pressures of a materialistic society, fathers cannot afford to reduce their role in the family to a financial one. Children need the protection, security, discipline, and love that the father can offer them, and fathers need to develop that bond with their children for the sake of their own peace and satisfaction.

As a second practical step, the final chapter of David Blankenhorn's book *Fatherless America* calls on fathers to fill these basic roles in the lives of their children: to provide, protect, nurture, and sponsor them. The term 'sponsoring'

---

[21] Hewlett and West, *The War Against Parents*: 165. These statistics are drawn from Jean Bethke Elshtain, 'Family Matters: The Plight of America's Children,' (July 14–21, 1993) *Christian Century*: 710.

[22] *LtF*: 13.

[23] *LtF*: 14.

captures the mentoring role fathers have toward their children, helping them build character and preparing them to face the future. "If mothers are likely to devote special attention to their children's pressing physical and emotional needs, fathers are likely to devote special attention to character traits necessary for the future, especially qualities such as independence, self-reliance, and the willingness to take risks."[24] One theme that emerges especially strongly in Blankenhorn's research is that mothers and fathers play very different roles in raising children, and that the child who has both kinds of love and nurturing has a tremendous advantage.

As a final suggestion, fathers can strengthen and deepen their relationship to God, so that they can mirror the fatherhood of God for their children. If a picture is worth a thousand words, a living example is priceless. Blankenhorn recommends that every father should take the following pledge: *Many people today believe that fathers are unnecessary. I believe the opposite. I pledge to live my life according to the principle that every child deserves a father; that marriage is the pathway to effective fatherhood; that part of being a good man means being a good father; and that America needs more good men.*[25] This is a pledge specifically directed toward fathers, but to the extent that any man seeks to imitate the fatherhood of God he will find that there are many who look to him for that specifically fatherly love that they have not received anywhere else. This is a task for every man, single or married, cleric or lay. Men are sorely needed in leadership roles in our communities, especially in areas that impact children and young people: coaching sports teams, scouting, youth groups, churches, chess clubs, even the PTA. There is a desperate need for men who can act as mentors to the victims of today's fatherlessness.

In a culture where most mothers are now working at least part time and more and more are working full time outside the home and where fathers are either overworked or absent, our children increasingly grow up in the *Default Mode*. Who is shaping our children in our absence? The remaining influential people in their lives are drawn from their schools, their peers, and especially the entertainment industry. None of these can be counted on to support the values and attitudes parents are hoping to instill. The problems in our public schools are well-documented, and I know of few parents with children in these schools who aren't tempted at one time or another by the home-schooling option, whatever its other merits or demerits. The state of the culture reflects itself in our schools and finds there some of its most avid and single-minded supporters. To take just one example, there are some in the school district of Lexington, Massachusetts, who wish to eliminate the terms 'mother' and 'father' from the school curriculum. The use of these terms discriminates, they say, against families with two parents of the same sex. We may sincerely hope that these forces are unsuccessful in their attempt to thus confuse the students, but we must also recognize that their past successes have already seriously distorted the picture of sexuality, marriage, and family life for our children.

[24] Blankenhorn, *Fatherless America*: 219.
[25] Blankenhorn, *Fatherless America*: 226.

Outside of school the public media, especially television, is shaping our children's minds. The average American teenager watches 22 hours of television a week. What do they see? Children who watch an average amount of TV see 8,000 murders and more than 100,000 other acts of violence during their elementary school years. Some networks come in for special mention here – MTV music videos average 20 acts of violence per hour, and 60 percent of programming on MTV links violence to degrading sexual portrayals. Standard children's programs are not much better. Such Saturday morning programs average 20–25 violent acts per hour.[26] Perhaps the shows our children watch are not of this kind, we tell ourselves, or perhaps the impact on them is not as bad as we fear. But at a minimum, when children are watching television or playing video games they are certainly not connecting to people. Further, their values are being strongly influenced by Hollywood, and it is safe to say that these fit poorly with what most parents want for their children.

We live in an increasingly violent and materialistic culture, and one which is also increasingly pornographic. We now face a widespread phenomenon of copycat violence, especially among teens imitating movies like *Natural Born Killers* or, even more sadly, the real-life actions of their peers in high schools across the United States. With the advent of the internet, many attitudes and vices that dared not speak their names are now all to eager to do so under the anonymity and privacy provided by the virtual world. Internet pornography has become a huge and wholly unregulated industry. Judge Robert Bork's chilling book *Slouching Towards Gomorrah* provides several hair-raising examples. "Users can download pornographic pictures as well as prose from the Internet. And there is a lot of both available. The demand, moreover, is for material that can't be easily found elsewhere – pedophilia, sadomasochism, eroticized urination, defecation, and vaginal and rectal fisting. Among the most popular are sex acts with a wide variety of animals, nude children, and incest."[27]

We may imagine that we can shield our children from this avalanche of cyber-filth, but that goal is quickly becoming the impossible dream. My own computer includes parental controls to block access to certain web sites and so-called 'chat rooms.' Nevertheless, one of my children, trying to find the ratio of males to females in our city, typed the word "men" in the search box and was bombarded by invitations to visit several sites directed toward homosexual men. Though he

---

[26] Hewlett and West, *The War Against Parents*: 149. Their statistics are taken from A. C. Huston et al., *Big World, Small Screen: The Role of Television in American Society*. Lincoln: University of Nebraska Press 1992: 53–54; Charles S. Clark, 'TV Violence' (March 26, 1993) *CQ Researcher*: 176; Leonard D. Eron, testimony on violence and the media, U.S. Senate Judiciary Committee, June 8, 1993: 3.

[27] R. H. Bork, *Slouching Towards Gomorrah: Modern Liberalism and American Decline*. New York: Regan Books 1996: 136. He cites Simon Winchester, 'An Electronic Sink of Depravity,' *The Spectator* (February 4, 1995): 9–11. The section quoted here is far less graphic than the actual samples of porno-prose provided by Winchester and referenced in Bork. It is not a book for the squeamish.

cannot access these sites, he now knows what is 'out there' so to speak, and several sites advertise with sample photos to whet the appetite. If this is the sort of thing our children find on supervised excursions on the internet, what about the many children who are left unsupervised and whose access to the toxic regions of cyberspace is unrestricted? The challenge for parents today can be all but overwhelming.

Solutions

In spite of such obstacles, we cannot afford to fall into a state of paralysis or despair. There are many things parents and each of us can do to make a positive difference in turning our culture into a more humane, more 'user-friendly' society. Large structural changes are certainly needed, and we can all work at some level for those larger changes. The authors cited here, David Blankenhorn, Robert Bork, Sylvia Ann Hewlett and Cornel West, all make several concrete proposals for changing laws and policies to better address the social problems they discuss. But we can also work in more immediate and personal ways to fight selfishness and consumerism in ourselves and in our children, and to reach out to the many around us who are in desperate need of that personal touch. David Blankenhorn's pledge for fathers is a great start, and we might also consider a pledge for families, committing ourselves to work for the ideal of the family so beautifully described by John Paul II: "Inspired and sustained by the new commandment of love, the Christian family *welcomes, respects and serves every human being,* considering each one in his or her dignity as a person and as a child of God."[28]

The only way families can begin to approach this ideal is the way of prayer. For Christian families in particular, we cannot reflect the face of Christ to others unless we have often looked at him. We must pray without ceasing, and we must teach our children to pray. If we don't have children, we must try to teach other people and their children. No one gets a waiver in the culture wars. One reason we need this practice of prayer so desperately is that without it, we will not know who we are, and we will not know who our neighbors are. Recall Christ's question to his disciples, "Who do you say that I am?" Of course this was for their benefit, not for his. But we would do well to ask him frequently, "Who do you say that *I* am?" It is so easy to listen instead to the television, to our acquaintances, or to the mindless magazines at the grocery checkout counters, and the message we hear there isn't always encouraging. If we spend time with God, we will know the joy that comes from hearing his voice: "Arise, my beloved, my beautiful one, and come."[29] This is the love that we can pass on to those around us; it is the source and summit of all other loves.

---

[28] *FC*: 64.
[29] *Song of Songs* 2:10.

Finally, we can light a candle. We must contribute in some positive way to creating a cultural climate that welcomes life and affirms human dignity. Perhaps we need to start behind the lines in this battle. We can teach and encourage modesty in our children and in young people generally. We can fight the power of the media in our culture and resist its dominance over our children. They do not need a television in their bedrooms; they may not even need a Nintendo. We can beg for better religious education (or create our own alternatives to it), and we can insist on better education in the schools about marriage and families. Minimally, we can remove our children from programs offensive to our beliefs. We can seek out likeminded persons and groups and join forces to contend for what is true and just and compassionate.

Finally, we parents must put our own children first. We may be genuinely limited in the time we can give them. We may not have employers who give us the flexibility we need and deserve. We may not have the freedom to rearrange our work schedules in such a way as to increase our presence in their lives. But if we can, we should. Most of all, we must let them know in every way we can that they matter to us, that we are deeply grateful for them, and that we at least want to be there for them always.

Since each believer is called by baptism to be another Christ, to "put on Christ" as St. Paul has it, we must be ready to make the words of Christ our own: "This is my body, given up for you." Perhaps these words apply most obviously to mothers, who shelter human life in their own bodies for many months and who sacrifice themselves in very physical ways, giving their time and strength to husband and children and work, in the home and outside the home. But husbands and fathers too must make these words their own, along with priests and religious and every person, married or single, who has a vocation to love. "This is my body – this is my strength, my time, my heart, the best years of my life – given up for you." Like every other way, the way of the family does pass through the cross; but "it is through the Cross that the family can attain the fullness of its being and the perfection of its love."[30] We have all the grace that is necessary to do God's will in our family life, even in this culture which can be so poisonous to the health of the family.

In his wonderful *Letter to Families*, John Paul II tells us that "Marriage and family are a true vocation which comes from God himself and is an apostolate: the apostolate of the laity. Families are meant to contribute to the transformation of the earth and the renewal of the world, of creation, and of all humanity."[31] In the context of the challenges described above, this can seem an impossible task. Dear Families, I know you're busy, but please save the world. Repeating the phrase he has made famous in 21 years as pastor of the universal church, the Holy Father tells us: "Do not be afraid of the risks! God's strength is always far more powerful than your difficulties."[32] The exhortation on the family appeared

[30] *FC*: 86.
[31] *LtF*: 18.
[32] *LtF*: 18.

on the Feast of Christ the King, 1981, and this is meant as a signal to us. Knowing the ultimate victory is his, we must be bold and full of hope, so that when Christ comes he will find us faithfully guarding our post in the all-important battle for the souls of our children.

The Culture of Life

3. Politics and the Culture of Life

13

Some problems of conscience in bio-lawmaking

ANTHONY FISHER OP

1. Introduction

A POLITICIAN AND MOTHER of seven girls has introduced a bill to ban female infanticide in her South Asian nation. While all homicide, at least after birth, is already technically illegal in her country, the law has long been ineffectual, being applied only to boy children; thousands of infant girls are killed with impunity each year. Mrs Nightingale Singh's plan is to make it clear by legislation – followed by pressure upon the police and prosecuting authorities – that to kill a healthy child, simply for being a girl, is a crime. She realizes that this will leave unaffected the many hundreds of *handicapped* babies of both sexes who are smothered each year – a tragedy in her eyes, though possibly less cruel than the lethal neglect called 'nursing care only' and 'demand feeding' suffered by handicapped children in the more primitive hospitals of the Western world. Her own opposition to all infanticide is well known, but she realizes that there is at present no realistic hope of getting an effective universal ban on the practice in her country.

The problem is: quite apart from the anti-population lobby and certain other conservatives who predictably support infanticide on demand, one of the pro-life groups has become her most vehement critic. This group, which claims to speak for all right-thinking pro-lifers, declares that by seeking only to ban sex-selection infanticide Mrs Singh is implicitly conceding both the legality and the morality of killing infants on other grounds such as handicap. The group accuses her of thereby engaging in 'intrinsically evil acts' herself as well as formally co-operating in the evil acts of others: she is promoting or at least acquiescing in infanticide and willingly sacrificing some handicapped children's lives in order to save some healthy baby girls. But one may not do evil in the vain hope that good may come of it, her critics remind her. The law, as it presently stands, is quite clear: no infanticide, full-stop. Trying to limit the harm by conceding a little infanticide would only further undermine the law and the pro-life message. And it would also leave her and her supporters excommunicate – an especially puzzling threat for Mrs Singh given that she is a pious Hindu.

Meanwhile Afro-MP Muhammed Ignatius Mboembe Le Vie is promoting an anti-cloning bill in the newly formed African Union. While cloning is being attempted for some extinct game animals and a low-cholesterol hippopotamus is being genetically engineered for the table, this science had not yet been applied to humans in the African Union. Le Vie is aware, however, that in America and Europe where such practices with respect to human beings have been authoritatively declared to be contrary to human dignity by parliaments or presidents, they are increasingly common practices and often funded by those same authorities. Le Vie thinks there is a very good chance of getting an Africa-wide ban on so-called 'reproductive' cloning (cloning intended to produce a live-born child) but is less confident of also achieving a ban on so-called 'therapeutic' cloning (an even more unethical kind of cloning, where embryos are created and destroyed to cannibalise them for medical applications). But there is very little chance of a ban on destructive human embryo experimentation in general.

Dr Le Vie plans to put up a bill banning all three practices, but is willing to fall back to a ban on cloning, or even to a ban on only reproductive cloning, as required by the vicissitudes of the political debate. He had considered going for a ban on all reproductive technologies that are profligate with early human life or that disintegrate life-making from love-making, but he realizes this would probably mean the bill got no hearing at all because of the power of the IVF lobby. Once again, however, he is opposed not only by those who favour laissez-faire in this area, but also by a group calling themselves the Defenders of African Family Values. DAFV declare that they cannot support any bill which does not at least go for a complete ban on all artificial reproduction, sex education in schools, and the public dissemination of the theory of evolution.

Meanwhile, in Aragon state, Spain, a physician-assisted suicide bill has widespread popular support and is likely soon to be passed. Provincial MP Don Miguel-Angel Vida thinks he will vote against the bill in any case, but is toying with proposing an amendment which would require that anyone who is to be assisted with suicide must first be given a pamphlet describing in graphic detail the last stages of death by poisoning and offering alternatives such as good palliative and pastoral care. He also plans to support an amendment by a pro-life colleague of another party which would require a one week 'cooling off period' between the consent to assisted suicide and its implementation.

Don Vida is uncertain, however. He wonders about the prudence of amendments which might seem to lend some credibility to the assisted suicide bill and the wicked practice it will condone; the consciences of a few weaker MPs and physicians may be appeased by the thought that 'at least there are safeguards' so that they will then vote in favour of the amended bill. Furthermore, Vida's proposal might itself be amended by his opponents, so that the mandatory information sheet given prior to consent would end up tame at best, if not actually pro-suicide. He wonders whether it might be best to take an absolute stand against the bill or even just to let sleeping dogs lie and hope the bill will fail. Maybe this generation should just give up on pro-life lawmaking, or simply refuse to co-operate with any law which broadens the range of legal homicide. He asks his elderly parish priest what he should do. The monsignor suggests prayers to San José Patron de la Buena Muerte and refers the question to a classmate who lectures at the seminary. The advice arrives three days after the final vote on the bill.

The complementary rôles of priests and laity in the formulation of public policy were described by the Second Vatican Council in its Constitution on the Church in the Modern World, *Gaudium et Spes*:

Secular duties and activities belong properly although not exclusively to the laity... Lay-people should know that it is generally the function of their well-formed Christian conscience to see that the divine law is inscribed in the life of the earthly city; from priests they may look for spiritual light and nourishment. Let the laity not imagine that their pastors are always such experts, that to every problem which arises, however complicated, they can readily give a concrete solution, or even that such is their mission. Rather, enlightened by Christian wisdom and giving close attention to the teaching authority of the Church, let the laity take on their own distinctive role.[1]

Regarding what they called "the difficult but very noble art of politics", the Fathers of Vatican II praised "the work of those who for the common good devote themselves to the service of the state and take on the burdens of office." Of politicians they counseled that "with integrity and wisdom, they must take action against any form of injustice and tyranny". Law-making has an important rôle to play in such action against injustice: by formally recognizing the duties and protecting the rights of all persons, families and groups in the community and proscribing any attacks upon those rights and persons.[2] In this context the responsibility of law-makers and those who influence them to protect the life of all members of the community from conception until natural death were reaffirmed by the Council[3] and have since been repeated very often by popes and bishops, as well as many other faithful Christians, clerical and lay.

But no politician can do everything, and good laws will only take us so far in building up a civilization of life and love. Morally sensitive lawmakers also face many dilemmas as to what kinds of law to seek, what to oppose, what to seek to ameliorate by amendment, and what to do as a means to such ends. This essay will focus on a particular group of *causæ conscientiæ* which I have often encountered in counselling politicians and their advisers engaged in the conventional political struggle in defence of innocent human life: the duties of a politician with respect to laws in the area of abortion, infanticide, embryo destruction, euthanasia or other crimes against life, especially in those situations where the laws are not presently, and are not likely in the near future to be, as 'perfect'[4] as the pro-life politician[5] would desire.

In considering such questions I cannot elaborate a full political ethic here, nor articulate all the principles to be followed or all the qualities to be cultivated in

---

[1] Vatican Council II, *Gaudium et Spes*: Pastoral Constitution on the Church in the Modern World (1965) (hereafter: *GS*): 43.

[2] *GS* 75.

[3] *GS* 27, 51.

[4] The language of 'perfect' and 'imperfect' bio-legislation has been common in ecclesiastical circles at least since the Symposium held by the Congregation for the Doctrine of the Faith in Rome 9–12 November 1994, 'Catholics and the Pluralist Society: The Case of Imperfect Laws' (*I Cattolici e la societa pluralista: Il caso delle 'leggi imperfette'*. Bologna 1996).

[5] I use this category to cover not only Catholic and like-minded Christian politicians, but all those who draw the same conclusions as articulated in Part 2 of this paper. Much of what I say will apply *mutatis mutandis* to those who advise, lobby and support them.

civic leaders. Nor can I describe the complex process of discernment appropriate in any political judgment. While relying upon the authoritative teachings of the Catholic Church I cannot elaborate as fully as I would like all the theological presuppositions which underpin those teachings, the levels of authority with which they have been proposed,[6] or the common ground such teachings have with the positions of many other Christians, pro-lifers and persons of good will. While I will often refer to abortion legislation in particular to illustrate the principles I will elaborate in this essay, many of them will apply *ceteris paribus* to other areas of bio-legislation such as those I outlined in my opening (fictitious) examples.

2. What politicians cannot rightly do with respect to bio-legislation

Since the Council a series of documents have offered some counsel to Christian politicians on the positive course reasonably to be taken with respect to the protection of human life. These have included declarations of the Congregation for the Doctrine of the Faith,[7] speeches of Pope John Paul II,[8] interventions by the Holy See at UN meetings, statements by national bishops' conferences, responses of individual bishops to Catholic politicians,[9] and much else besides – all culminating in the great encyclical *Evangelium vitæ*.[10] A number of positions, not uncommon in contemporary discourse and practice, have also been authoritatively refuted. Rather than rehearse the substantial argumentation offered in those texts, or offered by theologians who support those teachings, it must suffice for present purposes to summarize six positive conclusions regarding bio-politics:

(1) it is the duty of politicians to ensure that civil law serves the common good and reflects fundamental moral norms (especially those regarding basic human rights), and that it protects from unjust attack the vulnerable (including the unborn, disabled, frail elderly, sick and dying);[11]

[6] For some preliminary thoughts on this matter see A. Fisher OP, 'A guided tour of *Evangelium vitæ*'. 72 (1995) *Australasian Catholic Record*: 445–462. Here I am very much at odds with the view of, for instance, Francis Sullivan in K. Wildes & A. Mitchell (eds), *Choosing Life: A Dialogue on 'Evangelium vitæ'*.Washington DC: Georgetown University Press 1997.

[7] Congregation for the Doctrine of the Faith, *Quæstio de abortu*: Declaration on Procured Abortion (1974) (hereafter: *QDA*); *Jura et Bona*: Declaration on Euthanasia (1980) (hereafter: *JB*); *Donum vitæ*: Instruction on Respect for Human Life in its Origin and on the Dignity of Procreation (1987) (hereafter: *DV*) 3. See also *Catechism of the Catholic Church* (English ed., Sydney: St Paul's 1995 as corrected by the editio typica) (hereafter: *CCC*).

[8] Collected in a regular series of volumes appearing since 1978, *Insegnamenti di Giovanni Paolo II* (Vatican City: Libreria Editrice Vaticana).

[9] E.g. the debates of Geraldine Ferraro and Mario Cuomo with Cardinal O'Connor and others.

[10] John Paul II, *Evangelium vitæ*: Encyclical on the Value and Inviolability of Human Life (1995) (hereafter: *EV*).

[11] John XXIII argued that the common good is best safeguarded when personal rights and duties are guaranteed. The chief concern of civil authorities must therefore be to ensure that these rights are recognized, respected, co-ordinated, defended and promoted, and that each individual

(2) it is likewise their duty to lead rather than merely follow public opinion in such crucial matters, and to seek to ensure the widest possible consensus for the good on them;[12]

(3) far from being an imposition upon the consciences of others, laws which protect the vulnerable from the impositions of the strong reflect a healthy respect for human rights and fundamental moral norms, and assist people

is enabled to perform his duties more easily. For "to safeguard the inviolable rights of the human person, and to facilitate the performance of his duties, is the principal duty of every public authority". Thus any government which refused to recognize human rights or acted in violation of them, would not only fail in its duty; its decrees would be wholly lacking in binding force (*Pacem in Terris*: Encyclical on Establishing Universal Peace (1963) cited in *EV* 71). Likewise *DV* 3: "It is part of the duty of the public authority to insure that the civil law is regulated according to the fundamental norms of the moral law in matters concerning human rights, human life and the institution of the family. Politicians must commit themselves, through their interventions upon public opinion, to securing in society the widest possible consensus on such essential points and to consolidating this consensus wherever it risks being weakened or is in danger of collapse." Cf. *EV* 4, 20, 68.

The Catholic Church does *not* teach that all immoral activities can or should be proscribed at law: thus the Church does not counsel politicians to enact laws against adultery or lying even though it regards such activities as wrong. This view is proposed in very clear terms in the works of St Thomas Aquinas, e.g. *ST* 1–2, 96, 2.

It is sometimes suggested that abortion should be decriminalised on the grounds it is impossible to stop, women will seek abortions anyway and possibly achieve them by more dangerous ('backyard') methods, and the law will inevitably be ignored and brought into disrepute. Yet as *QDA* and *EV* 71 and 90 point out, it is a primary function of the criminal law to ensure that all members of society enjoy respect for their fundamental rights, such as the right to life: if the law does not act here, where can it act? If the Angelic Doctor thought that the law should not seek to prohibit all vices, he was clear that it should at least prohibit the more serious ones: "human laws do not forbid all vices, from which the virtuous abstain, but only the more grievous vices, from which it is possible for the majority to abstain; and chiefly those that are to the hurt of others, without the prohibition of which human society could not be maintained: thus human law prohibits murder, theft and such like." *ST* 1–2, 96, 2. Cf. *EV* 70–72.

QDA 20 observes: "It is true that civil law cannot expect to cover the whole field of morality or to punish all faults. No one expects it to do so. It must often tolerate what is in fact a lesser evil, in order to avoid a greater one. One must, however, be attentive to what a change in legislation can represent. Many will take as authorization what is perhaps only the abstention from punishment. Even more, in the present case, this very renunciation seems at the very least to admit that the legislator no longer considers abortion a crime against human life, since murder is still always severely punished."

Likewise *DV* 3: "The civil law ... must sometimes tolerate, for the sake of public order, things which it cannot forbid without a greater evil resulting. However, the inalienable rights of their persons must be recognized and respected by civil society and the political authority ... In various states certain laws have authorized the direct suppression of innocents: the moment a positive law deprives a category of human beings of the protection which civil legislation must accord them, the state is denying the equality of all before the law. When the state does not place its power at the service of the rights of each citizen, and in particular of the more vulnerable, the very foundations of a state based on law are undermined ...".

[12] *DV* 3.

to grow in virtue;[13] those whose religion part-motivates their political struggle in this area are thus not guilty of religious intolerance or imposition but merely assuming their proper rôle in a democratic polity;[14]

(4) on the other hand, laws that deny protection to certain classes of human beings undermine the common good and expose even the supposedly democratic state as tyrannical;[15] such laws are not morally binding[16] and must not be obeyed;[17]

(5) direct abortion and euthanasia are intrinsically and gravely evil, since they are the deliberate killing of innocent human beings and no circumstance, purpose or law can ever make them right;[18] they also attack family and

[13] *QDA* 20: "It is true that it is not the task of the law to choose between points of view or to impose one rather than another. But the life of the child takes precedence over all opinions. One cannot invoke freedom of thought to destroy this life." *DV* 3: "Recourse to the conscience of each individual and to the self-regulation of researchers cannot be sufficient for insuring respect for personal rights and public order ... The task of the civil law is to insure the common good of people through the recognition of and the defence of fundamental rights and through the promotion of peace and of public morality." *EV* 71: "the legal toleration of abortion can in no way claim to be based on respect for the conscience of others, precisely because society has the right and duty to protect itself against abuses which can occur in the name of conscience and under the pretext of freedom."

[14] Likewise those whose faith supports their action with respect to abortion law are no more guilty of 'imposing their beliefs' upon others than are their doctrinaire libertarian or secular opponents.

[15] *EV* 20, 70 talks of the "*tyrant State*, which arrogates to itself the right to dispose of the life of the weakest and most defenceless members."

[16] "Laws which authorize and promote abortion ... [are] radically opposed not only to the good of the individual but also to the common good; as such they are completely lacking in authentic juridical validity. Disregard for the right to life, precisely because it leads to the killing of the person whom society exists to serve, is what most directly conflicts with the possibility of achieving the common good. Consequently, a civil law authorizing abortion or euthanasia ceases by that very fact to be a true, morally binding civil law ... I repeat once more that a law which violates an innocent person's natural right to life is unjust and, as such, is not valid as a law. For this reason I urgently appeal once more to all political leaders not to pass laws which, by disregarding the dignity of the person, undermine the very fabric of society" (EV 72, 90).

[17] *EV* 73. Thus majority votes for abortion do not make it right any more than majority attitudes towards capital punishment, immigration or Aboriginal land rights; political leaders have a duty to lead, not merely to follow. Were they to collaborate in a social prejudice which excludes the unborn from respect and protection, they would be harming rather than serving the State, because they would be undermining the very bases of respect for law and the legitimacy of the state. Legalising abortion "contributes to lessening respect for life and opens the door to ways of acting which are destructive of trust in relations between people"; such laws are contrary to the good of individuals and the common good; indeed there is reason to doubt whether they are valid laws at all (*EV* 72). Thus no parliamentarian can hide behind majority opinion, renouncing the duty of forming and following his or her own conscience, even in the public sphere (*EV* 69).

[18] *EV* 57, 62, 65 etc.; cf. Fisher, 'A guided tour'. John Paul II here echoes Vatican II which had declared: "All offences against life itself, such as ... abortion, euthanasia and willful self-destruction, are criminal. They poison civilization, they debase the perpetrators even more than the victims ... they dishonour the Creator. Life must be protected with the utmost care

community;[19] this is a conclusion of well-informed natural reason, even unaided by faith, and therefore proper ground for political action even in an avowedly 'secular' society;[20] revelation mediated by the Church clarifies and confirms this conclusion and gives additional grounds for political action in any self-consciously Christian society or any pluralist democratic society with some Christian voters and leaders;[21]

from the moment of conception: abortion and infanticide are abominable crimes" (GS 27, 51). Likewise Pope Paul VI, Humanæ Vitæ: Encyclical on the Regulation of Birth (1968) (hereafter: HV) 14; Holy See, Charter on the Rights of the Family (1983), 4. The gravity with which the Church views the procurement of abortion is reflected in the latæ sententiæ excommunication under canon 1398 of the Code of Canon Law (1983).

There is some dispute about the status of the definitions in EV, and in particular whether they are proposed as an exercise of the 'ordinary' and/or the 'extraordinary' magisterium of the Church, whether of the papal and/or episcopal magisterium and/or the sensus fidelium. All of these kinds of magisterium seem to me to have been appealed to in the tradition and in EV itself, and for these reasons and others the present writer believes that Catholic teaching on the intrinsic evil of all direct abortion is proposed infallibly. The recent publication of John Paul II's Apostolic Letter motu proprio Ad Tuendam Fidem (1998) and of the CDF's accompanying Explanatory Note would seem to confirm that this teaching is intended to be at least an example of one "definitively proposed by the Church regarding faith and morals" and "necessary for faithfully keeping and expounding the deposit of faith, even if they have not been proposed by the Magisterium of the Church as formally revealed." Following Vatican II these documents suggest that the Catholic faithful are required to give "firm and definitive assent to these truths" and "whoever denies them would be rejecting a truth of Catholic doctrine and would therefore no longer be in full communion with the Catholic Church."

[19] EV 42–45, 53–67.

[20] On the basis of the teaching with respect to abortion in the Scriptures, the Christian tradition, natural law philosophy, and the magisterium of the Catholic Church, see: EV; J. Finnis, 'Abortion and healthcare ethics', in R. Gillon (ed), Principles of Health Care Ethics. Chichester: Wiley 1994: 547–558; M. Gorman, Abortion and the Early Church: Christian, Jewish and Pagan Attitudes in the Greco-Roman World. Downers Grove, IL: InterVarsity Press 1982; G. Grisez, Abortion: The Myths, the Realities, and the Arguments. New York: Corpus 1970; I. C. de Paula, 'The respect due to the human embryo: an historical and doctrinal perspective', in J. Vial Corea & E. Sgreccia (eds), The Identity and Status of the Human Embryo. Vatican City: Libreria Editrice Vatiana 1997: 48–73; and sources cited in these works.

On the basis of the teaching with respect to euthanasia, see: EV; A. Fisher OP, 'Theological aspects of euthanasia', in J. Keown (ed.), Examining Euthanasia: Legal, Ethical and Clinical Perspectives. Cambridge: Cambridge University Press 1995: 315–332; L. Gormally (ed), The Dependent Elderly: Autonomy, Justice and Quality of Care. Cambridge: Cambridge University Press 1992; L. Gormally (ed) Euthanasia, Clinical Practice and the Law. London: The Linacre Centre 1994; and sources therein.

[21] Catholic teaching on abortion, euthanasia etc., while accessible to reason unaided by faith, is also a matter of faith, since it is believed by Catholics not only on the basis of persuasive philosophical and sociological reasons but also on the authority of the Scriptures, the Christian tradition and the living magisterium of the Church. The gravity of the matter is all the greater when it is realized that such acts involve the killing of a being made in the image of God, that they are contrary not only to practical reason but also to God's will, and that they involve not only an attack upon a basic human value (life) but also the renunciation of a sacred trust. On the complex relationship between faith and reason in such matters see: John Paul II, Fides et Ratio: Encyclical on the Relationship between Faith and Reason (1998). On the implications of a more self-conscious focus on building a Christian society see Aidan Nichols OP's fascinating work Christendom Awake: On re-energising the Church in Culture (Edinburgh: T&T Clark, 1999).

and therefore

(6) politicians must act individually or in concert to ensure that the law prohibits all homicide, including abortion, embryo destruction, infanticide and euthanasia.[22]

The arguments which the Catholic Church (and others) present for these six claims are sophisticated, persuasive and, I believe, conclusive. Various things follow. Commonly heard counterproposals which are *incompatible* with Catholic teaching on bio-politics include:

(1) that abortion, euthanasia etc. are morally permissible;[23]
(2) that attitudes to abortion, euthanasia and the like are matters of 'private morality' or 'personal religion', and therefore should not influence public policy;[24]

---

[22] *EV* 68–74, esp 72.

[23] Some Catholics or other Christians openly declare themselves opposed to their Church's teaching on abortion or euthanasia, and yet claim they are believing and practising members of their church. Holding that direct abortion or euthanasia is always wrong, it is asserted, is not a 'core belief' for Christians in the way that, for instance, belief in Divine Revelation or the Trinity are; and conscience must have primacy in moral matters.

The Catholic Church, however, makes a clear distinction between a well-formed conscience, on the one hand, and arbitrary preference or intuition on the other (e.g. Vatican II, *Dignitatis Humanae* (hereafter: *DH*) 2, 3; *GS* 16; cf. *GS* 30 on not "wallowing in the luxury of a merely individualistic morality"). The moral character of actions is determined by *objective* criteria, not merely by the sincerity of intentions or the goodness of motives (*GS* 51), and all people are called to form their consciences accordingly. "The more a correct conscience prevails, the more do persons and groups turn aside from blind choice and try to be guided by the objective standards of moral conduct. Yet it often happens that conscience goes astray through ignorance which it is unable to avoid, without thereby losing its dignity. This cannot be said of the person who takes little trouble to find out what is true and good, or when conscience is by degrees almost blinded through the habit of committing sin" (*GS* 27).

Catholics seek to inform their consciences according to reason which grasps the natural law accessible to all; this is clarified, confirmed and possibly supplemented by divine revelation mediated by Church teachings. They believe that by "their faith, aroused and sustained by the Spirit of truth, the People of God, guided by the Magisterium, and obeying it, receives not the mere word of human beings, but truly the word of God." (Vatican Council II. *Lumen Gentium*: Dogmatic Constitution on the Church (1964), 12; cf. 25; John Paul II, *Veritatis Splendor*: Encyclical on Certain Fundamental Questions of the Church's Moral Teaching (1993) (hereafter: *VS*), ch. 2.) Given the consistency and gravity of Church teaching in this area, '(conscientiously) Catholic and pro-abortion' makes about as much sense as '(conscientiously) Catholic and anti-Eucharist' or 'Catholic and pro-rape'.

[24] Catholic teaching on human rights questions such as abortion is no more mysteriously religious or sectarian than its teaching against slavery, apartheid or unjust wars. To characterize these matters as 'private morality' or 'personal religion' is an evasion amounting to ethical relativism: cf. *EV* 70; Robert George, *Political action and legal reform in 'Evangelium Vitae'* (Washington DC: US Catholic Conference, 1996). Nor can the Christian legitimately privatize his or her religious beliefs. As Vatican II observed: "they are mistaken who, knowing that we have here no abiding city but seek one which is to come, think that they may therefore shirk their earthly responsibilities. For they are forgetting that by the faith itself they are more obliged than ever to measure up to these duties, each according to his proper vocation. Nor, on the

(3) that respect for the consciences of constituents, including those who do not believe abortion or euthanasia is wrong, requires their elected representatives make no laws which interfere with their right to exercise their conscientious beliefs in this area;[25]

(4) that politicians must respect and enact majority opinion on such matters, whatever it is;[26]

and therefore

(5) that a politician may initiate or should support (and a citizen may obey) a law which admits in principle the licitness of abortion or euthanasia.[27]

---

contrary, are they any less wide of the mark who think that religion consists in acts of worship alone and in the discharge of certain moral obligations, and who imagine they can plunge themselves into earthly affairs in such a way as to imply that these are altogether divorced from the religious life. This split between the faith which many profess and their daily lives deserves to be counted among the more serious errors of our age ... The Christian who neglects his temporal duties, neglects his duties toward his neighbour and even God, and jeopardizes his eternal salvation" (*GS* 43).

[25] *QDA* 20: "It is true that it is not the task of the law to choose between points of view or to impose one rather than another. But the life of the child takes precedence over all opinions. One cannot invoke freedom of thought to destroy this life"; *DV* 3: "Recourse to the conscience of each individual and to the self-regulation of researchers cannot be sufficient for insuring respect for personal rights and public order ... The task of the civil law is to insure the common good of people through the recognition of and the defence of fundamental rights and through the promotion of peace and of public morality."

EV 71: "The legal toleration of abortion can in no way claim to be based on respect for the conscience of others, precisely because society has the right and duty to protect itself against abuses which can occur in the name of conscience and under the pretext of freedom." Those whose religion part-motivated their struggle against slavery or the genocide of Australian Aborigines were not fairly charged with religious intolerance or imposition; and those whose faith supports their action with respect to abortion law are no more guilty of imposing their religion upon others than are their doctrinaire libertarian or secular opponents.

[26] *EV* observes, "the democratic ideal, which is only truly such when it acknowledges and safeguards the dignity of every human person, is betrayed in its very foundations" when legislators engage in a "tragic caricature of legality" in passing permissive abortion laws. "In the name of what justice," he asks, "is the most unjust of discriminations practised: some individuals are held to be deserving of defence and others are denied that dignity? When this happens, the process leading to the breakdown of a genuinely human co-existence and the disintegration of the State itself has already begun" (*EV* 20). Democracy is not infallible; it should not "be idolized to the point of making it a substitute for morality or a panacea for immorality ... The value of democracy stands or falls with the values which it embodies and promotes." If it fails to observe "the objective moral law which, as the natural law written in the human heart, is the obligatory point of reference for civil law" it easily becomes hostage to those "most capable of manoeuvring not only the levers of power but also of shaping the formation of consensus" (*EV* 70). Thus majority votes for abortion do not make it right any more than majority attitudes towards capital punishment, immigration or the rights of indigenous peoples; political leaders have a duty to lead, not merely to follow.

[27] "It must be clearly understood that whatever may be laid down by civil law in this matter, human beings can never obey a law which is in itself immoral, and such is the case of a law which would admit in principle the licitness of abortion. Nor can they take part in a propaganda campaign in favour of such a law, or vote for it ..." (*QDA* 21; cf. *EV* 59, 73, 90).

In addition to the range of things which a politician might not reasonably initiate, sponsor or by his affirmative vote legislate, there are also those actions which have the effect of assisting others in the liberalization of abortion laws and thus in the practice of abortion: this occasions concern about co-operation in another's evil. I do not need to rehearse the principles governing this kind of moral act here.[28] Suffice it to say that a legislator who favours permissive abortion, and therefore actively supports someone else's permissive bill or actively blocks someone else's restrictions to such a bill, engages in formal co-operation in the evil of the sponsor of the legislation. So too does one uninterested in the abortion issue who nonetheless supports such a bill or blocks such restrictions, hoping thereby to gain something else, such as appeasing certain opponents, keeping his or her seat, or horse-trading support for some other (possibly better) legislative objective. In such cases politicians can be guilty of formal co-operation in evil even if they disapprove of abortion and say so publicly. The sad reality is that some of the worst collaborators in permissive abortion régimes in recent decades have been politicians ostensibly opposed to abortion.

In his important reflection upon the implications of grievously unjust laws, Pope John Paul concludes that "Laws which authorize and promote abortion and euthanasia are therefore radically opposed not only to the good of the individual but also to the common good; as such they are completely lacking in authentic juridical validity. Disregard for the right to life, precisely because it leads to the killing of the person whom society exists to serve, is what most directly conflicts with the possibility of achieving the common good. Consequently, a civil law authorizing abortion or euthanasia ceases by that very fact to be a true, morally binding civil law" (*EV* 72). Here he is in the tradition of St Thomas who taught that "a tyrannical law, through not being according to reason, is not a law, absolutely speaking, but rather a perversion of law" (*ST* 1–2, 92, 1 ad 4) and that "unjust laws... are acts of violence rather than laws; because, as Augustine says (*De Lib. Arb.* i, 5), 'a law that is not just, seems to be no law at all.'" (*ST* 1–2, 96, 4).

[28] "In order to shed light on this difficult question, it is necessary to recall the general principles concerning *co-operation in evil actions*. Christians, like all people of good will, are called upon under grave obligation of conscience not to co-operate formally in practices which, even if permitted by civil legislation, are contrary to God's law. Indeed, from the moral standpoint, it is never licit to co-operate formally in evil. Such co-operation occurs when an action, either by its very nature or by the form it takes in a concrete situation, can be defined as a direct participation in an act against innocent human life or a sharing in the immoral intention of the person committing it. This co-operation can never be justified either by invoking respect for the freedom of others or by appealing to the fact that civil law permits it or requires it. Each individual in fact has moral responsibility for the acts which he personally performs; no one can be exempted from this responsibility, and on the basis of it everyone will be judged by God himself (cf. *Rom* 2:6; 14:12)" (*EV* 74). Cf. *VS* 78 and *EV* 73. These principles are explored very fully in G. Grisez, *The Way of the Lord Jesus*, vol. 3: *Difficult Moral Questions* (Quincy, IL: Franciscan Press, 1997), esp. pp. 871–898. A simpler treatment is: A. Fisher OP, 'Co-operation in evil'. 44/3 (1994) *Catholic Medical Quarterly*: 15–22.

3. What politicians can rightly do with respect to bio-legislation: the moral act of initiating or supporting an 'imperfect' abortion or euthanasia law

Having reviewed very briefly some commonly heard positions which are, in my view, excluded for politicians, I come now to consider what they reasonably *can* do. The applicable moral principles in this area are those concerning the intended object of the moral act, and concerning formal and material co-operation in an evil instigated by another person(s); there are also several virtues at issue which I will treat at the end of my paper.

In situations where abortion, infanticide, embryo experimentation, euthanasia and the like are already clearly illegal, leaders must remain vigilant lest such laws are flouted or diluted by permissive judgments in *causes célèbre*; they must seek to educate the public about the values underpinning and the benefits of maintaining such laws; they must counter those forces which will always be at work to undermine the civilization of life and love. Above all, perhaps, leaders must work to minimize not just the supply but also the demand for abortion and the rest: to ensure that public education, financial and social support, counselling and the like are more than adequate, so that unwanted pregnancy is rare and those who are troubled by their pregnancy are as fully supported as possible. Likewise the frail elderly, sick and disabled must not only be protected by laws but so loved and cared for by communities that killing them becomes unthinkable.

Would that most of us came from countries where the weakening of a well-nigh perfect legislative régime with respect to the protection of human life were the worry! The tragedy is that most of the Western world, at least, now operates under systems tolerant of thousands or millions of abortions per year and increasingly tolerant of embryo destruction and euthanasia at least by neglect. The 'culture of death', so tellingly identified by Pope John Paul II, is now predominant in the West and means that violence has become so commonplace that even practising Christians rarely reflect on just how bloody are the supposedly enlightened institutions and practices of their community.

Here we might distinguish several kinds of unjust bio-legal situations:

(1) where killing is presently *de jure* legal in some situations *due to constitutional law* – as is the case with respect to abortion in the USA according to a series of Supreme Court decisions supposedly interpreting the US constitution but actually unashamedly engaging in *eisegesis* and judicial legislation;

(2) where killing is presently *de jure* legal in some situations *due to statute law* – as is now the case with euthanasia in the Netherlands (as it was briefly the case in Australia's Northern Territory), and as it is the case with physician-assisted suicide in the US state of Oregon, with respect to abortion in the UK, much of Europe and the Western two-thirds of Australia, and with respect to destructive embryo experimentation in many jurisdictions;

(3) where killing is presently *de jure* legal in some situations *due to permissive interpretations by courts* of a *prima facie* restrictive statute – as was the case with respect to abortion in the UK before the 1967 Abortion Act, and is

the case today with respect to abortion in the Eastern states of Australia and increasingly in Ireland, and as was the case for a number of years with active euthanasia in the Netherlands (until its recent accommodation by statute) and as is the case with euthanasia by neglect in several jurisdictions, most notably Britain since the *Bland* case; and

(4) where killing is presently *de jure* illegal but *de facto* allowed in some situations either because the law is not enforced by the police, the prosecuting authorities and/or the courts, or because, while illegal according to the letter of the law, past experience and present realities indicate that a conviction is probably impossible under the present law – as is the case throughout much of the Western world today with respect to much bio-legislation.

In these situations the question immediately arises: are politicians bound to seek to change constitutions or to pass laws to make illegal practices such as abortion in all circumstances? And if the passage of such constitutional amendments or statutes is, for the time being, impossible without a miracle, are they bound, or at least permitted, to seek to pass laws which at least tighten up the situation in some way – so that at least some abortions, infanticides, embryo destructions or euthanasias which might otherwise occur would not? (Such a course of action has in fact been tried, and sometimes succeeded, in some places at some times.[29]) If such a restrictive yet still permissive bill is proposed, are pro-life politicians bound to support it, oppose it, or take some middle course?

What happens if someone from the other side, as it were, is making the running, proposing some new law to make access to abortion or euthanasia legal or more clearly legal or more broadly legal than it presently is? Suppose that the passage of such a bill seems very likely. Should or may a pro-life politician oppose such a bill at all stages, or support the bill at certain stages of the legislative process but not at others, in the hope of gaining some concession? Should such an MP, while opposing the bill as a whole, propose or support amendments to the bill which would, at least, tighten up the régime envisaged by the bill so that at least some abortions or euthanasias which might otherwise occur would not?

In *Evangelium Vitæ* paragraph 73, Pope John Paul II notes:

> A particular problem of conscience can arise in cases where a legislative vote would be decisive for the passage of a more restrictive law, aimed at limiting the number of authorised abortions, in place of a more permissive law already passed or ready to be voted on. Such cases are not infrequent. It is a fact that while in some parts of the world there continue to be campaigns to introduce laws favouring abortion, often supported by powerful international organizations, in other nations – particularly those which have already experienced

---

[29] For a thorough review of various attempts to ameliorate or enforce British abortion laws and the almost impenetrable obstacles to the passage of such laws, see J. Keown, *Abortion, Doctors and the Law: Some aspects of the legal regulation of abortion in England from 1803 to 1982.* Cambridge: Cambridge University Press 1988.

the bitter fruits of such permissive legislation – there are growing signs of a rethinking in this matter. In a case like the one just mentioned, when it is not possible to overturn or completely abrogate a pro-abortion law, an elected official, whose absolute personal opposition to procured abortion was well known, could licitly support proposals aimed at limiting the harm done by such a law and at lessening its negative consequences at the level of general opinion and public morality. This does not in fact represent an illicit co-operation with an unjust law, but rather a legitimate and proper attempt to limit its evil aspects.[30]

Following this text the Secretary of the Congregation for the Doctrine of the Faith, Archbishop Tarcisio Bertone SDB, wrote:

By virtue of their specific vocation, it is *mainly* up to lay Christians to engage with *imperfect laws* in present-day democracy. Three attitudes are possible here: (1) *Prophetic resistance*... may be justified if a lay Christian prefers to opt for the value placed in question by the law [here: absolute respect for life] rather than opt for the lesser evil [here: a less 'imperfect' abortion law etc.]... (2) *Collaboration*. A less radical attitude, or one involving greater collaboration, is permitted by the Church if it is possible to promote a lesser evil than that proposed by the law. We may remark that it is not the evil as such that is at issue here, *but the good, more specifically the good necessary to defuse or reduce the evil that the evil in question may produce*. In Christianity it is never permitted to do evil or use evil means to produce a good end; nonetheless each value, by the very fact that it belongs to what is good or what is true, asks to be respected. This attitude, that aims at what is good, within a situation characterized by what is evil, may be difficult to understand for those not directly involved in the political experience and unfamiliar with its complex ramifications. Just for this reason, this choice of what is good, in a situation characterized by what is evil, must be *publicly explained* by those who take such a decision on grounds of conscience. Once this effort has been made with all the necessary seriousness, the legislator must not let himself be tormented, or change attitude, as a result of the false interpretation that may be given to his gesture. (3) *Tolerance*. The third attitude is the tolerance of the evil expressed through an unjust law. Such tolerance can only be possible if resistance to the evil would involve a yet greater evil. Here too the object taken into consideration

---

[30] Likewise Cardinal Ratzinger wrote in May 1982 in response to a request from the US Bishops regarding the Hatch amendment: "according to the principles of Catholic morality, an action can be considered licit whose object and proximate effect consist in limiting an evil insofar as possible. Thus, when one intervenes in a situation judged evil in order to correct it for the better, and when the action is not evil in itself, such an action should be considered not as the voluntary acceptance of the lesser evil but rather as the effective improvement of the existing situation, even though one remains aware that not all evil present is able to be eliminated for the moment." Cited in R. G. Peters, 'Stopping Abortion: The Pragmatist's View', *Catholic Twin Circle* (17 Sept 1989).

by the act of tolerance is not the evil as such, but the good necessary to impede a greater evil.[31]

This important teaching has already occasioned considerable debate amongst faithful Catholics and their pro-life friends, such as Colin Harte in this very volume. To some it appears a contradiction: how can anyone who believes all abortion is wrong support "just a little abortion"? Is a spirit of appeasement or pragmatism being manifested in Vatican politics? Are we engaging in evil in the vain hope that good may come, trading some lives for others? Has despair of ever having sound laws and practices in this area resulted in a sell-out?[32]

I think not, but I recognize that understanding Catholic teaching in this area, like understanding the Christian Gospel on many topics, requires a certain amount of arduous and dispassionate thinking. And in the heat of political debate, in the face of urgency, amongst parliamentarians and public not well versed in the nooks and crannies of ethical theory, all led by media either unhelpfully simplistic or plain hostile, people may be inclined to dismiss such thinking as a luxury or unnecessarily convoluted. I believe this view is wrong, if understandable. A parallel might usefully be drawn, perhaps, with respect to Catholic teaching on the just war. It is complex and will not always deliver up a single clear answer on which wars are just ones and which ways of fighting them are just. Some will however be clearly unjust. And the complexities of the argument are no excuse for not doing the hard thinking. Too much is at stake to simply embrace "my country right or wrong" or a dogmatic pacifism. The same is true in our present discussion.

John Finnis has explained the application of these principles to abortion law reform as follows:

> [According to *Evangelium Vitæ*] the always illicit vote is [the vote] for a law as *permitting*, precisely *to* permit, abortion. This is always illicit, even if one is personally opposed to abortion and is voting for it only to keep one's seat and prevent euthanasia or genocide laws, or only to equalise the position of the poor and the rich. The kind of vote which... [*Evangelium Vitæ*] judges can be licit has as its object not: *to permit* abortions now illegal but rather: *to prohibit* abortions now legal or imminently likely otherwise to become legal. (Say: the existing law or the threatened alternative bill says abortion is lawful up to 24 weeks, while the law or bill for which the Catholic legislator is voting for says abortion is lawful up to 16 weeks.) Even though it is a

---

[31] T. Bertone, 'Catholics and pluralist society: "Imperfect laws" and the responsibility of legislators', in J. Vial Correa & E. Sgreccia (eds) *Evangelium Vitae. Five Years of Confrontation with the Society*. Vatican City: Libreria Editrice Vaticana 2001: 206–222, at pp. 218–219. Emphases in original.

[32] An example of a commentator who, while not openly critical of 'an incremental strategy, proposing or supporting laws that would limit abortion but allow it in some cases', is clearly deeply uncomfortable with it and ultimately concludes that such laws, while not excluded in principle, are always imprudent is Charles Rice, *The Winning Side: Questions on Living the Culture of Life*. Mishawaka, IND: St Brendan's 1999: 225–233.

vote for a law which does permit abortion, it is chosen by this legislator as a vote for a law which restricts abortion. That this restrictive law also permits abortion is only a side-effect – when we consider the act of voting in the perspective of the acting person – even though the side-effect of permission is as immediate as the object of restriction.[33]

The ink of these (and the surrounding) words of Professor Finnis was barely dry when lawmakers and pro-lifers in two different Australian jurisdictions were debating their implications for new laws. The sometimes bitter disputes during those legislative debates reflected confusion over some matters worth a little more and cooler attention from this distance because they are instructive about broader questions of conscience for bio-politics; there will no doubt be many echoes for those who have watched or participated more actively in efforts to reform bio-law here in Britain or across the various channels which separate her from the rest of us.

4. Some issues raised by recent Australian attempts to apply 'Evangelium Vitæ' 73

For those unaware of what happened in the antipodes in 1998–99 I will summarize the background very briefly.[34] In Perth, Western Australia, bills were introduced to legalize abortion on demand after a *cause célèbre* in which a doctor was charged with criminal abortion; some pro-life MPs, while opposing the bill(s) as a whole, promoted amendments which would at least restrict abortion in some ways. In Canberra, on the other hand, it was the pro-life parliamentarians in the local Australian Capital Territory assembly who initiated change: in a situation of *de facto* abortion on demand they sought to introduce at least some regulation, especially through requiring certain minimum information be given to women about foetal development and alternatives to abortion. In both cases the pro-life politicians achieved some limited success in a dreadfully hostile environment. And in both cases the vilification came as much from their pro-life friends as from their pro-abortion enemies. What were the points of contention? Four are worth mentioning here because they have wider ramifications.

4.1 *Whether* Evangelium Vitæ *73 applies to existing laws or to bills being debated or both*

First, there were some in Perth who asserted that *Evangelium Vitæ* §73 applied only to the introduction by pro-life MPs of new laws aimed at restricting abortion

---

[33] J. Finnis, 'The Catholic Church and public policy debates in Western liberal societies: the basis and limits of intellectual engagement', in L. Gormally (ed) *Issues for a Catholic Bioethic.* London: The Linacre Centre 1999: 261–273, at pp. 268–269.

[34] For fuller details see: Warwick Neville, 'Realpolitik, theology and the culture of death: abortion, politics and law in the Australian Capital Territory,' 10/4 (1998) *Bioethics Research Notes*: 37–39.

in a permissive régime, not to attempts to ameliorate by amendment permissive bills introduced to a legislature by someone else. (On this view Dr La Vie, and possibly Mrs Singh, might be justified in their actions but not Don Vida.) In Canberra, on the other hand, some people – sometimes the same people – asserted the opposite: *Evangelium Vitæ* sanctioned attempts to ameliorate by amendment other people's pro-abortion bills, but did not allow the introduction of new laws in a permissive régime which would restrict but not prohibit abortion. Yet in praising efforts "aimed at limiting the number of authorised abortions" the encyclical clearly refers *both* to promoting new, more restrictive laws in place of permissive ones already in place ("laws already passed") and to promoting restrictive amendments to other people's permissive bills ("laws ready to be voted on"). Either way, the Pope explains, when it is not possible to defeat a pro-abortion law or bill, a politician could in certain circumstances licitly support a proposal aimed at "limiting the harm done", without thereby being responsible for the far from perfect state of the law. Even had the Pope not been as clear as he was in fact, his principles clearly apply equally both to existing and to proposed laws.

4.2 Where 'existing law' is to be found

Another dispute in this context was over whether, in considering what *is* the present state of the law (the "law already passed"), one must refer only to a plain reading of existing statutes. The reason this was so important is that throughout much of Australia abortion has never been legalized by statute as it was in Britain in 1967; rather, courts have given permissive interpretations of *prima facie* restrictive abortion statutes and law 'enforcement' agencies have done little to enforce even those very liberal interpretations of the law. This has led to *de facto* abortion on demand: in fact Australia has a significantly higher abortion rate than Britain despite the more permissive British laws – it is now estimated that one in three Australian women has had or will have an abortion. Of course, even those peoples not blessed with a common law system, who must labour instead under codified criminal law, require authoritative interpretations and applications of their constitutions, statutes and treaties like any other country. In common law jurisdictions with some legislation and some customary law of precedent, it is even more clearly the case that the courts in part make the law. Law is not self-interpreting; indeed to the ordinary laity it often seems to mean something very different from its plain words. With respect to abortion this is very much the case: activist courts in the United States, Britain, Canada and Australia have discovered exceptions to the laws against abortion or rights to abortion hidden in words where no plain reader would have dreamed of finding them. The recent appalling US ruling in *Stenberg for Nebraska v Carhart* is only the latest of a long string of the like throughout the common law world. The same thing is happening with respect to euthanasia by neglect, especially for those given the death sentence 'PVS'. And galling as it is to those of us who are sure these are ideologically-driven misreadings of the law, until a superior court or legislator overrules those interpretations they are for our present purposes the law.

Furthermore, even accepting a plain reading of the statutes forbidding abortion in Australia, such statutes are manifestly not enforced by the police, the prosecuting authorities and/or the courts. It could well be argued that the statutes are therefore annulled by desuetude.[35] Several facts supported this view in West Australian and the Australian Capital Territory. First, the average woman in the Australian street thinks abortion is legal and governments, police and prosecuting authorities do nothing to disabuse her. Abortions are financed under the national health scheme, advertised in the media, approved by medical colleges, referred for and performed by doctors 'in good standing' and recommended by school counsellors. Furthermore, the first attempt in many years to initiate a case against a doctor who flagrantly broke the West Australian abortion statute led to the prompt repeal of that technical prohibition.

So what are we to make of an ineffectual law, ineffectual indeed for several generations? Catholic theology going back at least to St Thomas Aquinas has been well aware that black-letter laws are necessarily adapted "to time and place"; as Thomas observed, *consuetude et habet vim legis, et legem abolet, et est legum interpretatrix*: custom makes, unmakes and interprets laws.[36] Thus the Law, taken in the broad, capital-L sense of that which a particular legal system brings about, is in some senses more and in some senses less than the sum total of lower-case-l laws (statutes and precedents). And a lawmaker will properly take into account what the Law effectively achieves, or can be expected effectively to achieve, in making his decisions about what reforms of the Law and thus what particular laws he will support.

4.3 The prudence of ameliorative measures

A third point of dispute during the recent Australian debates was over the prudence of particular measures proposed in specific contexts – a matter about which morally and factually well-informed people may disagree even in ideal circumstances. There was entirely appropriate disquiet about the risk that the law would end up worse than it already was, or that a rare opportunity to make it better might be missed, about causing scandal either by action or inaction in these circumstances, about the helpfulness of particular wordings

---

[35] This raises the complex jurisprudential question of whether and when a law ceases to be such by virtue of desuetude. Such assessments are made on different bases in different jurisdictions and are provisional until an authoritative pronouncement of desuetude has been made by a superior court or the original law has been rescinded by the legislator. It might also be argued that some laws are ineffective for their primary purpose (in this case, protecting unborn human beings and their mothers from abortion) but effective for some other purpose (e.g. protecting the right of some institutions and individuals to refuse to provide such 'services').

[36] *ST* 1–2, 97, 3. Cf. Robert George, *Making Men Moral: Civil Liberties and Public Morality*. Oxford: Oxford University Press 1993, ch. 1.

and amendments to wordings, about the political minutiae of when to move and in concert with whom and all the rest. Some of these matters were of interest only to those involved at the time. But the claim by some critics that these measures were so imprudent as to involve wilfully wrong acts, negligence or immoral material co-operation in evil, deserves a little more attention.[37]

I have already dealt with immoral initiation and co-operation in the evil of legalizing or otherwise permitting offences against innocent life. *Evangelium vitæ* 73 makes it clear that support for imperfect laws is sometimes permissible, despite the material co-operation it might lend to offences against life. What are the reasons that might persuade a pro-life parliamentarian to engage in such material co-operation? One must examine these carefully and honestly, taking them seriously without overstating them. The most important one will be any unborn, handicapped or dying people the legislator believes might be saved, and any others (such as pregnant women) who might also benefit, even if not all can be saved or assisted. Politicians themselves can also have much at stake, as might those who rely upon them. And they might have various prior commitments and other responsibilities to take into account. So before supporting an imperfect bio-law the politician must ask: how important are the benefits expected from this activity, how extensive, how certain and for whom?

What are the relevant side-effects which would count against such material co-operation? Again, parliamentarians must examine these carefully and honestly, not ignoring them simply because they are unintended or minimizing them because of their enthusiasm for the benefits they hope to achieve by pursuing this course of action. The most obvious ill-effect of material co-operation is that it assists in another's wrong-doing, in this case the passage of a law permitting abortion. Thus the legislator must ask: what kind of loss or harm will result from the liberalization of abortion with which I am unintentionally co-operating, or from any other side-effects of my own activities? How extensive will the harm be, how certain is it to occur, and who will suffer it? Will my refusing to co-operate prevent the wrong – or will it go ahead regardless? Am I in a position to stop it or at least reduce the harm done? In what ways can I at least express my disapproval and try to convert hearts and minds to my way of thinking?

Another bad side effect of material co-operation is that it may corrupt the politician concerned. A person may find their strength of will on these matters affected by having, even once, co-operated materially in the evil of liberalizing abortion. They may become blasé about it, dulled to the evil side-effects, and happy enough to admit them as their own intention in the future. Or they may find themselves trapped in the company and schemes of others they thought allies who do not in fact share their scruples; the desire for solidarity and success

---

[37] Rice, *The Winning Side*, p. 233, addressing the American scene, asks "Although an incremental strategy of limiting abortion can be morally justified, does it make practical sense?" He responds "No. Period, paragraph, next case." This assertion seems to be based upon a disjunction between sound moral principle and virtuous practice: *EV* 73 certainly does not declare imprudent behaviour morally justified.

may then carry such a person along into formal co-operation with evil in the future, whether with respect to bad bio-law or some other moral 'compromise'.

A third ill-effect of such material co-operation can be that it corrupts others. Pro-life politicians who support imperfect bio-legislation may be misunderstood by others to be abandoning their pro-life position; they might thereby 'give scandal' to others who do not appreciate the distinctions between intentional ends and foreseen side-effects, formal co-operation and material co-operation etc. This might seriously impair the witness they could and should be giving to others. And their example might encourage others not only to co-operate materially, but even to co-operate formally, i.e. to advance even more permissive abortion legislation or to regard abortion less seriously. Pro-life politicians must be prepared at times to take a stance against an activity by privately or even fairly publicly refusing to co-operate even materially, and even at the risk of their political career; or, if they *are* co-operating materially, at least to take as active a part as is practicable in otherwise protesting against the evil practice they are unwillingly facilitating.

4.4 Underlying intentionality

A fourth area of concern in the late 1990s Australian debates of enduring interest was over the conception of the moral act underlying the Pope's argument, which some have impliedly rejected by accusing those who followed it of being intentionalists or subjectivists. Here we enter the deep waters of act analysis which *Veritatis Splendor* so helpfully plumbed for us, if not exhaustively, teaching among other things that

> The morality of the human act depends primarily and fundamentally on the 'object' rationally chosen by the deliberate will... In order to be able to grasp the object of an act which specifies that act morally, it is therefore necessary to place oneself in the perspective of the acting person. The object of the act of willing is in fact a freely chosen kind of behaviour... By the object of a given moral act, then, one cannot mean a process or an event of the merely physical order, to be assessed on the basis of its ability to bring about a given state of affairs in the outside world. Rather, that object is the proximate end of a deliberate decision which determines the act of willing on the part of the acting person.[38]

Even within the camp of those who support traditional Catholic moral teaching and subscribe to the centrality of the object of the moral act, there are differences of accent.

To give three examples: some years ago the British Bishops taught that the victim of rape is entitled to defend herself against the continuing effects of such an attack, including preventing the union of the rapist's sperm with her ovum,

[38] *VS* 78.

even by taking 'the pill' to prevent ovulation.[39] Interventions aimed at causing abortion after rape were, of course, excluded.[40] This cautious and nuanced position did not satisfy everyone. Some 'perfectionists' asserted that this episcopal teaching amounted to condoning the intrinsically evil act of contraception, at least in certain cases, and that it promoted the doing of evil that good may come of it. The Bishops explained that the object of taking the pill in such cases is *not* to sterilize one's chosen sexual acts in anticipation or retrospect, but to protect the woman from the continuing attack of the rapist (as his sperm made its way up her reproductive system); in this respect taking the pill is no more an act of contraception than would be the woman pushing her rapist away just as he was about to ejaculate. The complainants were not appeased by this explanation. Their thought would seem to have been: the object of an act can be seen from the outside, as it were; taking the pill is obviously engaging in contraception, an act which cannot be ordered to the good; 'subjective' intention is only relevant to ensuring that the act is free (and thus a genuinely human act at all), and may reduce responsibility or gravity, but it cannot affect the object which is 'objectively' known.[41]

Another example also hails from Britain: the teaching, a few years ago, that the Rubella vaccine was licitly used despite the fact that it is grown upon a cell line derived from an aborted girl.[42] Despite careful explanation of the remoteness of the abortion from the vaccinations, the difference of intended object, and the lack of any formal co-operation in the evil of abortion on the part of those giving or receiving the vaccine, there were those who thought it was intrinsically wrong to use the vaccine whilever it was cultured in this way.

A last example occurs at the other end of life. Advocates of euthanasia often suggest that intentionally killing a patient thought better off dead, withdrawing life-sustaining treatments because they are too burdensome, and giving high

---

[39] Catholic Bishops' [of England & Wales, Scotland, and Ireland] Joint Committee on Bioethical Issues, 'Use of the "Morning After Pill" in cases of rape'. 15/39 (31 January 1986) *Origins*: 633–638; and 'A Reply', 16/13 (11 September 1986) *Origins*: 237–238; cf. Pennsylvania Catholic Conference, 'Guidelines for Catholic hospitals treating victims of sexual assault'. 22/47 (6 May 1993) *Origins*: 81.

[40] It follows that measures such as the 'morning after pill' may only be used after rape when they involve no significant risk to the life of a developing embryo.

[41] They referred especially to *HV* 14: "In truth, if it is sometimes licit to tolerate a lesser evil in order to avoid a greater evil or to promote a greater good, it is not licit, even for the gravest reasons, to do evil so that good may follow therefrom; that is, to make into the object of a positive act of the will something which is intrinsically disorder, and hence unworthy of the human person, even when the intention is to safeguard or promote individual, family or social well-being. Consequently it is an error to think that a conjugal act which is deliberately made infecund and so is intrinsically dishonest could be made honest and right by the ensemble of a fecund conjugal life." Puzzling for these writers was the very next paragraph of the encyclical, 15: "The Church, on the contrary, does not at all consider illicit the use of those therapeutic means truly necessary to cure diseases of the organism, even if an impediment to procreation, which may be foreseen, should result therefrom, provided such impediment is not, for whatever motive, directly willed."

[42] See *The Tablet* 29 October 1994: 1391.

doses of pain-relieving agents to those in terrible pain, knowing that in the very frail this sometimes risks suppressing respiration, are all the same. But it is not only the pro-euthanasists who associate these different kinds of act: some 'perfectionists' from their opponent camp can be just as good at fudging these things. The thought here is again: you just know, from the outside as it were, that removing a ventilator from someone who is ventilator-dependent or giving a high dose of morphine is killing. Full stop. While appeasing their consciences with double talk of double effect and good intentions, such health professionals are engaging in murder, even if as a means to some merciful end.[43]

My point in raising these controversial examples is that I think that what was at issue in the debates between pro-lifers in Australia in the late 1990s – something which has also dogged the pro-life movement in many countries over the past decade or so – is similar. On the face of it, it is a difference over how 'hardline' one is about principle and how willing to compromise in order to achieve results such as saving babies' lives or relieving people's misery. But my suggestion is that unbeknownst to the disputants there is often a major metaethical difference between them, a difference of most basic principles. This very difference over the characterization of human acts has been as hotly debated between orthodox theologians of the Neo-Thomist and New Natural Law varieties as it has been between orthodox Christians and their utilitarian opponents inside and outside the churches.[44]

---

[43] This is despite the clear teaching in Congregation for the Doctrine of the Faith, *Jura et Bona*: Declaration on Euthanasia (1980); *EV* 65; the *Catechism*; and G. Grisez & J. Boyle, *Life and Death with Liberty and Justice*. Notre Dame, IN: University of Notre Dame Press 1979.

[44] On these matters see, for instance: G. E. M. Anscombe, *Intention*. Oxford: Blackwell 1957; J. Boyle, 'Praeter Intentionem in Aquinas'. 42 (1978) *The Thomist*: 649–665; J. Boyle, 'Toward understanding the principle of double effect'. 90 (1980) *Ethics*: 527–538; S. Brock, *Action and Conduct: Thomas Aquinas and the Theory of Action*. Edinburgh: T&T Clark 1998, ch. 5; A. Donagan, *The Theory of Morality*. Chicago: Chicago University Press 1977; J. Finnis, *Moral Absolutes: Tradition, Revision and Truth*. Washington, DC: Catholic University Press 1991 and J. Finnis, *Aquinas. Moral, Political and Legal Theory*. Oxford: Oxford Universtiy Press 1999; J. Finnis, G. Grisez and J. Boyle, 'Practical principles, moral truths and ultimate ends'. 32 (1987) *American Journal of Jurisprudence*: 99–151; R. P. George, *In Defense of Natural Law*. Oxford: Oxford University Press 1999; P. Hall, *Narrative and the Natural Law: An Interpretation of Thomistic Ethics*. Notre Dame, IN: Notre Dame University Press 1994; R. Hittinger, *A Critique of the New Natural Law Theory*. Notre Dame, IN: Notre Dame University Press 1987; J. Keenan, *Goodness and Rightness in Thomas Aquinas's 'Summa Theologiæ'*. Washington, DC: Georgetown University Press 1992, ch 4; A. Lisska, *Aquinas's Theory of Natural Law: An Analytic Reconstruction*. Oxford: Oxford University Press 1996; R. McInerny, *Aquinas on Human Action: A Theory of Practice*. Washington, DC: Catholic University Press 1992; G. Matthews, 'St Thomas and the principle of double effect', in S. MacDonald & E. Stump (eds) *Aquinas's Moral Theory*. Ithaca, NY: Cornell University Press 1999: 63–78; D. Nelson, *The Priority of Prudence: Virtue and Natural Law in Thomas Aquinas and the Implications for Modern Ethics*. Pennsylvania State University Press 1992; D. S. Oderberg, *Moral Theory: A Non-Consequentialist Approach*. Oxford: Blackwell, 2000; J. Searle, *Intentionality*. Cambridge: Cambridge University Press 1983; E. Vacek, 'Contraception again: in search of convincing arguments', in R. P. George (ed) *Natural Law and Moral Inquiry: Ethics, Metaphysics and Politics in the Work of Germain Grisez*. Washington, DC: Georgetown University Press 1998: 50–81; H. Veatch, *Swimming Against the Current in Contemporary Philosophy*. Washington, DC:

I will not venture much further into that particular quagmire in this essay. Suffice it to say that I think one cannot make sense of the Church's teaching on withdrawal of treatment, palliative care, care of victims of sexual assault, the permissibility of using drugs with a contraceptive effect for some genuinely therapeutic purpose, and the acceptability of certain vaccinations – any more than one can understand the Pope's teaching on the permissibility of certain less-than-perfect abortion laws – unless one accepts an account of the object of the moral act something like that proposed by Finnis, Grisez and associates. But one can also understand why, in a world where even the most unburdensome kinds of care (such as feeding and hydration) are routinely withdrawn from people no longer wanted, where babies and the elderly are sedated to death, where victims of rape or even of a night of carelessness are customarily treated with abortifacients, and where some 'Christian' politicians are unprincipled or plain cowards, such moral theorizing can seem to some of the pro-life troops to be a luxury almost designed to give comfort to the enemy.

One way of helping people to think about these things is to invite their thoughts on the complicity of God in the sins of the world and indeed the death of Christ, or the complicity of Jesus in the sickness of all those he did not cure, or the complicity of Jesus' disciples in the injustices of the Roman imperium which they helped finance by paying their taxes. Unsophisticated moralists, such as the great Lutheran theologian Jürgen Moltmann, suggest that yes, God was to blame: we are all caught up in the tragedy of unavoidable evil and God is no less complicit – indeed, given his power, he is perhaps more so. Since God sent Jesus into the world foreseeing he would be killed, and since God could have intervened to prevent it, we must say that *God killed Jesus*. So it is, Moltmann assures us, that on the cross we witness a breakdown of the relationship which constitutes the very life of the Trinity, the death of the Son but also of the Son's sonship and the Father's fatherhood, the utmost degree of enmity between the persons of God.[45] Offensive as this is to pious ears it reflects not so much the adolescent delight of the modern theologian in shocking as the failure of many contemporary minds to distinguish between what the scholastics called the *active* and *permissive* will of God or between *intentionality* and *foreseeability* in agents. In a world increasingly lacking the intellectual equipment to think about these things it is little wonder that politicians who support less than perfect legislation, and doctors who administer the pill after rape, and nurses who remove ventilators, are all thrown together with abortionists and other murderers.

Only by recovering a clear sense of God's horror at the sins of the world and the death of his innocent Son (as indeed of all his innocent children), of Jesus'

Catholic University Press 1990; D. Westberg, *Right Practical Reason: Aristotle, Action and Prudence In Aquinas*. Oxford: Oxford University Press 1994; and some of the contributions in R. P. George (ed) *Natural Law Theory: Contemporary Essays*. Oxford: Oxford University Press 1992, and Wildes & Mitchell, *Choosing Life*.
[45] J. Moltmann, *The Crucified God: The Cross of Christ as the Foundation and Criticism of Christian Theology* (trans. R. A. Wilson & J. Bowden) London: SCM Press 1974: 149–152, 214, 243; *The Trinity and the Kingdom of God* (trans. M Kohl) London: SCM Press 1981): 80–83.

bowel-churning pity in the face of the sickness and confusion of his fellows, and of the disciples' physical co-operation but moral non-complicity with the Roman oppressor – despite their own actions and inactions – can we begin to make sense of these things without blasphemy. Then we will see more clearly that persons do not intend everything that they tolerate; that people 'choose' that-which-they-foresee-but-do-not-purposely-bring-about in a morally very different sense from the sense in which they 'choose' that-which-they-purposely-bring-about-as-their-end-or-means-to-their-end. One may honestly intend the good such as it is in an imperfect bio-law while foreseeing but not intending the imperfection(s) in it.[46]

5. Some examples of reasonable stances for a pro-life politician vis-à-vis imperfect bio-laws

5.1 Opposition to permissive bio-laws at all stages

Should a pro-life parliamentarian support an imperfect bio-law? In any particular instance of such a law an MP might well form the view that, whatever its terms, bio-law reform in our current circumstances is likely to have the net effect of making abortion even more freely available and more commonly practised, or at least of confirming and codifying an already shameful situation. They might hold that the present (*prima facie* relatively restrictive) statutes are the best that is politically possible at this time and that if preserved such statutes have the potential for stricter interpretation and/or enforcement in the future. They might be persuaded that any new restrictions will be ignored in practice, much as current bio-legislation is in many areas, or that new loop-holes will emerge through which more people's lives would be put at risk. They might judge that a restrictive bill or restrictive amendments would be unlikely to be passed or would only be passed at the expense of some worse changes in other respects or in other areas. They might suspect that by giving support to an imperfect bio-law their witness against abortion etc. would be severely impaired and people would be scandalized. Or they might conclude that by refusing to be party even to restrictive amendments to an imperfect bio-law they will help to ensure the defeat of that law altogether. While recognizing that they have a *prima facie* duty to ensure (where no more is practicable) that at least some babies are saved, and also recognizing that one might support imperfect but restrictive bills or amendments with this in view without thereby intending any evil, some politicians may nonetheless judge that the likely or possible side-effects of even that degree of involvement by them would be so grave that the best course would be opposition to a particular imperfect bio-law from start to finish of its legislative progress.

---

[46] See G. Grisez, 'Human free choice and divine causality'. Edith Stein Lecture, Department of Philosophy, University of Steubenville, 29 March 2000. Unpublished.

Those pro-lifers who oppose restrictive but imperfect bills on these prudential grounds should be absolutely clear in their own minds (and possibly in their statements) that they are not opposing all imperfect abortion legislation *per se*, nor that they are accusing all pro-life supporters of such bills or amendments of intending permissive abortion, or of formal co-operation in evil, or of being willing to trade life for life, or even of imprudence. Rather, they make their own best judgment that by refusing to be party even to such efforts they will serve best the ultimate goals of creating a just and loving society, of saving babies and their mothers, of opposing the further corruption of our culture and our social fabric, and so on.

5.2 Support for some (restrictive) bio-law reform in a permissive situation

An alternative strategy for pro-life politicians, which also seems to me to fall within the terms of *Evangelium vitæ* 73, is to initiate or support a bill which, while continuing to allow some abortions, restricts it in some ways – thereby protecting at least some babies and their mothers. Parliamentarians have a strong *prima facie* duty to seek to protect the most vulnerable members of their community but sometimes that can only be achieved by the gradual erosion of a *de jure* or *de facto* permissive abortion régime through, among other things, imperfect abortion laws which at least introduce some restrictions not presently in practice.[47] While maintaining their ultimate goal of protecting the lives of all and being careful not to conclude too hastily that this is presently impossible, pro-life MPs will sometimes conclude that protecting *some* babies is all that they can do.

There are many kinds of restrictions to permissive bio-laws which pro-life parliamentarians may support if they have reason to believe such restrictions will, if passed, be effective. Some examples in the area of abortion laws (which would apply *ceteris paribus* to other areas of bio-lawmaking) include:

- restricting *the stage* of foetal development beyond which no abortions are permitted (e.g. 12 weeks);

---

[47] As St Thomas observed, "it seems natural to human reason to advance gradually from the imperfect to the perfect" (ST 1–2, 97, 1). In an unpublished advice offered to some pro-life groups during the Western Australian controversy, John Finnis suggested that if a legislator judged that Western Australian law is already widely permissive of abortion because it would be read as such by superior courts were it ever tested, the politician could in good conscience vote for a bill which, if enacted, "would accord real legal protection to some class of unborn babies who today are without that protection, even though the same Bill openly and plainly affirmed and ensured that some (perhaps many or most) other unborn babies remain unprotected (and are stripped of even 'paper' legal protection). That is to say, members holding the view I have described could cast such a vote (and agree in advance to do so) without immorally co-operating in the use of the legislative process to deprive human persons of their inalienable moral and human right to life."

- restricting *the reasons* for which abortion is permitted (e.g. excluding 'social' abortion or abortion on demand) or specifically prohibiting abortion on certain other grounds (e.g. sex selection);
- restricting *where* abortions may be performed (e.g. only in public hospitals) and *by whom* (e.g. only doctors) and licensing or otherwise restricting the number and activities of abortion providers;
- restricting government *funding* or private insurance for abortion;
- restricting access to particular *methods* of abortion (e.g. banning 'partial birth' abortion or RU486);
- requiring that more than one doctor *certify* that the abortion is appropriate;
- requiring that adequate *counselling* of the women involved be undertaken;
- instituting strict *information* giving provisions, including requiring that women seeking abortion receive adequate information about the unborn child, the risks of abortion, and alternatives to abortion;
- requiring *parental or guardian consent* to or at least notification of abortion performed on under-aged girls and court-consent to abortion performed on mentally handicapped women; and
- requiring a '*cooling off period*' between the time at which the doctor(s) certifies that an abortion may be performed and the actual abortion;
- provision for *exemption* on conscientious grounds of doctors, nurses, pharmacists and counsellors from any requirement that they perform, refer for, prescribe, dispense or otherwise co-operate in abortion;[48] and
- provision that no Church or other private institution can be required to provide such procedures on its premises.

[48] "The passing of unjust laws often raises difficult problems of conscience for morally upright people with regard to the issue of co-operation, since they have a right to demand not to be forced to take part in morally evil actions. Sometimes the choices which have to be made are difficult; they may require the sacrifice of prestigious professional positions or the relinquishing of reasonable hopes of career advancement. In other cases, it can happen that carrying out certain actions, which are provided for by legislation that overall is unjust, but which in themselves are indifferent, or even positive, can serve to protect human lives under threat. There may be reason to fear, however, that willingness to carry out such actions will not only cause scandal and weaken the necessary opposition to attacks on life, but will gradually lead to further capitulation to a mentality of permissiveness...

"To refuse to take part in committing an injustice is not only a moral duty; it is also a basic human right. Were this not so, the human person would be forced to perform an action intrinsically incompatible with human dignity, and in this way human freedom itself, the authentic meaning and purpose of which are found in its orientation to the true and the good, would be radically compromised. What is at stake therefore is an essential right which, precisely as such, should be acknowledged and protected by civil law. In this sense, the opportunity to refuse to take part in the phases of consultation, preparation and execution of these acts against life should be guaranteed to physicians, health-care personnel, and directors of hospitals, clinics and convalescent facilities. Those who have recourse to conscientious objection must be protected not only from legal penalties but also from any negative effects on the legal, disciplinary, financial and professional plane" (*EV* 74).

5.3 *Support for* restrictive amendments *to permissive bio-legislation but opposition to an unjust bill as a whole*

A third strategy consistent with *Evangelium vitæ* §73 that a pro-life legislator may reasonably adopt – at least in the Westminster system with which I am best acquainted – would be publicly to oppose an unjust bill from the beginning, on the basis that it is aimed, for instance, at permitting abortion on demand; then to vote *for* various amendments in the committee stage involving restrictions much like those proposed in the previous section; but to oppose the final bill as amended because it will, *in toto*, liberalize or confirm the *de jure* situation regarding abortion. Here the politician is facing a law "ready to be voted on" and does his or her best to improve that law.

As with the legislator who votes for a new, more restrictive but still imperfect law, MPs who support restrictive amendments must aim *not* at permitting abortion in all other circumstances (even though this is a foreseen side-effect), *nor* at lending respectability to abortion performed within these restrictive circumstances: their goal must be to place some obstacles in the way of abortion on demand in the hope that some abortions will thereby be prevented and some babies saved. The elimination of *all* induced abortion remains their goal, but in the meantime they propose or support amendments to a very permissive bill likely soon to be passed, with the goal of 'tightening up' that new law, hoping thereby to protect at least some unborn children who would not otherwise have the benefit of legal protection, even if not all.

To be licit, a legislator's support for an imperfect but more restrictive bio-legislation or for restrictive amendments to a permissive bill, must be aimed *not* at permitting abortion in some circumstances (even though this is a foreseen side-effect) but precisely at placing some obstacles in the way of abortion in the (not unreasonable) hope that some deaths will thereby be prevented. Of course, some supposedly pro-life politicians may disingenuously support such provisions with the real goal of permitting a 'moderate' or 'morally respectable' amount of abortion, or as a way of evading taking an open stand for or against abortion, or because they are willing to trade some lives for others. Genuinely pro-life supporters of such moves, however, will only support them if they are convinced that they will amount to a real restriction on the availability of abortion. Here there are important judgments of prudence and wisdom to be made about what actions will actually save lives, who else will be affected,[49] what messages will be conveyed to a morally unsophisticated public by an unhelpful media and what overall effect such moves will have upon culture and society.

The following things seem to me to follow both with respect to the introduction of additional but imperfect restrictions on abortion or restrictive amendments to permissive bills, and *ceteris paribus* to other areas of bio-legislation:

---

[49] E.g. an undesired effect of such moves might be that doctors who at present can plead the *de jure* prohibition of abortion against claims in tort for failure to provide an opportunity for an abortion find themselves without such protection.

- to avoid 'scandal' those supporting such imperfect legislation must voice a clear and public opposition to all abortion, and make it clear that in supporting such a bill they are not retreating from their judgment that the present permissive situation with respect to abortion is a serious violation of human rights;
- this strategy should not be adopted unless one judges that the new law or the amendments would be interpreted more literally and enforced more rigorously than existing statutes and that in supporting the law or amendments one is not wasting a real chance of persuading the authorities to interpret and enforce the present law more strictly;
- this strategy should not be adopted unless one judges that the net effect will be to increase, not diminish, the present protection of the lives of unborn children; and
- this strategy should only be adopted where it is likely to contribute not only to better laws but also to community education in respect for life.

I noted above that one matter of contention among pro-life parliamentarians is the stage in the political process at which MPs should engage privately in canvassing amendments or announce publicly their willingness to discuss or support restrictive amendments. Sometimes the earlier amendments are canvassed, the greater the likelihood that they will eventually be accepted, that other helpful amendments will be proposed, or that the promoters of a bill will be discouraged from persevering altogether. At other times, the earlier such amendments are proposed, the more likely they are to generate organised opposition from the proponents of a more permissive régime and the more likely they are to grant some respectability to the bill as a whole. These are again matters of prudent judgment for the politicians concerned, taking into account their best assessments of the present and likely future situation, the principles enunciated so far, and the process of discernment sketched briefly below.

6. Some virtues of a Catholic politician

6.1 The virtues of faith and political prudence

Because this paper has focussed on very particular *causæ conscientiæ* of pro-life politicians in the area of imperfect bio-legislation and what the *magisterium* of the Catholic Church might say to or imply about such questions, I have not focussed upon the bigger picture of the sense of vocation and kind of character that a politician should have or seek to cultivate. These would deserve much fuller treatment, and the present question would ideally be treated as part of that broader mission.[50]

---

[50] See, for example, G. Grisez, 'Patriotism, politics and citizenship', in his *Living a Christian Life*. Quincy, IL: Franciscan Press 1993, ch. 11.

I have argued that in the present circumstances many commonly espoused positions are ruled out for the faithful and prudent parliamentarian with respect to imperfect bio-laws, but that several remain as possible. Which of these is to be preferred will depend upon the fine detail of particular legal and political situations, the commitments and opportunities which present themselves to particular legislators in all the circumstances, and their best prudential judgment of what will work – without on the one hand adopting a perfectionist position which regards as immoral ever supporting imperfect laws, nor on the other hand being willing ever to engage in intrinsically immoral means even to achieve great goods. Whichever course were chosen, it should follow upon discussion with pro-life friends and allies. One would not be surprised if people of "good faith, moral probity, and legal competence" honestly disagreed about the *status quo*, the net effect of the passage of such imperfect legislation, or other matters involving judgments of prudence.[51]

At several points in this paper I have appealed to that earthly wisdom which is the virtue of prudence and that supernatural wisdom that is faith and a gift of the Holy Spirit.[52] Only by these great virtues and gifts can a person quickly and reliably apply the various appropriate principles with sensitivity to the range of people and values at stake. I have outlined several important principles here which virtuous lawmakers must bear in mind in their noble task. Two more, which I have hinted at along the way, would be these: we must never be willing to do even a little evil in order to bring about even a very great good; and we must with imaginative impartiality apply the Golden Rule to our situation, asking ourselves, for instance: were I one of the babies at risk, or one of the mothers seeking an abortion, or one of the old people marked for euthanasia, or some of the other politicians engaged in this great debate, or some of the voters I represent or people I influence, would I regard my action or inaction as fair? Having tried one's best to think these matters through and exclude thereby all unreasonable choices, politicians might conclude that there are still two or more paths open to them: then they must go for what seems best to them in the context of their particular temperament, gifts, opportunities, commitments and vocation.

If we are to have faith and prudence ourselves, we must cultivate certain attitudes of heart and mind: prayerfulness above all, a willingness to take counsel, humility, docility to truth, respect for our allies and an eagerness to learn from, work with and console them, self-criticism, imaginative impartiality and love for all. Of these habits of the heart St James wrote:

> Who among you thinks he is wise and understanding? Let him demonstrate this by a good life in the humility that comes from prudence... The wisdom which comes from above is first of all pure, then peaceable, gentle, compliant,

---

[51] This latter observation was made by John Finnis in his advice already cited.
[52] Cf. B. Ashley OP, *Living the Truth in Love: A Biblical Introduction to Moral Theology*. New York: Alba House 1996; R. Cessario OP, *The Moral Virtues and Theological Ethics*. Notre Dame, IN: Notre Dame University Press 1991.

full of mercy and good fruits, without inconstancy or insincerity. And the fruit of righteousness is sown in peace for those who cultivate peace.[53]

6.2 *The virtue of political courage*

In addition to faith and prudence, the task of the Christian legislator requires a great deal of fortitude: which ever of the various reasonable positions outlined above politicians take, they will meet a great deal of hostility from foes and even from those they might have thought they could count on as allies – those who share many of their views and sympathies. Taking such a stance, like taking a conscientious stance on many other contentious issues, can be at great personal cost, including some cost to one's prospects in one's party or electorate.[54] This should not, perhaps, be overestimated: even political opponents and voters who hold a different view are likely to respect a stance taken out of conviction rather than political ambition. But a degree of heroism may nonetheless be called for, and Christians will naturally turn to God, their church, their friends and families, for support in such situations; in the meantime, the Catholic politician must cultivate the virtue of courage.

> Called to serve the people and the common good, they have a duty to make courageous choices in support of life, especially through legislative measures. In a democratic system, where laws and decisions are made on the basis of the consensus of many, the sense of personal responsibility in the consciences of individuals invested with authority may be weakened. But no one can ever renounce this responsibility, especially when they have a legislative or decision-making mandate, which calls them to answer to God, to their own conscience and to the whole of society for choices which may be contrary to the common good.[55]

6.3 *Unity of purpose; diversity in strategies; charity in everything*

Vatican II taught that Christians "must recognize the legitimacy of different opinions" in political matters.[56]

> Often enough the Christian view of things will itself suggest some specific solution in certain circumstances. Yet it happens rather frequently, and legitimately so, that with equal sincerity some of the faithful will disagree with others on a given matter. Even against the intentions of their proponents,

---

[53] *Jm* 3:13–18.
[54] Cf. *EV* 74.
[55] *EV* 90.
[56] *GS* 75.

however, solutions proposed on one side or another may be easily confused by many people with the Gospel message. Hence it is necessary for people to remember that no one is allowed in the aforementioned situations to appropriate the Church's authority for their own opinion. They should always try to enlighten one another through honest discussion, preserving mutual charity and caring above all for the common good.[57]

Sadly this recognition of legitimate diversity is not always evident in bio-politics. Down through the ages even great saints have differed over what course was wisest in particular situations. We must therefore be loath to judge our confreres in the battle against abortion and euthanasia who differ from us on prudential matters. Nor can we rightly claim for ourselves a monopoly on prudence or on the authentic interpretation or application of principles about which there has as yet been no definitive clarification. Above all we must avoid the tendency to consider a person or a group less good-willed or less committed to the pro-life effort because they have a different legislative strategy from our own.[58] In this context, Archbishop Bertone, Secretary of the Congregation for the Doctrine of the Faith, recently noted that collaborations with less-than-perfect but better laws are not idle compromises with evil, but different ways of affirming truth and goodness. He scolded those who too readily brand the supporters of imperfect bio-laws as persons of faint heart or weak character, and those who write off the opponents of less-than-perfect bio-laws as extremists or extraterrestrials.[59] He suggested that the Church and the pro-life movement ought to be capable of generating diverse approaches to these matters while remaining, despite all the differences, within the bond of communion.

---

[57] GS 43.

[58] Cf. EV 91; Catholic Bishops' [of England & Wales, Scotland, and Ireland] Joint Committee on Bio-Ethical Issues 19/14 (1989) Briefing.

[59] T. Bertone, 'Catholics and pluralist society' noted that collaborations with less-than-perfect but better laws are "not idle compromises with evil, but different ways of affirming truth and goodness in the world, bearing in mind their concrete and often complex co-ordinates. In this respect, they are revealed as belonging to the same nature as the first attitude [of prophetic resistance], i.e. they form part of the dynamism intrinsic to the truth that tries to affirm itself in the world in order to redeem it and lead it definitively to the Trinitarian fullness. It follows from this that the person who tolerates imperfect laws or the person who collaborates with them [in the particular sense discussed above] must not be judged by his fellow-Christian, who actively resists them, as a person of faint heart or weak character, but as a brother who tries to bury in the infinitely diversified soil of the contemporary world 'a grain of mustard seed' (cf. Mt 13:31–32 and parallels) that could become, and in fact will become, a great tree.

"Contrariwise, the person who resists 'unjust laws' must not be considered by his fellow-Christian who tolerates them or collaborates with them, in the sense pointed out above, as a brother who has sprung from another planet or as an extremist cut off from reality, but rather as a true champion of truth in the world. Here the Pauline idea of the different charisms in a single Body might apply (cf. 1 Cor 12:1ff)... [T]he Church ought to be capable of generating her own heralds of truth and ensuring that they remain, despite all their differences, within the bond of communion." Op.cit. 219–220. (Emphasis in original.)

6.4 Humility and hope

I suggested earlier that humility is an important virtue for the politician in this area. Legislators must be aware that there is only so much they can do, especially with such blunt instruments as laws and social policies. As the Church's corrections of communism, fascism and, in some of its forms, liberation theology have made clear, there is a kind of heresy in the Enlightenment's notion that salvation for society can be found by law and policy. Vices like disrespect for innocent life certainly require the best efforts of the state to 'make men moral':[60] but in the end it will take more than this.

I suspect that for three decades now the Church and the pro-life movement around the world have over-estimated the power of bio-legislation. As the Psalmist warns us "put not your trust in princes" (*Ps* 146:3). There are many countries with very strong laws against abortion – at least on the statute books – but where, for the reasons discussed earlier, such laws are of little or no effect. The Pope has more than adequately identified the underlying ideological, economic and political causes of this. His chilling conclusion is well-known: there has emerged in the West "a culture which denies solidarity and in many cases takes the form of a veritable *culture of death*. This culture is actively fostered by powerful cultural, economic and political currents [and amounts to] a kind of conspiracy against life."[61] In the midst of such a dramatic conflict between the culture of death and the culture of life there is only so much lawmakers can do. This does not mean that efforts to hold the line and gradually to improve the legal situation are irrelevant: they may save some individual lives; and they may have an educative effect on society. But it does mean that much greater efforts are needed to get to the heart of why otherwise civilised societies have become so blind to the blood flowing in their streets. Without a massive re-evangelization of culture such laws are likely to remain largely dead letters.

John Finnis has observed that at the root of the present disarray and demoralization in Western Church and society is the practical elimination of transcendent hope. "It is obviously a precondition of sustainable engagement in public policy debates that one keep bright one's hope, and keep clear and firm the presuppositions of that hope."[62] We must pray that, in living out the imperative to be 'unconditionally pro-life' in a new century and millennium, politicians, pro-life activists, lobbyists and their sympathizers, will always hold fast to that hope, even when the political scene is difficult to negotiate and potentially demoralizing. For in the end we know that we side with Him who came so that we might have life, and have it to the full.[63]

---

[60] "The purpose of law is to make men moral": *ST* 1–2, 92, 1, *sed contra*, citing Aristotle, *Nicomachean Ethics* 2, i.

[61] *EV* 12.

[62] Finnis, 'The Catholic Church and public policy debates in Western liberal societies: the basis and limits of intellectual engagement': 266.

[63] *Jn* 10:10.

The entire creation has been groaning till now in an act of giving birth, as it waits for the glory of the children of God to be revealed (Cf. *Rm* 8:22). Let Christians therefore be convinced that they will yet find the fruits of their own nature and effort cleansed of all impurities in the new earth which God is now preparing for them, and in which there will be the kingdom of justice and love, a kingdom which will be fully perfected when the Lord will come himself.[64]

---

[64] Synod of Bishops, *Justice in the World* (1971): 75–76.

14

Some recent treatments of the private defence of innocent human life

J. L. A. GARCIA

Introduction

My topic is private (that is, unauthorized) defense of innocent human life through active resistance to anti-life behavior. By active resistance I mean efforts not just to dissuade individuals or influence public policy, but to obstruct, burden, or prevent those who procure, or who regularly perform or assist in such activities as elective abortion, physician-assisted suicide, mercy-killing, and so on. Since all the discussion of these 'point-of-event' activities I have seen concentrates on violent resistance to abortion, so shall I.[1] I should say immediately that I do not see the matter as especially important socially, politically, personally, or even morally.

It is not socially important, because the incidents are relatively few, and seem not to stem from any deep social pathology, save that involved in the wall of protection that surrounds abortion. Nor has it great political significance, as it calls for no change in our laws or their theories, nor in our discourse on public matters, save insofar as it dramatizes the urgency of our assaults on life.[2] Personally, I have no stake in the issue from my own commitments or behaviour. Even at its most violent, the deeds of its agents pale morally before those of its targets. So, active resistance, when it turns violent, is rather a distraction from important pro-life concerns, and one often raised with the object of diverting discussion of our society's widespread, heinous, and generally accepted crimes against genuinely innocent human life. Its chief danger is as such a diversion, and as a misdirection of effort better devoted to other initiatives. As for resolutely non-violent interventions, I can see no serious moral objection in principle, given the gravity of the atrocities in question, to the kinds of 'sidewalk counseling' of those considering abortion and those who work in 'abortuaries' common in the

---

[1] Some forms of active resistance, of course, may not occur at the site of the abortion, say damaging an abortionist's car at a stop light. I ignore the matter, as nothing hinges on where the act of prevention is made, though the fact could affect whether the act is a last resort in preventing an attack that is imminent.

[2] Surely, as a social matter, it matters no more than do recent acts of violence against anti-abortion protestors, and much less than does the injustice inherent in abortion itself. (On the former topic, see B. Clowes, 'The Plague of Pro-abortion Violence', *Human Life International Reports* April 2000: 9–14.)

United States, even if under immoral and illegal restrictions, nor to most efforts to slow or impede their work, nor to shame them out of them.[3] So does abortion skew our thought that I once heard a prominent bioethicist, when talk turned to anti-abortion counseling, speculate on a right *not* to be informed. Such fancies are not to be taken seriously, and I see little basis for inquiry into imagined moral difficulties posed by nonviolent action against abortion.

Several years ago, after some attacks in Florida, the magazine *First Things* ran a piece entitled "Killing Abortionists: a Symposium." The title must have been meant to shock.[4] Here after all, were professional men, gunned down as they went about their all-too-common, socially accepted practice. In response, the title conjures a picture of dons in turtle-neck and tweeds, puffing their pipes, talking in their accustomed 'On the one hand, on the other hand' mode, engaging in detached conversation, entertaining the kind of mild disagreement we expect among reasonable people on complex issues. A symposium! On killing medical people and their assistants going about their business in providing medical care and services! Where is the horror? Where the vehemence? Where the denunciation? The title suggests it is conspicuously absent.

Actually, and (I think) unfortunately, the brief pieces therein do not live up to this enticing prospect. Denunciations predominate, and they are often intemperate, unfair, and excessive, charging the killers with "hypocrisy", and with setting themselves up as "prosecutor, judge, jury, and hangman", comparing them to "anarchists and terrorists", and so on. Surely, it was particularly unwarranted and unkind for some to suggest that the person who kills an abortionist therein so lowers herself as to approach the latter's debased state.[5] Robert George was the chief exception. Tongue firmly in cheek, he declared himself "personally opposed" to the killings but "unwilling to impose" his view on others, who need to follow their own consciences. He urged "policies aimed at removing the root causes of violence against abortionists", as well as waiting periods and "nonjudgmental counseling", rather than the brute instrument of legal coercion against those inclined to kill. I find admirable and right-headed Professor George's refusal to join the hand-wringing. We should save our outrage for what is more straightforwardly outrageous, in victimizing more innocent victims. Some

[3] Publicizing names, addresses, etc. of abortionists or their minions should, in charity, be interpreted as efforts to shame, unless there is clear and specific evidence to the contrary, rather than as the veiled threats and intimidation their opponents often assume them to be.
[4] H. Alvare, et al., 'Killing Abortionists: a Symposium'. *First Things* December 1994: 22–31. Other contributors included Hadley Arkes, Francis Canavan, Jean Garton, Robert George, Nat Hentoff, Richard Land, Roger Cardinal Mahoney, Frederica Mathewes-Green, Bernard Nathanson, John Cardinal O'Connor, Ralph Reed, Ann Swidler, Terry Schlossberg, Ronald Sider and Keith Pavlischek, and George Weigel. For some responses, see 'Correspondence: Pro-Life, Anti-Violence'. *First Things* March 2001: 4–7.
[5] For similarly unqualified and problematic denunciation, see Cardinal O'Connor, 'We simply abhor killing...' *Catholic New* York March 18, 1993: 5. An episcopal authority offers somewhat more nuanced critical assessment in Archbishop Oscar Lipscomb, '"You shall not murder": a Pastoral Instruction on this Moral Teaching of the Catholic Church'. *Catholic Week* November 19, 1993: 3–4.

Christian intellectuals have recently moved the discussion beyond knee-jerk condemnations of forms of pro-life resistance that cross into illegality and even violence. That is to the good. Because I fear some of their thinking may involve under-examined and perhaps unwarranted criticism of such activity, I will describe and discuss three such treatments. I wish neither to advocate nor condemn such activity in general, nor really to stimulate further discussion of a topic I think too often a distraction. Still, we do need to give it some thought from time to time, and it is better if that thinking is more nuanced and judicious rather than less. I hope I can make a small contribution to that. One preparatory and prefatory remark: I suspect some pro-life people feel uncomfortable with the subject because of the nagging thought, perhaps a fear, that if such direct resistance is morally permissible it is incumbent on them, on pain of hypocrisy, themselves to engage in it. That, of course, does not follow. Even if, as I shall suggest, some arguments offered against various forms of inhibitory, forceful, and even violent resistance fail convincingly to show it is necessarily, always, or normally illicit for people in roughly our situations, they may well have sufficient force to enable us to feel and to be justified in choosing other forms of opposition and declining to participate in these.

Grisez's concerns

In responding to the two hundredth, and last, question in his *Difficult Moral Questions*, Germain Grisez asks us to imagine a conversation with someone who supports active, but generally not violent, anti-abortion resistance. He places four arguments against violent resistance, specifically, against killing abortionists, in this interlocutor's mouth: (i) that such killing leaves no room for the repentance Christians should wish evildoers, (ii) that it undermines the pro-life position publicly to promote death, (iii) that it is counterproductive because it inflames pro-death forces, (iv) that it "serves as a bad example for many sorts of extremists."[6] Grisez adds some additional concerns: (v) unlike some cases considered also by Robert Audi, whose work I engage below, where someone violently defends a threatened child against a solitary attacker, killing the abortionist does not really rescue the child, because she or he remains at the mercy of a mother bent on her destruction, in a society that makes available to her abundant assistance and encouragement; (vi) such attacks provoke such backlash that abortion becomes more entrenched, better protected, and more frequent.

Grisez quickly concedes that none of the first four objections is decisive. Each allows that under "appropriate conditions" violent resistance might be permissible.[7] According to traditional Catholic morality, defensive attack, even using lethal force is sometimes permissible, even when it results in foreseen but

---

[6] G. Grisez, *The Way of the Lord Jesus, vol. 3: Difficult Moral Questions*. Quincy, IL: Franciscan Press 1997: 844–847, at p. 846.
[7] Grisez, *Difficult Moral Questions*: 847.

unintended death.[8] So, its precluding repentance, its complicating for the simpler-minded the nature of informed pro-life reasoning, and its encouraging those who need dissuasion from violence, cannot always be decisive. These are possible, unfortunate, and unintended side-effects, requiring that actions risking them have some proportional reason, but they do not at all preclude there ever being such reason. In any event, they are not inevitable.

Grisez does not make a similarly explicit concession with respect to the fifth argument, that from the abortionist's status as a mere agent of the mother, who can normally find another such willing agent. However, it is on all fours with the others. The prospective bad result may not be unavoidable, and it would not be a conclusive consideration even if it were. Indeed, there is another difficulty with this argument. To say, as Grisez does, that a defensive attack "would therefore be pointless" because it might lead to a larger number of abortions slights the great good done simply in rescuing this child now. Saving this innocent constitutes a powerful case for a proportional reason for defensive attack on the malefactor, in cases where there is no comparably effective and less violent (or otherwise costly) alternative available. Grisez does not need my reminder that Christian ethics focuses our love on individuals not on such dubious abstractions as 'the greater good' or 'the good of the greater number.' When, in 1999, three firefighters in Worcester, Massachusetts went in search of their trapped colleague, they risked – and, tragically, lost – a greater number in service to a lesser. This manifested not their bad mathematics but their moral sensitivity to, and their living of, such virtues as camaraderie, loyalty, and bravery. Grisez knows this all too well, and has argued with some care and vigor against consequentialism.[9] Nevertheless, I cannot see how his argument here shows due appreciation for its pertinence.

In the end, Grisez suggests that, in light of their likely short-term bad effects, violent defensive attacks on isolated, individual abortionists "would be pointless unless" part of a larger campaign of violence that would constitute "starting a revolution with no prospect of success." Let us turn to Christopher Tollefsen's discussion, which develops this sort of objection in somewhat greater detail.

Tollefsen's critique

Tollefsen considers three ways of conceiving a violent anti-abortion attack on an abortionist, considers the requirements of justifying each of them, and concludes that such an attack fails to meet standards of moral permission, no matter which

---

[8] 'Lethal force' is legally defined as force likely sufficient to cause serious bodily injury or death, according to Rice and Tuskey. See C. Rice and J. Tuskey, 'The Legality and Morality of Using Deadly Force to Protect Unborn Children from Abortionists'. 5 (1995) *Regent University Law Review*: 83–151, at p. 105.

[9] See, especially, G. Grisez, 'Against Consequentialism' 23 (1978) *American Journal of Jurisprudence*: 21–72; J. Finnis, G. Grisez, and J. Boyle, *Nuclear Deterrence, Morality and Realism*. Oxford: Oxford University Press 1987: 249–269.

of the three ways it is conceived. It cannot be justified as (i) punishment, because justly administered punishment is reserved to the state. Nor can it be justified as a (ii) defense, because just defensive attacks must "have a reasonable chance of success", whereas "Given the available resources, it is highly unlikely that violence could actually prevent an abortion from taking place." Finally, it cannot be justified as part of a just rebellion because (following Alan Donagan) Tollefsen maintains that an uprising is just (that is, permitted by justice) only when "it can reasonably be predicted that the rebellion will succeed in righting the wrong."[10]

I think Tollefsen correct to view attacking an abortionist to punish her for her actions as an immoral arrogance.[11] The dangers (indeed, certainty) of procedural injustice in private determination of guilt, and execution of punishment for it, are so great that we would do better simply to forgo punishment in situations where the state is set against its exercising its responsibilities. Moreover, some of those involved in anti-abortion violence have sometimes slipped into the rhetoric of punishment and vengeance. However, I think Tollefsen's insistence on likely overall success as a condition of permissibility is excessive.

The moral relevance of failure and possible bad results derives from the necessity of having proportional reason for actions likely to cause as much suffering as defensive violence or civil rebellion are prone to do, even when undertaken for good causes. As we observed above, a reasonable chance at success in saving *this* child from *this* attack is already grave reason to act for that end, by launching a defensive attack when it is sufficiently likely to prevail. I do not see why that last phrase need be interpreted to require that it be more likely to succeed than to fail. That someone is in desperate need, as the child facing imminent abortion is, already constitutes strong reason to do something in hope of helping, even if chances of success are bleak and what one does is also likely to do harm. That is so even when the probability of the harm times its magnitude exceeds that of the probability of success multiplied by its value. (To the limited extent those are quantifiable and knowable.) Not counting bad theology, I know of no good argument to show that we are required to act only for the *greater* good, rather than simply for a good that is *proportionate* (or, if the relevant goods and evils are not commensurable, at least, *not* disproportionate) to the harm envisioned.

---

[10] C. Tollefsen, 'Donagan, Abortion and Civil Rebellion'. 11 (1997) *Public Affairs Quarterly*: 303–312, at p. 310, quoting A. Donagan, *The Theory of Morality*, Chicago: University of Chicago 1977, p. 109. Also see Tollefsen, p. 308: "the force used [in licit defense] must have a reasonable chance of success ... violence used when one is unable to save is impermissible." Presumably, in the latter, Tollefsen means that defensive force is impermissible when it is (or should be) *recognized* as impossible.

[11] It is my impression that some defenders of the morality of violent attacks that have been made against abortionists and their willing helpers may fail adequately to distinguish protective, punitive, and revolutionary attacks. See, for example, M. Bray, *A Time to Kill*, Portland, Oregon: Advocates for Life 1994, and various articles that appeared in the early 1990s in the magazine *Life Advocate*. (Bray was convicted and imprisoned in the destruction of abortion facilities.) As my title indicates, my interest here is solely in such acts considered as acts in defense of life against present homicidal menaces.

I make no claim that an agent is morally required to act in defense of life at risk of great harm to herself, or to her intended beneficiary. However, we should take care not irresponsibly to criticize others for doing so.

Tollefsen thinks, in light of its likely failure, any relevant instance of anti-abortion violence is "most plausibl[y] intrepret[ed]" as "political in nature … [and as undertaken] with [politically] reformatory purposes in mind."[12] I am unsure what hermeneutic drives this interpretive claim, and I suspect it may involve the same under-appreciation of acting desperately to save the single life, even if only briefly, that I earlier suggested may have crept into Grisez's writing. Tollefsen sometimes talks of some accurate action-descriptions being superior to others, and faults some for being "incomplete." However, the adequacy of any description is always contextual, and no workable (and therefore finite) description of any event (or physical object) can be "complete". For these reasons, I think Tollefsen's claim that these acts "must be described as a sort of pre-revolutionary activity" contextual, unestablished, and iffy. I also think it morally inconclusive both because it relies on unsupported assumptions about the probability of failure, and because his assumptions about the alleged need that any just defensive attack (or rebellion) have a high chance of success suffers the same flaw as Grisez's. The Church has recently come in for more than a little criticism for its leaders' alleged unwillingness to act with noble if doomed resistance to oppression. Her historical institutional hostility to active (even violent) resistance by slaves and on their behalf – the noble *causes* of John Brown, Nat Turner, David Walker, and even Spartacus, whatever our misgivings about some of their actions – is also problematic, a further ground for that recollection, reflection, and repentance recently urged. There are times when short-term failure is more likely than long-term success. However, we are ill-advised to make this alone the basis of our moral response to gross injustice, lest ill-informed conscience make (not so much cowards as) 'do-nothings' of us. Again, I know Tollefsen is no consequentialist and I am confident he would acknowledge the force of these considerations in principle. My complaint is only that he does not appear to me fully to appreciate the force that applying them here has in militating against the position he affirms.

Audi's complaints

Audi offers a long and complex discussion of active and violent defense of innocent human life against abortionists. I can hope here only to comment on a few points from his discussion. Audi discusses this topic in the context of a wider, over-riding concern for civic peace in a liberal democratic, pluralistic society. His goal is to delegitimize violence against abortionists (especially, its private use) to protect their prospective victims. He anticipates that the defensive attacker and those sympathetic to her will justify (defend the permissibility of)

---

[12] Tollefsen, 'Donagan, Abortion and Civil Rebellion': 310.

such attacks on the grounds that the abortionist possesses a murderous intent, an intent to kill an innocent person. Audi's first step toward criticizing this claim is to urge abandonment of the rhetoric of 'murder' in respect to abortion. He wants "to reduce the inflammatory language" in hopes therein of "remov[ing] some significant barriers to mutual understanding and perhaps open some paths to partial resolution."[13]

Of course, those of us who think discussion of abortion too often obscured, denatured, and de-sensitized by a bloodless and vague rhetoric of 'choice' (to do what?), of the 'products of conception', of so-called 'reproductive rights' that characteristically turn out against reproduction, of 'a certain late-term abortion procedure' (as some demurely call partial-birth abortion), and so on are unlikely to join this bandwagon. We think the discussion sometimes needs more accurate language, which is likelier to trigger appropriate responses of outrage. Why, then, should we accede to Audi's urging that we eschew talk of 'murder'? Because "Murderers are not only dangerous to innocent people ... they are heinous and often clever criminals who must both be stopped and punished."[14] Of course, Audi here seems merely to assume one of the principal points at issue. He presupposes that anything ordinary people involve themselves in must be pretty innocent. Those of us who remember the United States' history of slavery, of *de jure* racial segregation, of forced sterilization, and so on, should know better than that. Audi blinds himself to what, adapting Jules Feiffer's nice phrase in a way he might not like, we can call our "little murders." If they're so little, so commonplace, done by folks so much like you and me, then they can't be murders, right? Well, wrong.[15]

Audi has better reasons to offer than that, of course. Even if we are right to think that a human fetus (I follow Audi's term) is an innocent person, perhaps we should not so quickly assume, that someone, such as the abortionist, who means to kill her or him therein intends to kill an innocent person. The abortionist may not recognize the unborn as human persons, Audi reasons, and thus may lack the vicious intent to kill the innocent. We ought immediately to note and question Audi's undefended assumption that it is appropriate to treat personhood as the central issue here. What marks the human fetus as morally different from a cat fetus (or an adult cat) is that it is importantly like us in its prospective future, in its ultimate capacities and potential, in its origin, and its past – in short, in what it is. After all, it is conceded that the conceptus is a "product of reproduction", something conceived, begun. This, however, is not a mere by-product of the process, but its eponymous, central goal and *telos*. Yet, if that is so, it is

---

[13] R. Audi, 'Preventing Abortion as a Test Case for the Justifiability of Violence'. 1 (1997) *Journal of Ethics*: 141–163, at p. 145.

[14] Audi, 'Preventing Abortion as a Test Case for the Justifiability of Violence': 145.

[15] One feels tempted to offer Audi a practical compromise: we will agree to "remove the notion of murder from the candidates to describe the kinds of abortion at issue", that is, agree to forgo its use, if the pro-abortion side agrees to label the acts as presumptively unjustified homicides. Of course, even Audi will not agree to that, so his appeals to moderation appear to be merely one-sided advocacy.

what makes reproduction to be re-productive, the making again of one of us: someone's son or daughter, brother or sister, etc. Why then need we ever enter the murky realm of personhood rather than stay on the firmer and hard-won ground of equalitarian humanism, that is, by taking it that human rights reside as such in humans, whether or not they meet some ginned-up (and, usually, rigged) criterion of personhood?

We ought also observe that traditionally what is said to justify defensive attack, when nonviolent alternatives are not available or would not avail, is not chiefly the agent's personal guilt, on which this issue of her intentions bears, but whether the action itself is unjust aggression.[16] That position is not unproblematic, raising the difficulty of why the virtue or vice of an *action* matters to how its *agent* is to be treated, how the former can be established independently of the agent's virtue or vice in performing it, and why, when these are out of harmony, it is the former rather than the latter that is decisive. Nevertheless, it is a line of defense open to someone who takes the position with which Audi here engages, and he ought to have said more about why he thinks the agent's personal vice decisive for the permissibility of defensive attack on the abortionist, when this is not at all an uncontroversial assumption.

Having entered those reservations, let us nevertheless set them aside, and consider, first, Audi's view that the abortionist may act without any intent to kill, and, second, his view that the abortionist may not recognize that her victim is an innocent person, and so intend to kill her or him without therein intending to kill a person.

Of course, it has long been recognized in Roman Catholic medical ethics that someone may licitly perform an action that terminates a pregnancy, and therein the life of an unborn child, without homicidal intent and without sin. These are so-called 'indirect abortions', as in the case of removing a mass of malignant tissue that contains a fetal human. Here, one acts foreseeing the abortifacient result but not intending it. (Or, as it is sometimes misleadingly said, without intending it 'directly'.) Audi wants to expand on this idea, and suggests a physician "might . . . argue that, in the case in which the development of the pregnancy will harm the patient's mental and emotional condition, removing the fetus is a regretted [and unintended] effect of adopting a policy of protecting her mental and emotional health." He immediately acknowledges that "this may be an inadmissible application of the principle of double effect."[17] However, he does not drop the idea for that reason, suggesting in a footnote that "the issue seems to be when one *does* something as a means rather than producing it as an effect consented to", and adding that "Some might argue that just as the appendectomy causes the [unintended] abortion, the adoption of the plan to

[16] See, for example, D. Oderberg, *Applied Ethics*. Oxford & New York: Blackwell 2000: sec. 5.2.1, pp 191–198. Also see Pope John Paul II's encyclical letter *Evangelium Vitae*, sec. 55, and the passage in Aquinas, *S. T.* 2–2, 64, 7, there cited.

[17] Audi, 'Preventing Abortion as a Test Case for the Justifiability of Violence': 149.

protect one's patient's health is what causes (via one's agency, to be sure) the [unintended] abortion."[18]

It is difficult to find much merit in this suggestion, which should have died with Audi's recognition that it was "an inadmissible application" of double effect reasoning. Audi seems to mean that it is a valid application, though one that religious authorities, for their own reasons, will not allow (admit). The problem, however, is deeper than that: the proposed application makes no sense. The agent may regret the abortion, but that is just a matter of her feelings. What matters morally is not her feelings but her will, whether she intends to perform an abortion. I can make no sense of the claim that she does not intend that in this kind of case. After all, she aborts the fetus pursuant to her "policy" of health-protection and, thus, as part of her *plan*. That is to say, she does it on purpose, with intent.[19] Again, she does it for the sake of an effect that follows precisely from the abortion, not merely from something else which is alone aimed at and which is caused along with the unsought abortion. Thus, she must intend to abort, causing it not merely as a *side*-effect consented to, but as a means to her end of health. Without some such explanation we are left in the dark as to why Audi's physician performs the abortion, because we cannot explain how she means to get from her act to her goal of saving health unless we treat the abortion as intended as a means to the goal (or a part of it).

Recall that Audi has a back-up position, because he also thinks that, even if the abortionist does intend to kill the fetus, and even if in fact that fetus is a person, she may nonetheless not recognize her victim as an innocent person. In that case, Audi thinks, she may intend to kill without intending to kill a person. What should we say here? Would such failure of recognition show that her intention is not to kill an innocent person? Would it show that her intention is itself morally innocent? Even if the former answer is affirmative, that does not show that the latter also is. Her failure to recognize the other as a person, let alone as an equal, may result from vicious willfulness, from an immoral blinding of moral perception, or hardening of heart. We know this from reflection on racial prejudice and similar phenomena. Indeed, Lawrence Blum and others have suggested it is one of the central functions of the moral virtues to help us perceive and appreciate the moral stakes in the situations we encounter, and lack of such virtue is vice.[20]

Audi appears to recognize this possibility and, if I understand what he is up to, is concerned to show that rejecting the unborn human's personhood can be reasonable, and thus need not open the abortionist to charges of intellectual or moral vice in acting as she does. He attempts this by offering grounds for rejecting

---

[18] Audi, 'Preventing Abortion as a Test Case for the Justifiability of Violence': 151, and note 13.
[19] White and Bratman, among others, understand intent precisely in terms of plans. See M. Bratman, *Intention, Plans and Practical Reason*. Cambridge, Mass: Harvard University Press 1987, and A. R. White, *Grounds of Liability*. Oxford: Oxford University Press 1985, esp. pp. 72–75.
[20] See L. Blum, *Moral Perception and Particularity*. Cambridge: Cambridge University Press 1994.

three secular arguments for personhood.[21] By showing that disagreement about whether the conceptus is a person can be reasonable, he means to acquit the abortionist of the charge of morally culpable intent, which charge if it were vindicated might legitimate violent attacks on her in defense of life.[22]

The first line of inference that Audi discusses he calls "the genetic argument". It reasons from the premises that the conceptus already possesses all necessary genetic information for personal development and that this development is normally realized by a natural process, to the conclusion that the human unborn is, from its earliest stages, a person. It closely resembles what Audi calls "the human life argument" which holds simply that because "there is biological human life at conception", the human unborn is a person. Since the premises of the genetic argument are only somewhat more detailed versions of the latter's premises, and since they reason to the same conclusion, I will here treat these two together as 'the genetic human life argument'. Audi rejects this argument as invalid, maintaining that it shows only that the unborn is a being that is human not a human being, that it is "a potential person" not a person. Moreover, he claims, whatever rights such an entity may have, "those of an actual person tend to take priority in any case of conflict".

We can consider these three responses in order. I do not doubt there are senses of the term 'being' which disallow, as Audi says, inference from 'X is a being' and 'X is human' to 'X is a human being'. This would be true of a clump of dead human tissue considered as a 'being', for example. However, the unborn human is a being in a stronger sense, since it is an organized system with its distinctive internal program of development and a genetic coding different from that of either its (genetic) mother or (genetic) father. It must be a human *some-thing*, yet it is not a tumor, nor waste, nor a body part in the ordinary senses in which an ovary or an ovum is. It seems most reasonable, rather, to deem it a distinct human substance (not independent, of course), a member of the species.

---

[21] He also briefly treats two arguments for fetal personhood that are explicitly religious. These, however, are less pertinent and I shall ignore them.

[22] If I understand Audi's implicit wider strategy, it is to show that defensive attacks against abortionists, even when conscientiously motivated, violate principles of good citizenship and public action nowadays usually discussed under the rubrics of 'neutral principles' and 'public reason'. See, especially, R. Audi, 'Separation of Church and State and the Obligations of Citizenship'. 18 (1989) *Philosophy and Public Affairs*: 259–296; also see J. Rawls, *Political Liberalism* (pbk. edn.) New York: Columbia University Press 1996: 243 note and ff., suggesting an argument that legally protecting unborn humans from early abortion may be "unreasonable." (This argument is weakly repudiated at pp. lv, note and ff.) I shall not engage that issue here. However, I will note that I cannot see why reasonable disagreement, even if that were what is involved in abortion, should here yield constitutional protection for abortion and moral protection against conscientious attacks on abortionists and their amanuenses. After all, we might instead respond to this disagreement with the social drawing of a line motivated by the superordinate humanistic presumption for protection of innocent life. Constitutionalizing protection of abortionists and even of abortion, as is current in the United States, only makes it more difficult to change the legal order as may seem advisable in response to further social reflection, persuasion, and information-gathering.

That, of course, is what 'the genetic human life argument' is meant to show, and Audi's response is insufficient to warrant rejecting its conclusion or even its validity, when modified along the lines I have indicated.[23]

Audi's second response to 'the genetic human life argument' was that it shows only that the unborn human is a potential person. It is important that Audi presupposes that the term 'potential' acts here as what Peter Geach called an '*alienans* adjective': a potential person need not be a person *tout court*. However, if that is so, it tells only what the human unborn will *become*, but may not yet *be*. It does not tell us what it now *is*. I think this response also inadequate. After all, the persons we ordinarily encounter are constantly developing, and even developing as persons. So, noting that an entity is developing personal features does not entail that is not already a person. The question, then, remains, developing or not, what is the developing human fetus? One attractive answer is that it is already a person with the potential for further development *inter alia*, in precisely those characteristics in virtue of her developmental capacity for which she is a person: thought, will, and the rest. For Audi's moral defense of the abortionist to go through, then, he must show anyone ought to presume that the person whose thinking is in question, i.e., the abortionist, has a better way of conceiving of the human unborn and comes to that conception through a thought process untainted by moral vice. Failing that, Audi has not shown the abortionist reasonable – and, he supposes, therein without fault – in refusing to accept and treat the human unborn as a person. Thus, Audi has not given us adequate reason to suppose the abortionist is innocently without the intent on whose basis Audi's imaginary anti-abortion attacker seeks to justify (show to be permissible) her violence against the abortionist.

The third response Audi makes to what I have called the 'genetic human life argument' is that while the unborn, not yet a human being and still subpersonal, may have rights, any such rights must give way morally to any conflicting rights of "an actual person." If there were such entities as merely potential persons (i.e., things that are not, but will normally become, persons), and if they had some kinds of rights, then I suppose it would be reasonable to say, abstracting from the particulars of the rights involved, and assuming other things equal, that a right of theirs gives way to a right of yours. However, this is only in the abstract. Once we know what the particular rights involved are, it could turn out that whatever normative force the rights of the imagined merely potential person lack, on account their bearer's sub-personal ontic inferiority, they gain simply for being rights to more important things. Audi explicitly acknowledges this in a footnote: "The priority [of actual persons' rights to the rights of merely potential persons] does not imply that just any right of a[n actual] person is stronger than

---

[23] I realize the topic has more complexity than I do or can do justice to here. For philosophical arguments for fetal humanity and against the moral permissibility of direct abortion, see, *inter alia*, P. Lee, *Abortion and Unborn Human Life*. Washington, DC: Catholic University of America Press 1996, and S. Schwarz, *The Moral Question of Abortion*. Chicago: Loyola University Press 1990 (also available online at ohiolife.org).

every right of a potential person, such as its right not to be killed."[24] Yet this undermines the relevance of Audi's claim of normative priority to the issue he is discussing. For it seems precisely to be the right of the fetal human (considered now, I think fancifully and insultingly, as one of Audi's merely potential persons) *not to be killed* that the abortionist (and, we should note, the importuning mother) threatens and which, aside from cases where continued pregnancy or live delivery puts the mother's life at risk, must conflict with a lesser right, if it conflicts with any rights at all.[25] Why then ought we favor some lesser, weaker right of what is uncontroversially a person over the conflicting right of the unborn, when the latter's right would unquestionably be a central and stronger right once the latter 'became' a person? On this crucial part of his case, Audi provides no detail. Here, I think, his defense of the abortionist falters at a crucial juncture.

The last of Audi's arguments that concerns us is what he calls "the wedge argument." It is the familiar 'slippery slope' argument that, because there is no non-arbitrary line to mark off when the developing entity becomes a person, it must be one from the start. It is a familiar fact that such arguments are invalid, and Audi points this out. However, he seems not to notice it closely resembles a different but stronger argument. According to this different argument, if an entity has rights at one stage in its development but not at another, then there must be some morally decisive difference between its existence at the two stages. It then points out the failure of the defender of abortion to make a convincing case just where that salient difference lies. It is birth, of course, that is most commonly presented as marking the pertinent change and transition. Audi notes that birth marks a biological, psychological, social difference in life, observing that neglect of this fact in most discussions may be owing to the discussants' being predominantly male.[26] However, birth is not alone in marking significant change in life, and Audi does not explain why it is only the changes that occur at birth that make such a dramatic moral difference. Why ought not attaining the age of reason, or adolescence, or some other such turning point, make a moral difference of consequence comparable to that such thinkers claim for birth? And, if they do not, why does birth? More important than the question of the *magnitude* of the change birth supposedly marks, Audi does not adequately justify his view of its *nature*. Why think the state *from* which the entity changes is one in which she was disentitled to our concern or protection?

---

[24] Audi, 'Preventing Abortion as a Test Case for the Justifiability of Violence': 147, note 9; emphasis retained.

[25] For ease of exposition, here I employ the philosopher's common practice of talking of negative rights, rights not to have things done. In fact, for reasons I cannot here explore, I think we would do better to say that in such cases we do not so much violate a distinctive (negative) kind of right, but violate a 'positive' right (to life) in a distinctive, and especially egregious, way. The rest of my argument would then have to be modified accordingly: it is not so much that the abortionist presumptively violates a more important (negative) type of right but presumptively violates the right to life in an especially heinous way. For more on the topic, though not couched in the language of rights, see J. L. A. Garcia, 'The New Critique of Anti-Consequentialist Moral Theory'. 71 (1993) *Philosophical Studies*: 1–32.

[26] Audi, 'Preventing Abortion as a Test Case for the Justifiability of Abortion': 149.

Of course, even if no one of these differences is morally crucial, it might still be that the differences that occur at birth make a decisive moral difference when taken collectively. Still, that approach requires some explanation of what it is that makes this collection of irrelevancies jointly decisive, when no one of its elements is.

What I conclude from these inquiries is that Audi fails in what he needs, even by his own assumptions. First, he assumes that what would be needed, within relevant contexts, to justify a violent attack on an abortionist in defense of human life is for her to have some culpably bad intention. Second, he argues that an abortionist may not intend the abortions it is her business to perform. Third, he seems to assume that someone's intentions will not be culpable or otherwise morally objectionable insofar as they involve (or only involve) mental states it is reasonable to have. Fourth, he appears to assume that in this kind of case, at least, showing it can be reasonable to reject certain arguments for a position, here, about the personhood of the fetus, makes it reasonable to reject the thesis with which the arguments conclude. I have tried to provide grounds to doubt each of these assumptions, as well as the arguments Audi defends and the reasons he offers for rejecting the arguments he disputes.[27]

[27] We should add a few words on Audi's discussion of a moral 'presumption of innocence' for both the abortionist and her behavior. (See Audi, 'Preventing Abortion as a Test Case for the Justifiability of Violence': sec. III.) Let us first distinguish a *looser* construal, which consists simply in the claim that the *conjunction* that grounds guilt (that is, objectively disordered conduct and *mens rea*) needs to be established (e.g., beyond 'reasonable doubt'), from the *stricter* construal, which claims that *each* of its *conjuncts* needs to be so established. Even on the stricter construal, such a presumption admits of defeat. In a society like ours, where scientific and moral information about the unborn human is readily available, ignorance is fairly easily avoided by responsible agents, especially, by those who consider engaging in abortion as a career and have not only a special responsibility but also (unlike many young mothers of the unborn) ample leisure and calm circumstances in which to find and assess the relevant information. Moreover, any decent person should recognize a presumption of rights and dignity whenever dealing with a human organism, even if she temporarily allows, for the sake of objective consideration and argument, the possibilities of lessened rights and subpersonal humans. All this must weigh heavily against any supposed initial presumption of innocence. It may in fact serve to establish a presumption of *viciousness* in those who routinely perform or aid abortions.

In any case, why think we ought "presume" actions (act-tokens?) "innocent"? Does Audi suppose this presumption to be a moral duty, or only something epistemically virtuous (but perhaps supererogatory)? If the latter, to whom is it owed? On what basis? And in what would an action's (act-token's?) being "innocent" consist? What is the relevant contrast term? We blame *agents* for their actions; we do not blame the actions themselves. Perhaps an act-token can be called 'blameworthy', but when we say that we seem to be making a claim about its suitability as a basis for blaming its agent for performing it. In any case, what is the *use*, the *good*, the *point* of Audi's here distinguishing a second (kind of) presumption of innocence? If the presumption is supposed to be epistemically warranted, what warrants it? Note also that any valid presumption of innocence in apparently homicidal action must accompany a presumption of entitlement to protection that the potential victim possesses. Because of the latter presumption, in choosing what is normally and recognizably immoral, an agent loses the presumption of innocence in actions violating the protection to which another is presumptively entitled.

Conclusion

I return to my initial remarks. Here I have meant neither to praise nor to condemn conduct, only calmly to reflect upon and assess some discussions of a matter of intellectual interest but little practical urgency. This topic is of minimal importance practically, serving chiefly to distract us from the serious matter of abortion's inherent injustice to the minor one of the sometimes unjustified violence to which its horror drives some. Thoughtful silence here may be better than ill-considered denunciations, which are more reflexive than reflective.

   I have *assumed* that abortion normally kills a human being, and argued for the presumption that it is intentional and against the claim that those who perform or willingly facilitate abortions normally merit a presumption that their thinking is reasonable and their actions innocent. My discussion has found wanting various arguments that violent attacks against abortionists (let alone, on their deadly facilities and instruments) are in principle (or even normally) immoral in circumstances like ours. In so arguing, I recognize, of course, that there may be available intellectual defenses of those arguments or conclusions that I have not considered. I confess that I do not know just when such actions are permissible and when impermissible. It is, I think, a more difficult matter than many on either side of the abortion dispute have acknowledged. If we should not be so sure that active and even violent resistance to abortion is always and inherently impermissible, that does not entail that it is always, often, or ever the best course, or even a permissible one in this or that situation.[28] There are reasons that militate against it, and even if they do not show such conduct always forbidden, they may suffice to rebut any suggestion that it is obligatory. My suggestion is that we practice tolerance here, recognizing and accepting a plurality of legitimate approaches to our society's abortion atrocities, and that we respond with justice and charity toward all, the unborn victims, the medical victimizers, and those who sometimes go to extremes – justifiably or not – in protecting the former against the latter. The genuine problems involved in anti-abortion violence will disappear as our culture of death gives way to a culture of life. Let us all act, in our various

   In any event, any presumption of innocent, as contrasted with guilt, may be irrelevant to the issue. For preventive violence is usually said to require objectively unjust aggression, not guilt. Of course, the simple fact that you are a threat or danger to me is insufficient to justify my using violence against you; nor would your doing something that *would* be immoral if *otherwise* chosen suffice to justify it. So, there must be something vicious in the agent's will, even if she is drunk, or drugged, or insane, or whatever, even if her guilt is thereby mitigated. Violent *defense* is not justified by guilt as punishment is, but I think that the factors that justify will also always involve the person defensively attacked in guilty behavior. What matters is that the abortionist is *not* drunk, or drugged, or insane, or anything of the sort. Audi in fact seems to want to stress that the agent may be reasonable. However, is she is, then she also should have it in her power to know better.

[28] For a careful argument in support of some forms of violent resistance, see J. K. Fitzpatrick, 'A Pro-Life Loss of Nerve?' *First Things* December 2000: 35–38. See also Bray, *A Time to Kill*. As far as I can see, nothing I say here commits me to accepting either their arguments or their conclusions.

ways, to hasten that day, resisting the temptation to demonize those who respond to the imperative of defense in ways we rightly do not deem as always obligatory on us all. Illegal violence against legally protected abortionists and their aides will end when legal abortion does. For now, if resort to violence against abortion is not to become commonplace, what is important is that we insist on legal, nonviolent means that are safe and reasonably effective in resisting and preventing abortions. That means repudiating and reversing recent measures meant to oppress and harass sidewalk counselors, "rescuers", and even protestors, abridging their rights of free speech. On this, fair-minded people on all sides ought agree and join forces.[29]

[29] I am grateful to Professors Christopher Tollefsen and Richard Stith for their kindness in sharing with me their own work, and to both of them and Mr Richard Doerflinger for recommending to me and providing me with a number of relevant readings. I am also indebted to Luke Gormally and The Linacre Centre for inviting my participation in the Centre's Conference, *The Great Jubilee and the Culture of Life*, and for directing my attention to these topics.

The Culture of Life

4. Medicine, the Developing World and the Culture of Life

15

A preferential option for poor mothers

R. L. WALLEY

I AM MOST HONOURED to have been given this opportunity to present this paper. I am a professor of obstetrics and gynaecology in Newfoundland, Canada, and have nearly thirty years of experience of training both undergraduates and specialists in obstetrics and gynaecology, as well as twenty years experience in developing new approaches to the care of poor mothers in West Africa, in accord with the magisterial teaching of the Catholic Church.

The Second Vatican Council called for a preferential option for the poor. Mothers at the dawn of the third millennium are, in the opinion of many of us clinicians, among the poorest of the poor, both in body and in spirit. Because of the ethic of 'reproductive health' (the euphemism for abortion and contraception) that presently dominates the practice of obstetrics, it appears to many, even within our Church, that we as Catholics have no place in maternal health care, given our ethical position. This paper will review briefly the present tragic state of health of mothers and their unborn children throughout the world and the inappropriate, unethical and destructive solutions which currently dominate the practice of obstetrics and gynaecology, and the problems that we Catholics have in continuing to have a presence in the care of these mothers. But there will be an element of optimism to the review, presenting as it does a new professional initiative for the care of poor mothers.

Maternal health and the new Millennium

During this Millennium Jubilee the entire world is confronted with the thought of a birth that took place 2000 years ago. As Christians we celebrate the 2000th anniversary of the most important event in human history, the Incarnation, which began miraculously in Nazareth some 266 days before the most important birth in history, in Bethlehem. However, Pope John Paul II, in his Apostolic Letter for the millennium, *Tertio Millennio Adveniente*, has reminded us that we also celebrate the most important motherhood ever:

> The Father chose a woman for a *unique mission* in the history of salvation: that of being the Mother of the long awaited Saviour. The Virgin Mother responded with complete openness.[1]

[1] Pope John Paul II, *Tertio Millennio Adveniente* 1994: 54.

245

The conclusion that any reasonable person must come to after reviewing current world mortality, morbidity and abortion statistics is that the world cares very little for mothers and for their unborn children. It is an international disgrace that in our time so many mothers should give their lives having their babies, or sustain terrible birth injuries simply because they did not receive adequate care. It is unconscionable that millions of mothers should be subjected to the indignity of having their unborn children destroyed in their wombs, supported by the most powerful leaders in our world and paid for with our taxes. Sadly, the professions of obstetrics and gynaecology have colluded in the victimisation of the unborn child and now serve mothers, in most parts of the world, more frequently with death than life, having seemingly nothing better to offer.

Christian health professionals in particular have a special responsibility to develop new ways of providing the sort of care for mothers and babies to which they have a right, ones based on life and hope, rather than on death and despair. A group of Catholic health professionals has adopted a preferential option for poor mothers and their unborn children.

Maternal mortality, morbidity and abortion

The World Health Organisation estimates that each year 585,000 mothers die from causes related to pregnancy and childbirth, of which 99% occur in the developing world. While infant mortality levels are 10 times higher in developing than in developed countries, maternal mortality in developing countries is more than 100 times that of industrialised countries. Each time a woman becomes pregnant, given existing levels of health care in developing countries, she runs a risk of dying, and the risk adds up over her lifetime. The lifetime risk for a mother in Africa is enormous. It is estimated that 1:16 mothers will die as a direct result of complications during pregnancy and delivery, compared to 1 in 7000 in North America and Europe. There are five main causes: haemorrhage, infection, induced abortion, high blood pressure, and obstructed labour.

In addition to the mothers that die, there are many more who suffer serious but non-fatal childbirth injuries, the most common being obstetric fistulae. Fistulae occur because of unrelieved obstructed labour. Because the bladder or rectum or both are trapped between the head of the baby and the bones of the pelvis, pressure necrosis results, which in turn leads to fistulae or abnormal connections to the birth canal, which further results in the mother becoming incontinent. The mother leaks urine and faeces continuously down her legs and is therefore wet, filthy and foul smelling and is consequently rejected by her husband, family and society. Tragically, she is also often regarded as having been unfaithful to her husband and is condemned and ostracised. There are tens of thousands of these mothers who need loving care, through surgery, excellent nursing care, rehabilitation and counselling.

Obstetric fistula has been termed by the World Health Organisation the "forgotten disease", because while common in developed countries 100 years ago, it is now no longer seen, because mothers are healthier and receive better care. Obstetric fistula is another form of genital mutilation, which has not had the same degree of media attention as has female circumcision. However, the consequences for a mother, in terms of discrimination, are far worse.

The problem with numbers is that they sanitise suffering. So let me put a more personal spin on the suffering of mothers. In the first twenty years that I had been a practising specialist in Canada, I was never actually present at a maternal death, or ever had a mother under my care die. Having now worked for nearly twenty years in mission hospitals in West Africa, I have been associated with such tragedies all too frequently. I would like to illustrate the reality with two stories of the death and suffering of two mothers from my own experience in Nigeria.

A maternal death

One Saturday evening at St Luke's Hospital, a sister obstetric colleague and I were called to the maternity ward where a young mother at term with her third child had just been admitted in a moribund condition. She had been seen in the antenatal clinic some weeks before and had been well but for some reason had not returned until now. On examination she was barely conscious, and pleaded with us to help her. Her distraught husband was at her side. We started to assess her condition. The woman was severly anaemic, jaundiced, and her pulse and blood pressure indicated that she was in shock but she was not in labour. However, as sister examined her abdomen to determine if the baby was alive and I started to put up an i/v, the mother died. I recall that moment clearly as I was holding her hand. Both of us then watched helplessly as the movements of the baby in the uterus ceased.

The husband, realising what had happened, broke down and wept uncontrollably and called on God and us to help him. For both of us, even the missionary sister-doctor with thirty years of experience of tragedy in Africa, this was a profound emotional experience. The sister, close to tears herself, said to me as we walked back to the house, that "any woman who dies giving birth to a new life, no matter what she may have done in the past, must go straight to God". This mother had set out like most mothers to make a very "special gift of self", but she had ended by losing her life.

Grace's story

Grace's story, one of awful suffering, is typical of what many endure. At the age of fourteen, when working in a gas station, she became pregnant by a passing taxi driver. When she came to deliver there was no money to go to hospital, so she tried to deliver alone. Grace's labour did not progress properly as there was insufficient room for a baby to pass through the bony pelvis. Her mother called a traditional birth attendant (TBA).

247

After two days in complete obstructed labour she became dehydrated, her uterus and bladder ruptured and her dead baby remained undelivered. The TBA tried a few futile, drastic manoeuvres to deliver the dead infant. When it became obvious that she was near to death the TBA told her mother to take Grace home. A little later a village woman helped Grace deliver the macerated and infected dead baby.

A few days later the fistulae became evident and so the local native doctor tried to solve the problem by inserting herbs into the birth canal. When this failed, some women tried 'drying her out' by pouring boiling water over her vulva. This compounded the problem by causing extensive burns to the inside of her legs. Grace was infected and close to death.

The villagers managed to contact one of the Medical Missionaries of Mary (MMMs) who then took Grace to one of their hospitals close by. There Grace was resuscitated, and her burns dressed. Her condition improved a little but the relatives seeing what had happened to Grace decided to take her back to her village. There she lay on her face in great pain, covered in flies for weeks. One of the MMMs went to see how she was. On arrival in the village the sister was led to Grace's hut by the awful smell coming from it. There she found Grace in a pitiful state. She was then taken to another of the MMMs' hospitals which specialises in the treatment of obstetric fistula. In addition to these awful problems, Grace was found also to be crippled as she had developed foot drop caused by the prolonged obstructed labour which damaged the nerves supplying the leg muscles. Grace is one of the lucky ones who has survived. Over the last three years she has required many operations to close the fistulae and for skin grafts, and much physiotherapy. As if this were not enough suffering for one person, Grace has lost much more: the only baby she will ever have and even the chance of having a husband. Sadly, Grace has run away from the safety of the hospital.

The disparity between maternal mortality and morbidity rates, between developed and developing countries, is greater than any other commonly used measure of health status. Deaths as a result of pregnancy complications are the number one cause of death and disability among women of reproductive age, world-wide. The incidence of deaths from this cause is twice the incidence of deaths caused by any other condition, including AIDS, malaria, TB or sexually transmitted diseases. There is no single cause for male mortality in this age group that comes close to the magnitude of maternal mortality and morbidity. The tragedy is that the solutions to this suffering have been known for decades and cost very little. Simply put, mothers in our world at the beginning of the new millennium are being neglected basically because motherhood is not of political importance.

The world's response

During the last twenty-five years technology has served mothers and babies well. The rates of maternal deaths in developed countries have fallen to what are sometimes called irreducible minimums. Our mothers no longer die from haemorrhage, infection, or pregnancy induced hypertension because they have access to emergency transport; to well trained specialists in obstetrics and anaesthesia; to obstetrical nurses or midwives; to high risk intensive care facilities with sophisticated ultrasound and labour monitoring equipment; to blood transfusion; and to appropriate antibiotics and effective medications.

In spite of all the developments in knowledge and medical technological developments we are in one of the darkest ages of medical history. There exists a modern black death, when mothers and their babies in the developing world are still dying and suffering in an unprecedented way because they do not have access to the basics, to safe, clean and dignified facilities in which to give birth, to clean water, to electricity, to simple communications such as a telephone or to safe and rapid transport to hospital when complications develop. All of which we in the affluent world take for granted. We have perfected the barbarism of abortion and now force it on poor mothers in developing countries.

The Save Motherhood Initiative was launched at the first international safe motherhood conference in Nairobi in 1987 and a 'call to action' was issued to do something about maternal mortality. Unfortunately the response has been inadequate despite being issued many times since. The reasons for this failure according to authoritative opinion are:

- Missed opportunities that could have been used to rescue mothers from death.
- Muddled thinking.
- Mistaken priorities, for example hospitals which do not have the basic equipment to provide emergency obstetrical care.
- The reduction in development assistance by the world's richest countries to 0.3% of gross national product, which is less than half of what it should be.
- The promotion by governments, their funding agencies and international health organisations of what is now known as 'reproductive health', which is simply a euphemism for abortion and contraception. It is estimated that billions of dollars are spent by our governments and private agencies on birth control programmes but only a small fraction is spent on emergency obstetric care which would help mothers survive their pregnancies – care that we do not deny ourselves. To become a maternal death a mother must be pregnant! How can birth control pills or condoms help a mother with obstetric labour or who is bleeding to death from a postpartum haemorrhage? In my experience the women who die want to be mothers but are poor, young and have no influential voice to speak on their behalf, and are denied emergency care which could be readily available and inexpensive. This is culpable neglect by our world which has no concern for the 'unimaginable suffering' of mothers and which has adopted a 'conspiracy of silence'. There is not the will or compassion to do what is necessary.

This year marks the 50th anniversary of the UN Charter of Rights. Among these rights is the right to proper medical care. The Beijing Conference of Women identified twelve critical areas of concern one of which was the right of women to the "highest attainable standard of physical and mental health". However, the needs of mothers were not given the same emphasis. The focus must, however, be on mothers, who are important for their own sake, for their young children, who will die if their mother dies, which in turn may lead to the deaths of their families. Maternal mortality does not have the same political clout as, for example, AIDS or landmine injuries. As the Secretary-General of the UN recently pointed out on World AIDS day, "AIDS is the most publicised of all diseases". It is a pity that the deaths of mothers does not receive the same degree of attention.

During the last year I have visited northern Albania (to look at the situation among Kosovo refugee mothers), Ethiopia, Ghana and, in April this year, East Timor. Health care for mothers in all these areas is extremely poor.

Mention must be made of the consequences of abortion for the care of pregnant women. We must be quite clear about what is happening: it is no less than a holocaust. Abortion currently dominates international health policy. It is a policy which arises from poverty of thought and more seriously from the poverty which results from lack of love. So-called 'unwanted pregnancy' is now considered a disease to be treated with either surgery or with new medical 'treatments', i.e. abortifacients, such as the progesterone blocking agent RU 486 or methotrexate and misoprostol. Despite the many advances in modern perinatal medicine and obstetrical care which have almost eradicated maternal deaths and markedly reduced perinatal deaths in the developed world, deaths from abortion continue to rise throughout the world.

In Canada during the last twenty years the abortion rate has doubled, with 106,658 abortions performed in 1995. Of all pregnancies 1:5 is deliberately terminated; we have no laws which restrict abortion. The once Catholic province of Quebec has one of the highest abortion rates in the western world. In my home provice of Newfoundland and Labrador in 1995, 506 children were destroyed in the Health Science Centre alone and an additional unreported number in a local private abortion clinic. This amounts to destroying at least one kindergarten class per week. Our provincial government is now the largest provider of abortion services since it pays for all abortion services.

Obstetricians and gynaecologists provide their skills to destroy babies but make little effort to reduce the number of abortions. Normally all maternal or perinatal deaths are investigated and discussed in depth to determine if they could have been prevented. In spite of knowing so much about the unborn child, specialists in obstetrics and gynaecology have connived in devaluing the human being in the womb, thus making it so much easier to destroy. It defies belief that the most powerful man in the world would twice veto a bill which would have outlawed the obscenity of partial birth abortion. We are dominated by a culture of death.

The health needs of mothers are not exactly those of women generally. Mothers need special concern and care. Mothers frequently die alone, in agony from obstructed labour or in terror from haemorrhage, or suffer the extreme indignity of fecal incontinence, or suffer in silence and despair following an abortion. It is not good enough for us to simply discuss these problems; it is incumbent on us all to provide practical solutions.

The Catholic Church and maternal health care

Many Catholic health professionals presently involved with the provision of reproductive health care agree with Cardinal Ratzinger's opinion, expressed in his opening address to the Extraordinary Consistory of Cardinals held in 1991, that the Church "is losing ground in its efforts to protect the unborn, the handicapped, the sick and the weak".

Despite the consistent teaching of the Holy Father and the bishops, clearly laying out the Church's teaching, most recently in the encyclical *Evangelium Vitae*, the Church still seems to be failing to get its point across even to its own. The concerted effort of pro-life organisations throughout the world, over the last thirty years, to educate politicians and the general public about the humanity of the unborn child and the evil of abortion has fallen well short of its goal. Abortion has become as acceptable as contraception even to many Catholics in the west and is rapidly becoming so in developing countries as 'reproductive health' programmes are forced on them. As a consequence, the numbers of abortions world-wide are increasing. To break the vicious circle it is even more urgent than ever to reaffirm forcefully and professionally the Church's teaching on the inviolability of innocent human life. The Pope writes:

> In addition to making public declarations at every opportunity, bishops should exercise particular vigilance with regard to the teaching being given in Catholic seminaries, schools and universities, and the practices being followed in Catholic hospitals and clinics; they should support projects which seek to offer practical help; and they should encourage scientific reflection and legislative or political initiatives which would counter the 'death mentality'.

Unfortunately, the Church previously one of the largest providers of health care, especially for mothers, is now in many places rapidly getting out of the business or does not seem to have an idea as to what it could or should be doing to remedy the situation. The obstetrics and gynaecology unit in the Catholic hospital in which I held my appointment for nearly twenty years closed because, as the Sister Administrator stated in the press, "we cannot provide the services (abortion/sterilisation) to which the community is entitled". In return the hospital was 'compensated' with psychiatry, and vascular and chest surgery. It seems that this Catholic hospital has lost the courage to stand up for those for whom it was founded. Mothers have been abandoned, and the only door open to them is to the abortion clinic to help them in their time of distress.

The Catholic obstetrician

I would like to tell you something about what has happened to the Catholic obstetrician and gynaecologist over the past thirty years during which I have been in practice. Obstetricians used to be trained with one simple objective, which was to ensure that all pregnancies, as far as was humanly possible, should result in a live and healthy mother and a live and healthy baby. This requires special obstetrical skills and also general surgical and medical training. When I started residency training I was struck by the following statement from the preface to the obstetricians 'bible', *Williams Obstetrics* (then in its 16th edition):

> Happily we live and work in an era in which the foetus is established as our second patient with many rights and privileges comparable to those previously achieved only at birth.

Obstetricians and midwives share a unique and privileged vocation in the service of life, as assistants to the co-creators of new life. During the last thirty years there have been great advances in foetal-maternal medicine, which have made the outcome of childbirth for mothers and their babies a much safer business in the developed world.

Back in the early 1970s it was not anticipated, even by the Church leadership, that dark changes were about to occur that would turn maternal healthcare upside down and force many obstetricians to make serious decisions about their lives and careers. Almost overnight, abortion and contraception became basic to the healthcare of women. This had profound ethical and practical significance for Catholics in practice or in training. No other branch of medicine has been so affected by comparable developments.

It has not been appreciated that many obstetricians of my generation who decided to remain loyal to their Faith had, from the very beginning of these developments, to take a fundamental stand in defence of human life. This often caused them and their families considerable pain. Some saw their careers ruined, others were forced to leave their homes and country to continue in the speciality, and yet others had to abandon the speciality. In very personal ways Catholic specialists and their families have been subjected to professional and social ostracism and have become an 'embarrassment' because of their public stand.

Catholic ob/gyns who have remained faithful to the teaching of the Magisterium are viewed as ultra-conservative, professionally outdated and even possibly negligent, and are widely treated with displeasure by the profession. Thus the Catholic ob/gyn is in danger of going the same way as the dinosaur, having been frozen out by the abortion/contraception asteroid. This should be a source of grave concern to everyone.

It is not surprising that very few Catholics are entering obstetrics and gynaecology, as residents in training are exposed to one-sided, ill-informed and prejudiced views by those determined to change the way obstetrics and gynaecology is practised. In many parts of the world it is common to require those in training to participate in abortion or contraception as part of the training, and many in consequence come to divorce what they do from what they believe. It is significant that the more recent editions of *Williams Obstetrics* have dropped the reference to the foetus as a second patient. This is not unconnected with the development by obstetrians of the hideous procedure of partial birth abortion.

The questions that must be considered are: What effect does all this have on women and mothers? Where will they obtain opinions and treatment for their health problems which are in accordance with their moral convictions? Are women being unduly influenced by doctors or nurses who do not understand or care about religious convictions? Can Catholics still be relevant in the care of mothers and their unborn children? The answer to the last question is in my opinion a clear 'Yes' but we must be innovative and, indeed, courageous. But this begs the next question: *Who* is going to provide these services?

MaterCare International

It was Pope John Paul II, in his encyclical *Evangelium Vitae*, who issued an urgent appeal to all, but in a special way to Catholic health professionals, to do something extra for life:

> To all members of the Church, *the people of life and for life*, I make this most urgent appeal, that together we may offer this world of ours new signs of hope, and work to ensure that justice and solidarity will increase and that a new culture of human life will be affirmed, for the building of an authentic civilization of truth and love.[2]

> *A unique responsibility belongs to healthcare personnel: doctors, pharmacists, nurses, chaplains, men and women religious, administrators and volunteers.* Their profession calls for them to be guardians and servants of human life.[3]

> A special task falls to *Catholic* intellectuals, who are called to be present and active in the leading centres where culture is formed, in schools and universities, in places of scientific and technological research, of artistic creativity and the study of man... A specific contribution will also have to come from *Universities*, particularly from *Catholic* Universities, and from *Centres, Institutes and Committees of Bioethics.*[4]

In response to these invitations, a small international group of Catholic obstetricians and gynaecologists began asking themselves whether, if they did not do something, anyone would. This stubborn few believed that if they held to their moral principles they could continue to be truly effective in caring for mothers and their unborn babies, and that there are mothers around the world who still want the sort of care that they can provide. In October 1995 the group established MaterCare International (MCI) which has adopted a preferential option for poor mothers and their unborn children. The intention was not to develop a talking shop but to develop new practical initiatives of maternal service, training and research, in accordance with the teaching of the Gospel of Life, in

---

[2] *Evangelium Vitae*: 6. Emphasis in original.
[3] *Evangelium Vitae*: 89. Emphasis in original.
[4] *Evangelium Vitae*: 98. Emphasis in original.

order to contribute to the reduction of maternal mortality and morbidity rates by 75% in the next ten years and to the elimination of abortion throughout the world. As *Evangelium Vitae* asks, MCI intends to place itself:

> ... at the service of a new culture of life by offering serious and well documented contributions, capable of commanding general respect and interest by reason of their merit.[5]

MCI is developing a revolutionary structure for the 21st century, without large buildings with expensive overheads, but with a small international central agency linked to national groups that support flexible reference centres, distributed throughout the world, all linked together through modern communication and information technologies.

The international centre, currently located in Canada, will provide the specialist support for national support centres. The centre presently consists of an obstetrician, a professor of nursing, a secretary and a volunteer board. In the future we hope to have a staff that will reflect the unique, international, interdisciplinary, diverse vocational character and experience of our Church, and will include an administrator, medical and nursing directors, a theologian-ethicist, a health educator, a communications expert, and support staff.

National centres have been legally established in Canada, Ireland, the UK, and are in process of being established in the USA, Ghana, and Australia, and are planned for Portugal and East Timor. These centres raise funds from private or government sources, carry out projects in different countries or supply consultants to help with these projects. The international board meets quarterly by international conference call. At the last meeting we linked Canada, Ireland, the UK, Ethiopia, Ghana and the USA for one hour, all for $500. In the future we aim to set up a method for international teleconferencing using the internet, which is free.

All of this may seem to some idealistic and unrealistic, but we have confounded the sceptics by showing that we too can be successful in providing services, and in teaching and research, and that we can obtain public money without compromising ourselves in order to do so; we just had to be as gentle as the dove, as crafty as the snake, and as determined as the terrier with a trouser leg.

In 1998, MCI began its first programme, which is the evaluation of a model emergency obstetric service to reduce maternal deaths and injury in a rural area of Ghana. The first phase of the development of an oral prostaglandin which could be used by untrained traditional birth attendants in villages, when faced with life-threatening postpartum haemorrhage, when medical help is not immediately available, has been completed. Recently, in principle approval was given by the minister responsible for the Canadian International Development Agency to develop a sixty-bed treatment and rehabilitation centre for mothers with obstetric fistulae, which will also have a special interest in training nurses and doctors in the management of these patients.

---

[5] *Evangelium Vitae*: 98.

MCI is also developing an advocacy role on behalf of mothers by informing the general public of the 'unimaginable suffering' of so many mothers not only in developing countries but in crisis situations.

MCI organised an emergency service for Kosovar refugees based in an Austrian Military Field Hospital in northern Albania which was put on hold when hostilities ceased. MCI has been asked to develop a rural antenatal service in Kosovo itself.

A major new initiative is in East Timor. East Timor has twenty-three doctors for a population of 700,000, none of whom are trained in obstetrics. There is only one general hospital in the entire country, located in Dilli, which at the time of my visit had one foreign obstetrician on a three month contract. Some deliveries are performed by locally trained midwives and more complicated vacuum and forceps deliveries by general practitioners. However, most mothers deliver at home without professional help. There is an excellent clinic at San Antonio Motael in Dilli, at the time of my visit doing a small number of normal deliveries but without adequate equipment. This clinic could be expanded into a facility providing level one obstetrical care at reasonable cost.

The proposal is to provide essential obstetrical care at San Antonio Motael clinic which will include: safe caesarean section, forceps and vacuum delivery, and manual removal of placenta, anaesthesia, blood transfusion, and medical treatment for severe anaemia, hypertension, and infection, and resuscitation of the new-born. Training programmes in obstetrics for East Timorese doctors and nurse/midwives will also be included. Obstetrical consultants from overseas will be required to help out for short terms for the foreseeable future.

MCI is also developing an obstetric fistula teaching CD which will be made available free of charge and which also will be available on MCI's website.

MCI is not just for the developing world; it is concerned about the general future of obstetrics and gynaecology. Three years ago we tried to set up an international meeting to discuss the training of future specialists but without success. MCI is in full support of a recent initiative of the Pontifical Council for Healthcare Workers to convene a meeting, later this year, of interested Catholic obstetricians, so that "a more organised and united effort can be made to meet the challenges of the secularised culture of our times". We believe that there still remain throughout the world academic and hospital departments of obstetrics and gynaecology which could offer quality residency courses and electives consistent with a pro-life ethic.

MCI has developed a website (www.matercare.org) with a unique fundraising mechanism known as LifeSaver, which relies on individuals making *free* daily donations, sponsors and advertisers who pay the donations, and the extraordinary power of the internet.

We have also developed a quarterly newsletter, and a video about maternal mortality and obstetric fistula. Our interests are also in providing distance learning for doctors and nurses in, for example, natural family planning.

We also have in mind to establish an email or internet consulting and advisory service for anyone who would like a second opinion about any subject related to the care of mothers or about individual problem cases.

255

MCI is also in the process of applying to the United Nations for official non-government organisation status.

To be successful we need colleagues to join in and help, but most importantly we need the guidance and support of the Church hierarchy, starting at the very top, and we also need the support and encouragement of pro-life and Catholic women's groups, and pro-family organisations everywhere.

The Millennium – a golden opportunity

Pope John Paul II, in his Apostolic Letter, *Tertio Millennio Adveniente*, points out that the millennium jubilee is also a celebration of the motherhood of Mary. In a small way all mothers share in a special way in the motherhood of Mary, through their own birthing experiences and also, sadly in many circumstances, through death and injury they share in the suffering and death on the cross of her Son and in the sufferings of Mary at the foot of the cross – especially when they suffer the loss of a child. The Holy Father reminded us that the motherhood of the Virgin Mary

> ...which began in Nazareth and was lived most intensely in Jerusalem at the foot of the Cross, will be felt during this year as a loving and urgent invitation addressed to all the children of God, so that they hear her maternal voice: "Do whatever Christ tells you". (cf. *Jn* 2: 5)[6]

All of us are called to be involved in the celebration of the Great Jubilee. We have a golden opportunity, but, more importantly, an obligation, to show our love and concern for the welfare of mothers. We must 'breathe life' back into obstetrics and we think we have found a way of doing so.

---

[6] *Tertio Millennio Adveniente*: 54.

16

Combating the spread of AIDS

SR DR MIRIAM DUGGAN

COMING FROM AFRICA, the continent hardest hit by the AIDS pandemic, the topic of life and death, and how to survive, is uppermost in one's mind. Consider these recent statistics[1]:

- with 34 million people living with HIV, and 11.6 million people having already died, AIDS to-day is regarded by many as the worst plague ever to have hit mankind. It should be noted that 23.3 million of the people living with HIV are in Sub-Saharan Africa; 95% of the 11.2 million AIDS orphans are in Sub-Saharan Africa. We are in the midst of the biggest world war ever, mankind versus a tiny virus. Unfortunately the virus is gaining ground at the rate of 16,000 new cases daily according to UNAIDS report.[2]

In Sub-Saharan Africa where I have worked for the past 31 years, I have seen the great tragedy of this pandemic, as I have cared for thousands of young people suffering from Aids. I have seen their dreams shattered, their families torn apart, so many young people orphaned, extreme poverty, and major setbacks in development in some countries. Coupled with this is the terrible strain on the already overstretched health services, and the frequent lack of the basic drugs to relieve pain, while drugs which might slow down the progress of the disease are completely outside the reach of the majority of African people.

The HIV/AIDS pandemic is devastating Africa and jeopardising the continent's future. On the 10th of January this year, the UN Security Council met specifically to discuss the problem and called the HIV/AIDS pandemic the most serious factor in the economic and political destabilisation of Africa.

It is against this background that I present this paper to you.

In Dec. 1991, 50 people from various Christian denominations within Africa, and who were involved in AIDS care and prevention programmes, met in Dakar, Senegal, prior to an International Conference, to try and put our experiences and thoughts together as to what is the answer to the AIDS crises in Africa. How can the further spread of the virus be stopped? From that meeting we came up with the following Statement of Belief.

---

[1] It should be noted that figures given in this paper are those available to the author when the paper was presented in July 2000.
[2] World Health Organisation Report 1998.

Statement of belief

"We believe that individuals and whole communities have the inherent capacity to change attitudes and behaviours. The power to fulfil this capacity is often denied or is not exercised.

"This power must now be recognised, called forth and supported from both within and without. This will enable people to initiate and sustain behaviours that promote a healthy state of mind, body, spirit and environment. A critical component in this process is a supportive response to those living with HIV in the community.

"We recognise that behaviour change at individual and community level in the present HIV pandemic is a complex and on-going process. It is inextricably linked to such basic human values as care, love, faith, family and friendship, respect for people and cultures, solidarity and support.

"The present pandemic affects everyone. Our experience as affected and infected individuals proves that behaviour change is possible. We believe that *behaviour change is the most essential strategy in overcoming the HIV pandemic*".[3]

This statement brings out the fact that people have the inner capacity to change behaviour, but in the messages that are given these days that capacity is often denied. For example, we hear from many organisations "young people to-day are promiscuous, and therefore give them the condom" instead of encouraging them to turn away from high risk behaviour. Joy Engelsman, Senior Associate of Youth for Christ has this to say: "Kids are being sold out. They are being told sex is great and that they cannot abstain. They are given condoms and the green light. We should be telling them the opposite". We must begin to tell young people that they can have good values in their lives and that they can live behaviours that promote a healthy state of mind, body, spirit and environment. Our behaviours are very much linked with the values and attitudes we uphold.

Probably the most important line in the statement is the last one: "We believe that behaviour change is the most essential strategy in overcoming the AIDS pandemic". It was realised that more and more information was being given on the ways the HIV virus spreads, and more and more statistics were being published each year, but nothing was changing; only the numbers of those infected were increasing. It was realised that information or awareness about the spread of the disease was only the first step. There was a great need to look at the root causes for the spread of the disease. What were the underlying behaviours that led to the spread of the disease? What were the good values society was ignoring? At what places were the risks high? What was the fertile soil the HIV virus had found?

Sr. Kay Lawlor, MMM, at that time working in Kitovu Hospital, Uganda put together a programme called *Education for Life: A Behaviour Change Process*, based on the helping skills model of Gerard Egan, which is a behavioural and problem solving approach. As used in the Education for Life programme, it is

[3] Statement of Belief. ICCASA AIDS Conference, Dakar, Senegal 1991.

designed to facilitate a person's movement through the various stages involved in the changing of behaviour.[4,5]

Since 1992 I have worked with this programme in several African countries, and I believe this programme can go a long way in preventing the further spread of HIV. A workshop can last three to six days depending on the level one is working with. The core of the process can be visualised in the following diagram:

THE BEHAVIOUR CHANGE PROCESS

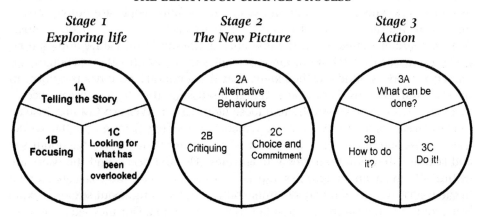

Stage 1. Exploring life is facilitated by:

(a) Telling the story.
(b) Focusing.
(c) Looking at what has been overlooked.

Stage 2. The New Picture is facilitated by:

(a) Calling forth alternative goals.
(b) Critiquing them.
(c) Making choices and commitments.

Stage 3. Action is facilitated by:

(a) Asking what can be done.
(b) Planning how to do it.
(c) Doing it.

The underlying principles are:

• Know and accept the present reality.
• Choose and commit self to a possible new behaviour.
• Act.

---

[4] Sr. K. Lawlor MMM, *Education for Life: A Behaviour Change Process*. Booterstown, Co. Dublin: MMM Communications.
[5] G. Egan, *Skilled Helper*. Monetery, CA: Books/Cole Publishing Co., 1986.

Participants going through this process are helped to make responsible, informed and life-giving choices.

Guided questions are given for each sub-section. These are discussed in small groups and presented at the plenary group where further discussion takes place. Role-playing is used to answer some of the questions.

For example, in Stage I questions about relationships, about what happens at night-clubs, disco halls and rave concerts are discussed. Questions are raised relating to drugs, alcohol and their role in the spread of AIDS. It is well recognised that in places where there is an abuse of alcohol and people are out of control the prevalence rates of HIV are high. The root cause may be the alcohol abuse. Questions are discussed about the influence of the media on values and culture, and how repeated watching of amoral soapies and anti-Christian messages can influence people's minds to the extent that the amorality becomes the norm in society, and governs behaviour. When discussing this topic African people frequently refer to pornography and loose living as our Western Culture, instead of recognising it as an evil culture which is spreading throughout the world. Sadly, most young people to-day seem to be getting their knowledge about sex and sexual behaviour from glossy magazines, TV, and peers, and the peers are getting it from TV and magazines. Especially in urban areas, there is a breakdown in the traditional African way of aunts and uncles teaching about sex and sexual behaviour, and the Churches often fall short in this area. Our messages are often too negative ('Don't do this or that as it is sinful'), rather than bringing out the wonderful gift of sexuality, the mystery of procreation, and how it should be cherished.

Questions around freedom, and the often false concept of freedom, are discussed, helping people to see that the only true freedom is the freedom to make responsible choices, and to be accountable for the consequences of one's choices.

'Safer sex', 'safe sex', and the many issues around condoms are openly discussed, helping people to understand that the sex which is truly safe is sex within marriage, with a life-long faithful partner: sex as God has ordained it. Participants are helped to see through the many confusing messages given to-day in regard to AIDS prevention and the condom, and to understand the difference between "The condom will prevent" and "The condom will reduce the risk", bringing home the realisation that the risk is very high when we are speaking about a disease that kills. Failure rates are not just percentages, they are lives. Unfortunately, due to the crisis situation everyone is looking for a quick solution, and the condom has been promoted to Governments as the answer.

As a doctor and gynaecologist I never cease to be amazed at the way condoms are promoted to youth as the answer to AIDS when we know the failure rates in preventing pregnancy, know the breakage rates, know they often are not afford-able, and when we know that people under the influence of drugs and alcohol rarely use them. In my estimation the free and indiscriminate distribution of condoms in schools and the wide advertising of them in a glorified way has encouraged more young people to become sexually active, because they believe the device will ensure safety. It is interesting to note that in the USA, Congress have put aside 230 million dollars to promote a change in behaviour among teenagers, after years of making condoms available in schools and colleges.

In Stage 2 of the process alternative behaviours and values are discussed. It is important to look at alternatives, as one of the reasons people fail to change is because they fail to look at alternatives. These new values and behaviours are then critiqued, with a view to seeing how possible it is to live them in to-day's society, and in particular with a view to seeing how to overcome negative peer pressures, and how to make responsible choices, choices that will give life. What are the values one wants in one's life? Participants are helped to commit themselves to sustaining a good pattern of behaviour, or to change from a pattern of 'at risk' behaviour to a new pattern of life-giving behaviour.

The third stage is devoted to planning how to put into action the new desired behaviour; a group may also plan how they will support each other in their new desired behaviour.

In this process the participants themselves come up with the new patterns of behaviour and values that they want. All the facilitators do is give the guided questions, and facilitate the dialogue. One does not go into a group and tell them that they need to change their behaviour, rather one helps them to discover what behaviours they need to change. In this way they own the decisions, and it is much more likely that they will live out their commitments.

In order to heighten the dynamic of the process a few short inputs are given on the gift of sexuality and the gift of procreation, condom data, current statistics on Aids, and how values influence attitudes and behaviour. Various skits, songs, times of reflection, liturgies are used by the facilitators in order to bring out or emphasise a message.

While working with this process it was realised that the groups making the most consistent and effective use of the process have recognised and incorporated an element necessary for bringing about a sustainable change, that is the element of faith. Using the power of prayer, and the Word of God and times of reflection, brought a depth into the programme. The Word of God has many powerful references in regard to life, values, and Christian living. In many instances what is most needed in changing behaviour is self control, which is one of the fruits of the Holy Spirit. Praying for the gift of the Holy Spirit in people's lives has often helped them to change from addictive behaviours where they felt helpless to help themselves.

"God's gift was not a spirit of timidity, but the Spirit of power and love and self-control." (2 Tim 1:6)

"When self-indulgence is at work the results are obvious: fornication, gross indecency and sexual irresponsibility; idolatry and sorcery; feuds and wrangling, jealousy, bad temper and quarrels; disagreements, factions, envy; drunkenness, orgies and similar things.... What God's Spirit brings is very different: love, joy, peace, patience, kindness, goodness, trustfulness, gentleness and self-control." (Gal 5:19–20, 22)

I have been amazed how, during inbuilt times of prayer and reflection, participants in the programme have been challenged and touched deeply and in God's grace have been able to make a commitment to a new way of life. This has not only been with school-going youth but with adults, prostitutes and street children and people in all walks of life.

The programme can be conducted for many different age groups and the questions geared to the needs of a particular age group. It can also be carried out in various ways, either using a block period of 3–5 days or on a weekly basis.

This programme can be used with people of different faiths, with respect for their beliefs. We have trained leaders of different religions in this programme, where they use their beliefs to strengthen and support the process. All major religions that I have been able to study hold marriage as sacred, and forbid pre- and extra-marital sex. Working with a group where there are people from different faiths can be very enriching as they listen to what is expected of them by the different religions.

This programme has been used to help rehabilitate prostitutes and street children. With these one needs to allow much more time for the programme, and build in sessions on self-worth and self-image, and it may also be necessary to address the reasons why these youths are in prostitution, and offer alternative sources of income.

Youth Alive

After the workshops had been running for some months, it became obvious that for young people who had made a commitment to wait until marriage before having sex, or who had turned away from sex, drugs and drinking habits, the ongoing support of a group was important. To meet this need Youth Alive clubs were established as positive peer support groups. The sense of belonging is very important to youth. In our discussions they often said that the reason they indulged in sex, drank alcohol or took addictive drugs was because they wanted to belong to the group. The challenge was to turn the negative peer pressure into positive peer pressure. This is what Youth Alive groups are about. It is more than a club, it is a way of life. These groups are now very active in several African countries.

Youth Alive mission statement

"We are a pro-life organisation with a mission to reach out to influence positive attitudes and behaviour change.

"We have a vision that sees young people fulfilling their dreams and ambitions with respect for humanity.

"We shall endeavour to promote a healthy state of mind, body and spirit in our nation."

Objectives

- To educate youth regarding HIV/AIDS.
- To help them grow in awareness of correct spiritual, moral, and cultural values and to character build so that they can live these values.
- To encourage and assist youth to develop their talents fully.
- To promote pro-life policies for youth both locally and internationally.
- To promote a healthy state of mind, body, spirit and environment for all people.

Knowing that young people have a lot of energy which needed to be tapped and channelled in a positive way youth were trained to give 'Education for Life' programmes to other youth, as well as to be involved in giving 'Adventure Unlimited', which is a character building programme for 9–14 year old groups.

Follow-up on-going formation workshops are conducted in the clubs, and thus the slogan "ABC for AIDS Prevention", which for many groups means "Abstinence, Be Faithful and Condom" became "Abstinence, Be Faithful and Character-Building".

Talent shows, music, drama and sports are promoted in the clubs, and where possible the youth go out into the community to bring their positive messages through song and drama, rallies and marches.

In many communities they are involved in activities to help people living with AIDS or to support orphans.

Being involved in these activities has helped to build their confidence and sense of self-worth, and one quickly realises that good role models and positive peer pressure can be a powerful force to bring about change.

One of the first countries that focussed on Behaviour Change as a way of preventing the spread of AIDS was Uganda, which was once looked upon as the AIDS capital of the world. Behaviour Change was the No 1 policy for AIDS prevention in the country and it had the full support of President Yoweri Museveni. You may recall when he was invited to speak at the International AIDS Conference in Florence he had this to say;

> In the olden days you offered us the magic bullet of penicillin, now we are being told to protect our lives by a mere bit of rubber. In a country like mine where people have to walk 5 km to get an aspirin, do you think that they will go there to get a condom? That is why I am asking my people to go back to our time-tested culture of no pre-marital sex and faithfulness in marriage. Young people need to be taught discipline, self-control and at times sacrifice.

These programmes, and the establishment of Youth Alive clubs, spread rapidly to many parts of the country. In 1996 The Rockefeller Foundation sponsored the Rural Development Women's Consultancy group to carry out an evaluation of the programmes, going to various schools, and parishes where the activities had been.

The evaluation showed very clearly:

- a great reduction in the sexual activity of those who had taken part in the programme as compared to those who had not.

263

Views on Youth Alive Club activities

Percentage of respondents exposed to YAC activities showing how YAC has been useful to them by sex and district of residence.

Ways	Female				Male			
	Kla	Jinja	Pallisa	Luweero	Kla	Jinja	Pallisa	Luweero
Provided information on AIDS and ways of preventions	98.2	100.0	100.0	100.0	91.3	96.2	100.0	92.9
Helped to change behaviour	81.7	98.1	100.0	85.2	87.2	92.3	95.8	100.0
Helped develop talents in Music, Dance, Drama, etc.	86.2	94.4	92.7	77.8	82.6	92.3	95.8	64.3
Helped make friends	96.3	92.6	97.6	70.4	95.7	96.2	95.8	78.6
Taught how to care for others	97.2	100.0	92.7	88.9	82.6	96.2	95.8	100.0
Taught how to care for those suffering from AIDS	88.1	92.6	85.4	92.6	91.3	96.2	83.3	85.7
Strengthened Christian Faith	91.7	96.3	100.0	74.1	87.0	96.2	100.0	100.0
Others	34.9	18.5	24.4	3.7	26.1	19.2	33.3	0.0
Should YAC continue? (YES)	99.1	100.0	100.0	100.0	100.0	96.2	100.0	92.9

Source: Compiled from survey.

- a far higher number of young people who had never engaged in sexual activity among those who had attended a workshop compared to young people who had not attended a workshop.

And there was another side to it: youth who had done the programme were far more active in community and church activities.[6]

The table above will give you samples of how youth have been helped through the activities of Youth Alive.

I believe that the impact of these Education for Life programmes, and the establishment of Youth Alive clubs and similar other church programmes focussing on behaviour and values have in no small way contributed to the fact that the prevalence rate for HIV infection in Uganda has fallen from 28.9% to 9.8% according to the UNAIDS figures for 1999, showing that AIDS can be prevented. Uganda is the first country in Africa to register a significant drop in the spread of the virus.

Kenya

In 1993 the programme spread to Kenya and Tanzania.

A participative evaluation carried out by Premese Africa of the programme in Kenya showed that it was having an impact on youth.

[6] *Evaluation of Youth Alive, Uganda.* Rural Development Women's Consultancy Group, Uganda.

264

Of those trained in the programme:

- 78% had changed their sexual behaviour.
- 12% had stopped indulging in alcohol.
- There was a greater positive self-image among youth who had done the programme.
- Young women were more assertive of their right to say 'no' to sex.
- There were more positive attitudes towards people living with HIV/AIDS.[7]

Already in Kenya in some areas there was evidence that the prevalence rates among youth had begun to drop, e.g.

- Nakuru prevalence rate: from 27% to 24.6%.
- Ngumbi prevalence rate: from 24.01% to 22%.

Zambia

In Zambia since 1998, 420 Education for Life Programmes have been conducted involving 22,583 youth, and Youth Alive Clubs established widely throughout the country. In a recent evaluation carried out the following was stated to be the case:

- Most youth who had gone through the programme indicated that they were abstaining from sexual activity and refraining from drug abuse.
- Most youth stated that abstaining from sexual activity was not only best but was also possible.
- Most youth said that the programme had made a meaningful impact on their lives.
- Many of the youth had become involved in Church programmes.[8]

A recent report from UNAIDS has indicated that the prevalence rate among young people in Zambia had dropped from 24% to 13% especially in the under-25 years group,

Zimbabwe

Since April 1999, 'Education for Life – a Behaviour Change Process' workshops have been held in a number of places all around the country. While it is still too early to make a detailed assessment of the impact of the programmes, they have been received with great appreciation and enthusiasm. A number of individuals have come forward to say how the programme was a turning point

---

[7] *Participatory Evaluation of Education for Life Programme, May 1997–September 1999.* Premese Africa, P.O. Box 25942, Nairobi, Kenya.

[8] Institute of Economic and Social Research, University of Zambia, *Evaluation of the Youth Alive Zambia Behaviour Change: Report* (May 2000).

for the better in their lives. In one of the secondary schools, the headmaster commented that there was a marked improvement in the discipline and performance of a class of students who had been through the programme. Also an increasing number of young people are volunteering to help in the facilitation of programmes and in other Youth Alive activities.

Programmes have also started in Tanzania, South Africa and Botswana, but it is probably too early to know of any impact they are having in these countries at present.

Many other groups with similar messages are becoming active, such as, Youth for Christ, Worth the Wait, True Love Waits, and Free Teens. The more groups that take on this kind of approach the greater the chance of bringing about a change in society and in the environment.

Conclusion

The AIDS pandemic is indeed a very tragic one, but maybe instead of dwelling on the magnitude of it, it is preferable to see the challenge it is offering to people of good will, to look beyond the misery and to read the signs of the times. A tiny virus is baffling the minds of great scientists, and yet we have the answer to it – or a large part of the answer – within our grasp. Is it not an invitation to mankind to return to the Creator's law, a call to conversion?

If one makes a study of all the literature that has come out on AIDS prevention over the years one will notice a shift in the emphasis from 'know your sex partner, use a condom', to the new emphasis on having one life-long partner.

If you look at the following diagram taken from the Zimbabwe AIDS figures you will note that 92% of the spread is through sexual activity. This we have within our power to change, and the 7% which is mother to child transmission will also reduce as there will be less mothers infected.

92% spread by sexual contact;
  7% spread from mother to child;
  1% spread by other ways, i.e. needles,
     scarification, etc.

In an article by R. B. Marwood, published in *The British Journal of Hospital Medicine*, entitled 'AIDS – A Conspiracy of Misinformation',[9] he stated that "Church Leaders proclaim abstinence as the only real protection. I fear they are correct. It would seem that virginity and faithfulness will once again become fashionable".

If society addressed the root causes for the spread of the virus and returned to the values of no pre-marital sex and faithfulness in marriage AIDS could be

[9] R. B. Marwood, 'AIDS A Conspiracy of Misinformation'. 37 (1987) The British Journal of Hospital Medicine: 99.

drastically reduced. If the millions invested in Latex rubber as a prophylactic were instead invested in addressing the root causes I think the outcome would be much more beneficial to society.

An important line in the 1991 'Statement of Belief' (from the Dakar meeting) which I quoted earlier is: "A critical component in this process [of behaviour change] is a supportive response to those living with HIV/AIDS in the community." It is very important that those living with the virus are not rejected or isolated. It has been well shown that in a climate of acceptance, in which people can speak about the disease they are suffering from and feel accepted, there is less likelihood that they will go and spread it, and people will go more freely to be tested and find out their status. In Uganda, thanks in no small way to Philly Lutaaya, a popular singer who went down with AIDS in the late eighties, but who used his songs to educate and warn others, and who encouraged people to come out and speak about the disease, many people spoke out and many support groups were formed, who actively participated in AIDS prevention programmes. To these men and women a great debt of gratitude is due. The young person who speaks out and tells other young people not to take the risks that led to them getting the virus can have a great impact. This is only possible when others reach out in compassion, not judging or condemning, but meeting people where they are.

Having worked in several African countries and witnessed many lives changing I am convinced that there is a great challenge to the Church to promote the culture of life through helping people to look at values and behaviours that need to change not only to prevent AIDS but also to improve the quality of our lives together, to stabilise family life, and promote Christian living.

A second challenge is to have a Gospel response to those living with the virus and to be to the forefront in care and support.

Maybe in the years to come historians will look back and say this was a special moment in salvation history when God called to his people and looked for a response. The question is how will we have responded? Will we have been to the forefront promoting the Culture of Life?

I would like to conclude with a quotation from the book of *Deuteronomy*:

See to-day I set before you life and prosperity, death and disaster. If you obey the commandments of Yahweh your God, that I enjoin on you to-day, if you love Yahweh your God and follow his ways, if you keep his commandments, his laws, his customs, you will live and increase, and Yahweh your God will bless you in the land which you are entering to make your own. But if your heart strays, if you refuse to listen, if you let yourself be drawn into worshipping other Gods, and serving them, I tell you today, you will most certainly perish: you will not live long in the land you are crossing the Jordan to enter and possess. I call Heaven and earth to witness to you today: I set before you life or death, blessing or curse. Choose life, then, so that you and your descendants may live in the love of Yahweh your God obeying his voice and listening to him. (Dt 30:15–20)

Supplementary Papers

17

Eugenic genetic engineering as a manifestation of the culture of death in human genetics

THOMASZ KRAJ

THE ENCYCLICAL LETTER *Evangelium Vitae* (*EV*) of John Paul II, issued in 1995, introduced into the public debate two important notions: *the culture of life* and *the culture of death*. These two notions refer to two fundamental and radically different attitudes towards man. The former is based on the Gospel and follows its logic, while the latter stands in contradiction to the Good News. The Encyclical Letter of John Paul II is the response of the Church to the devaluation of human life in the contemporary world. Not only does this devaluation manifest itself in the increasingly widespread practice of abortion and euthanasia but also in the belief that these are socially and morally valid ways of resolving human problems. According to the Pope the basis of the culture of death consists in subjectivism carried to an extreme, "a *notion of freedom,* which exalts the isolated individual in an absolute way" (*EV* 19) and the promotion of the self understood in terms of absolute autonomy (*EV* 20,68). In the culture of death there is no place for God, the truth of Creation and human responsibility to the Creator.

The same logic and the same concept of man may be traced in some projects of biotechnology. One of these projects is *eugenic genetic engineering* (EGE), which is a good example of how the culture of death gains its territory in human genetics. What is eugenic genetic engineering? EGE is a non-therapeutic genetic intervention with the aim of creating human beings with pre-established qualities. However, EGE is concentrated not so much on an individual as on his or her genes, on designing the human genetic make-up, especially with the aim of securing advantages for the human race. The term *eugenic genetic engineering* in bioethical literature has two meanings: the strict meaning given above and the broader meaning which concerns various efforts aimed at the birth of healthy offspring. The term EGE in this paper is used in the strict sense.

EGE would require two types of genetic intervention: eugenic germ-line engineering (EGLE), which would resemble germ-line genetic therapy (GLGT), and human cloning by nucleur transfer. To bring out the way in which EGE projects manifest the culture of death one must clarify, first, the intended purpose of both interventions and, then, the concept of man they are based on.

Eugenic germ-line engineering and human cloning as eugenic proposals

The procedure used for EGLE would be similar to that used for GLGT. The range of changes proposed by eugenicists, and especially the requirement that they be permanent, calls for a GLGT-type intervention rather than somatic gene therapy.[1] EGLE is simply distinguished by the purpose for which it is performed. GLGT is aimed at a therapeutic alteration of a pathological state, whereas EGLE aims at a re-modeling of the human genetic make-up to secure genetic enhancement. There are three types of possible enhancement: physical, which would involve physical powers of the human body and its longevity; intellectual, concerning such traits as intelligence or memory; and moral, concerning attitudes and behaviour especially as they affect interpersonal relationships. The idea of using EGLE arises from observation of the dependence of some traits or forms of behaviour on genetic factors.

EGLE might be thought to be a relevant response to the requirements of global competition and modern technology which depend on the availability of particular skills. Eugenic germ line engineering, employed with caution and prudence, might be thought to have a contribution to make to the global competition for skilled workers

Human cloning (which is already being attempted) is thought to have the advantage over eugenic germ-line engineering of being more predictable. While in the case of EGLE it is impossible to exclude interaction among genes and random mutations, which could diminish or even cancel out any improvement, the intended outcome of cloning might be more secure, at least after the experimental stage. Transmission of genetic material from one generation to another by cloning would allow us both to reduce the risk of a genetic disorder[2] and to increase the chance of passing on some positive feature. The intact genotype (which could also be engineered before the procedure) is transmitted to offspring, thus securing the birth of someone with more predictable characteristics than is normally the case.

The most important eugenic uses for human cloning which have been suggested include:

- production of a large number of identical individuals predestined to special tasks within the community;[3]
- production of identical twins separated in time, so as to have "copies" of children with some desired features.
- copying of an adult individual. His or her copy could grow as his or her offspring.

[1] H.T. Engelhardt Jr., 'Human Nature Technologically Revisited'. 8 (1990) *Social Philosophy & Policy*: 191.

[2] J. Fletcher, *The Ethics of Genetic Control. Ending Reproductive Roulette*. Buffalo: Prometheus Books 1988: 154; K. Bayertz, *GenEthics. Technological Interventions in Human Reproduction as a Philosophical Problem*. Cambridge: Cambridge University Press 1994: 69.

[3] P. Ramsey, *Fabricated Man. The Ethics of Genetic Control*. New Haven: Yale University Press 1970: 71; R. Rhodes, 'Clones, Harms and Rights'. 4 (1995) *Cambridge Quarterly of Healthcare Ethics*: 285.

Some objections to eugenic genetic engineering

In this section I shall mention some practical and moral objections to EGE; in the next I shall raise more fundamental objections.

Proposals for EGE in its two forms (human cloning and EGLE) invite a number of objections relating to its feasability. Such proposals seem to rest on erroneous biological assumptions, which overemphasize the role of genes in an organism's growth (genetic determinism), the biological significance of certain correlations (e.g. between proteins and their "phenotypic" manifestations) and which see evolution as an aimless process which should be subordinated to the requirements of human (in this case, eugenic) reason. EGE proposals also tend to overestimate our genetic knowledge and our ability to control genetic processes in living organisms, especially with the help of the techniques postulated by eugenicists which at present either do not exist (EGLE) or are still experimental (cloning).

There is also a problem concerning the novelty of eugenic manipulation since any new intervention on humans requires thorough testing on animals. But how do you test on animals the enhancement of typically human traits like intelligence or certain spiritual abilities? Thus eugenic projects necessarily presume experiments on human beings which are non-therapeutic, very risky and performed with the intention of killing the subject in the case of mishap at the embryonic or foetal stage. Furthermore, both EGLE and cloning rely on generating human beings outside the context of marital union, i.e. through IVF or other laboratory procedures (cloning) which are wrong both because of the mode of generation and because (if successful) they will be lethal for many human embryos generated

The risks posed by EGE are not restricted to those immediately affected. Since EGE involves human germ-cells (prior to or subsequent to the generation of embryos) it would necessarily result in modification of future generations. This means that features acquired by the child will be naturally passed on to its future offspring, thus exposing future generations to risk, since long-term effects of an initial manipulation are hardly predictable.

These objections make it sufficiently clear that EGE is hardly compatible with respect for human life and human health. The root of what is objectionable about EGE, however, lies in the understanding of human life which underpins such proposals. Eugenic proposals in human genetics represent a particular anthropological position which cannot be harmonized with what the Pope calls the culture of life and love.

Anthropology of eugenic genetic engineering

Proponents of eugenic genetic engineering are convinced that there is an absolute novelty in the situation of man in the era of genetic revolution. Rapid developments in modern technology have created a fascination with new possibilities and the prospect of man's limitless self-modification. The adherents of eugenics are convinced that neither existing anthropology nor ethics is able to provide criteria for evaluating the new situation. They therefore see an urgent need to prepare new standards to help man to adjust to the new situation. The activity through which man will meet the new challenge raised by genetic knowledge is human auto-manipulation (self-manipulation, self-alteration).

The advocates of EGE reject the notion of there being some features proper to the human being which science and medicine should respect. They call this view biologism or physicalism and claim that there are compelling reasons for changing the natural human condition.

Human self-alteration, however, raises the question of human nature, which is traditionally thought to impose limits to auto-manipulation. For proponents of eugenic manipulation, human nature is something merely physical. On the one hand it is a foundation of man's subjectivity, but on the other hand it constitutes a reality extraneous to human subjectivity. Human nature belongs, then, to the outside world. It does not belong to the essence of man and seems rather to be an obstacle, which should be overcome with the help of genetic technology. The notion of human nature is very important in the analysis of moral problems connected with cloning and EGLE, because the normative character of nature has always been widely recognized, i.e. what was a distortion of healthy human nature was acknowledged to be morally questionable.[4] The advocates of EGE claim that they also reject what is against human nature. According to them, however, it is man who decides freely and independently what is natural and what is not.[5] Man who changes his nature overcomes in this way his finitude, his "inability to accomplish all that he wills."[6] The full realization of humanity is: to be in control. Our purported dominion over the 'nature' which is extraneous to our subjectivity is the foundation for man's claim to full autonomy and limitless freedom. The anthropology underlying radical eugenic aspirations postulates a new creation, a new 'Genesis', in which man replaces God. Science and technology are believed to offer this possibility.

Critical analysis of eugenic anthropology

There are two fundamental questions to resolve in relation to eugenic genetic engineering: Who is man? What is his nature? According to proponents of EGE the human being is composed of two elements: human subjectivity (which involves our spiritual abilities) and its biological foundation. The essence of man consists only in the first element, while his biological nature is simply raw material and the starting point for human self-manipulation. The present form of human biological nature is an outcome of accidents and natural selection. It

---

[4] L. Palazzani, 'Personalism and Bioethics'. 10.1 (1994) *Ethics & Medicine*: 9; L. Palazzani, 'La natura nel dibattito bioetico'. (1998) *Seconda navigazione*: 204–226; R. Spaemann, 'Naturale e innaturale sono concetti moralmente rilevanti'. (1998) *Seconda navigazione*: 184–203.
[5] R. Chadwick, 'The philosophy of human nature'. 10 (1996) *Medical Humanities Review*: 9.
[6] Ramsey, *Fabricated Man. The Ethics of Genetic Control*: 159.

has no normative value and may be changed practically at will.[7] However, human observation and intuition indicate that human influence on our own nature is rather limited. The human being is a fully integrated structure, a **unity** of two elements, spiritual and material (corporeal):

> A human being is not a purely spiritual entity, but a being at once spiritual and physical – *corpore et anima unus*. I am not a mere soul, even if my soul survives death. Rather, I am a biological being – an animal – sharing biological characteristics with non-human animals, but in a way that is fully human. My biological nature is not 'subpersonal', not something separate from what I am myself; rather, it has the moral importance of the nature of a human person.[8]

If eugenic aspirations are in part motivated by an ideology of limitless autonomy, we should note how little in practice their realization would amount to genuine exercises of autonomy. For autonomy is a matter of *self-determination*, but EGE is always a matter of what we propose to do to *other* human beings who have no possibility of consenting to the ways in which we propose to manipulate them. So the reality we are talking about is not autonomy but the freedom to dominate.

On what grounds would choices be made to preside over a humanly engineered 'evolution' of mankind when choice is to be unconstrained by considerations of what is compatible with nature? All we seem to be left with is a radical subjectivism: "there are no objective criteria for establishing which physical characteristics or behaviours should be 'improved' and in what measure... Even if it was possible to suppose a perfect objective intervention, there would still be no objective criteria for deciding who should be the recipient of such interventions".[9] In this perspective any abuse becomes legitimate if performed in the name of human autonomy and freedom.

The freedom which purports to legitimate eugenics involves a paradox. If what we have in mind is the freedom of individuals to carry out eugenic genetic modifications then, were they to be successful, the effect would be to produce constraining determinants in the lives of those on whom they had been carried out. Moreover, the subjective values on which they had been based would have been imposed on a future generation.

A claim to unrestricted freedom leaves no room for God or for the recognition of moral norms. It is a fundamental truth of Christian doctrine, repeatedly affirmed in the teaching of the Magisterium (and reasserted in *Evangelium Vitae*), that every human being is created by God. What is more, man is created

---

[7] Engelhardt, 'Human Nature Technologically Revisited': 191.

[8] Working Party of the Catholic Bishops' Joint Committee On Bioethical Issues, *Genetic Intervention on Human Subjects*. London: The Linacre Centre [on behalf of The Catholic Bishops' Joint Committee on Bioethical Issues] 1996: 16.

[9] L. Palazzani, 'Genetic engineering and human nature', in: P. Doherty, A. Sutton (eds) *Man-made man*. Dublin: Open Air/Four Courts Press 1997: 55.

in the image of God, redeemed by Jesus Christ and called to eternal life. Because of this every human being has a great dignity which requires recognition of his or her fundamental human rights. The right to life is the most basic of such rights. Furthermore, human life should begin in a human way, i.e. as a result of the union of husband and wife. A human life is the life of a human person. The human being is "a person, that is, a being which, on the one hand, represents invariantly the species man, and on the other is something new, one of a kind, not reproducible, with a uniqueness that goes beyond the simple individuation of its common type."[10] EGE does not recognize man as a person with his unique individuality; the human being is treated as an artifact which in the case of EGLE would be produced *de novo* and in the case of cloning re-produced or copied.

EGE is closed to the dimension of life as God's gift. The logic of love, which should resemble God's love, is replaced by the logic of manipulation, production and manufacturing. Instead of receiving the unconditional acceptance proper to love the human person who might result from EGE would be viewed as the more or less successful (and therefore more or less acceptable) product of the manipulation attempted. Where technology and the free market predominate the process of objectifying children is inevitable. At first the child is made *for* the parents and *for* their happiness. The next step is a consumerist attitude along something like the following lines: "I want a boy, of a good height and general fitness, and I want him next year, not this, and I want to have one in reserve in case I lose him."[11] Thus the child not only becomes one of many goods which serve to satisfy the needs of parents, but is also treated as an article which happens to be ordered at the surgery rather than the supermaket.

Were EGE to succeed it would seriously distort parent-child relationships. If parents have gone to the trouble of having a specifically pre-programmed child they will have correspondingly specific expectations of that child. Such expectations about a child's future create psychological pressure (a kind of tyranny) which reduces the child's freedom. The use of sophisticated genetic tools may also make parents see themselves as absolved from the duty of educating the child: "let the genetic intervention do the job instead of me." All this is incompatible with the acceptance of children for who they are and the commitment to their moral development, i.e. their growth towards genuine freedom, which are at the heart of authentic family life.

To sum up, the prospective employment of EGE is both incompatible with respect for the dignity of human beings and extremely dangerous not only for the individuals directly involved but also for various human communities and groups, future generations included.

---

[10] J. Ratzinger, 'Man Between Reproduction and Creation: Theological Questions On the Origin Of Human Life', in: Smith R.E. (ed) *Trust the Truth. A Symposium on the Twentieth Anniversary of the Encyclical 'Humanae vitae'.* Braintree MA: The Pope John Center 1991: 371.
[11] B. Tobin, 'Deliberately cloning human beings: on the significance of even contemplating it!'. 8/1 (1997) *Bioethics Outlook:* 5.

Conclusion

Pope John Paul II writes that there is rejection of God at the root of the culture of death:

> Here especially one sees that "at the heart of every culture lies the attitude man takes to the greatest mystery: the mystery of God." ... Where God is denied and people live as though he did not exist, or his commandments are not taken into account, the dignity of the human person and the inviolability of human life also end up being rejected or compromised (*EV* 96).

The characteristic traits of the culture of death outlined in the Encyclical *Evangelium Vitae* are exemplified in the project of *eugenic genetic engineering*. They are:

- the unrestricted autonomy of the individual with its related subjectivism and relativism of values (*EV* 19,20,68).
- the treatment of man as if there were no difference between him and other creatures. Man is seen as mere raw material for eugenic manipulations (*EV* 22).
- the negation of the human dignity and personal uniqueness of each human being (*EV* 23) together with the pretension of deciding whose life is worth living and whose not, who may live and who should die (*EV* 66).
- the devaluation of human sexuality (*EV* 23).
- non-therapeutic experimentation on human embryos and their killing as a result of experimental procedures or mishaps (*EV* 14,63,89).

EGE is only one example of the culture of death in the context of biotechnology. The Second Vatican Council in the Constitution *Gaudium et spes* teaches that the purpose of any culture is the perfection of human bodily and spiritual qualities and the promotion of authentic values, which render the life of various communities more human (*GS* 53). The question which arises in discussion of eugenic projects is precisely the question about the humanism of these proposals, the humanism on behalf of which the whole enterprise claims to be undertaken. More than three decades ago the late Paul Ramsey captured the demise of humanism which EGE portends:

> Speaking of the man-God only in the future tense, these new messiahs (or, if one prefers, these new cultic bearers of an absolute biological future) must necessarily speak of humanism in the past tense as well. The crucial point is that they propose to take up where *humanism* left off... It is not Christianity alone but man as well that the revolutionary biologists have left behind in their flights of grasping after godhead. No values at all are being produced, no values are even in conflict, if men come to subsist in a world in which the sole judgment to be made is... that men "simply want to try it scientifically."[12]

---

[12] Ramsey, *Fabricated Man. The Ethics of Genetic Control*: 146–147.

It should be clear, then, why the message of *Evangelium Vitae* is so crucial for the contemporary world. The Encyclical unmasks publicly the true intentions and plans of the advocates of the culture of death and calls on all of us to defend the genuine humanism of the culture of life and love.

18

Wojtylan insight into love and friendship: shared consciousness and the breakdown of solidarity

SCOTT FITZGIBBON[1]

ONE OF POPE JOHN PAUL II's encyclicals identifies the virtue of solidarity.[2] A document from the recent Synod for Europe refers to a "crisis of solidarity."[3] The Holy Father, in recent speeches, states that "the century now beginning ought to be the century of solidarity"[4] and encourages the development of a "culture of solidarity."[5]

To refer to solidarity is to refer to close affiliations: friendships, households, marriages, and the bonds among citizens, partners, members of the staffs of

[1] This article benefitted greatly from the assistance afforded by Professor Mark F. O'Connor, the Director of the Arts and Sciences Honors Program at Boston College, who, with the help of his student Adelina Jedrzejczak, translated portions of Karol Wojtyla's book *Osoba i Czyn*. He is the source of quotes in English from that Polish original *infra*. He also generously discussed several points of interpretation, but final responsibility for them rests not on his shoulders but on mine.

Thanks are also extended to Dean John Garvey of Boston College Law School and to several members of the faculty of Boston College Law School who commented on an oral presentation of an early version of this work in June of 2000.

Finally my thanks for generous financial assistance to Darald and Juliet Libby.

[2] *Sollicitudo rei socialis* 1987: 38.6. 80 *Acta Apostolicae Sedis*: 513. An English translation (provided by Vatican Press) is in J. Michael Miller (ed), *The Encyclicals of John Paul II*. Huntington, Indiana: Our Sunday Visitor, Inc. 1996: 426–77.

[3] *Instrumentum Laboris* for the Synod Of Bishops – Second Special Assembly for Europe, in *L'Osservatore Romano*, Weekly Edition in English, November 18, 1999. *See* John Paul II, Message to Prof. Sergio Zaninalli, Rector of the Catholic University of the Sacred Heart, May 5, 2000, in *L'Osservatore Romano*, Weekly Edition in English, May 24, 2000 at 9 ("The value of solidarity is in crisis, perhaps mainly because there is a crisis in the only experience which could guarantee its objective and universal value: that communion between persons and peoples which the believing conscience traces back to the fact that we are all children of the one Father, the God who 'is love' ....").

[4] John Paul II, Address to the Diplomatic Corps, January 10, 2000, in *L'Osservatore Romano*, Weekly Edition in English, January 12, 2000, at 1 (the entire phrase is in italics as there published). *See* John Paul II, Address to the Ambassador of France, June 10, 2000, in *L'Osservatore Romano*, Weekly Edition in English, June 21, 2000, at 4 ("It is .... important to develop an ever greater European consciousness in our contemporaries which, mindful of peoples' roots, mobilizes them to form a community of destiny through a political will which seeks to unite them").

[5] John Paul II, Homily of November 12, 2000, in *L'Osservatore Romano*, Weekly Edition in English, November 15, 2000, at 2.

hospitals, and the faculties of universities. To warn of a crisis of solidarity is to observe that there has been a crisis of affiliation; a crisis of *philia*. During the Twentieth Century it often seemed as though man were losing his nature as a political animal (as Aristotle called him),[6] and as a "house-hold-maintaining animal" (as Aristotle also called him) and a *koinonikon* or partnership-forming creature.[7] It seemed as though man were losing his capacity to be a *culture-forming*, culture-belonging animal: a creature which forms and nourishes a life-sustaining culture rather than a culture of death. To recommend a century of solidarity is to propose a deeper understanding of the structures of close affiliation.

To pursue a deep understanding of the person and how he forms community was the major academic project of Professor Karol Wojtyla prior to his election as Pope John Paul II. His philosophical writings, his plays, and his poetry shed light from several new directions. This article describes some of his major insights and extends them. It shows how they help explain modern crises of solidarity.

I. The nature of affiliation: the traditional Aristotelean approach based on will and reason[8]

Aristotle emphasizes what the affiliates will or intend. "To be friends, [people] must be mutually recognized as bearing good will and wishing well to each other."[9] Further components are mutual knowledge[10] and reciprocity. Friendship, at least in its higher form, involves "reciprocal choice of the absolutely good and pleasant,"[11] and therefore reciprocal reasoning and

---

[6] *Politics* 1253a 2–9 (Jowett translation in J. Barnes (ed), Volume II. *The Complete Works of Aristotle*. Princeton, New Jersey: Princeton University Press 1984: 1986–2129). Aristotle also identifies man as *politikon* in *Politics* 1278b 19–21, in *Nicomachean Ethics* 1097b 12, 1162a 17–19, and 1169b 17–19 (hereinafter referred to as *Nicomachean Ethics*), and in *History of Animals* 488a 8–10. Here and throughout this article the translation of the *Ethics* quoted is that by W. D. Ross (revised by J. O. Urmson) in J. Barnes (ed), Volume II. *The Complete Works of Aristotle*: 1729–1867.

[7] *"oikonomikon zoon"* and *"koinonikon anthropos."* Aristotle, *Eudemian Ethics* 1242a 22–24. In context: "[M]an is not merely a political but also a household-maintaining animal, and his unions are not, like those of the other animals, confined to certain times, and formed with any chance partner, whether male or female, but ... man has a tendency to partnership with those to whom he is by nature akin." Here and throughout the translation of the *Eudemian Ethics* quoted is that by J. Solomon in Volume II. *The Complete Works of Aristotle:* 1921–1979.

[8] See generally S. Stern-Gillett, *Aristotle's Philosophy of Friendship*. Albany, New York: State University of New York Press 1995; A. Price, *Love and Friendship in Plato and Aristotle*. Oxford: Clarendon Press 1989.

[9] *Nicomachean Ethics* 1156a 3–4. See *id.* 1155b 33 ("[G]oodwill when it is reciprocal being friendship") and 1156a 10 ("wishing well" is a component of friendship).

[10] "For many people have goodwill to those whom they have not seen but judge to be good or useful .... but how could one call them friends when they do not know their mutual feelings?" *Id.* 1156a 1–3. *See id.* 1167a 23–24.

[11] Aristotle, *Eudemian Ethics* 1237a 31–32.

judging[12] and "sharing in discussion and thought."[13] Another element is expressed by the verb *philein*, which can mean "to love" but also encompasses less intense attitudes.[14]

The Aristotelean approaches rest on the firmest of foundations. In any human action the will is central; in any good action *good will* is central. Good will means freely and knowingly choosing the good and so involves the reason. Fullness in Aristotelean virtue is never a matter of just *doing* good things; excellence involves activity for the right reasons, with the participation of the mind and a correct disposition of will:

> ... [S]ome people who do just acts are not necessarily just, i.e. those who do the acts ordained by the laws either unwillingly or owing to ignorance or for some other reason and not for the sake of the acts themselves ... so is it, it seems, that in order to be good one must be in a certain state when one does the several acts, i.e. one must do them as a result of choice and for the sake of the acts themselves.[15]

But this classical approach, at least if you interpret it narrowly, seems to be incomplete. Parties to an intense and lasting love, for example, would tell us that their relationship reaches to depths not fathomed by terms such as good will, good wishes, and agreement. Players in a drama of affiliational disfunction can attest that their troubles go deeper than disagreement and ill will. Participants in the Twentieth Century's crises of solidarity – young Americans during the period of the War in Vietnam, for example – await a kind of ethics and anthropology deeply understood by Homer and Shakespeare but not successfully depicted in the language of classical academics.

---

[12] Since choice involves "consideration and deliberation." Aristotle, *Eudemian Ethics* 1226b 8. "Choice arises out of deliberate opinion." *Id.* at 1226a 8–9. "[C]hoice is deliberate desire ... I call it deliberate when choice is the source and cause of the desire ....". *Id.* at 1226b 18–20.
[13] *Nicomachean Ethics* 1170b 11–12.
[14] It is translated with forms of the verb 'to love' in the Ross translation of the *Nicomachean Ethics*. But it can mean something different from *eros* and from *agape*, and can be found, according to Greek usage, not only between parent and child and husband and wife but also between host and guest. See the definition in *A Greek-English Lexicon Compiled by Henry George Liddell and Robert Scott*. Oxford: Clarendon Press 9th ed. 1940: 1933 and authorities cited. A discussion of Greek words for love and related matters, with extensive references, is contained in C. Spicq, *Theological Lexicon of the New Testament*. Peabody, Massachusetts: Hendrickson Publishers (James D. Ernest, trans.) 1994: 8–22. *Philein* is discussed at some length in the *Rhetoric*, where Aristotle states: "We may describe friendly feeling [*philein*] towards anyone as wishing for him what you believe to be good things, not for your own sake but for his, and being inclined, so far as you can, to bring those things about." *Rhetoric* 1380b 34–1381a 1 in Volume II. *The Complete Works of Aristotle* 2152–2269. This seems to require complete unselfishness, but in the ensuing passage Aristotle uses the term for one's disposition towards the enemies of enemies (1381a 16–17) and "to those who are willing to treat us well where money is concerned" (1381a 20–21).
[15] *Nicomachean Ethics* 1144a 14–20.

2. The nature of man: some Wojtylan insights

Wojtylan writings, without rejecting Aristotelean thought[16] contain an anthropology enriched by the addition of a supplementary component: that of *consciousness*.[17]

2.1 *Consciousness*

Wojtyla's view of consciousness and its connection with love can best be understood through his play *The Jeweler's Shop*.[18] Teresa and Andrew, a young couple recently engaged, encounter one another as though by chance in a city street Andrew says:

> I met Teresa when she had just paused
> in front of a large window ...
> I stopped by her quietly and unexpectedly –
> and suddenly we were together
> on both sides of the big transparent sheet
> filled with glowing light.
> And we saw our reflections together,
> because behind the widow display
> is a great, immense mirror
> ... [W]e found ourselves all of a sudden
> on both sides of the great mirror
> – here alive and real, there reflected...[19]

Soon Teresa and Andrew find themselves standing in front of a jeweler's shop. Again, in front of a window – Teresa and Andrew are looking at wedding rings. This time the window *becomes* a mirror. Teresa says:

> ... [T]he window has turned into a mirror of our future;
> it reflects its shape.
> ... I already saw, as in a mirror,
> myself, in a white wedding dress, kneeling with Andrew...[20]

---

[16] The Aristotelean elements are prominent, for example, in K. Wojtyla, *Love and Responsibility*. London: William Collins & Son 1981 (H.T. Willetts, trans.).

[17] Some recognition of this element appears in *Nicomachean Ethics* 1170b 11–12, where it is stated that a friend develops a "consciousness of the existence of his friend" which is "realized in their living together and sharing in discussion and thought."

[18] K. Wojtyla, *The Jeweler's Shop*, in *The Collected Plays and Writings on Theater*. Berkeley & Los Angeles, California: University of California Press 1987: 278–322 (B. Taborski, trans.) (hereinafter referred to as *The Jeweler's Shop*). The play is subtitled "A Meditation on the Sacrament of Matrimony, Passing on Occasion into a Drama."

[19] *Id.* at 285.

[20] *Id.* at 288 & 287: these passages appear in the opposite order from that set forth above.

And then later Andrew says that the mirror was:

> not an ordinary flat mirror but a lens absorbing its object.
> We were not only reflected but absorbed.[21]

Teresa and Andrew, entering one of the closest of all affiliations, stand before glassy surfaces which represent media of experience and thence media of solidarity.

The mirror is a metaphor which also appears in Wojtyla's poetry[22] and in his philosophical writings – especially his book *Osoba i Czyn*[23] and its controversial English edition *The Acting Person*.[24] The Wojtylan mirror is not only a medium for the reflection only of the self. Not at all – a wide mirror displays the surrounding scene as well.[25] Nor is it a medium for the reflection only of current,

---

[21] *Id.* at 292. The next sentence is: "I had an impression of being seen and recognized by someone hiding inside the shop window."

[22] *See* 'The Samaritan Woman Meditates', in *Easter Vigil and Other Poems*. New York: Random House 1979: 13 (J. Peterkiewicz, trans.):

> I – yes I – conscious then of my awakening
> as a man in a stream, aware of his image,
> is suddenly raised from the mirror and brought
> to himself, holding his breath in amazement,
> swaying over his light.

[23] K. Wojtyla, *Osoba i Czyn*. Krakow: Polskie Towarzystwo Teologiczne 1969: 35–36 (hereinafter referred to as *Osoba i Czyn*). The Polish word here translated 'mirror' is *odzwierciedlenie*.

[24] K. Wojtyla, *The Acting Person*. Dordrecht: D. Reidel Publishing Co. 1979: 31 (A. Potocki, trans.; A.-T. Tymieniecka, ed) (hereinafter referred to as *The Acting Person*). The controvery concerns whether *The Acting Person* is faithful to *Osoba i Czyn* and to Wojtyla's thought. See, e.g., K. Schmitz, *At the Center of the Human Drama: The Philosophical Anthropology of Karol Wojtyla/Pope John Paul II*. Washington, D.C.: Catholic University Press 1993: 60 n. 6 ("gravely misleading in important passages, and, ... because of an unstable rendering of important technical terms, simply muddled"); see also the discussion on page 59 and page 155 n. 48. But then, *The Acting Person* is not just a translation: it is endorsed by Wojtyla in the preface as an "improved presentation" (page ix). (And see page xiv: "I thank the editor, A.-T. Tymieniecka, who, guided by her excellent knowledge of the philosophical environment of the West, gave to my text its final shape .... although the basic concept of the work has remained unaltered.") Some say that the revision process was hijacked by Tymieniecka once Wojtyla had become too busy to keep involved. This view seems to be embraced, accompanied by insider's familiarity, in G. Weigel, *Witness to Hope: The Biography of Pope John Paul II*. New York: HarperCollins Publishers, Inc. 1999: 174–75 n. 8. But apparently *some* of the revisions, at least, came from the pen of Wojtyla. See S. Gregg, *Challenging the Modern World: Karol Wojtyla/John Paul II and the Development of Catholic Social Teaching*. Lanham, Maryland: Lexington Books 1999: 56 n. 26 (noting that "there is little question that Wojtyla revised parts of AP throughout the 1970's in anticipation of its English publication").

Doubts about *The Acting Person* do not undermine the conclusions of this article, since the relevant passages of that book are consistent with *Osoba i Czyn*. Under the guidance of Professor Mark F. O'Connor, the Director of the Arts and Sciences Honors Program at Boston College, correspondences are identified in some of the footnotes *infra*.

[25] See *The Acting Person* 31: "Consciousness is ... The reflection, or rather the mirroring, of everything that man meets with in an external relation by means of any and all of his doings ... " This closely follows *Osoba i Czyn* at 36.

contemporaneous phenomena: the Wojtylan mirror not only receives and reflects: it retains and records.[26] Teresa observes: "The window absorbed my person at various moments and in different situations... I am also convinced that our reflection in that mirror has remained forever, and cannot be extracted or removed. A little while later we concluded that we had been present in the mirror from the beginning...[27]

The Wojtylan mirror is a metaphor for consciousness. In Wojtylan thought, the mirror is the repository and reflector of what has been encountered or comprehended.[28] It is not the mind as a whole, not even the 'conscious' mind as a whole; it is not the will nor the thinking, analyzing, reasoning activity of the mind.[29] Rather, it is the medium upon which those things which we experience or understand are preserved, 'penetrated', 'illuminated',[30] and reflected back to the inner self.[31] Consciousness is, Wojtyla says at one point, "understanding."[32]

John of the Cross, on whom Wojtyla wrote a doctoral thesis, uses the metaphor of the mirror to similar purpose, referring to:

> ... an archive and storehouse of the understanding, wherein are received all forms and images that can be understood; and thus the soul has them within itself as it were in a mirror, having received them by means of the five senses, or... supernaturally; and thus it presents them to the understanding... [E]ven as the five outward senses represent the images... of their objects [on the mirror]... even so, supernaturally,... without using the outward senses, both God and the devil can represent... many things to the soul...[33]

---

[26] See *The Acting Person* 31 ("once the action is accomplished consciousness still continues to reflect it."). This closely follows *Osoby i Czyn.*

[27] *The Jeweler's Shop* 292.

[28] *The Acting Person* 31–32 (closely following *Osoba i Czyn* 35–36).

[29] See A. Damasio, *The Feeling of What Happens: Body and Emotion in the Making of Consciousness.* New York: Harcourt Brace & Company 1999: 198–99: "Extended consciousness is not the same as intelligence. Extended consciousness has to do with making the organism aware of the largest possible compass of knowledge, while intelligence pertains to the ability to manipulate knowledge ..."

[30] *The Acting Person* 33: "[W]e attribute to consciousness the specific quality of penetrating and illuminating whatever becomes in any way man's cognitive possession." (This closely follows *Osoba i Czyn* 35.) Compare Damasio, *The Feeling of What Happens: Body and Emotion in the Making of Consciousness* 315:

> It all begins modestly, with the barest of senses of our living being related to some simple thing inside or outside the boundary of our bodies. Then the intensity of the light increases and as it gets brighter, more of the universe is illuminated ... Under the growing light of consciousness, more gets to be known each day, more finely, and at the same time.

[31] *The Acting Person* 36 ("consciousness can mirror actions and their relations to the ego"). (This closely follows *Osoba i Czyn* 39.)

[32] *The Acting Person* 32: "Consciousness is, so to speak, the understanding of what has been constituted and comprehended."

And in Teresa of Avila the mirror also contains Christ or reflects His image:

> On one occasion, when I was reciting the Hours with the community, my soul suddenly became recollected and seemed to me to become bright all over like a mirror: no part of it – back, sides, top or bottom – but was completely bright, and in the centre of it was a picture of Christ Our Lord as I generally see Him. I seemed to see Him in every part of my soul as clearly as in a mirror...[34]

Wojtyla's references to consciousness reflect his interest in the phenomenologist philosophers, and especially Max Scheler[35] (who defined "consciousness" as "everything that comes to appearance in inner perception"[36]). Phenomenologists tend towards an exclusivity of subjectivism which, if not flying to the extremity of denying that there are goods or facts outside of experience, does place feeling and experiencing front and center epistemologically, making them the sources of man's knowledge: the person "has no access to knowledge which does not go through an emotionalized consciousness" and no knowledge of the good except as emotional values – the resonance of experience in "the sounding box of his interior conscience."[37] But of course Wojtyla and the entire Catholic tradition assert that there is a reality and good independent of what one experiences of them; and that one can learn about them in ways other than by the resonances of experience – for example by discourse and reasoning.[38] Consciousness serves these projects rather than supplanting them.[39]

---

[33] *Ascent of Mount Carmel* Book II, Ch. XVI, in Volume I. *The Complete Works of Saint John of the Cross Doctor of the Church.* Wheathampstead: Anthony Clarke 1974: 123 (E. Peers, trans.). For metaphors along similar lines, see *Spiritual Canticle* Stanza XII in Volume II. *The Complete Works of Saint John of the Cross Doctor of the Church* 236–38. ("The propositions and articles which faith sees before us she calls a silvered surface." "[W]hen they are in clear vision they will be in the soul as a perfect and finished painting.")

[34] St. Teresa of Jesus, *The Life of the Holy Mother Teresa of Jesus.* Ch. XL, in Volume I *The Complete Works of St Teresa of Jesus.* London: Sheed and Ward 1975: 292 (E. Peers, trans.).

[35] *See The Acting Person* xiv. ("The author of the present study owes everything to the systems of metaphysics, of anthropology, and of Aristotelean-Thomistic ethics on the one hand, and to phenomenology, above all in Scheler's interpretation, and through Scheler also to Kant, on the other hand.") Wojtyla's studies of the phenomenologists are detailed in G. Williams, *The Mind of John Paul II: Origins of His Thought and Action.* New York: Seabury Press 1981: Chapter 5.

[36] M. Scheler, *Formalism in Ethics and Non-Formal Ethics of Values: A New Attempt Towards the Foundation of an Ethical Personalism.* Evanston, Illinois: Northwestern University Press 1973: 392 (M. Frings & R. Funk trans.).

[37] R. Buttiglione, *Karol Wojtyla: The Thought of the Man Who Became Pope John Paul II.* Grand Rapids, Michigan: William B. Eerdmans Publishing Co. 1997: 57–58 (characterizing the views of Max Scheler). A detailed account appears in Williams, *The Mind of John Paul II: Origins of His Thought and Action* Chapter 5.

[38] See *Osoba i Czyn* Chapter Four: "Our ability to create thoughts is not ... nearly as important as our ability to distinguish between what is true and what is not true. The mind allows us to maintain a connection with reality ..."; *The Acting Person* 158: "Thinking and comprehending are the manifestation of [the mind's] ... intellectual function ... its practical function consists in the evaluating and distinguishing of what is true and what it not ... [T]he mind in these two functions allows man to keep alive the widest possible contacts with reality."

2.2 *Consciousness as orienting knowledge towards the self*

The person as portrayed in Wojtyla's writings, is "the interaction of two structures": one of cognition, playing upon the realia of the world; the other that of consciousness, which "subjectivizes" knowledge.[40] You may know a thing, but until you put it into some important relation to yourself you lack full consciousness of it.[41]

Consciousness is the subjective side of knowledge. It is the 'personalist' side of knowledge. It is that aspect of knowing which orients things to the self. It is knowledge from one's own perspective.[42]

Things relate to the self in many ways. They can cause physical sensations like heat and pain, they can cause grief or joy, they can affect plans and projects, and they can *receive* the effects of our actions as well. As a person develops and the range of his activities widens, he extends the ways in which he intersects with the *realia* of the world and so widens and enriches his consciousness.[43]

2.3 *Consciousness of one's self and one's actions*

Consciousness mirrors not only the surrounding environment but also the self. The mirror displays to Teresa and Andrew not only their surroundings but also themselves, and their context – their situation in time and place. A recent study by a prominent neurologist (Damasio) states that: "consciousness...

---

[39] This seems to be conveyed by a very complex passage in *The Acting Person* 159:

> Man's consciousness has indubitably a mental character, but even so its proper function does not consist solely in searching for truth and distinguishing it from fallacy, because this belongs to judgments. Consciousness in its mirroring function draws its significative contents from the active intellectual and practical processes that are directed towards truth.

The corresponding paragraph of *Osoby i Czyn* states: "[T]he internal dynamism of the mind... leads to recognizing the truth... The mirroring or reflexive function of consciousness no longer plays an active part – instead it draws its meaning from those actions of the mind which are directed towards truth."

[40] *The Acting Person* 58 n. 26.

[41] A recent study of consciousness by a prominent neurologist states:

> [C]ore consciousness occurs when the brain's representation devices generate an imaged, nonverbal account of how the organism's own state is affected by the organism's processing of an object, and when this process enhances the image of the causative object, thus placing it saliently in a spatial and temporal context.

Damasio, *The Feeling of What Happens: Body and Emotion in the Making of Consciousness* 169.

[42] See Damasio, *The Feeling of What Happens: Body and Emotion in the Making of Consciousness* 198: "Extended consciousness is... the capacity to be aware of a large compass of entities and events, i.e., the ability to generate a sense of individual perspective, ownership, and agency, over a larger compass of knowledge than that surveyed in core consciousness."

[43] His wider, and enriched "extended consciousness" is the basis for a solid "sense of self" and the ground of personal stability and integrity. *Id. passim.*

places [the] ... person at a point in individual historical time, richly aware of the lived past and of the anticipated future, and keenly cognizant of the world beside it."[44] In consciousness "we step into the light of mind and we become known to ourselves."[45] Another recent study by leading neurologists (Edelman and Tononi), similarly, describes the development after early infancy of a "higher-order consciousness" which presents a "discriminable and nameable self."[46] And a recent book by a philosopher of the mind (Flanagan) identifies the development of a "deep" kind of self-consciousness and the emergence of "self-represented identity."[47]

Furthermore – here is a crucial Wojtylan insight – consciousness reflects the person's *actions*. "Consciousness accompanies and reflects or mirrors the action when it is born and while it is being performed; once the action is accomplished consciousness continues to reflect it ..."[48] Through his consciousness, the person can discern himself as an acting person. He becomes "aware of both the fact that he is acting and the fact that it is he who is acting."[49] He acts in the fullest sense of the term "action" only when he acts with this awareness. The topic sentence of *Osoba i Czyn* states: "The only action that deserves to be termed as such is the conscious doing of a person."[50]

---

[44] *Id.* at 16.

[45] *Id.* at 315.

[46] G. Edelman & G. Tononi, *A Universe of Consciousness: How Matter Becomes Imagination*. New York: Basic Books 2000: 175.

[47] O. Flanagan, *Consciousness Reconsidered*. Cambridge, Massachusetts: MIT Press 1992: 194–95.

[48] *The Acting Person* 31 (closely following *Osoba i Czyn*).

[49] *The Acting Person* 31 (closely following *Osoba i Czyn*).

[50] This is the second sentence of Chapter One ('conscious' is *wiadomy*). (And see the first sentence of paragraph five: "An action is conscious doing.")

The Acting Person at first appears to depart from this emphasis: there the second sentence in Chapter One reads, "It is only man's *deliberate acting* that we call an 'act' or 'action'." (Emphasis in original.) This is followed by a sentence not contained in *Osoba i Czyn*:

> Nothing else in his acting, nothing that is not intended and deliberate, deserves to be so termed. In the Western philosophical tradition a deliberate action has been seen as the *actus humanus*, the human act, with the stress laid on the aspect of purpose and deliberate-ness; it is in this sense that the term is used, even if implicitly, throughout this book, since only man can act purposely and deliberately. (p. 25)

But this apparent departure is actually a change only in organization. The edition adds the heading "The Act in Its *Traditional* Interpretation" (emphasis added) over the first two paragraphs and saves Wojtylan departures for later. On the next page it states: "[T]he term 'human act' or 'action' as such contains a definite interpretation of action as conscious acting ... [This interpretation] accounts for the experiential facts as a whole and brings out most meaningfully all that is essential in them." (p. 26)

Another important text on these matters is K. Wojtyla, *Person and Community: Selected Essays*. New York: Peter Lang 1993 (T. Sandok, trans.) and especially 'The Person: Subject and Community' in *id.* at 219–61.

2.4 Consciousness in the service of self-knowledge

Reflection on what is displayed by consciousness is basic to self-knowledge. Reflection on one's actions, especially,[51] since *actus humanus* is a complex phenomenon. "[H]ow deep are human deeds," Wojtyla exclaims in one of his poems.[52] Andrew, about to take one of life's big steps, can see not only the project of getting engaged and married, but also himself as a taker of steps and a performer of projects. He can learn that he is a self-possessing, self-governing being. In this and many other ways he can progress, with the aid of consciousness, in the construction of what a recent study refers to as the "autobiographical self";[53] and can progress in stability, integrity, and a "sense of self."[54]

This deeper, developing self is itself reflected in consciousness. "Consciousness is ... the reflection, or rather the mirroring, of everything that man meets with in an external relation by means of any and all of his doings ... and all the things happening in him. This is all mirrored in consciousness. 'Contained' in it, so to speak, there is the whole man, as well as the whole world accessible to this concrete man."[55] Consciousness, thus, has a deeper structure which leads Wojtyla to construct metaphors more complex than that of the mirror. In *The Jeweler's Shop*, the mirror becomes a lens, absorbing what it reflects. In Wojtyla's poem *Looking into the Well at Sichar* the mirroring surface of the water covers another surface:

> Look now at the silver scales in the water
> where the depth trembles
> like the retina of an eye recording an image.[56]

---

[51] See *Osoba i Czyn* Chapter One paragraph 3: "an action is a source of knowledge about a person."

[52] K. Wojtyla, 'A Bishop's Thoughts on Giving the Sacrament of Confirmation in a Mountain Village', in *Easter Vigil and Other Poems* 67, 68:

> The surface connects with the hidden plane,
> frontier running untouched by sight;
> thoughts rise to the eyes like moths to the pane,
> they silently shine in the pupils – deep,
> how deep are human deeds.

[53] Damasio, *The Feeling of What Happens: Body and Emotion in the Making of Consciousness* (*passim* and especially at 172–76).

[54] *Id. passim.*

[55] *The Acting Person* 31 (closely following *Osoba i Czyn*). Compare Damasio, *The Feeling of What Happens: Body and Emotion in the Making of Consciousness* 224: "The idea each of us constructs of ourself, the image we gradually build of who we are physically and mentally, of where we fit socially, is based on autobiographical memory over years of experience and is constantly subject to remodeling."

[56] *Easter Vigil and Other Poems* 9.

2.5 Consciousness of incompleteness: transcendence

An important attribute reflected in consciousness is that of incompleteness. Action involves "a tendency away from what is incomplete towards an appropriate fullness... The tendency toward fulfillment of oneself shows that this self is somehow incomplete... [T[he human self is revealed to itself ... as a tendency toward self-fulfillment."[57]

Andrew can discern that he suffers from the human condition of insufficiency. He can realize that when he acts in major matters – for example becoming engaged, getting married – he seeks to complete or fulfill himself.

Self-fulfillment ultimately involves transcendence. Transcendence – "inseparably connected" with self-fulfillment – is a surpassing or "a going-out-beyond or a rising-above."[58] "[T]ranscendence ultimately converge[s] in a single source, which constantly resounds within the human being..." "Transcendence is the spirituality of the human being revealing itself."[59]

2.6 Ethical consciousness

Consciousness is that aspect under which truths about the good are known and embedded and "felt" and discerned in one's interiority[60] in a way which deploys them as applicable to one's own activities. Andrew can discern his character as a moral person: the goods he has embraced; and the goods (or bads) towards which his actions tend. His consciousness can appropriate and personalize the goods of his actions.

2.7 Will and Reason: Aristotle revisited

All of this can enrich the Aristotelean understanding in several ways. For example, consider the Aristotelean point that the good of an action involves not just doing a good thing but understanding the action and its goodness:[61] with Wojtylan insight we can add that full understanding of an action requires a full and illuminated consciousness. And consider the Aristotelean view that action is good insofar as aimed at good ends: with Wojtylan insight we can add that the reflexive good of self-knowledge can be among those ends.

---

[57] Wojtyla, 'The Person: Subject and Community', in *Person and Community: Selected Essays*, at 232–33.
[58] *Id.* at 233.
[59] *Id.*
[60] See *The Acting Person* 155 (referring to man's "experience" of the good).
[61] See text at note 15, *supra*.

3. The nature of affiliations: a richer account based on Wojtylan anthropology[62]

3.1 *Consciousness within affiliations*

Andrew and Teresa show us consciousness as it emerges within an affiliation. Andrew observes:

> Here we both are, we grow out of so many strange moments,
> as if from the depths of facts, ordinary and simple though they are.
> Here we are together. We are secretly growing into one
> because of these two rings.[63]

When they are together, side by side, each sees the world as the other sees it. Each sees a sort of display as it appears to the other. Andrew and Teresa look into the same mirror. As John Paul II puts it in his *Original Unity of Man and Woman*, a couple "participates in perception of the world."[64] When you are in love, you see the world with her, and she with you.

Each sees the world, and each sees the other. Andrew is conscious of Teresa; Teresa is conscious of Andrew. As the Pope once said about Adam and Eve: "They see and know each other ... with all the peace of the interior gaze."[65]

Each is aware of the other and makes the other a part of his consciousness – penetrated, illuminated, preserved, and reflected back towards the inner self – so that the other and her doings become a part of his life; a component of his "autobiographical self."

Each sees the other not only superficially but also intimately; each sees the other in all of her complexity; each sees and knows the other's *consciousness*. In 'The Person: Subject and Community', Wojtyla states that "[T]he basic dimension of interpersonal community ... is reducible to treating and really experiencing

---

[62] For discussions of Wojtyla's views on affiliations, see R. Hogan & J. LeVoir, *Covenant of Love: Pope John Paul II on Sexuality, Marriage and Family in the Modern World*. San Franciso, California: Ignatius Press. 2d ed. 1992; K. Doran, *Solidarity: A Synthesis of Personalism and Communalism in the Thought of Karol Wojtyla/Pope John Paul II*. New York: Peter Lang Publishing 1996; M. Shivanandan, *Crossing the Threshold of Love: A New Vision of Marriage in the Light of John Paul II's Anthropology*. Washington, D.C.: Catholic University Press 1999; P. Simpson, *On Karol Wojtyla*. Belmont, California: Wadsworth 2001.

[63] *The Jeweler's Shop* 287.

[64] John Paul II, *Original Unity of Man and Woman: Catechesis on the Book of Genesis*. Boston, Massachusetts: Saint Paul Editions 1981: 95. The phrase refers to Adam and Eve.

[65] *Id.* at 100. The "interiorizing" or "subjectivizing" view of friendship is a characteristically modern one. See D. Konstan, 'Reciprocity and Friendship', in C. Gill, N. Postlethwaite & R. Seaford (eds), *Reciprocity in Ancient Greece*.Oxford: Oxford University Press 1998: 281 ("A sociologist and historian of friendship sums up the current consensus: 'friendships are voluntary, unspecialized, informal and private ... Friendships so conceived turn on intimacy, the confident revelation of the self to a trusted other, the sharing of expressive and consummatory activities ... The behaviour of friends to each other is appropriately interpreted through knowledge of the other's inner nature' ...") quoting A. Silver, 'Friendship and Trust as Moral Ideals: an Historical Approach', 30 (1989) *European Journal of Sociology*: 274–97.

'the other as oneself.'"[66] He refers to "relationships in which human beings mutually reveal themselves to one another in their personal human subjectivity."[67] He refers to "[t]he constitution of the *I* of another in my consciousness and will."[68] (Some modern philosophers think "interpenetration of consciousness" is impossible, but a persuasive rebuttal appears in a fairly recent book by Owen Flanagan.[69]) Love and close friendship involve solidarity of consciousness.

And since the consciousness of the individual has a complex structure, each can be conscious of the other in a rich and complex way. Andrew can be conscious not only of Teresa's consciousness of her surroundings, but of how she has oriented her awareness of the world towards her inward self; he can "see things from her perspective." And he can see how she is conscious of herself, and maps and remaps her consciousness as her life evolves.

Andrew's consciousness of Teresa embeds what she knows; what she has identified to be good; her knowledge of herself and her incompleteness and insufficiency. It includes awareness of her suffering:

> ... that discreet suffering
> which at the time I did not want to know,
> and today am willing to regard as our common good.[70]

Andrew is conscious of how her actions reflect her insufficiency, of how they aim at transcendence, and of how they imply her spiritual destination. So Andrew's consciousness of Teresa, as he embraces his solidarity with her, embeds and brings these characteristics of Teresa into his own consciousness, "absorbing" them.[71] In "I-thou" relationships, "[t]he *thou* stands before my self as a true and complete 'other self'."[72]

---

[66] In Wojtyla, *Person and Community: Selected Essays* 244–45.

[67] *Id.*

[68] *Id.* at 204. *See also* John Paul II, *Original Unity of Man and Woman: Catechesis on the Book of Genesis*: 87–88 & 94 (observing that the biblical depiction of Adam and Eve as naked together but not ashamed "[u]nquestionably describes their state of consciousness; in fact, their mutual experience of the body – that is, the experience on the part of the man of the femininity that is revealed in the nakedness of the body and, reciprocally, the similar experience of masculinity on the part of the woman." "The words of Genesis 2:25, 'they were not ashamed,' do not express a lack, but, on the contrary, serve to indicate a particular fullness of consciousness and experience...").

[69] *Consciousness Reconsidered* 87–107. "Phenomenological opacity is a matter of degree... Understanding another involves conceiving of the other's experiences... [It] involves imaginatively taking on what we think things are like for the other, and this typically requires bracketing out to some extent what we think things are like for ourselves." *Id.* at 105–106.

[70] *The Jeweler's Shop* Act I Scene I.

[71] And consider Wojtyla's poem 'The Samaritan Woman':

> It joined us together, the well;
> the well led me into you.
> No one between us but light
> deep in the well, the pupil of the eye
> set in an orbit of stones.

Further, Andrew can be conscious of how Teresa's consciousness of himself is structured. Andrew can be conscious of himself *in the way that* she is conscious of him. Because he knows her well, he can see how he looks to her. As Aristotle states: "[t]o perceive a friend must be in a way to perceive one's self. And to know a friend to know one's self...". These unique features of close affiliations afford special opportunities for self-knowledge and development. Andrew, seeing himself through Teresa, can understand his own nature better – from a different angle – more deeply – than were he to remain unaffiliated.[73]

Further, Andrew can be conscious of Teresa's awareness of his *actions*. Actions seen through the mirror of friendship have a unique appearance, since they are displayed "from the outside." When you act alone, you focus on the object of your action – your goal and the things that lead to it. When you act in the presence of a friend, you can in a way see the action as he does. This insight is expressed by Price:

> [I]n perception we become transparent to what we are perceiving, so that perceiving it and perceiving ourselves are the same mental act (something like seeing outside and seeing through a window)... [But if] I see a friend looking into my eyes, his looking is to me not transparent (as it is to him) but opaque, so that I see him looking into my eyes without thereby seeing them myself.... It is from him that I can learn most easily to distinguish the perceiver from the perceived; I then generalize to my own case... in my own person, my projects are (to extend the metaphor) transparent on to their objects, so that my focus is upon the objects, not my pursuit of them; but joining in those projects with a friend I become conscious of his pursuing them, and so conscious in a new way of pursuing them myself (for we are pursuing them together). I thus become explicitly aware of myself not just abstractly as an agent, but as an agent with a certain character, thereby achieving not a bare self-consciousness but a real self-knowledge.[74]

Andrew's consciousness of himself as a person who acts because he is afflicted with insufficiency and incompleteness can be supplemented and enhanced by his affiliation with Teresa. She knows him well and sees what lies behind his strivings. He may experience a degree of shame when he allows her to observe

Within your eyes, I,
drawn by the well,
am enclosed.

Easter Vigil and Other Poems 12.

[72] Wojtyla, 'The Person: Subject and Community' in *Person and Community: Selected Essays* 245. The sentence continues: "which, like my own self, is characterized not only by self-determination, but also and above all by self-possession and self-governance.".

[73] In a somewhat similar way, a person's knowledge of his inmost self is promoted by his friendship with God. Professor Wojtyla's understanding of this insight through his studies of John of the Cross is discussed in Buttiglione, *Karol Wojtyla: The Thought of the Man Who Became Pope John Paul II* 46–48.

[74] Price, *Love and Friendship in Plato and Aristotle* 121–22.

these unimpressive circumstances. But if he does not try to hide them – if he allows her to participate in his full self – he will come to know himself better through her love.

Andrew's knowledge of himself as a person who seeks to transcend his limitations by acting – who seeks to complete himself by what he does (for example by getting engaged) – can be enhanced by Teresa's consciousness of this dimension of his nature; and hers by his. Each can see how the other tends towards a spiritual destination. "The *thou* stands before my self as a true and complete 'other self,' which, like my own self, is characterized not only by self-determination, but also and above all by self-possession and self-governance. In this subjective structure, the *thou* ... represents its own transcendence and its own tendency towards self-fulfillment."[75]

3.2 The ethical dimension

Andrew is aware of Teresa's "ethical consciousness" – of the goods (and bads) towards which her actions tend and her own appropriation or personalization of these goods (and bads). Aware of how he looks through her eyes – "seeing himself from the outside" – and how he must appear in the light of her ethical consciousness, Andrew can appraise his own ethical situation more wisely.

3.3 The vertical dimension

Solidarity of consciousness can lead on to what we might call a "solidarity of transcendence." As Andrew stands with Teresa before the great mirror, he comes to see, as he tells us, that the mirror is "not an ordinary flat mirror:"

> but a lens absorbing its object.
> We were not only reflected but absorbed.[76]
> I had an impression of being seen and recognized by someone ...
> inside the shop window.[77]

Someone who turns out to be the Jeweler, into whose presence Teresa and Andrew are together transported: the Great Author, it seems, of the solidarity of love.

Teresa and Andrew are present not only each in the other's consciousness but also in the consciousness of God. God is conscious of them. He sees them as they are, He sees their hearts and minds, and therefore of course He is aware of their consciousness and how they participate in seeing the world together. It is the genius of the Wojtylan metaphor of the mirror/lens, with Teresa and Andrew

---

[75] Wojtyla, 'The Person: Subject and Community' in *Person and Community: Selected Essays* 245.
[76] *The Jeweler's Shop* 292.
[77] *Id.*

on one side and the Jeweler on the other, that it reflects and contains and transmits this complex set of relationships.

Teresa becomes aware of God's awareness of her. Andrew becomes conscious of God's consciousness of him. Teresa and Andrew are "absorbed" and transported through the lens. They participate in a solidarity of consciousness with Him.

John Paul II, at a general audience in 1980, said much of this in a discourse on Adam and Eve:

> [T]he man and the woman see themselves, as it were, through the mystery of creation: they see themselves in this way, before knowing 'that they are naked'. This seeing each other is not just a participation in 'exterior' perception of the world, but has also an interior dimension of participation in the vision of the Creator Himself – that vision of which the Elohist text speaks several times: 'God saw everything that he had made, and behold, it was very good' (Gn 1:31).[78]

3.4 What about reason, will and the good? Towards a synthesis

Solidarity of consciousness is not the whole story of course. Not at all: affiliation involves the will and reason just as Aristotle stated; and not only from their "personalist side."[79]

It seems that friendship starts with reason and will. Making friends starts with appreciating each other's good aspects. It starts with the parties' establishing a sort of reciprocity around their commonly willed good. Understanding and will are there at the beginning, and they endure as the fundamental ligaments of friendship. Then, as this process progresses – as the friends understand one another better and concur on common aims and projects – their consciousnesses interface as well. As the good of the other party comes into view and the good ends towards which a reciprocity could be put become apparent, the consciousness expands and embraces the other party and the commonality.

Where interpenetration of consciousness has developed, reasoning together and willing the mutual good take on several new dimensions. Knowledge of one another – reasoning or thinking about one another – then includes subjective awareness: "discover[ing] the other in [the] self" and "discover[ing] himself in the other."[80] Willing the other's good comes to include willing the enhancement of the other's consciousness. Andrew and Teresa help one another

---

[78] John Paul II, *Original Unity of Man and Woman: Catechesis on the Book of Genesis* 99.

[79] "[I]n friendship . . . the decisive part is played by the will. I desire a good for you just as I desire it for myself. . . . [Friendship brings about a] 'doubling' of the subject, the doubling of the 'I': my 'I' and your 'I' form a moral unity, for the will is equally inclined to both of them, so that *ipso facto* your 'I' necessarily becomes in some sense mine, lives within my 'I' as well as within itself." Wojtyla, *Love and Responsibility* 90–91.

[80] *Id.* at 131.

see the world together in a richer way, and in a way that makes it more fully their own. Andrew can give himself more fully by presenting himself to Teresa's awareness in a way which is authentic and genuine. Wojtyla in his book *Love and Responsibility* refers to "choosing oneself in another, and the other in oneself."[81] The chorus in *The Jeweler's Shop* announces: "Love... becomes thought and will."[82] Love and solidarity involve a complex interplay of consciousness, reason and will.

4. How these Wojtylan insights can assist in understanding crises of solidarity

If, then, consciousness plays a major role in affiliation, distortions of consciousness should constitute a major explanation for pathologies of affiliation. This hypothesis can be supported by a sampling of scientific literature.

4.1 Certain pathologies of consciousness

Professor Edwin Shneidman in *The Suicidal Mind* reveals that in attempted suicides, "the diaphragm of the mind narrows and focuses on the single goal of escape to the exclusion of all else – parents, spouses, children.... Suddenly, they are just not in the picture."[83] Dr. Shneidman calls this phenomenon "constriction."[84] Dr. Jonathan Shaw in *Achilles in Vietnam* describes the cases of soldiers who go berserk, attacking the enemy in a murderous rage:

> [T]he cognitive universe is simplified to a single focus. The berserker is ... blind to everything but his destructive aim. He cannot see the distinction between civilian and combatant or even the distinction between comrade and enemy.[85]

These soldiers suffer a disruption of the consciousness in which many experiences are outright forgotten, as are entire stretches of time, the identities of comrades; even the names of comrades.

---

[81] *Id.* The passage continues: "Love is impossible for beings who are mutually impenetrable – only the spirituality and the 'inwardness' of persons create the conditions for mutual interpenetration, which enables each to live in and by the other."

[82] At 291. In fuller context:

> Love – love pulsating in brows,
> in man becomes thought
> and will:
> the will of Teresa being Andrew,
> the will of Andrew being Teresa.

Comparable points about the will and reason as components of solidaristic communities appear in Part 7 ("Participation") of *The Acting Person*.

[83] E. Shneidman, *The Suicidal Mind* New York: Oxford University Press 1996: 60.

[84] *Id.* at 59.

[85] *Achilles in Vietnam: Combat Trauma and the Undoing of Character*. New York, New York: Simon & Schuster 1995: 86–87.

Dr. Judith Herman, in *Trauma and Recovery*, describes the pathologies caused by combat, captivity or torture:

> For the common soldier, war has the feel – the spiritual texture – of a great ghostly fog, thick and permanent... You can't tell where you are, or why you're there, and the only certainty is overwhelming ambiguity. In war you lose your sense of the definite, hence your sense of truth itself...[86]

In former concentration-camp prisoners, "[t]he experience of the present is often hazy and dulled, while the intrusive memories of the past are intense and clear. A study of concentration camp survivors found this 'double consciousness at work.' "[87]

Herman further reports damage to consciousness of the self; loss of "basic sense of self", and "inability to maintain one's own separate point of view while remaining in connection with others."[88] Another phenomenon she reports is loss of faith and trust: a "crisis of faith" and "pervasive distrust of community."[89]

4.2 *Certain pathologies of affiliation*

These studies also report extensive disruptions to marriages, to community and to other affiliations. The Vietnam-war berserker studied by Shaw experienced, while in Vietnam, a phenomenon in which the "cognitive universe [was]... simplified to a single focus.... [B]lind to everything but his destructive aim... [h]e cannot see the distinction between civilian and combatant or even the distinction between comrade and enemy"[90]; he is "cut off from all human community.... No living human has any claim on him, not even the claim of being noticed and remembered."[91] In later life he was especially liable to marital failure and divorce. Similar breakdowns are reported among the victims of combat, captivity or torture studied by Herman: "Traumatic events... shatter the sense of connection between individual and community, creating a crisis of faith. Lifton found pervasive distrust of community and the sense of a 'counterfeit' world..."[92] "The dialectic of trauma operates not only on the survivor's inner life but also

---

[86] J. Herman, *Trauma and Recovery*. New York, New York: Basic Books 1997: 53, quoting T. O'Brien, 'How to Tell a True War Story', in *The Things They Carried*. Boston: Houghton Mifflin 1990: 88.

[87] Herman, *Trauma and Recovery* 90, quoting R. Jaffe, 'Dissociative Phenomena in Former Concentration Camp Inmates', 49 (1968) *International Journal of Psycho-Analysis*: 310–12.

[88] Herman, *Trauma and Recovery* at 52–53.

[89] *Id.* at 55.

[90] Shaw, *Achilles in Vietnam: Combat Trauma and the Undoing of Character* 86–87.

[91] *Id.* at 86.

[92] Herman, *Trauma and Recovery* 55, citing R. Lifton, 'Concept of the Survivor', in J. Dimsdale (ed), *Survivors, Victims, and Perpetrators: Essays on the Nazi Holocaust*. New York: Hemisphere 1980 and also citing R. Lifton, *Home from the War: Vietnam Veterans: Neither Victims nor Executioners*. New York: Simon & Schuster 1973.

in her close relationships. It results in the formation of intense, unstable relationships that fluctuate between extremes."[93]

4.3 Why and how these affiliational consequences ensue

Various pathologies of consciousness can be mapped onto the various functions of consciousness within affiliational structure:

- Even basic recognition and awareness of the other can be occluded by "constriction of consciousness" reported by Shneidman and the failures of awareness reported by Shaw.
- "Seeing the world together" with someone else is impossible where one of the parties sees only the "fog" reported in Herman or whose picture of the world is distorted beyond what is recognizeable through the eyes of others. Penetrating through "phenomenological opacity" so as to see the world as someone else does requires, as Flanagan writes, "bracketing out to some extent what things are like for ourselves,"[94] and this is difficult for someone whose own experiential life is befogged or clamorous.
- Putting aside shame and taking the risk of solidarity by allowing another person to see one's insufficiency and incompleteness is difficult to one whose self-regard – whose consciousness of self – is damaged by trauma as reported by Herman.
- A solidaristic pursuit of transcendence is impossible for those who have despaired of meaning, abandoned trust, and lost their faith.
- Ethical solidarity is impossible to enter into with someone who has revealed himself to be morally depraved; and the direct victim of depravity may by traumatic extension lose the ability to form ethical solidarity with anyone. Shaw reports that some Vietnam soldiers lost control after their superiors led them into massacres or gave medals for conduct which violated the laws of war: in other words after being subjected to experiences which led them to apprehend that the mirror of solidarity with certain of their superiors reflected images that they could no longer bear to behold.[95] Consciousness constricts out of revulsion at the badness of an affiliate or out of horror at the ends to which an affiliation is devoted. Consciousness constricts; reciprocity and mutuality of consciousness end; the withdrawing party is no longer engaged in the process of making himself available to the consciousness of the other; both are self-concealing and ashamed. In an important set of homilies in 1979 and 1980, the Pope offered a similar account of the disaffiliation which ensued upon mankind's first sin: Adam and Eve became ashamed.[96] Disclosing one's insufficiency

[93] Herman, *Trauma and Recovery* 56.
[94] *Consciousness Reconsidered* 106.
[95] This is the point of the title of Shaw's book: Achilles goes berserk after his commander, Agamemnon, betrays him by appropriating his rightfully won prize of war, the girl Briseis.
[96] John Paul II, *Original Unity of Man and Woman: Catechesis on the Book of Genesis, passim* and especially at 89–91. See Shivanandan, *Crossing the Threshold of Love: A New Vision of Marriage* 121–25.

becomes impossible; seeking transcendence together or even separately becomes embarrassed. The parties to what was once a close affiliation cease to know one another; they cease to act together or will the same things: when the pathology runs its course all the ligaments of the affiliation come unbound.

5. Conclusion

All of this may help shed some light on what John Paul II called the "crisis of solidarity". *The Jeweler's Shop* places Teresa and Andrew in the commercial district of a city. The business centers where the postmodern City of Man offers its wares include the Planned Parenthood clinic, the pornography parlor, and someday soon perhaps the euthanasia center. If there is a "great, wide mirror" in the windows of these shops – where the Culture of Death advertises its wares – many reasonable people wish to avoid being reflected by it. Still less absorbed into it or brought through it, into the presence of whoever or whatever is at work on the other side of the lens.

The Holy Father, in a recent speech, has invited us to make this new century a "century of solidarity."[97] Let us make sure, so far as can be, that the Teresas and Andrews of our children's generation, as they walk together down streets of shops and houses, encounter not only the warehouses and lodgings of the culture of death, but that they also peer occasionally into a wide and welcoming doorway of a Roman Catholic Church, a Catholic hospital, a hospice, a creche, or simply an open and thoroughly human face of a good-hearted person who will encourage them not to be ashamed of their sense of incompleteness; but to know that seeking transcendence is not futile and nothing to be ashamed of, either in oneself or in one another.

[97] *See* note 4, *supra.*

19

The science and politics of stem cell research[1]

RICHARD M. DOERFLINGER

In both the United States and the United Kingdom, advances in culturing embryonic stem cells have prompted campaigns to change or evade laws against funding certain kinds of destructive human embryo research. In what follows the public policy debate in the United States will be reviewed, with occasional references to significant differences between the American and British situations.

1. The policy options in embryonic stem cell research

The U.S. policy debate began in earnest with a December 1998 congressional hearing conducted by Senator Arlen Specter, Chairman of the Senate Appropriations Subcommittee on Labor, Health and Human Services and Education. On that occasion and many times since, Senator Specter described embryonic stem cells as "a veritable fountain of youth" for treating and even curing a wide variety of diseases. Scientific witnesses hailed the promise of these unspecialized and versatile cells, which are capable of reproducing themselves as well as a wide variety of more specialized cell types, and described three ways to obtain them.

First, one could harvest the cells from live human embryos created by *in vitro* fertilization which are found to be 'in excess of clinical need'. Such harvesting would invariably destroy the embryos. This method, championed by researchers at the University of Wisconsin, ultimately became the central focus of new guidelines for "human pluripotent stem cell research" issued in final form by the National Institutes of Health (NIH) in August 2000.[2] The decision to fund this research required some creative bookkeeping. Since 1996 a congressional rider to annual health care spending bills (known as the Dickey amendment after its sponsor, Congressman Jay Dickey of Arkansas) has prohibited federal funding of research in which human embryos are harmed or destroyed.[3] The NIH

---

[1] It should be noted that this paper was revised for publication prior to President Bush's decision of 9 August 2001 on Federal funding of stem cell research. It therefore does not deal with the debate about that decision.

[2] National Institutes of Health Guidelines for Research Using Human Pluripotent Stem Cells, 65 *Federal Register* 51976–81 (25 August 2000). Implementation of these guidelines has been suspended by the Bush Administration pending further review.

[3] The current version of this law is Section 510 of the Labor/HHS appropriations bill for Fiscal Year 2001, H.R. 5656 (enacted through Section 1(a)(1) of H.R. 4577, the FY '01 Consolidated Appropriations Act, Public Law 106–554).

guidelines evaded the intent of this law by instructing researchers in how to destroy human embryos for their stem cells, while directly providing government funds only for the research on the resulting stem cells. In this way no federal funds would be directly traceable to the act of destruction, and the NIH could pretend to be conforming to the Dickey amendment.

Second, "embryonic germ cells" could be harvested from fetal tissue after induced abortions, a technique developed at Johns Hopkins University in Baltimore, Maryland. These cells, the precursors of sperm and egg, were found to retain their "pluripotency" or ability to produce cells of widely varying kinds for a much longer time than other body cells. This approach was ultimately also incorporated into the NIH stem cell guidelines, though it could have been funded without new regulatory action because Congress enacted a law in 1993 authorizing funding for fetal tissue transplantation research (42 USC §289g-1 et seq.). The 1993 law provided that such tissue may be used in federally funded research only if the researcher does not participate in the abortion or influence its timing or method, and only if the unborn child is dead before tissue is harvested.

Third, embryos could be created in order to be killed for their stem cells, using cloning to produce a genetic match with each patient. At the December 1998 hearing this was proposed by Dr. Michael West of Advanced Cell Technology in Worcester, Massachusetts as the only sure way to prevent patients' bodies from rejecting embryonic stem cells as foreign tissue. This approach would require a further step that has generally been rejected even by many who otherwise support human embryo research: the special creation of human embryos solely for the purpose of research that will destroy them. Dr. West offered to ameliorate the ethical difficulties by engineering fatal defects into these embryos in advance, so they would be incapable of developing past the embryonic stage – his argument being that in such a case, destroying the embryos for their cells would not create a net increase in embryonic deaths (over and above those already ensured by the researcher's manipulation of the embryo).[4]

The first difference between the American and British debates is that in the U.S., serious political discussion has focused on the first of these three scenarios. The debate on use of fetal tissue from abortions is largely seen by U.S. lawmakers as resolved – though this debate may be revived by recent evidence of commercial trafficking in such tissues, and by studies suggesting that use of fetal tissue to treat Parkinson's disease has been disappointing and even sometimes harmful. The use of cloning or any other technique to create embryos solely for stem cell research, on the other hand, has been set aside as showing too extreme a disrespect for developing human life. To a greater degree, the British debate has emphasized the problem of rejection of foreign tissue and has concentrated on cloning as a way of creating embryos for research.

---

4 "The goal is to create a developing mass of mostly human cells that's crippled enough to prevent its development into a person, yet healthy enough during the first week of existence to produce the crucial 'stem cells' that scientists want to collect." R. Weiss, 'Can Scientists Bypass Stem Cells' Moral Minefield?', *Washington Post*, 14 December 1998 at A3.

The British Parliament's decision to allow what some call 'therapeutic cloning' will, of course, have repercussions on the American scene. In 1999 the California-based Geron Corporation, which had funded the Wisconsin and Johns Hopkins studies but expressed no interest in Dr. West's approach, announced that it had acquired Roslin Bio-Med of Scotland to combine the cloning expertise of Dr. Ian Wilmut's team with Geron's growing expertise in stem cell research.[5] Increasingly such biotechnology companies may become international conglomerates, performing the more controversial elements of their work in whatever country finds them socially and legally acceptable. For his part, Dr. Wilmut announced in 1999 that genetically matched transplant tissue from cloned embryos may be available within five years.[6]

It remains a constantly repeated refrain in the American debate, however, that the only human embryos to be destroyed for government-funded stem cell research will be those which "would have been discarded anyway" by fertility clinics. The reality is actually more complex.

The NIH guidelines for federally funded stem cell research allow the use of embryos deemed by fertility clinics to be "in excess of clinical need." In current practice, the clinics ask parents to choose among several options for disposition of any embryos they do not presently need for efforts to have a liveborn child. Generally parents are asked whether the embryos should remain frozen for possible later use, be donated to another couple for reproductive purposes, or be discarded; some clinics also offer the option of donating the embryos for fertility research. Under the NIH guidelines, the option of donating these embryos for federally funded stem cell research is simply added to this list, and is to be offered *at the same time as all the other options*.[7] The assumption that this option will be chosen only by parents who would otherwise have chosen to discard the embryos is arbitrary and almost certainly false.

2. Ethical and legal problems

Authorizing the use of live human embryos for destructive research is unprecedented in U.S. government policy. A review of some past ethical and legal decisions related to this issue will illustrate what a radical departure the NIH guidelines are.

- The NIH's Human Embryo Research Panel in 1994, and President Clinton's own National Bioethics Advisory Commission (NBAC) in 1999, were both unanimous in their general support for destructive human embryo research. Yet both advisory bodies conceded that the embryo is a developing form of human life that deserves "respect" (though neither body held that the

---

[5] Geron Corporation Press Release, 'Geron Acquires Roslin Bio-Med and Forms Research Collaboration with the Roslin Institute', 4 May 1999, www.geron.com/pr_050499.html
[6] A. Ballantyne, 'Transplant clones within five years', *The Sunday Times*, 16 May 1999.
[7] National Institutes of Health Guidelines, note 1 supra at 51980.

embryo merits full protection as a human person). They also recognized the continuity of human development from the time of fertilization onward, using the term 'embryo' for all stages of early development. This marks a second difference between the American and British policy debates, because British law has codified the notion that the embryo in its first two weeks of development has the lesser status of a 'pre-embryo'. The U.S. is fortunate that most of its major policy deliberations on this issue occurred after the scientific community had begun turning away from the misleading and politically motivated idea of the 'pre-embryo'.[8] In U.S. policy, justifying harmful human embryo research requires arguing that human lives which deserve respect should nonetheless be destroyed for the benefit of others.

- Since 1975, U.S. federal regulations have protected all unborn human offspring as 'human subjects' if they have begun to implant in the womb.[9] The blastocyst-staged embryos to be destroyed for their stem cells under the NIH guidelines are at the same stage of development as embryos beginning to implant. Denying these embryos any protection as human subjects seems to require arguing that mere location completely determines the moral and legal status of a member of the human species.

- The NIH guidelines contradict the standards enacted by Congress in 1993 for fetal tissue research following induced abortion. Such tissue may not be used unless it is harvested *after* fetal death occurs from an abortion performed for other reasons; researchers may not influence the timing or manner of the abortion (42 USC §289g-1 et seq.). In embryonic stem cell research, the live embryo is destroyed specifically for the sake of the research in ways dictated by the needs of that research. In effect, the researcher's harvesting procedure *is* the abortion.

- At least nine states prohibit even privately funded experiments harming human embryos. In some of these states, such as Michigan and Pennsylvania, conducting such an experiment is a felony. (Ironically, Pennsylvania is the home of the U.S. Senate's leading advocate for destructive embryo research, Senator Arlen Specter.) The most recent of these state laws, enacted by South Dakota in 2000, also prohibits research using stem cells that one knows were obtained by destroying a human embryo.[10]

- While proponents argue that these embryos "would be discarded anyway", Congress has consistently rejected such arguments in the case of the child in the womb. The unborn child who "will be aborted anyway" has the same protection in federally funded research as the child intended for live birth (42 USC §289g). Congress's policy judgment has been that any harm to the

---

[8] See R. Doerflinger, 'The Ethics of Funding Embryonic Stem Cell Research: A Catholic Viewpoint'. 9 (1999) *Kennedy Institute of Ethics Journal*: 137–50 at 138–9, 147 notes 1 and 2.

[9] U.S. regulations protecting human subjects in federally funded research define a "human subject" as a "living individual" subjected to research (45 CFR §46.102(f)). Subpart B of Part 46 provides special protections for fetuses as human subjects. "Fetus" includes "the product of conception from the time of implantation" (45 CFR §46.203(c)).

[10] S.D. Codified Laws §§34-14-16 to 34-14-20.

unborn that is planned by private parties gives the government no special authority to do harm of its own.

This last point raises a third difference between the American and British policy debates. Under Britain's Human Fertilization and Embryology Act of 1990, all permissible human embryo research is licensed and supported by the government. By contrast, the American situation is that of a "free enterprise" system. Much medical research (including, thus far, all research requiring the destruction of human embryos) is supported by private funds; privately funded research is not federally regulated as such, though (as noted above) it must comply with any relevant state laws. Federal regulations such as those protecting human subjects in medical research apply directly only to projects which receive federal funds, though the Institutional Review Boards established by major research institutions to ensure compliance with these regulations do review other research, and generally use the federal regulations as a convenient 'gold standard' for privately funded research as well.

The disparate treatment of privately and publicly funded research in the American system has been denounced by some British observers as mere hypocrisy.[11] Potentially it is something far more healthy, for it retains a means by which government may encourage morally and socially responsible approaches to a problem even where it may lack the will or the constitutional authority to prohibit irresponsible approaches outright. This is the path taken in the U.S. on the abortion issue, where the U.S. Supreme Court has barred legislators from placing meaningful restrictions on abortion itself: Federal lawmakers, and their counterparts in most states, still exercise a policy judgment preferring childbirth over abortion by providing public funding for the former but not the latter.

In the American system, then, a specific authorization of federal funds for destructive human embryo research would be seen as giving government's "seal of approval" and active encouragement to research that destroys some human lives for the sake of possible help to others. Conversely, a denial of such funding may send a message of disapproval but it does not bar private investors from exploring the possibilities of embryonic stem cell research.[12] It declares that the government will confine its own efforts to avenues which most American taxpayers agree are morally responsible.

3. The moral relevance of alternatives

The outcome of the U.S. debate on federal funding may depend in large part on new developments in areas of research that do *not* rely on the destruction of

[11] Editorial, 'Ethics can boost science'. 408 (16 November 2000) *Nature*: 275.

[12] For example, the research center that pioneered the use of embryonic germ cells from fetal tissue recently received a single $58.5 million private donation to expand its work. See Johns Hopkins University Press Release, 'Hopkins Launches Cell Engineering Institute With $58.5 M. Gift', http://hopkins.med.jhu.edu/press/2001/JANUARY/010130.HTM

human embryos. U.S. lawmakers may support embryonic stem cell research if they see it as the only feasible way to obtain cures for devastating diseases; their enthusiasm will vanish if the same goals can be achieved in less controversial ways.

Even NBAC's 1999 report, despite its broad support for funding human embryo research, concluded that because the embryo deserves respect as a form of human life "the derivation of stem cells from embryos remaining following infertility treatments is justifiable *only if no less morally problematic alternatives are available for advancing the research.*"[13] Therefore the growing promise of adult stem cell research and other alternatives has assumed great ethical and political significance.

Adult stem cell transplants have been used in human patients for decades – primarily to preserve one's immune system or the ability to replenish one's blood supply in patients subjected to chemotherapy and radiation treatments for various forms of cancer. Until two years ago, however, most researchers assumed that stem cells could not be found in most adult organs, that non-embryonic cells could not be cultured effectively outside the body, and especially that adult stem cells were capable of only a very narrow repertoire of cell types – that hematopoietic (blood-producing) stem cells, for example, could produce only the various types of blood cells. Today all these assumptions are in full retreat due to new evidence of the versatility of these cells, as well as new discoveries regarding stem cells from placentas and umbilical cord blood.

Adult stem cells are already in clinical use to help patients with cancer, leukemia, corneal damage, bone and cartilage breaks, severe combined immune deficiency, and other ailments.[14] Adult pancreatic islet cells have shown new promise in alleviating Type I diabetes.[15] In animal trials, adult pancreatic stem cells have proved more effective than their embryonic counterparts in treating diabetes.[16] Meanwhile, recent trials in transplanting embryonic stem cells into

[13] National Bioethics Advisory Commission, *Ethical Issues in Human Stem Cell Research* (Rockville, MD: September 1999), Volume I at 53.

[14] For detailed information and citations see generally the Web site of Do No Harm: The Coalition of Americans for Research Ethics, www.stemcellresearch.org; current clinical uses of adult stem cells in human patients can be found at www.stemcellresearch.org.currentaps.htm.

[15] A recent review of ways to provide insulin-producing islet cells for human transplants concludes that "the most promising is generation of beta cells from pancreatic duct cells. It is inherently a shorter biological step to make a beta cell from a duct cell than it is from other possible cells, such as embryonic stem cells and haemopoietic stem cells." P. Serup et al., 'Islet and stem cell transplantation for treating diabetes'. 322 (6 January 2001) *British Medical Journal*: 29–32.

[16] V. K. Ramiya et al., 'Reversal of insulin-dependent diabetes using islets generated *in vitro* from pancreatic stem cells'. 6 (March 2000) *Nature Medicine*: 278–82 (adult pancreatic stem cells used to keep diabetic mice healthy without insulin injections); G. Vogel, 'Stem Cells Are Coaxed to Produce Insulin'. 292 (27 April 2001) *Science*: 615–17 (embryonic stem cells produced only 1/50 of the needed supply of insulin and the treated diabetic mice died).

the brains of animals have produced some disturbing results, as the cells formed growths containing a variety of other cell types and caused surrounding brain cells to die.[17]

The ability of adult stem cells to produce tissues of widely varying kinds is increasingly difficult to deny. Mesenchymal stem cells from bone marrow can be used to produce bone, cartilage, fat, and cardiac muscle.[18] They now also seem capable of producing liver tissue for transplantation.[19] Adult neural stem cells can be directed to produce blood cells.[20] In one especially promising study, researchers funded by the NIH and the Christopher Reeve Paralysis Foundation have demonstrated that "adult marrow stromal cells can be induced to overcome their mesenchymal commitment and may constitute an abundant and accessible cellular reservoir for the treatment of a variety of neurologic diseases."[21] As if to rival this study, human fat – certainly an "abundant and accessible" resource in the United States – has also become a source of stem cells that can be directed down a variety of developmental pathways.[22]

Many of these advances contradict an assumption held as dogma by many cell biologists until recently. It was thought that only embryonic stem cells were capable of cutting across the broad categories of human cell types arising from each of the three basic embryonic germ layers – ectoderm, mesoderm and endoderm. Now it seems that any stem cell with the complete human genome can be reprogrammed by environmental signals to produce almost any other type of cell. Moreover, adult stem cells may be far safer for human therapies than embryonic cells, because they seem more docile to their surroundings and do not continue to proliferate in uncontrolled directions after being transplanted. Moreover, use of a patient's adult stem cells (modified by new environmental signals or even by gene therapy) to repair and regenerate that patient's own damaged tissues would avoid all problems of tissue rejection, obviating any need to explore the controversial realm of "therapeutic cloning."

The new findings are given additional significance by recent advances in multiplying adult stem cells in culture. Further refinement of these techniques should greatly enhance the ease and effectiveness of using adult stem cells in

---

[17] G. Vogel, 'Stem Cells: New Excitement, Persistent Questions'. 290 (1 December 2000) *Science*: 1672–4, at 1674.

[18] R. Lewis, 'Human Mesenchymal Stem Cells Differentiate in the Lab'. 13 (12 April 1999) *The Scientist*: 1.

[19] S. Okie, 'Bone Marrow Cells Offer Hope for Liver Therapies'. *The Washington Post*, 27 June 2000 at A3.

[20] D. Josefson, 'Adult stem cells may be redefinable'. 318 (30 January 1999) *British Medical Journal*: 282.

[21] D. Woodbury et al., 'Adult Rat and Human Bone Marrow Stromal Cells Differentiate Into Neurons'. 61 (2000) *Journal of Neuroscience Research*: 364–70, at 364.

[22] R. Weiss, 'Human Fat May Provide Stem Cells', *Washington Post*, 10 April 2001 at A1; P. Zuk et al., 'Multilineage Cells from Human Adipose Tissue: Implications for Cell-Based Therapies'. 7 (2001) *Tissue Engineering*: 211–28.

cancer and leukemia treatment, in future transplantation therapies, and as a vector for somatic cell gene therapy.[23]

Nor are cells from adults the only emerging alternative to embryonic stem cells. Fetal bone marrow obtained after spontaneous abortions (miscarriages) are many times richer in stem cells than adult bone marrow, and less susceptible to rejection by a recipient's immune system.[24] And there are early indications that umbilical cords and placentas, now routinely discarded four million times a year after live births in the United States, harbor stem cells with a versatility rivaling that of embryonic cells.[25]

Proponents of embryonic stem cell research have reacted to this evidence in interesting ways. Some have simply tried to deny the evidence, at times even suppressing findings that their own organizations have produced.[26] Others acknowledge there are alternatives, but insist that the government must fund both embryonic and adult stem cell research to see "which one will be best" for different uses. But that argument simply overlooks the challenge presented to scientists by President Clinton's bioethics advisors: if workable alternatives can be found, funding research that requires destroying human embryos is ethically irresponsible. Simply proceeding to fund all approaches, including those requiring such destruction, would be responsible policy only if the human embryo had absolutely *no* moral value or status. Research animals are treated with more respect than that.

It is the view of this author that direct destruction of innocent human life at any stage is inherently wrong regardless of any benefits that may accrue from

---

[23] See: D. Colter et al., 'Rapid expansion of recycling stem cells in cultures of plastic-adherent cells from human bone marrow'. 97 (28 March 2000) *Proceedings of the National Academy of Sciences of the USA*: 3213–8 (adult stem cells amplified a billion-fold in six weeks, retaining their multipotentiality for differentiation); E. Rosler et al., 'Cocultivation of umbilical cord blood cells with endothelial cells leads to extensive amplification of competent CD34 + CD38- cells'. 28 (2000) *Exp. Hematol.*: 841–52.

[24] A.G. Wu et al., 'Analysis and characterization of hematopoietic progenitor cells from fetal bone marrow, adult bone marrow, peripheral blood, and cord blood'. 46 (August 1999) *Pediatric Research* 163–9.

[25] N. Wade, 'Company Says It Can Derive Stem Cells From the Placenta', *The New York Times*, 12 April 2001 at A22; Cryo-Cell International Press Release, 'Cryo-Cell Subsidiary's Collaboration with University of South Florida in Research Program for the Treatment of Neurodegenerative Diseases with Umbilical Cord Blood Detailed at AAAS Annual Meeting', 20 February 2001. www.cryo-cell.com/press_releases/pr58.htm

[26] In one egregious example, actor Christopher Reeve testified on behalf of the Christopher Reeve Paralysis Foundation in April 2000 that embryonic stem cell research is necessary for advances in treating spinal cord injury because, among other things, adult stem cells cannot be made 'pluripotent' and thus able to produce a significant supply of nerve cells. Testimony of Christopher Reeve before the U.S. Senate Appropriations Subcommittee on Labor. Health and Human Services and Education, 26 April 2000. His own foundation's study showing that bone marrow stem cells can provide an abundant supply of nerve cells for transplant had been submitted for publication the month before. That study begins with the sentence: "Pluripotent stem cells have been detected in multiple tissues in the adult, participating in normal replacement and repair, while undergoing self-renewal." D. Woodbury et al., note 20 supra at 364.

it. But even for those who do not hold to this moral absolute, or who recognize a lesser status for embryonic human life than for later stages of human development, recent advances in adult stem cell research and other alternatives should be greeted as the most ethically responsible way to pursue medical progress. If these alternatives turn out to be as promising as they now seem, any destruction of developing human life for research purposes can be set aside as unnecessary.

20

Countering the contraceptive mentality

HELEN DAVIES

Introduction

THE DEVELOPMENT of the culture of death in the twentieth century cannot be separated from an all-pervading 'contraceptive mentality'. The roots of this attitude lie in the ideology of population control; we are told large families need to be discouraged because the world is over-populated. In this context the words 'family planning' have come to mean avoiding having children rather than planning for them. This paper takes it as evident that the contraceptive mentality is inculcated early and extensively, and parents need to be aware how this is done. It is the openly stated aim of the International Planned Parenthood Federation to influence children's sexual behaviour to such an extent that when "when they reach the point of their life where the use of contraception becomes a possibility they will choose contraception as naturally as breathing".[1]

A spiritual contagion

This mentality could be likened to a disease of the collective soul of a nation. Untreated it leads to the debilitation of the body politic and, because it bears no positive fruit, ultimately to the death of a civilisation. A nation without a pro-life culture is facing the threat of a diminishing population, a fact amply borne out by the European experience. The antidote to this spiritual contagion lies in a return to the fear of God and observance of His laws. 'Fear' is used here in the sense of 'respect and reverence', and the laws particularly referred to are those to do with the transmission of life and the role of the family.

Church teaching

In the Catholic context this implies a return to the teaching of the whole Faith, not just the pick-and-mix variety so prevalent in this area. The rejection of the prophetic encyclical *Humanae Vitae* in 1968 epitomised the hold the contraceptive mentality had amongst both clergy and laity. The encyclical continues to be

---

[1] Dr Alan Guttmacher MD, former President of Planned Parenthood, quoted in *Washington Star News*, 3 May 1973.

largely untaught. It is only by learning what the Church teaches about God's plan for marriage and the family that we will be able to pass it on to our children. This is where a major failure has allowed the contraceptive mentality to flourish.

The arguments of the world are pervasive and delivered into our homes by the 'experts'. In the terminology of a pseudo-morality, we are told the only 'responsible sex' is 'safe sex', safe that is from the risk of 'unwanted pregnancy' or sexually transmitted disease. This mantra is given out to all, without thought, reflection or balance. Almost unconsciously we are affected by it to varying degrees. Many have been persuaded that the use of contraception is a necessary lesser evil than abortion, not realising how closely the two are linked. Once the child has been spiritually rejected it is not a far step to that child's total rejection by abortion if it is unintentionally conceived. Where contraceptives fail, abortion becomes the necessary back-stop. In other words, the contraceptive mentality precedes the abortion mentality. In such a society sexual union becomes devalued to the level of a recreational pastime, and fertility debased to consumer transactions of buying and selling (as, for example, in 'surrogate motherhood').

Innocence – sanctuary of childhood

The resistance to this mentality starts in the home. Parents give life to their children and live with them; they have a unique opportunity to know and understand them as individuals. Part of their vocation as parents is to educate and form their children to be chaste. It is their responsibility and their prerogative. The recent guidelines from the Holy See state that other educators can assist them in this task but that their role is always subsidiary and subordinate, and that this task is best undertaken within the family.[2]

In this context the years of childhood innocence are an important developmental safeguard. These years up to puberty allow the child to develop at his or her own pace, to see things through the eyes of a child, to think as a child. Innocence enables them to live in the world of adults without being burdened with adult matters. It is a vital sanctuary in growth towards maturity, enabling them to concentrate on acquiring skills and learning appropriate to their stage of development. It also helps parents to form their children to be chaste, answering their questions with discernment and reverence, giving them only as much information as they judge they need at the time. This formation is therefore gradual and on-going, and it will often be non-verbal, in that example speaks louder than words. It will also consist of encouraging their child's natural modesty in a way that looks on the body as God's wonderful creation to be respected and honoured.

Because of the unique importance of this private communication with their child, parents must resist anybody or anything which could undermine it. The

---

[2] Pontifical Council for the Family, *The Truth and Meaning of Human Sexuality. Guidelines for Education within the Family.* 1995. See sections 23, 40 and 145.

innocent child possesses something which they may need to be reminded of – a sense of wonder, the spiritual attribute that is the first step towards being able to pray. Indeed such chidren may contribute in no small way to the salvation of their parents; "Unless you become like little children you shall not enter the Kingdom of Heaven". (*Mt* 18:3)

Sex education – an outgrowth of the contraceptive mentality

It is only by the gradual inculcation of virtue allied with the teaching of the Faith that parents will lay the foundation for chastity, which includes an apprenticeship in self-mastery. Those who would invade the sanctuary of innocence with sex education disrupt this private communication between parent and child. Sexual information is given in the classroom often to mixed classes of boys and girls. Chidren are given permission to treat such information like any other subject in the curriculum, to talk about intimate sexual matters openly and without embarrassment, either in the classroom or outside it. Their natural reticence is undermined and most of all their modesty, which is the guardian of chastity. The mystery and sacredness of human sexuality is trivialised and debased. This happens now, even in Catholic primary schools, where children are expected to be fully conversant with the correct names and functions of the genital organs and with facts about sexual intercourse, before they move on to secondary school. Sometimes parents realise what is happening only when their child brings home an explicit worksheet from school. When they protest they are told: "You are the only ones to complain". However, they are right to complain because what is happening is making their task of training their children to be chaste more difficult. This premature sexualisation of innocent children is not education; it is a form of manipulation, and it plays into the hands of those who wish to inculcate the contraceptive mentality.

Sex education continues in secondary school, often under different headings: 'Personal, Social and Health Education', 'Relationships', or even under the guise of 'Religious Education'. The emphasis on sexual anatomy and function goes well beyond that needed for the biology of human reproduction. Pubertal changes are covered in detail and discussions are encouraged on sexual behaviour, sexual orientation, sexually transmitted diseases, AIDS, contraception and abortion. Videos are used, often with graphic scenes such as childbirth. I have been told of girls so traumatised by these lessons that they refuse to communicate at all on these issues with their mothers.

All this would be bad enough if those giving this information understood and accepted the Church's teaching on marriage and family life. But with the wide-spread contraceptive mentality presently prevailing amongst many Catholics it would be wishful thinking to believe they did. The stage is set for the perpetuation of the contraceptive mentality into the next generation, and the wisdom and riches of the Church's teaching is simply not communicated.

Nothing of what is said here is intended to suggest that teachers are happy about giving classroom sex education; many are not but find themselves pressurised to do so. They are offered incentives to attend training courses largely organised by those who promote contraception. These will attempt to rid them of their uneasiness by subjecting them to open and candid discussions on sexual matters. They will thus lose their ability to be shocked and become 'sex educators', able to talk to teenagers in a language they will understand. Parents, of course, are not capable of doing this, or so the received wisdom has it. What seems to be forgotten is all this is that communication skills with teenagers will never be a substitute for the proper teaching of sexual morality.

"And lead us not into temptation"

Failure to understand and teach what the Church teaches about original sin and grace and temptation explains why 'sex education' has gained a place in the curriculum of Catholic schools. Because of the brokeness of our human nature caused by the inheritance of original sin, the human will must be strengthened by supernatural grace to fight temptation and avoid the occasions of sin. Information about sex in a public setting destroys the necessary privacy and intimacy which should surround this subject, otherwise such information can easily become an occasion of sin. This is why the *Guidelines* issued by the Pontifical Council for the Family insist that any sexual information of an intimate nature given to children should be given privately and individually, preferably by the mother to her daughter and by the father to his son.[3] It is only in exceptional cases that they may delegate this task, and even then it must still be done individually, something not possible in a school classroom.

Those who promote sex education lessons say that they will be giving children the information to make 'the right choices'. If they mean choosing contraception "as naturally as breathing", then thirty years of such educational programmes in the state schools have accompanied an alarming increase in the extent and consequences of early sexual activity. Yet the prescription remains the same – 'more and better sex education' – but possibly with a different name.

Choosing to be chaste, however, is not based on information but on formation. Formation is a gradual, ongoing process, and chastity requires the exercise of virtue, of prudence and modesty. It is neither prudent nor modest to expose adolescents in a group setting, and on a systematic basis, to images or situations which have the potential to be sexually arousing, either physically or in the imagination. Discussions in such settings are impossible to regulate; questions raised by the more 'street-wise' members of the group easily violate the privacy and modesty of their more reticent peers. To promote sex education in group settings is not to create "an atmosphere favourable to the growth of chastity".[4]

---

[3] *The Truth and Meaning of Human Sexuality*: 67.
[4] See Pope Paul VI, Encyclical Letter *Humanae Vitae*: 22.

Conclusion

The contraceptive mentality attacks the roots of Catholic culture. It drives a wedge between creatures and their Creator, and between man and woman. It particularly devalues motherhood and the gift of fertility. In the case of sex education imposed on children outside the family, it undermines the uniquely important role the family plays in the transmission of beliefs and values.

To combat this mentality we need parents who see the child as a gift from God, and take seriously their vocation to educate their children in chastity. These parents will be guided by the wisdom of Church teaching and will have access to education about the natural methods of family planning. They will then find that their children imbibe the truths of God's plan for procreation almost unconsciously in all its beauty, and that they are, as it were, immunised against the contraceptive mentality. If for serious reasons they are unable to carry out this part of their vocation then they may request assistance. But it comes in that order: the request comes before the assistance, and the assistance to the child is always private and individual.

We also need priests and teachers who are filled with hope, who aspire to purity of heart and who know and teach the true Faith without ambiguity. They will understand the support that parents need to fulfil their vocation, and that parents can be re-catechised through their children. They will be like beacons in the contraceptive night of darkness. Young people will be given a vision of marriage and parenthood which inspires and challenges them to be mothers and fathers the Church truly needs. Strong in their knowledge of what it teaches, protected when they need protection, they will be ready to found a true culture of life.

21

The culture of life and the quality of life ethic: an either/or?

CHRISTOPHER KACZOR

IT IS A DAUNTING TASK to talk about quality of life. "An on-line search of the phrase QOL in Medline, Cinahl, Psyc-Info, Eric, and Social Science Abstract provided a list of 16,021 articles published between 1993 and 1998.... Since 1993, there have been over 4,000 articles published about QOL relating to health."[1] The term arose in sociological discussions, spread to psychology, and entered health care ethics. Health related quality of life considerations inform, at least for some ethicists, medical judgments on a wide range of issues. Quality of life judgments have played a role in the discussion of prenatal diagnosis and selective abortion, in treating or failing to treat handicapped newborns, and in the care of the elderly. Scholars have also adduced these judgments in the discussion of how to treat PVS patients as well as those with terminal diseases. Negative quality of life judgements have been the cry of those who consider themselves compassionate and in a German version (*lebenunwertes Leben*) the cry of the Nazis. As James Walter and Thomas Shannon have suggested its meaning "ranges from judgments about whether one should live at all, to the conditions under which one will live, to evaluations of life-style, and to considered judgments by patients about how medicine corresponds to their beliefs and aspirations."[2] Quality of life considerations pertain to at least three different issues: (1) the definition of, judgments about, and uses of quality of life, (2) the criteria that guide and establish the assessment of quality of life,[3] and (3) the mode by which we know the criteria have been fulfilled.[4] This paper hopes to differentiate different senses and uses of the term 'quality of life' and discuss which of these senses are compatible with a health care ethic advancing the culture of life as described by John Paul II in *Evangelium vitae*. Thus, my discussion will focus primarily on judgments, definitions, and uses of quality of life in coming to

---

[1] B. Haas, 'A multidisciplinary concept analysis of quality of life' 21 (1999) *Western Journal of Medicine*: 728 ff.

[2] J. Walter and T. Shannon (eds) *Quality of Life: The New Medical Dilemma*. New York: Paulist Press 1990: 1.

[3] Cf. T. Gill and A. Feinstein, 'A critical appraisal of the quality of quality of life measurements'. 272 (1994) *Journal of the American Medical Association*: 619.

[4] This hermeneutic is suggested in J. Walter, 'Proportionate reason and its three levels of inquiry: structuring the ongoing debate', in C. Kaczor (ed.) *Proportionalism For and Against* Marquette: Marquette University Press 2000: 393.

decisions in health care and not the clinical criteria or modes of knowing the criteria have been fulfilled.[5] First I will say a word about inappropriate uses of quality of life, uses that exclude certain human beings from being considered persons or that deem them to have a 'wrongful life'. Secondly, I will address suffering and dependency in the culture of life, and finally there will be a word about how quality of life considerations might legitimately enter into discussions of health care ethics.

The term 'quality of life' appears just twice in Pope John Paul II's encyclical *Evangelium vitae*. The term's use in the encyclical reflects the ambiguity of the phrase in the literature. Quality of life is first used as a term of reprobation, as a way of devaluing suffering human persons. John Paul II writes:

> The eclipse of the sense of God and of man inevitably leads to a practical materialism, which breeds individualism, utilitarianism and hedonism. Here too we see the permanent validity of the words of the Apostle: "And since they did not see fit to acknowledge God, God gave them up to a base mind and to improper conduct" (*Rm* 1:28). The values of being are replaced by those of having. The only goal which counts is the pursuit of one's own material well-being. The so-called "quality of life" is interpreted primarily or exclusively as economic efficiency, inordinate consumerism, physical beauty and pleasure, to the neglect of the more profound dimensions – interpersonal, spiritual and religious – of existence.[6]

On this view, only those actually or potentially living this "good life" merit our concern and consideration. Those human beings that lack this actuality or potentiality have a life not worth living.

However, the passage in question does not indicate that it is quality of life as such that is problematic but rather a certain interpretation of it, the "so called 'quality of life'" as the pope says. Indeed, later John Paul II suggests a more positive meaning of quality of life:

> Another welcome sign is the growing attention being paid to the *quality of life* and to *ecology*, especially in more developed societies, where people's expectations are no longer concentrated so much on problems of survival as on the search for an overall improvement of living conditions.[7]

Quality of life in this context includes the quest to make life worth living, to humanize our way of life above mere survival. This quest must be understood not merely in terms of material well-being but also social, moral, and religious

---

[5] On this, see A. Leplege and S. Hunt, 'The problem of quality of life in medicine'. 278 (1997) *Journal of the American Medical Association*: 47–50; T. Gill and A. Feinstein, 'A critical appraisal of the quality of life measurements'. 272 (1994) *Journal of the American Medical Association*: 619–624; and G. Guyatt and D. Cook, 'Health status, quality of life, and the individual', 272 (1994) *Journal of the American Medical Association*: 630–631 for an introduction to these complex questions.

[6] John Paul II, *Evangelium vitae*: 23.

[7] John Paul II, *Evangelium vitae*: 27. Emphasis in the original.

development. The meaning here is not so much medical as social, not clinical but personal and interpersonal.

Evangelium vitae thus reflects various meanings of the term quality of life, some noxious to an ontological valuing of each human person; others entirely commensurate with and even demanded by an affirmation of the unique value of every human being. But what of quality of life in health care ethics? Are the so called sanctity of life and quality of life ethics completely opposed or might they be in some respects reconciled?

Illustrating uses of quality of life that undermine recognizing the dignity of all human beings are those arguments denying that respect is due human beings in early stages of development. Pro-abortion and pro-infanticide arguments of Mary Anne Warren, Michael Tooley, and Peter Singer have presupposed a functional evaluation of human beings and used it to justify their ethical views.

Typically, it is noted that the fetus lacks some capacity, for instance rationality, or does not excercise this capacity to the requisite degree, and hence the unborn child cannot be considered as worthy of the respect given to other human beings. Thus, abortion is morally permissible and should be legal on demand and without limit.

From the perspective of the culture of life, judgments about the humanity and the personhood of any member of the class *homo sapiens* should be inclusive rather than exclusive. The human person must be accorded an ontological value rather than a functional one. The ontological view has a decisive advantage over the functional view insofar as any functional view arbitrarily excludes human beings from being considered truly persons. First, the functional view must choose some standard by which to separate those that are merely human beings from those who are also persons. Recently, the proposed standard has been rationality. Different cultures have proposed other standards, however, such as the ability to reproduce, attractiveness, racial or sexual characteristics, usefulness to the community, or some other desired characteristic. Given this standard, further choices must be made about the degree of the characteristic needed by the human being if that human being is to count legally and/or morally as a person, a being due respect. In so far as characteristics such as rationality are matters of degree, invariably an arbitrary standard must then be chosen to distinguished the protected and valued class of human beings from the unprotected and unvalued class. Of course, a standard of morality based on arbitrary choices hardly merits the title, and so functional evaluation is incompatible with right reason.

Secondly, from an historical perspective, the arbitrariness of these choices has led to innumerable catastrophic injustices by whites against blacks, men against women, rich against poor, Aryans against Jews, etc. The lessons of history indicate the gross danger of adopting an exclusive rather than an inclusive point of view with respect to the personhood of any human being. The authors of the U.N. Declaration on Human Rights crafted it precisely to avoid such arbitrary and exclusive judgments.

One might also add that from the perspective of Christian belief the mission of Jesus indicates that the poor, rejected, and unloved, just as much as the rich, accepted, and loved, merit our respect and kindness. As John Paul II writes in *Evangelium vitae*:

> In a special way, believers in Christ must defend and promote this right [to life], aware as they are of the wonderful truth recalled by the Second Vatican Council: "By his incarnation the Son of God has united himself in some fashion with every human being". This saving event reveals to humanity not only the boundless love of God who "so loved the world that he gave his only Son" (*Jn* 3:16), but also the incomparable value of every human person.[8]

Christ's interaction with various 'marginalized' human beings, such as tax collectors, prostitutes, the Samaritan woman, lepers, and so forth offers a model of Christian interaction with those whom society deems 'unwanted', especially the so called unwanted child.

Unfortunately, quality of life concerns, understood as judgments about which humans have personhood and which lack personhood, are not confined to discussion about abortion. Quality of life judgments, understood as the functional evaluation of human beings who must merit personhood, run through many other concerns of medical ethics. Ethicists have used functional evaluation of human beings in justifying active euthanasia, in not treating handicapped infants as persons, in removing organs from living but neurologically damaged patients, and in removing nutrition and hydration in order to kill PVS patients. Functional evaluation of human beings is one way of describing what John Paul II calls the "culture of death". Clearly, this sense of quality of life is incompatible with the inclusivity of a culture of life that affirms the intrinsic dignity and fundamental equality of every human being regardless of circumstance.

This malignant sense of quality of life is not the only way in which the term can be used. Understood within the context of the culture of life, quality of life, on my view, can be an element in making decisions about what sorts of treatments should be given to a patient. It is here that a sanctity of life ethic parts from a vitalistic ethic which demands that we extend the duration of human life as much as possible regardless of the burdens or benefits of the treatment to the patient and others.[9] If a patient's condition or quality of life is such that treatments provide no real benefit but rather impose a heavy burden, the treatment need not be given even if such treatment would extend the life of the patient.

As John Keown has pointed out, it is the *treatment* and not the *life of the human person* that is burdensome. Even if the duty to prolong life is not without exception, human life is always a gift and never a burden. Thus the idea of life itself being a burden, 'wrongful life' as it is sometimes called, must be rejected. Many ethicists maintain that life in itself has no intrinsic value but only instrumental value. Living as such, they maintain, is not beneficial or good especially

[8] John Paul II, *Evangelium vitae*: 2.
[9] J. Keown, 'The legal revolution: from "sanctity of life" to "quality of life" and "autonomy"', in L. Gormally (ed) *Issues for a Catholic Bioethic*. London: The Linacre Center 1999: 233–260.

when life is connected with severe suffering and when death would bring release from this suffering as well as, hopefully, rest with God. Even some who explicitly reject a merely instrumentalist account of the value of human life, sometimes speak as if life itself were burdensome. For example, James Walter and Thomas Shannon state: "The specific issue here is whether the burdensomeness of the life preserved by the offering of nutrition/hydration can or should be part of the overall assessment of burden in the determination of ordinary/extra-ordinary...[10]" Typically, such beliefs in 'wrongful life', or the idea that some lives are not worth living, rest on at least two philosophical mistakes.

The first mistake is a Cartesian/Neo-Platonic conception of the person as a duality of two substances, body and soul. Death, it is argued, is ontologically evil for the body of a person but good for the Christian person brought into a new life.[11] Human persons, however, are a unity of body and soul; they are ensouled bodies.[12] Since human beings are not pure spirits merely using or possessing their own bodies, but rather human beings *are* their bodies (but not, of course, *merely* their bodies), what is evil for the human body is evil for the human person. Since death is not a good for the human body, but rather a privation of a due good, the death of a person's body is not a good for that person. Hence, in an ethics in which one is enjoined to want and seek the good for oneself and others (love your neighbor as yourself), in the realm of com-mutative justice, intentional killing of human beings has no place.[13]

The second mistake in speaking of persons with low quality of life as having a 'wrongful life' is the lack of requisite conceptual distinctions between good and evil. The fact that some evil brings about some good or some good brings about some evil does not change the nature of evil into good or good into evil. Let us say that I am tortured, imprisoned, and blinded by captors from whom I even-tually escape. Following my escape, I become a more loving, generous, and sensi-tive person. It does not follow that because good resulted from my experience that being tortured, imprisoned, and blinded are goods for my captors or me. The forgiveness of sins is a great good, and forgiveness of sins comes about only *because of* sin, but we certainly cannot conclude from these observations that sin itself is a good. In a similar way, we cannot reason that since eternal life is a great good, and death brings about eternal life, then death is a good. We cannot reason that since relief of pain is a good, and death brings a relief of pain, death is a good. Although many evils may be connected with life (severe

---

[10] J. Walter and T. Shannon, 'The PVS Patient and the Forgoing/Withdrawing of Medical Nutrition and Hydration'. In Walter and Shannon (eds) *Quality of Life: The New Medical Dilemma.* New York: Paulist Press 1990: 214.

[11] D. Thomasma, 'Assisted Death and Martyrdom'. 4.2 (1998) *Christian Bioethics*: 112–142, at 130.

[12] P. Lee, 'Human Beings are Animals', in R. George (ed) *Natural Law and Moral Inquiry.* Washington D.C.: Georgetown University Press 1998: 135–151.

[13] I cannot defend this claim here, but interested readers should see Christopher Kaczor, *Proportionalism and the Natural Law Tradition.* Washington, D.C.: The Catholic University of America Press, 2002.

pain, debilitation, sickness), these evils must all be conceptually distinguished from life. That is, just because an evil such as sickness is found in conjunction with a good such as life does not mean that sickness is a good or life is an evil any more than the pain associated with staring at the sun would make eyesight an evil. Eyesight, like life, is an intrinsic good of human persons even if connected with or a necessary condition for various evils.

However, those in the debates about what does or does not constitute burdensome treatment often implicitly assume the belief that some lives are not worth living both for the dependent individual and for those who care for the dependent individual. Suffering and dependency can be construed as unmitigated evils.

From the perspective of religious faith, such a belief cannot be accepted. Suffering can be meaningful when the one suffering offers this suffering for that which is lacking in the Mystical Body. As it says in *Col* 1:24: "I am now rejoicing in my sufferings for your sake, and in my flesh I am completing what is lacking in Christ's afflictions for the sake of his body, that is, the church." As John Paul II wrote in his Apostolic Letter *Salvifici Doloris*:

> Every man has his own share in the Redemption. Each one is also called to share in that suffering through which the Redemption was accomplished. He is called to share in that suffering through which all human suffering has also been redeemed. In bringing about the Redemption through suffering, Christ has also raised human suffering to the level of the Redemption. Thus each man, in his suffering, can also become a sharer in the redemptive suffering of Christ.[14]

Within the Christian experience, suffering can draw one closer to Christ and help the entire Church, indeed the entire world. The one caring for those in need by offering support, love, and treatment follows the model of Jesus and indeed cares for Jesus. "Whatsoever you do for the least of these you did for me" (*Mt* 25:40). The perfection of the mystical body of Christ is accomplished through the suffering of the Body of Christ and the imitation of Christ's care for the suffering, both of which give meaning to suffering.

One might also note that health-related quality of life, understood in its subjective aspect of life satisfaction, rather than as an objective evaluation of biological function (objective health status), remains remarkably high on average even when biological function is poor. In the words of Alain Leplege and Sonia Hunt in a recent article from the *Journal of the American Medical Association*: "There is ample evidence that, as an individual comes to terms with the fact of long-term illness, adjustments occur that preserve life satisfaction, and individuals can consider their quality of life as good even when there are severe limitations on their physical ability."[15] For instance, patients with asthma reported high quality

---

[14] John Paul II, Apostolic Letter *Salvifici Doloris*: 19.
[15] A. Leplege and S. Hunt, 'The problem of quality of life in medicine'. 278 (1997) *Journal of the American Medical Association*: 48.

of life, regardless of severity of illness or medical condition, if they experienced the giving and receiving of love, had a positive approach to everyday events, and took pleasure in life.[16]

These considerations might be enriched by also calling to mind recent philosophical reflection on why dependency ought not be considered an unmitigated evil to be avoided at all costs. In his recent book, *Dependent Rational Animals*, Alasdair MacIntyre writes:

> We ... need to learn how to dissociate the evaluation of personal qualities and of reasoning from physical appearance and from manner of presentation. In so doing we may discover what we had not hitherto suspected: that we have not up till now been able to separate ourselves from feelings of dislike, disgust and even horror in responding to the facial appearances of certain types of other and so we have not been able to exercise critical judgment in respect of those feelings; that we have been lacking in adequate self-knowledge in failing to understand the full range of judgments that are influenced irrelevantly by such feelings; and that, in responding to those whose appearance has affronted us, we have assumed that from them at least we could have nothing to learn. We discover, that is, in our encounters with the disabled hitherto unrecognized sources of error in our own practical reasoning.[17]

Thus, through such encounters, which would seem to be of benefit only to the one receiving care, the caregiver also learns lessons that might not otherwise be available. Even in the case where the one given care cannot communicate, is passive, gravely disabled, or in a persistant vegetative state, one may recognize opportunities for growth. As MacIntyre argues:

> What they give us is the possibility of learning something essential, what it is for someone else to be wholly entrusted to our care, so that we are answerable for their well-being. Everyone of us has, as an infant, been wholly entrusted to someone else's care, so that they were answerable for our well-being. Now we have the opportunity to learn just what it is that we owe to such individuals by learning for ourselves what it is to be so entrusted.[18]

Such lessons provide those who care for the gravely disabled a great good. The benefit in situations of care for the dependent is simply not one way. Thus, not just theological considerations but also philosophical ones suggest that the dependency of even the most disabled person should be considered not simply as a burden for others.

Although the patient's life is always beneficial to him and often to others, not all treatments are. In order to determine which treatments are beneficial and which are burdensome the condition or, one might say, the quality of the life

---

[16] Cf. Leplege and Hunt, 'The problem of quality of life in medicine': 50.

[17] A. MacIntyre, *Dependent Rational Animals: Why Human Beings Need the Virtues* Chicago: Open Court 1999: 137.

[18] MacIntyre, *Dependent Rational Animals* 138–139.

of the patient must be taken into account. Determining which treatments offer very little benefit, while imposing significant burdens, requires evaluation of the quality of life, or what one might call both the objective health status and subjective health status of the patient in question.

How then ought one to evaluate 'quality of life' understood as an evaluation of the worthwhileness of treatment (not of patients)? William E. May's article "Criteria for Withholding or Withdrawing Treatment" offers perhaps the best account so far of how quality of life considerations, understood in the restricted sense, may enter into determinations about which treatments are burdensome. After critiquing Kevin O'Rourke's interpretation of Pius XII's address to a congress of anesthesiologists, May writes:

> [M]edical treatment is 'extraordinary' or 'disproportionate' and hence not morally obligatory if *objectively discernable features in the treatment itself, its side-effects, and its negative consequences impose grave burdens on the person being treated or on others.* Excessive burdensomeness is the major criterion, therefore, for determining whether or not to withhold or withdraw medical treatments. Excessive burdensomeness is, one could say, the genus. Species of excessive burdensomeness include riskiness of the treatment, the excessive pain of the treatment, the severely negative impact the treatment will have on the subject's life, treatments judged morally or psychologically repugnant, and treatments that would be too costly and severely imperil the economic security of the patient, the patient's family, or the community.[19]

The list given by May is helpful, and we might add with him a few more "species." Clearly a treatment that is futile, not medically indicated or even counter-productive, should be considered extraordinary and should be withdrawn. Also classified as extraordinary are treatments that interfere with a person's spiritual duties or aspirations, as Pius XII noted in his address to anaesthesiologists.[20]

In this way, quality of life considerations are both 'objective' or having to do with the objective health status of a patient or treatment and 'subjective' or having to do with the relationship between the proposed treatment and the pursuit of the vocation or aspirations of the patient. One aspect of quality of life is objective because it involves considerations that might be empirically measured and verified such as a treatment's being medically counterindicated due to the patient's physical condition. What may be beneficial treatment to an otherwise healthy patient might be burdensome treatment to someone with a terminal illness. Similarly, the risk associated with a treatment or the likelihood of its benefit are not connected with the plans, aims, or goals of a patient. The benefit of a proposed treatment is linked with the over-all condition that the patient is likely to have after the treatment. In the words of Germain Grisez, "[E]ven if

[19] W. May, 'Criteria for Withholding or Withdrawing Treatment'. 57.3 (1990) *Linacre Quarterly*: 88.
[20] Pius XII, 'The Prolongation of Life: An Address to an International Congress of Anesthesiologists' 1957 as cited by May, 'Criteria for Withholding or Withdrawing Treatment': 89.

they are not dying, comatose and other severely mentally disabled persons stand to benefit far less from many sorts of treatment than do most other people, and it is reasonable to provide those sorts of treatment only to persons who will benefit more from them."[21] Thus, a given treatment that may be ordinary treatment for an otherwise healthy patient may be disproportionate or extraordinary for a comatose patient not precisely because the burden of treatment differs but because the benefit of treatment differs.

The other aspect of quality of life, the subjective health status of a patient, cannot be determined on empirical grounds alone. One reason for considering a treatment burdensome is the severely negative impact a treatment may have on the patient's lifestyle or vocation, and this will be determined by what sort of lifestyle or vocation a patient has chosen and a considered judgment about how the treatment will impact this lifestyle or vocation. A young father might consider a treatment to be excessively burdensome whose side-effects would be debilitating. On the other hand, an elderly and more sedentary person, without obligations of child care, may consider debilitation as endurable given the alternatives. Similarly, that a treatment is morally or psychologically repugnant must be considered not so to speak a priori but in the concrete situation of the individual who assesses 'quality of life', that is, his or her own condition even as subjectively assessed, in addition to individual goals, beliefs, and aspirations, in coming to a decision about the treatment.

Some aspects of quality of life contain both objective and subjective elements. Excessive pain of the treatment is determined in part by the condition of the patient both physically and mentally. A treatment that causes excessive pain to one patient, due to the patient's physical condition or psychological constitution, may not cause excessive pain to another. Some people bear a great deal of pain well; others are extremely sensitive.

In coming to an evaluation about whether a treatment is ordinary or extraordinary, i.e., obligatory or not obligatory, one should first consider the objective health status of the patient and then the subjective health status. If the treatment is risky, linked to noxious side-effects, or extremely expensive, then that treatment is extraordinary regardless of the subjective health status of the patient. Other treatments may be ordinary in an empirically verifiable sense, but extraordinary due to the vocation, aspirations, sensitivity to pain, or other not empirically verifiable characteristics of a patient. All of these quality of life concerns are fully compatible with an affirmation of the intrinsic dignity of every human being. However, insofar as the noxious meaning of the term is most common, we may not want to speak about quality of life even though the term can be used to capture both the objective and subjective aspects of health status important in coming to decisions about treatment. However in certain objective and subjective senses, 'quality of life' judgments are fully compatible with the culture of life, even if we should for prudential reasons not want to use the term 'quality of life'.

---

[21] G. Grisez, 'Should nutrition and hydration be provided to permanently comatose and other mentally disabled persons?', 57.2 (1989) *Linacre Quarterly*: 30–43, at 42.

22

Challenging a consensus: why *Evangelium Vitae* does not permit legislators to vote for 'imperfect legislation'

COLIN HARTE

1. Introduction

Evangelium vitae 73 has been widely interpreted as teaching that a Catholic or other morally upright legislator may rightly *vote for a law which tolerates or permits abortion* if this restricts abortion more than the existing law or than a law which might otherwise be enacted. Although it is not found in the encyclical the term 'imperfect legislation' has become widely used to describe this sort of restricting law, and my use of the term in this paper will be in accordance with how it is now commonly understood.[1]

This paper does not attempt to provide a comprehensive argument against voting for 'imperfect legislation' itself, but has the more limited objective of establishing that *Evangelium vitae* does not teach that a legislator may vote for such legislation. The encyclical's teaching must, of course, be viewed in the context of the magisterium's wider teaching (which had not previously addressed this question directly). This includes the teaching, restated with clarity in *Evangelium vitae*, with respect to such questions as the relationship between the moral law and the civil law, the foundational and conditional aspects of participation in democratic societies, and the need to respect as a fundamental requirement of authentic social structures the inviolable and inalienable right to life of every human being. The encyclical's guidance to legislators faced with 'imperfect legislation' is offered as a development of the principles already clearly articulated in the magisterium's teaching and which this paper does not repeat.

---

[1] The term 'imperfect law' was used most notably in the title of a symposium organised by the Congregation for the Doctrine of the Faith held a few months before the publication of *Evangelium vitae*, entitled "Catholics and the Pluralist Society – The case of 'imperfect laws'" (Rome, 9–12 November 1994). Given that the symposium was held precisely to discuss the question addressed in *Evangelium vitae* 73, it seems somewhat surprising, given the general view that the encyclical authorises votes for 'imperfect legislation', that this term was not used in the encyclical itself. Of course, if the encyclical does not, as I argue, authorise votes for 'imperfect legislation' there would be no need for it to use the term. The symposium's proceedings were published in Italian: J. Joblin & R. Tremblay (eds) *I Cattolici e la Societa Pluralista: Il Caso delle 'Leggi Imperfette'*. Bologna: Edizioni Studio Domenicano 1996.

Given his pre-eminence in contemporary deliberations on moral, political and legal theory, the view of Professor John Finnis on this question merits particular respect, and it is for this reason that I cite him as the principal proponent of the view which this paper is challenging.

2. Understanding 'Evangelium vitae' 73

2.1 A 'problem' and a 'solution'

What guidance or instruction, then, does *Evangelium vitae* (*EV*) give to legislators? The disputed part of *EV* 73 is the final paragraph (*EV* 73.3) which can be sub-divided into three sections: a) a presentation of the problem which needs to be addressed, b) an explanation of how the problem has arisen, and c) the proposed 'solution' to this problem. These sub-divisions are not specified in the normative Latin text or in the official translations, but their identification – particularly that of a) the problem, and c) the solution – helps to avoid the sort of confusion and misinterpretation which has arisen. The full, official English translation of *EV* 73.3 is:

> [*a) The problem*]
> A particular problem of conscience can arise in cases where a legislative vote would be decisive for the passage of a more restrictive law, aimed at limiting the number of authorised abortions, in place of a more permissive law already passed or ready to be voted on.
> [*b) Why the problem has arisen*]
> Such cases are not infrequent. It is a fact that while in some parts of the world there continue to be campaigns to introduce laws favouring abortion, often supported by powerful international organisations, in other nations – particularly those which have already experienced the bitter fruits of such permissive legislation – there are growing signs of a rethinking in this matter.
> [*c) The solution*]
> In a case like the one just mentioned, when it is not possible to overturn or completely abrogate a pro-abortion law, an elected official, whose absolute personal opposition to procured abortion was well known, could licitly support proposals aimed at *limiting the harm* done by such a law and at lessening its negative consequences at the level of general opinion and public morality. This does not in fact represent an illicit cooperation with an unjust law, but rather a legitimate and proper attempt to limit its evil aspects.[2]

[2] [*The problem*] De conscientia nominatim agitari potest quibusdam forte evenientibus casibus, cum legatorum suffragia necessaria sunt ut strictiori legi faveatur, quae scilicet circumscribat abortuum lege admissorum numerum pro laxiore lege quae iam viget vel suffragiis probanda ... [*The solution*] Superiore in casu, quoties vitari antiquarive non potest abortus lex, liquet legatum, qui palam alioquin vulgoque abortui adversetur, suffragari licite posse illis consiliis quae eiusmodi legis *damna minuere velint* et perniciosum effectum extenuare qui sive culturam sive moralitatem publicam respicit. Hac enim agendi ratione officium suum non praestat illicitae vel iniustae legi; potius vero aequus opportunusque inducitur conatus ut eius iniquae cohibeantur species.

Our concern lies with what is presented as 'the problem' and 'the solution' and not with the middle section. The first point to note is that one cannot state 'the problem' as though that were 'the solution'. For example, if a child asks a teacher whether $2 + 2 = 5$, and the teacher replies that the answer is clearly apparent if the child uses a calculator, one cannot say that the teacher has answered that $2 + 2 = 5$; that is the problem that has been posed, not the solution. With respect to the teaching of *EV* 73, however, many distinguished commentators have failed to note the distinction between the problem posed and the solution. For example, Professor Finnis says that in *EV* 73 the following 'statement' is found:

> a Catholic elected legislator whose absolute personal opposition to procured abortion is well known can, in a legislative vote decisive for the passage of a bill, licitly give his or her support to a bill for a law which permits abortion but less permissively than the existing law or than a bill which will otherwise be passed and become law.[3]

My disagreement with what Professor Finnis says at this point is not based on a difference of *interpretation*, but rather on a recognition that the 'statement' to which he refers is not to be found anywhere in the encyclical; it is, rather, his version of what he thinks is taught, a version which is flawed because he has failed to differentiate what is written as the 'problem' and as the 'solution'. The encyclical indisputably *does not state* that a legislator can "licitly give his or her support to a bill for a law which permits abortion but less permissively than the existing law or than a bill which will otherwise be passed and become law" as Professor Finnis and some other distinguished commentators have claimed.[4] To be precise, it states (i.e. teaches) that "when it is not possible to overturn or completely abrogate a pro-abortion law, an elected official ... could licitly support proposals aimed at *limiting the harm* done by such a law and at lessening its negative consequences at the level of general opinion and public morality." The question which needs to be addressed is what exactly is meant by this somewhat obscure reference to "proposals aimed at limiting the harm done by such a law...". Does this mean that a legislator can support *any* legislative proposal or are some proposals acceptable and others not?

We are, of course, trying to establish not simply what might be practically effective, but what is truly ethical, and an answer to the question of what "proposals" might be ethically supported requires a consideration of jurisprudential and legislative matters relevant to abortion legislation. An awareness of two particular types of unjustness in law is a relevant starting point.

---

[3] John Finnis, 'The Catholic Church and Public Policy Debates in Western Liberal Societies: The Basis and Limits of Intellectual Engagement'. In L. Gormally (ed) *Issues for a Catholic Bioethic*. London: The Linacre Centre 1999: 261–273 at 268.

[4] For example, Professor Mgr Livio Melina states as the teaching of *EV* 73 what is, in fact, identified as "the problem," in his paper 'La Cooperacion en Acciones Moralmente Malas Contra la Vida Humana'. In R. Lucas Lucas (ed) *Commentario Interdisciplinar a la 'Evangelium Vitae'*. Madrid: Biblioteca de Autores Cristianos 1996: 467–490, at 481.

2.2 Intrinsic and extrinsic unjustness in laws

In the abstract one cannot say whether a just income tax law should specify that 20%, 50% or even 80% of one's income should be taxed; similarly, one cannot say whether the maximum speed on public roads should be set at 20, 50 or 80 miles per hour. The justness or unjustness of much human law depends on the concrete situation and different jurisdictions at different times may legitimately choose from a wide range of options, the justness or unjustness of specific legislative measures being judged by *extrinsic factors* – i.e. the circumstances. Laws, however, which fail to protect human life – such as those which tolerate or permit abortion, killing the newborn, euthanasia or murder generally – or those which specifically permit (i.e. do not merely tolerate) other moral evils, can be judged to be *intrinsically unjust*; a consideration of extrinsic factors such as whether the previous law permitted or tolerated other or greater evils does not affect the fundamental unjustness of such laws. St Thomas Aquinas makes a distinction between unjust laws which are contrary to the divine good, and those which are contrary to the human good, and this distinction would appear to correspond with the distinction between intrinsic and extrinsic unjustness in laws.[5]

The teaching of *EV* 73.3 is prefaced by a short paragraph that has been frequently overlooked (*EV* 73.2) which states that *it is never licit to vote for an intrinsically unjust law.*

> In the case of an intrinsically unjust law [de lege ... suapte natura iniqua] such as a law permitting abortion or euthanasia, it is therefore never licit to obey it [eidem se accommodare] or to 'take part in a propaganda campaign in favour of such a law, or vote for it [latis suffragiis sustinere]'.[6]

Consideration of extrinsic factors must generally be considered before judging whether it serves the common good to enact a specific legislative measure,[7] but

---

[5] Cf. St Thomas Aquinas, *Summa Theologiae* 1–2, 96, 4.

[6] *EV* 73.2. The sentence includes part of a quotation from the Congregation for the Doctrine of the Faith's *Declaration on Procured Abortion* (18 November 1974), which expresses a similar view: "It must in any case be clearly understood that a Christian [hominem] can never conform to a law which is in itself immoral [legi intrinsece inhonestae], and such is the case of a law which would admit in principle the liceity of abortion [si lex feratur quae principium liceitatis abortus recipiat]. Nor can a Christian take part in a propaganda campaign in favour of such a law, or vote for it [Is praeterea non potest esse particeps alicuius motus publicae opinionis, qui eiusmodi legi faveat, neque potest latis suffragiis sustinere]." n. 22.

[7] Aquinas' definition of law as "nothing else than an ordinance of reason for the common good, made by him who has care of the community and promulgated" (*S Th* 1–2, 96, 4) is worth recalling. The common good is "the sum total of social conditions which allow people, either as groups *or as individuals*, to reach their fulfilment more fully and more easily" [my emphasis] (Vatican Council II, *Gaudium et spes* 26) and my contention is that 'imperfect' legislation specifically excludes from protection (by either tolerating or permitting abortion) some individuals who should be included for protection within that particular legislation. John Paul II notes that the common good is "the good of all and *of each individual*" [my emphasis] (*Sollicitudo rei socialis* 38) and that "it is impossible to further the common good without acknowledging

intrinsic unjustness can be discerned as a property of the measure itself. When deciding whether to vote for specific measures which affect abortion it is not sufficient merely to judge them 'imperfect' (a judgment often made without defining what precisely is meant by the term); it is necessary to judge *whether they are just* and, hence, whether they truly *are law*.

If it is never licit to vote for an intrinsically unjust law, as taught by *EV* 73.2, the first consideration when judging the licitness of voting for any 'imperfect' legislation is precisely the norm dictated by that legislation. Law is, after all, a dictate or statement of norms[8] – some of which are of an absolute moral nature, others of a relative political nature. Any discussion about the licitness of voting for 'imperfect' legislation cannot focus solely on the goals or motivations or intentions of those promoting it or the consequences of enacting it, but must focus primarily on the concrete legislation under consideration which has *an objective purpose/intent* irrespective of the subjective motives or intentions of those voting for it.[9] A difficulty emerges when discussing what sorts of legislation might be supported because one tends, inevitably, to refer to concise *illustrations* of legislation which may or may not correspond with the reality of concrete legislative proposals. For example, how does one represent legislation to lower the upper limit for abortions from, say, 24 to 16 weeks? Does one present an illustration of legislation which states: "Abortion is permitted up to 16 weeks"[10]; or: "Abortion is prohibited after 16 weeks"; or: "Abortion is not punished by law up to 16 weeks"; or: "Abortion is tolerated up to 16 weeks"; or: "Abortion is permitted

and defending the right to life" (*EV* 101). 'Imperfect' legislation, by promoting the good of *some* in a legislative context which calls for the promotion of the good of *all* people, undeniably fails to promote the common good. Although Aquinas does not refer to 'justness' in his definition of law this is implicit in his inclusion of rationality as a condition. Cf. N. Kretzmann, 'Lex iniusta non est lex' 33 (1988) *The American Journal of Jurisprudence*: 99–122, at 114.

[8] Aquinas also speaks of law as a "dictate of practical reason" ("nihil est aliud lex quam quoddam dictamen praticae rationis..." *S Th* 1–2, 91, 1). Professor Finnis objects to the common translation of "dictamen" by "dictate" claiming "it is unsound, in so far as 'dictate' suggests arbitrariness and even abuse of power"; see his *Aquinas: Moral, Political and Legal Theory*. Oxford: Oxford University Press 1998: 256. Although the term "dictate" is widely used (for example, the English text of *EV* 71 translates "normas *edere*" with "*dictate* norms") Professor Finnis raises a legitimate concern that the term "dictate" might be misunderstood. My point, however, is that law must be judged primarily in terms of what it 'dictates' – or 'states', 'commands', 'specifies', 'prescribes', etc – and not solely in terms of its *effect*.

[9] The objective purpose/intent of laws which prohibit all or some abortions remains constant, although the subjective intention of those voting for such laws might vary. One legislator might vote for such laws because he recognises the right to life of the unborn; another legislator might be indifferent to the right to life of the unborn (and might even be positively pro-abortion) but vote for such laws as a means of gaining favour with his constituents so that they will be willing to vote for him at the next election.

[10] Professor Finnis uses the example of lowering the limit to 16 weeks, and provides illustrations stating "Abortion is lawful up to 16 weeks" and "Abortion is permissible up to 16 weeks," in his paper 'Unjust Laws in a Democratic Society: Some Philosophical and Theological Reflections'. 71 (1996) *Notre Dame Law Review*: 595–604 at 600–601; cf also 'The Catholic Church and Public Policy Debates...': 268–269.

up to 16 weeks and prohibited after 16 weeks"; etc.? Can distinctions be identified between any of these illustrations which affect the justness of voting for such legislation? And do these illustrations adequately represent the reality of the situation in a particular legislative assembly where legislators might, for example, be considering an Amendment Bill specifying that the words "24 weeks" in an existing Abortion Act simply be substituted by "16 weeks"? Whatever defects there may be in particular illustrations the underlying principle must always be that legislators vote for *just legislation*. The *intrinsic unjustness* of legislation that violates the moral law can always be detected, and the teaching of *EV* 73 is clearly predicated on the illicitness of voting for such legislation (*EV* 73.2).

2.3 Primary and secondary aspects of abortion legislation

Any attempt to promote just legislation which affects abortion requires a recognition, which has not generally been acknowledged, that abortion laws typically contain two distinct types of law.[11] The first type refers to the victims whose intentional killing is either *permitted* or *tolerated*, the law granting greater or less protection depending on such factors as whether the child has reached a certain gestational age, was conceived after rape, is socially inconvenient or has a disabling condition etc. For the purposes of the present discussion (and notwithstanding the different meaning associated with the term in a general legislative context) I shall refer to this as *the primary (abortion) legislation*, and it can be condemned as unjust and unacceptable if it denies the right to life of even one human being whose right to life should always be safeguarded. In other words, the primary abortion legislation is predicated on the denial of the right to life of some or all unborn children. The law need not specifically *permit* abortion to be unjust primary abortion legislation; it is also unjust – intrinsically unjust – if it *tolerates* abortion, such that some or all abortions are regarded as unpunishable acts or if the law specifies that some abortions (e.g. those performed after x weeks, or those performed, say, for reasons of social convenience) are prohibited, the legality of other abortions (e.g. those before x weeks, or those performed, say, for allegedly 'medical' indications) not being specified.[12]

---

[11] This point does not seem to have been recognised in any of the literature on the subject of abortion law reform. For example, see A. Fisher OP, 'On the duties of a Catholic politician with respect to abortion law reform, with particular reference to *Evangelium vitae* 73' (1998), at http://www.priestsforlife.org/articles/imperflefisher.html. He presents for consideration 15 different measures which in his view might be supported to counter permissive abortion laws, yet does not seem to recognise that there are fundamental differences in the types of law being proposed. In my view no more than five of the measures Fr Fisher proposes could be enacted as just laws.

[12] Civil law can often tolerate, without permitting, moral evil (for example, some immoral sexual acts), but violations of the fundamental right to life can be neither permitted nor tolerated, as indicated in *EV* 71 and its reference to Aquinas' teaching at *S Th* 1–2, 96, 2: "Human laws do not forbid all vices from which the virtuous abstain, but only the more grievous vices from which it is possible for the majority to abstain; and chiefly those that are to the hurt of

A consequence of denying the right to life of any unborn children is that one has to consider how that primary legislation will be practically implemented. If abortions are permitted or tolerated various questions arise. Where will they be performed? Who will perform them? Will they be publicly funded? Will counselling be required beforehand? Can hospitals opt out of providing abortion services? Can medical and administrative personnel opt out of involvement if they have a conscientious objection? etc. These practical questions dealing with the implementation of the primary legislation can be regarded as *the secondary legislation*, and they can be distinguished in two ways. First, there are measures predicated on the legality (and hence the acceptability/justness) of abortion. They regulate abortion in such a way that abortions can be procured provided that certain conditions are fulfilled, e.g. they may specify a requirement of counselling or a cooling off period before an abortion. Such measures being predicated on intrinsically unjust legislation that permits or tolerates abortion can always be judged themselves to be intrinsically unjust. Secondly, there are measures that are predicated on other rights or duties and not on abortion *per se*. Such measures might be based on the right of doctors not to be obliged to act in ways which violate their integrity as doctors (hence a measure stating "Doctors have a right not to participate in abortion procedures"), society's right to prevent chemical companies producing noxious substances (hence a measure stating "The manufacture of [the abortion pill] RU486 is prohibited") or the right of citizens to have their taxes spent on morally good projects (hence a measure stating "Public money shall not fund abortion"). These illustrations are for measures that are not intrinsically unjust.

2.4 Considering the justness of four possible ways to limit abortion

The ways in which just changes may be made to abortion legislation depend considerably on the specific legislative systems of different countries. Codified

others, without the prohibition of which human society could not be maintained: thus human law prohibits murder, theft and such like." By including murder within the category of vices which human law *must* prohibit there would appear to be no doubt that Aquinas would also have judged that abortion *must* be prohibited by human law. Just as a law which states "Murder is prohibited if the victim is aged between 3 and 72" does not prohibit "murder" but only "some murders" (and, therefore, by implication "tolerates" other murders), likewise a law which states "Abortion is prohibited after 16 weeks" does not prohibit "abortion" but only "some abortions." There is a distinction between laws which permit and tolerate abortion; however, the distinction does not justify voting for one and not the other. Analogously, though on an entirely separate subject, one can make a distinction between Catholics who have contracted a merely civil marriage and those living together as though they were married. John Paul II notes that the situation of those in the former category "cannot of course be likened to that of people simply living together without any bond at all, because in the present case [i.e. those in a civil marriage] there is at least a certain commitment to a properly-defined and probably stable state of life... Nevertheless, not even this situation is acceptable to the Church." (*Familiaris consortio* 82) Any remarks I make about the unjustness of laws which 'permit' abortion also apply to laws which 'tolerate' abortion.

systems present different opportunities from those of the UK and other countries where the abortion law is established by one or more Statutes or judicial judgments. Bearing in mind the distinction, stated above, between primary and secondary legislation, there would appear to be four general ways in which one might attempt to limit abortion in a UK-type non-codified system.

(i) Changes to particular Acts are often made by Amendment Acts, and one could consider whether an Abortion Act might be justly amended. The key consideration is that the justness of any Amendment Act is determined by judging the justness of the original act to which it refers, *as amended* by the Amendment Act. If some abortions will still be permitted or tolerated under the terms of a previous Abortion Act after the enactment of an Amendment Bill, the Amendment Bill can be judged to be *intrinsically unjust* and a violation of the moral law which prohibits all abortions.

(ii) One could try to prohibit some categories of abortion, not by introducing an Amendment Bill but by introducing separate legislation to prohibit some categories of abortion (i.e. the *primary legislation*). Such legislation might lower the time limit during which abortions could take place or prohibit 'social' abortions, but in so doing it would tolerate if not specifically permit earlier or 'hard case' abortions. Because such legislation would make an illicit *distinction of persons* – granting protection to some but not to others in a context which requires that the right to life of all the unborn should be safeguarded – it can be judged to be intrinsically unjust.

(iii) Abortions can be limited by enacting separate *secondary legislation* (i.e. legislation which is not an Abortion Amendment Bill). As indicated above, some secondary legislation is predicated on the legality of abortion itself (e.g. "Counselling [or a cooling-off period] is required before an abortion") and can be rejected as intrinsically unjust. It is possible, however, to enact just legislation stating, for example, that: "Doctors have a right not to be involved in abortion procedures"; or: "Public money may not be used to finance abortions." A legislator could not, however, vote justly for a measure – even though it would have the same practical effect – which stated that "Doctors have a right to decide whether or not to be involved in abortion procedures"; or: "Abortions can take place provided that they are not funded by public money"; because these latter proposals are predicated on the licitness of abortion, and can be judged to be intrinsically unjust.

(iv) In addition to voting for a Bill to be enacted as law, legislators encounter various votes, e.g. votes concerning amendments to particular clauses, during the passage of a Bill. The issues surrounding this are complex, but legislators may have many opportunities to vote justly – either voting for, against or abstaining – depending on the proposals with which they are faced. They may have the possibility of casting a vote justly which could affect positively the overall outcome of an unjust law, without having supported any unjust aspects of the law or the law in its entirety. For example, during the passage of a Bill a pro-abortion legislator might introduce a clause to extend the categories according to which abortion would be permitted, and a pro-life legislator could justly *vote against* the amendment. A pro-life legislator could also *vote in favour* of an amendment stating that medical personnel could not be obliged to participate in any procedure if they had any ethical objection to it.

2.5 Distinguishing just and intrinsically unjust proposals which affect abortion

Having considered the justness of these four ways of limiting abortion, let us return again to the teaching of *Evangelium vitae* 73: "When it is not possible to overturn or completely abrogate a pro-abortion law a legislator... could vote for proposals aimed at limiting the harm done by such a [i.e. abortion] law..."

The Pope does not teach that legislators can vote for a "law" (i.e. an abortion law) which stops some categories of abortions whilst tolerating or permitting others. He refers, rather, to voting for "proposals" ("consiliis") and in so doing one might, perhaps, argue that this unusual choice of term – proposal – was adopted purposely in order to avoid the mistaken view that a legislator could vote licitly for an "abortion law" (which is what 'imperfect' legislation is). There is no indication that the Pope is suggesting that pro-life legislators may support intrinsically unjust proposals (i.e. that they support evil to do good), and the teaching of *Ev* 73.2 would appear to rule this out as an option.[13] If it is a requirement that the proposals be just, as appears to be the case, the only sorts of proposals they could support are those I have referred to above: just measures dealing with secondary legislation, and proposals encountered during the passage of legislation which can be justly supported.

3. Questions posed by 'Evangelium Vitae' 73

If, contrary to my view, *EV* 73 should be interpreted as teaching that morally upright legislators may vote justly for 'imperfect' legislation, certain questions would have to be considered, some of which I shall address here:

---

[13] Some writers have attempted to square the circle. John Finnis acknowledges that *EV* 73.2 teaches that "it is never licit to vote for a law permitting abortion." He also believes that *EV* 73.3 teaches that a legislator can vote for a law which does (as he acknowledges) permit abortion if this is chosen as a means of restricting abortion, and claims that the two propositions are consistent; see Finnis, 'The Catholic Church and Public Policy Debates...': 269. Leslie Griffen overcomes a conflict between her interpretation of *EV* 73.3 and the preceding paragraph *EV* 73.2 by misrepresenting what is taught: "Politicians should *in most cases* not vote for abortion laws... As a rule, Catholics are never supposed to vote for "intrinsically unjust" abortion laws. But the encyclical *identifies one exception to this rule*; the Pope states that *in some circumstances* Catholic politicians may vote for laws that permit some abortion" [my emphasis]; see L. C. Griffen, 'Evangelium Vitae: Abortion'. In K. W. Wildes SJ and A. C. Mitchell (eds) *Choosing Life: A Dialogue on 'Evangelium Vitae'*. Washington DC: Georgetown University Press 1997: 159–173, at 170.

3.1 If EV 73 teaches that 'imperfect' legislation can be supported, what is the purpose of voting for it?

If one surveys the literature presented by the pro-life movement to justify campaigns for 'imperfect' or 'incremental' legislation the main (and often the only) reason given is that it seeks to *save lives*. For example, in a publication stating its "aims, ethics and activites" the Society for the Protection of Unborn Children explained its policy to support legislation to stop some abortions (irrespective of whether the legislation permitted or tolerated other abortions):

> The principal focus of the pro-life political campaign in Britain is to tighten the current law to stop the practice of abortion on demand: a realistic legislative objective which would save as many unborn lives as possible in as short a time as possible.[14]

Although this view is widely held it is noticeably not cited in *EV* 73 to justify what is taught. Rather, the encyclical provides two reasons for supporting the said "proposals."

First, the proposals are aimed at "limiting the harm done by such a [i.e. abortion] law." The essence of an abortion law is that the right to life of some or all unborn children is denied (i.e. the primary legislation). Just secondary legislation has as its subject other legitimate considerations – the proper allocation of public money, the rights and duties of doctors, legitimate hospital regulations etc – and abortion is considered as one object (among several possible objects) in relation to the particular subject. Any primary legislation measure, such as one which attempts to lower the time limit for abortions with a Bill stating "Abortion is permitted up to 16 weeks, and prohibited after 16 weeks," does not have the effect of "limiting the harm done" by a particular abortion law but rather replaces that particular abortion law with another (albeit less extensive) abortion law. By contrast, a proposal stating public money may not be used to pay for abortions (or any other just measure which involves secondary legislation) does not constitute an abortion law, yet does "limit the harm" done by the primary legislation which is the essential part of an abortion law. The point is clearer, perhaps, if one considers that one would attempt to "limit the harm" done by a hurricane not by restricting the physical force of the hurricane itself, but by *secondary* measures such as having securer buildings, removing objects from open spaces, taking cover in safe areas, etc. Acting in this way one is not *limiting the hurricane*, but the harm which might otherwise be done by it. Similarly, the "proposals" referred to in *EV* 73 are not aimed at "limiting abortion" (as some commentators have claimed) but aimed at "limiting the harm" of an abortion law.[15] In fact, the

---

[14] SPUC, *Our Aims, Ethics and Activities*. London: SPUC Publications 1997: 27.

[15] The distinction is not noted by some writers. John S Rock SJ writes: "John Paul states that an elected official whose absolute personal opposition to abortion is well-known could support proposals aimed at *limiting abortion*, when it is not possible to overturn or completely abrogate a pro-abortion law" [my emphasis]; J. S. Rock SJ, '*Evangelium Vitae*: Some Highlights'. 64.1 (February 1997) *Linacre Quarterly*: 5–15, at 13.

only words emphasised by italics in *EV* 73.3, as if to highlight the point I am making, are the words "limiting the harm."

Secondly, the proposals are aimed "at lessening its [i.e. the abortion law's] negative consequences at the level of general opinion and public morality". This is not an entirely satisfactory translation of the Latin which refers not so much to the effect of voting for such proposals on "general opinion" but rather on the "culture" of the society in which these proposals will be enacted.[16] Properly understood, the focus is on how voting for the permitted "proposals" improves the "culture and public morality," and little attention seems to have been paid to what this actually means. The term "culture" which, as the Second Vatican Council teaches, refers to "all those things which go to the refining and developing of man's diverse mental and physical endowments"[17] has many facets, including the institutions (understood either in a physical or social sense) which contribute to society. If, as the Council teaches, there is a duty to respect "the right of every man to human and civil culture in harmony with the dignity of the human person, without distinction of race, sex, nation, religion, or social circumstances"[18] one cannot appeal to the concept of culture in order to justify voting for a measure to prohibit some (but not other) abortions because in so doing one will be failing to respect the cultural (and other) rights of those excluded by the law. Furthermore, in view of the fact that the measure would specifically treat the most vulnerable of the unborn (i.e., younger babies, those conceived after rape/incest, those likely to be born disabled) in a way which further marginalises their status in society, the culture would be *negatively affected* by such a measure. By contrast, secondary legislation measures ensuring that doctors have a right not to participate in abortions, or that public money may not be used to fund abortions, would, within the limited terms of reference of such measures, uphold with integrity the social or institutional structures to which they refer, thereby contributing positively to both the culture and public morality.

3.2 If EV 73 teaches that 'imperfect' legislation can be supported, does it justify supporting it on the grounds that it is licit 'cooperation' in evil?

Some writers have argued that legislation to lower the abortion time limit, or to stop some abortions for 'social' but not other reasons, can be justified as permissible material cooperation in evil. It is claimed that support for this view can be found in the final sentence of *EV* 73 in which the Pope says, with reference to voting for the permitted "proposals": "This does not in fact represent an illicit cooperation with an unjust law, but rather a legitimate and proper attempt to

---

[16] "suffragari licite posse illis consiliis quae eiusmodi legis damna minuere velint et perniciosum effectum extenuare qui sive culturam sive moralitatem publicam respicit" (*EV* 73). The Spanish and Italian text translate the Latin literally as "cultura."

[17] Vatican Council II, *Gaudium et spes*: 53.

[18] *Gaudium et spes*: 60

limit its evil aspects." The statement is commonly interpreted as teaching that a legislator who votes for what is commonly regarded as "imperfect" legislation is making a *licit cooperation* with an unjust law.

Professor Finnis' support for legislation to limit abortion appears to be based on an argument that voting for it can be justified as permissible material cooperation:

> Sec. 73 of *Evangelium Vitae* concludes with the words: "This does not in fact represent an illicit cooperation with an unjust law, but rather a legitimate and proper attempt to limit its evil aspects." The wording is a little incautious, for the sentence is dealing with two things at once. It is implicitly saying *first* what I have been saying, that such a vote need not be *formal* cooperation in the wicked choice to permit abortion up to 16 weeks... But the sentence at the end of sec. 73 is also saying, secondly, that the legislator's non-formal but obviously real material cooperation in enacting the new law which does in fact permit abortion up to 16 weeks can be justifiable. The incautiousness in the wording is twofold. On the one hand, the sentence says, not "*can be*" (as I did) but "*does in fact* represent a legitimate and proper attempt" etc. The legitimacy of material cooperation depends upon many factors, not all of which are considered by the paragraph. "Does" should be read as meaning "can be, provided all relevant conditions are fulfilled."[19]

The purpose of this paper is to clarify the precise teaching of *Evangelium vitae* and not to examine exhaustively each of the arguments that have been presented to justify voting for 'imperfect' legislation. A detailed response to Finnis' argument will have to wait until another occasion[20] but, in brief, a major shortcoming with his view seems to be his failure to assess adequately the goodness (which can also be regarded as the justness) of the actual measure for which a legislator is voting to be enacted as law. The legislative measure is part of the 'matter' of the act which makes up the 'external' action.[21] Because, as St Thomas teaches, the interior act of the will and the external action, considered morally, are one act,[22] the morality of the act of voting for *any* legislation requires a determination to be made as to the goodness or badness – the justness or unjustness – of the matter intrinsic to the external action, i.e. the legislation. If, as I have argued, some (and, indeed, many) measures to limit abortion can be judged to be intrinsically unjust, the act of voting for such measures – the moral act – can be judged to be morally bad in every instance because of the defect in the matter. Whether or not an action can be judged to be permissible material cooperation in evil, (the 'cooperation in evil' being justified according to the conditions of the 'double effect' principle), depends on whether the action performed can be judged to be a good action, and in the instance of voting for

---

[19] Finnis, 'The Catholic Church and Public Policy Debates...': 269.
[20] See C. Harte, 'Good acts by bad Acts?'' to appear in J. Merecki SDS and T. Styczen SDS (eds) *A Problem of Conscience: Towards an Understanding of a Disputed Papal Teaching* (forthcoming 2002).
[21] Cf. St Thomas *S Th* 1–2, 20, 2.
[22] Cf. *S Th* 1–2, 17, 4; 20, 3.

'imperfect' legislation a favourable judgment cannot be made because of the defect in the matter.[23]

Can one argue that my view conflicts with the teaching of *EV* 73 which appears to say that a legislator voting for the sorts of measures I believe cannot be supported is not making "an illicit cooperation with an unjust law"? A problem with this argument is that it depends on a translation which does not correspond with the normative Latin text, which states "Hac enim agendi ratione officium suum non praestat illicitae vel iniustae legi..." This translates literally: "Acting in this way [i.e. by voting for the said "proposals"] he or she [the pro-life legislator] does not give his or her office to [i.e. does not support or vote for] an illicit or unjust law..."[24] The Latin text, as can be seen, does not mention "cooperation" and makes no reference whatsoever to the principle of permissible material cooperation. The adjective "illicit" is not linked to the legislator's action (or "cooperation") but rather is linked to "law." A legislator who votes to prohibit some but not all abortions – say, to lower the upper limit from 24 to 16 weeks – by means of an Amendment Bill or by a measure of the form "Abortion is permitted up to 16 weeks and prohibited after 16 weeks" *is voting for an unjust and illicit law.* The sort of 'proposal' approved in *EV* 73 is clearly not this sort of measure because the text specifies that a legislator voting for the permitted "proposals" *would not be voting for an illicit or unjust law.*[25]

---

[23] Professor Finnis, and those who share his view, commonly cite the teaching of *Veritatis Splendor* 78 to justify the action of a pro-life legislator voting for 'imperfect' legislation: *"The morality of the human act depends primarily and fundamentally on the 'object' rationally chosen by the deliberate will, as is borne out by the insightful analysis, still valid today by Saint Thomas..."*(VS 78). The text includes a footnote referring to St Thomas' teaching at *S Th* 1–2, 18, 6, (a reference that tends to be overlooked by critics of my view), which refers precisely to the dimensions of the interior and external act. It is insufficient for either myself or opponents of my view simply to cite *VS* 78 as a supporting text without developing the argument more fully. My forthcoming paper 'Good acts by bad Acts?' provides a fuller treatment of this aspect of the question of voting for abortion legislation.

[24] The official English translation is: "This does not in fact represent an illicit cooperation with an unjust law."

[25] One critic of my view objected that it does not make sense to speak of an "illicit law." If he is correct, this is a criticism of the Latin text and not of my translation which is consistent with the Latin. However, I do not believe the objection is valid. An illicit law is one which is not permitted, a "law" which is "unlawful." This is an entirely appropriate description of a law which, in violating the moral/divine law, can be judged to be intrinsically unjust, and "not a law" (cf *EV*72). Professor Fr Tadeusz Styczen SDS rightly, in my view, refers to a "law against life" as an *"absurdity"*; see his 'Ethics as the theory of natural law facing the "law against life",' in Pontifical Academy for Life et al., *Medicine and Law: For or Against Life?* Vatican City: Libreria Editrice Vaticana 1999: 217–237, at 217. He asks rhetorically: "Can man, a rational and free being, ever give assent to the absurdity of 'law against life,' for whatever reason? Can he ever make such use of his freedom as to employ it against truth?" (p. 218). The term "illicit law" seems particularly appropriate in the light of the teaching of *EV* 73.2 that it is never licit to vote for an intrinsically unjust law. It is not licit to vote for such a law, because the law itself is not licit. Irrespective of a legislator's subjective intention when voting for 'imperfect' legislation (which, as I noted above at 2.2, may or may not be a good intention) *the objective purpose/intent* of such legislation is to permit or tolerate some or many abortions. It is still,

With respect to the argument that suggests that *EV* 73 advances the view that voting for 'imperfect' legislation can be justified as permissible material cooperation, one also notes that this view requires, at least for Finnis, a criticism of the text itself as being "a little incautious." Finnis acknowledges that his argument based on "material cooperation" is not directly taught in *EV* 73, but that the text is "implicitly saying... what I have been saying." The Latin text, however, indicates that neither the English translation nor Finnis' interpretation of it are consistent with what the Pope is actually teaching.

3.3 If EV 73 teaches that 'imperfect' legislation can be supported, can only pro-life legislators vote for it?

The 'solution' given in *EV* 73 does not state that *any* legislator may vote for the 'proposals' to which it refers but specifies merely that some legislators – those "whose absolute personal opposition to procured abortion was well known" – may licitly support them, a qualification which on the one hand might seem to support Finnis' view that the text is dealing with the issue of material cooperation, but which on the other poses a difficulty for his view which also needs to be addressed.

Finnis argues that a pro-life legislator's vote for a proposal such as "Abortion is permitted up to 16 weeks and prohibited after 16 weeks" (when the previous limit was higher) would not be *formal cooperation* in the continued permission for abortion up to 16 weeks, but that it would be *material cooperation* which (according to Finnis' argument) could be regarded as a side-effect of a good act of voting to stop abortions after 16 weeks.[26] According to Finnis a pro-life legislator's vote for such legislation can be judged morally acceptable because although the legislator would be voting (as Finnis admits) "for a law which does permit abortion"[27] he would not be voting to permit "precisely to permit" the pre-16 week abortions,[28] but rather, as it were, voting to permit them, precisely to prohibit those after 16 weeks.[29] By contrast, a legislator who is not pro-life but opposes late abortions might, though he would be acting in a way

---

objectively, a "law against life" and would thus, as Professor Styczen describes such a law, be "an anti-law acknowledged as a law; it is lawlessness identified with lawfulness; in the language of logic it may only be described as contradiction: (p. ~p), while in everyday language it is called the absurd" (p. 219).

[26] 'The Catholic Church and Public Policy Debates...' 269. Cf. also 'Unjust Laws in a Democratic Society...' 601.

[27] Finnis, 'The Catholic Church and Public Policy Debates...': 269 (quoted above in 3.2).

[28] Finnis, 'The Catholic Church and Public Policy Debates...': 268.

[29] My purpose in this section is not to provide a point by point critique of Finnis' argument but to indicate a practical difficulty with his argument. (In my view his suggestion that "the always illicit vote is for a law as permitting, precisely to permit abortion" (p. 268) – which in practical terms indicates Finnis' support for a law "permitting, precisely to prohibit," a notion which is not only a contradiction in terms but inadequate, as it overlooks the objective reality of the measure being supported – is a particularly weak part of his argument.)

which is behaviourally no different from that of the pro-life legislator, be casting his vote precisely to stop abortion after 16 weeks whilst also in fact *cooperating formally* in the evil of permitting, *precisely to permit*, those abortions prior to 16 weeks. Indeed, even if a legislator did not support permission for all the abortions allowed up to 16 weeks, but willed that only some of those abortions be permitted (say, those up to 10 or 12 weeks, or those carried out up to 16 weeks for eugenic but not social reasons) there would still be some element of formal cooperation in evil in voting for the measure. It therefore seems to be consistent with Finnis' view that the Pope should include as a qualification that those legislators voting for the "proposals" (interpreted as meaning 'imperfect legislation') be those "whose absolute personal opposition to procured abortion was well known".

In effect, the qualification would indicate – especially if it is viewed as an indication that the Pope is endorsing the act of casting certain legislative votes because they can be judged to be permissible material cooperation – that *a totally pro-life legislator* can licitly vote for 'imperfect' legislation (if this is what "proposals" refers to) because such a vote can be judged to be a good action, *whereas a legislator who is not totally pro-life cannot licitly vote for the same measure* because he would not be performing a good action, but *doing evil*. If the pro-abortion legislator would be doing evil (a judgment required by Finnis' analysis) he should avoid voting for 'imperfect legislation', and pro-life legislators and campaigners should not lobby him to vote for it because this would be an incitement to do evil. In reality, the success of any measure to limit abortion usually requires the support of legislators who favour some, and possibly many, abortions (because if a majority of legislators were totally pro-life they would normally be able to enact legislation which conformed to the moral law), and experience shows that pressure to encourage them to vote would often be necessary. If, as the analysis indicates, this constitutes pressure to do evil, applying such pressure cannot be legitimately undertaken and the prospects for 'imperfect' legislation being successfully enacted would often be greatly reduced if not negligible. There would therefore be little point in promoting such legislation.

Why, then, should the Pope have included the qualification that legislators voting for (what I have argued must be) *just* measures be known to be absolutely opposed to procured abortion? One answer is that legislative procedures are often complex – as noted above at 2.4(iv) – and without a public statement of his or her pro-life stance the reasons for a pro-life legislator's legitimate vote for just 'secondary' legislation might be misunderstood. For example, a pro-life legislator could vote during the passage of an abortion bill for just amendments to prevent public funding of abortion, or to ensure that medical personnel have a right not to engage in any procedures with which they have an ethical objection. Some pro-abortion (or 'pro-choice') legislators might also be willing to support such measures. In view of the possibility that pro-life legislators might be mistakenly viewed as supporting the underlying pro-abortion aspects of the legislation, or as supporting the measures for the wrong reasons (e.g. it might be thought that their fundamental concern was the rights of medical personnel or the use of public money, and not the right to life of the unborn) it is appropriate, as both a witness to their pro-life convictions, and to avoid scandal, that the reasons for their actions be publicly known. Indeed, given that the primary objective of law is to protect life, and the foundations of human society are radically undermined when laws fail to do this, one might assume that the actual or prospective undermining of society by legislation that fails to protect each human life, automatically requires from morally upright legislators a public declaration in favour of the right to life.

3.4 If EV 73 teaches that 'imperfect' legislation can be supported, does this depend on there being a more permissive law currently in force?

Whatever is meant by the term "proposals" one must acknowledge that voting for them does not depend on the prior existence of an abortion law. The 'solution' given in *EV* 73 says that a legislator can vote for the permitted proposals "when it is not possible to overturn or completely abrogate a pro-abortion law". Yet again, the English text is not a satisfactory translation of the Latin "quoties vitari antiquarive non potest abortus lex" which makes it clearer that the two relevant situations with respect to voting for the permitted "proposals" are those of either (i) being unable to avoid the enactment of an abortion law which has not yet been enacted [vitari], or (ii) being unable to overturn or repeal an existing abortion law [antiquari]. Other translations, such as the Italian [quando non fosse possibile scongiurare o abrogare] reveal these two conditions more clearly.[30]

If the term "proposals" refers to 'imperfect legislation', then *EV* 73 must be understood as teaching that a legislator may vote for a law permitting or tolerating abortion up to 16 weeks *even if the previous law prohibited all abortions*, if he is voting for this in order to prevent a law permitting or tolerating even more abortions. Professor Finnis supports this view, saying that *EV* 73 states that a legislator could "licitly give his or her support to a bill for a law which permits abortion but less permissively [i] than the existing law or [ii] than a bill which will otherwise be passed and become law."[31]

I have argued that *EV* 73.3 must be understood in the light of *EV* 73.2 which states that "in the case of an intrinsically unjust law . . . it is never licit to . . . vote

---

[30] The "problem" stated in *EV* 73 refers to casting a legislative vote for a law "in place of a more permissive law already passed or ready to be voted on." Although this quotation might appear to provide a more favourable illustration of my point, the teaching of *EV* 73 is to be found, as I demonstrated earlier, in what is stated as the 'solution' not the 'problem'.

[31] Finnis, 'The Catholic Church and Public Policy Debates . . .': 268. ["In *Evangelium Vitae* (1995) sec. 73 you find two statements: (i) it is never licit to vote for a law permitting abortion, (ii) a Catholic elected legislator whose absolute personal opposition to procured abortion is well known can, in a legislative vote decisive for the passage of a bill, licitly give his or her support to a bill for a law which permits abortion but less permissively than the existing law or than a bill which will otherwise be passed and become law. Are these two statements consistent? Someone may say that they are not. . . But the objection is, I think, mistaken, and the two statements are consistent."]

for it". Although I have argued that this statement indicates that it is never licit to vote for any 'imperfect' legislation (which in restricting abortion to certain categories can always be judged to be intrinsically unjust) it must, surely, apply *at least* to the law which originally tolerates or permits abortion. If it is "never licit" to vote for this original law, and if *EV 73* also teaches that 'imperfect legislation' may be supported to prevent the enactment of an original law which will otherwise tolerate or permit even more abortions, then *EV 73* contradicts itself. The whole section would be rendered meaningless.

4. Authoritative explanations and clarifications of *EV 73*

Since the encyclical was published only two notable indicators have been given as to how *EV 73* should be understood.[32] In the first, given to journalists at the first presentation of the encyclical on 30 March 1995, Cardinal Joseph Ratzinger stated, without deviating from the Pope's phraseology, that "the elected official can support proposals aimed at 'limiting the harm...and lessening the negative consequences' (n 73)." The clarification that Cardinal Ratzinger provided, which immediately followed this sentence and which also concluded his commentary on this section of the encyclical, was brief but highly significant: "Of course, he can never vote for injustice to be declared justice."[33] This statement corresponds with what I have presented as a true translation of the Pope's concluding remarks in *EV 73* ("Hac enim agendi ratione officium suum non praestat illicitae vel iniustae legi"), which teach that in voting for the permitted "proposals" a legislator is not voting for a law which can be judged to be illicit or unjust. It indicates that the teaching of *EV 73* is predicated on a view that one cannot vote for unjust measures, and not that erroneously applied principles of material cooperation in evil provide legislators with a justification for voting for measures which can be judged to be unjust.

The second noteworthy indicator came nearly five years later when Pope John Paul II, in a discourse to mark the fifth anniversary of *Evangelium vitae*, alluded to the teaching of *EV 73*, saying:

[32] After this paper was prepared the Secretary of the Congregation for the Doctrine of the Faith (CDF), Archbishop Tarcisio Bertone SDB, published a noteworthy paper, 'Catholics and Pluralist Society: "Imperfect laws" and the Responsibility of Legislators', in J. Vial Correa and E. Sgreccia (eds) *Evangelium Vitae: Five Years of Confrontation with the Society* [Proceedings of the Sixth Annual Assembly of the Pontifical Academy for Life, 11–14 February 2000] Vatican City: Libreria Editrice Vaticana 2001: 206–222. Archbishop Bertone's interpretation of *EV 73* is in line with the 'consensus' view that I am challenging, and a response to some of his arguments, notably that voting for such legislation can be viewed as a choice for the lesser evil, can be found in Colin Harte, 'Inconsistent Papal Approaches towards Problems of Conscience?' 2 (2002) *The National Catholic Bioethics Quarterly*: 99 – 122. It is clear from Archbishop Bertone's frequent use of the expression "it seems to me" that he is putting forward a personal view and not an official CDF interpretation of *EV 73*.

[33] Cardinal Joseph Ratzinger: Presentation of *Evangelium vitae* to Journalists (30 March 1995). Full text in *L'Osservatore Romano*, English edition, 5 April 1995, pp 1–2.

Do not leave anything undone in the attempt to eliminate legalized crime or at least to limit the harm of such laws, keeping in mind the radical obligation to respect the right to life of every human being from conception to natural death, even if he is the last and least gifted.[34]

The reference to "limit[ing] the harm of such laws" repeats the language of *EV* 73, but here the Pope presents for the first time, in connection with how one should "limit the harm," the important qualification that one must keep in mind the radical obligation to respect the right to life of every human being, even if he is the last and least gifted.[35]

Although the question being addressed in this paper requires an analysis which fully respects its ethical, jurisprudential and legislative dimensions, its subject matter is always the human person – the human person who has an "almost divine dignity"[36] as a result of the Incarnation. Leaving aside, as it were, the question of law, my particular objection to legislative measures to limit abortion – that is, by what I have labelled the primary legislation – is that such measures always make an illicit, and arbitrary, distinction of persons in which the rights of some are protected, whilst the fundamental rights of others are overlooked and thus denied. This illicit distinction of persons is compounded by the fact that the weakest are treated, *contrary to all principles of justice, solidarity and basic human decency*, in an unfavourable way. Attempts to limit abortion by 'imperfect' legislation will always focus on stopping the sorts of abortions which society is generally less inclined to favour, and the good end of saving some lives, through the bad means of an intrinsically unjust law, is inevitably accompanied by an increased marginalisation of those excluded by such measures. The experience of many countries, consistent with what logic would suggest, is that *the most vulnerable babies* – younger babies, those conceived after incest or rape, those likely to be born disabled, i.e. those to whom the Pope refers as the "last and least gifted" – will be excluded from so-called 'imperfect'

---

[34] John Paul II: Address to participants at the 6th General Assembly of the Pontifical Academy for Life, commemorating the 5th anniversary of *Evangelium vitae*, 14 February 2000, n. 4. Reprinted in Vial Correa and Sgreccia (eds) *Evangelium Vitae. Five Years of Confrontation with the Society*: 9–11, at p.10.

[35] The focus of John Paul II's remarks in his address of 14 February 2000 assumes particular significance because this was his first public statement in connection with *EV* 73 since the encyclical was published. Given the importance of the teaching of this section it seems curious that the Pope had not already referred to it, especially as he had addressed many gatherings in the previous five years where clarification or even a mere re-statement of the teaching would have seemed appropriate. For example, he did not raise the issue in his address to the World Pro-Life Congress organised by the Pontifical Council for the Family (3 October 1995); addressing the Pontifical Academy for Life he mentioned the "problem area" of law but did not refer directly to the teaching of *EV* 73 (20 November 1995); most notably, perhaps, he offered no words of clarification when addressing a Symposium at the Vatican on the specific issue of 'Evangelium vitae and Law' (24 May 1996); the issue was also avoided in his address at the Vatican to participants in the 2nd European Meeting of Politicians and Legislators (23 October 1998).

[36] "dignitatem quasi divinam" (*EV* 2).

laws. The Pope's clarification that attempts to "limit the harm" done by pro-abortion laws must keep in mind the "radical obligation to respect the right to life of every human being from conception to natural death, even if he is the last and least gifted" would appear to support the view that 'imperfect' legislation to limit abortion, at least insofar as it makes an illicit distinction of persons, is not permissible.[37]

5. Conclusion

Much contemporary discussion of "the problem of conscience" considered in *Evangelium vitae* 73 has adopted the terminology of 'imperfect legislation' without establishing what precisely is meant by the term. A particular objection to the term itself – a term which barely predates the 1990s in its current usage – is that it obscures the point which must ineluctably be established: whether *the specific measure* for which a legislator is voting is *just or unjust*. Although I have accepted the commonly used definition for the purpose of this paper, the term 'imperfect legislation' is, in fact, inherently ambiguous. Some writers suggest that *all* human laws are "imperfect." Others may use the term solely for laws which *limit* a moral evil (irrespective of whether this is achieved by a just or unjust measure); or for *any* unjust law which violates the moral law; or for a (just) law which does not exactly fulfill the true desires of the legislator who supported it merely as a political compromise; or for a law which, due to flaws in its drafting, fails to be as effective as envisaged. I think that those *just* laws which limit abortion by what I have labelled 'secondary' legislation can be considered 'imperfect', in the sense that if just primary legislation prohibiting all abortions were enacted such secondary legislation would not be required. This, however, is not the sense in which 'imperfect' legislation is now commonly understood, and because of the inherent ambiguity of the term it would be preferable not to use it at all with respect to laws limiting abortion. Insofar as it is employed nowadays without making a distinction between *just* and *unjust* measures the term 'imperfect legislation' should be rejected as counterproductive to serious attempts to resolve the moral question addressed by *EV* 73.

John Paul II highlights the unacceptability of attempts to "limit the harm" of abortion laws by measures which amend (i.e. do not repeal) the 'primary' legislation. These fail to respect the right to life of every human being, specifically those whom the Pope refers to as "the last and least gifted," and, consistent with what he states earlier in *Evangelium vitae*, amount to an unjust discrimination:

> How is it possible to speak of the dignity of every human being when the killing of the weakest and the most innocent is permitted? In the name of what justice

---

[37] The Pope's remarks on 14 February 2000 refer solely to what I have labelled the 'primary' legislation. He does not address the question whether 'imperfect' (insofar as it may be unjust) secondary legislation might be supported, but the clarification by Cardinal Ratzinger that a legislator "can never vote for injustice to be declared justice" has already answered this point.

is the most unjust of discriminations practised: some individuals are held to be deserving of defence and others are denied that dignity?[38]

The unjustness of laws authorising such discrimination can be discerned by the light of human reason, but for those whose lives are informed by faith in the person of Jesus Christ a more compelling reason can be proposed for reflection and acceptance. A vote for 'imperfect' abortion legislation (at least with respect to the primary legislation) always involves excluding from protection at least one unborn human being *who is rightly entitled to protection* and with whom Christ, through His Incarnation, has in a certain way become united.[39] Because that child's person cannot be separated from the person of Christ the exclusion of the child also means an exclusion of Christ.[40] We ignore at our peril His teaching: "In so far as you neglected to do this to one of the least of these, you neglected to do it to me" (*Mt* 25:45).

One may profitably consider the principal rationale for voting for 'imperfect' legislation. The predominant view seems to be that it would be better to have a law tolerating or permitting fewer abortions, than a law tolerating or permitting more abortions. Furthermore, that it would be better *to vote for a law* permitting or tolerating a limited number of abortions – say, if pregnancy occurs after rape or if the child is likely to be born disabled – than to live in a society with an existing or proposed law permitting or tolerating hundreds of thousands, possibly millions, of abortions each year. I do not question the commendable zeal on the part of those seeking to save human lives. But how does this rationale for acting differ from the judgment of Caiaphas who held that it was expedient that one man should die for the people so that the whole nation perish not (*Jn* 11:50)? Are not pro-life campaigners and legislators effectively making the same judgment about those excluded from protection by so-called 'imperfect' legislation, as Caiaphas made about Jesus Christ? And are they not thereby implicated, as Matthew 25:45 teaches, in Caiaphas' judgment? Or should Caiaphas' judgment, which tradition has condemned, be applauded as a means of saving innumerable lives?

EV 73 is an extraordinary section, not least because for such a long period of time it has been commonly understood, unlike the content of any other papal encyclical, as teaching precisely the opposite of what it would appear, in fact, to teach.[41] The significance of its teaching cannot be overstated, not only with respect to the precise question it addresses, but also with respect to its profound implications for other important questions concerning engagement in secular political, legislative, executive and judicial bodies. One can say, without

---

[38] *EV* 20.

[39] Cf. *Gaudium et spes* 22.

[40] Cf. *EV* 104.

[41] The misunderstanding has not been restricted solely to those who believe that legislators may rightly vote for 'imperfect legislation'. Professor Fr. Arthur F Utz OP, for example, argues that a moral justification cannot be found for such votes, and criticises what he perceives to be the teaching of *EV* 73 because in his view it supports a morally indefensible action: 'Das Unheil der Nr 73/74 der Enzyklika Evangelium Vitae'. 28 (1998) *Theologisches*: 307–310.

exaggeration, that the ramifications of the teaching of this section will be as momentous in the area of social and political morality as the teaching of *Humanae vitae* has been in the area of conjugal morality.

This paper has not attempted to present, with respect to the main ethical, jurisprudential and legislative dimensions of the question, a comprehensive argument against voting for 'imperfect legislation' itself. It has, rather, sought to establish that *EV 73 does not teach*, in spite of the widely held view to the contrary, that this sort of legislation can be supported. Amongst other things, this paper has not highlighted how faulty practical applications of concepts like solidarity and (correctly understood) political democracy would appear to feature as major aspects of the misinterpretation of *EV 73*. In particular, it has not explored the cogent Christological aspects of the question, but proposes for acceptance the interpretation presented here, as both an authentic interpretation of the Pope's teaching and a necessary precondition for understanding the question in its Christological dimension. Though the teaching of *EV 73*, properly understood, makes demands and has what might appear to be 'restrictive' implications for legislators and others engaged in promoting the right to life as a matter of a public policy, nevertheless, as part of the 'Gospel of Life' it should be received as "good news" (cf *EV 1*). Far from 'restricting' legislators it liberates them from a precarious legal positivism, thus enabling them to appreciate the ethical and transcendent nature of this question which finds its ultimate answer, as do all questions, in Jesus Christ.[42]

[42] I am grateful to many people for their comments on an earlier draft of this paper, and in particular for the helpful assistance of Alison Davis, Damian P. Fedoryka, Fr Kevin L. Flannery SJ, Fr Jaroslaw Merecki SDS, David Paton, Helen Watt, and Ted Watt.

Contributors

Cardinal Thomas J Winning was Archbishop of Glasgow from 1974 till his death on 17th June 2001. He was Chairman of the Catholic Bishops' Joint Bioethics Committee from its establishment in 1983 until the time of his death.

Archbishop George Pell is Archbishop of Sydney; at the time of the Conference he was Archbishop of Melbourne.

Bishop Donal Murray is Bishop of Limerick. He succeeded Cardinal Winning as Chairman of the Catholic Bishops' Joint Bioethics Committee.

Kateryna Fedoryka Cuddeback is an Associate of the Population Research Institute, Front Royal, Virginia.

Helen M Davies is a retired General Practitioner, with a particular interest in fertility and in the training of teachers of Natural Family Planning.

Richard M Doerflinger is Associate Director, Secretariat for Pro-Life Activities, National Conference of Catholic Bishops of the United States, and Adjunct Fellow in Bioethics and Public Policy, National Catholic Bioethics Center.

Sr Miriam Duggan FMSA is Superior General of the Franciscan Missionary Sisters for Africa. She is a gynaecologist who has worked as a missionary doctor in Africa for over 30 years.

Fr Dermot Fenlon is a priest of the Birmingham Oratory. He was formerly a Fellow of Gonville and Caius College, Cambridge, and a University Lecturer in History.

John Finnis is Professor of Law and Legal Philosophy in the University of Oxford, and Biolchini Professor of Law in the University of Notre Dame, Indiana. He is a Fellow of University College, Oxford, and a Fellow of the British Academy.

Fr Anthony Fisher OP is Director of the John Paul II Pontifical Institute for Marriage and the Family (Australia Campus), Melbourne, Episcopal Vicar for Healthcare, Archdiocese of Melbourne, and Regent of Studies, Australian Dominican Province.

Scott FitzGibbon is Professor of Law at Boston College.

Jorge L A Garcia is Professor of Philosophy at Boston College.

Laura L Garcia is Adjunct Professor of Philosophy at Boston College.

Robert P George is the McCormick Professor of Jurisprudence and Director of the James Madison Program in American Ideals and Institutions at Princeton University.

Luke Gormally is a Senior Research Fellow at The Linacre Centre for Healthcare Ethics, London, and a Research Professor at The Ave Maria School of Law, Ann Arbor, Michigan. He was Director of The Linacre Centre from 1981 to 2000.

Colin Harte has been active in the pro-life movement for nearly 20 years and has written a thesis related to the topic of his paper.

Fr Richard Hogan is a priest of the Archdiocese of St Paul and Minneapolis and Associate National Director of Priests for Life.

Christopher Kaczor is Assistant Professor in the Department of Philosophy in the Bellarmine College of Liberal Arts at Loyola Marymount University, Los Angeles.

Fr Thomasz Kraj is a priest of the Archdiocese of Cracow and Assistant Professor of Bioethics in the Pontifical Academy of Theology, Cracow.

Monsignor Livio Melina is Ordinary Professor of Moral Theology at the Instituto Giovanni Paolo per Studi su Matrimonio e Famiglia at the Pontifical Lateran University, Rome.

Fr Carlo Lorenzo Rossetti is a priest of the Diocese of Rome and Professor of Theology at the Pontifical Lateran University.

Robert L Walley is Professor of Obstetrics and Gynaecology at Memorial University of Newfoundland, and Medical Director of MaterCare International.

Index[1]

abortion: 6, 8, 23, 49, 50, 51, 62–70
passim, 200, 202, 205; and moral
pluralism: 52–53, 58, 59, 62–70; and
public reason: 62–70; Church's
teaching on: 201; deaths from: 250;
has corrupted practice of medicine: 9;
imposed on developing countries: 6;
nonviolent action against: 228;
research into attitudes to: 162–164;
right against: 60; 'right' to: 15 (*see also*:
Thomson, Judith Jarvis); violent
resistance to (*see also*: private defence)
227ff; ways to limit legislatively:
328–330
abortion debate, reframing the: 164
Abortion Law Reform Association: 29, 46
abortion laws, permissive (variety of possible
restrictions to): 218–219
abortion legislation, primary and secondary:
327–328
act analysis: 213–217. *See also*: causing
death as side-effect; foresight of
consequences; intention; John Paul II,
Pope: *Veritatis Splendor*
Advanced Cell Technology Inc: 300–301
AIDS: 156, 257–267 *passim*; and behaviour
change: 258–267; and condom use:
260–261; and Education for Life
Programme (*see*: Education for Life);
and Youth Alive (*see*: Youth Alive);
impact on Africa: 257; spread of: 257
American Foreign Policy and zero
population growth: 28
Anglican Christianity: 27
Anscombe, Elizabeth: 3–4
anthropology, Christian: 149. *See also*:
human being; human body; human
person; human soul
apostasy: 47–48

Aquinas, St Thomas: 16, 20, 24, 25, 58,
104, 105, 111, 139, 199, 204, 218
n.47, 234, 325, 326, 327–328
Aristotle: 17, 21, 280–281, 289
Arnold, Thomas: 38, 39
Audi, Robert (on violent resistance to
abortion): 232–239
Augustine, St: 9, 24
Australia: abortion incidence and rate in:
160, 161, 210; assisted reproduction
in: 160; attitudes to abortion in: 161;
attitudes to euthanasia in: 161;
attitudes to life issues in: 161–162;
Catholic religious practice in: 159;
debates about *Evangelium Vitae* #73 in:
209–217; embryo exploitation in: 160;
pro-life situation in: 160; religious
situation in: 159–160
authority of Church to teach moral truth:
173–176
autonomy, ideology of: 275, 277; and
culure of death: 6–7
AVSC (Access to Voluntary and Safe
Contraception): 77

Bangladesh, coercive population control in: 82
baptism and conversion: 135
Bentham: 31
Bertone, Archbishop T. (on 'imperfect'
legislation): 207–208, 224 and n.59,
338
bioethics (as secularist discipline): 96ff
birthrates: 155–156
bishop, role of (in promoting the Gospel of
Life): 162, 164–168
Bland case: 206
Blankenhorn, David: 186–188
Bork, Judge Robert: 189
Boyle, Joseph: 24

---

[1] Names which occur merely as a part of bibliographical references in the footnotes are not
included in this Index.